Her Secret Service

Claire Hubbard-Hall is a writer and historian who specialises in the history of secret intelligence. She has held lecturing posts in several British universities and is an honorary Associate Professor of Intelligence History. She has contributed to television documentaries and written for popular history magazines. *Her Secret Service* is her first book. She is based in Lincolnshire, UK.

Her Secret Service

The Forgotten Women of British Intelligence

Claire Hubbard-Hall

WEIDENFELD & NICOLSON

First published in Great Britain in 2024 by Weidenfeld & Nicolson,
an imprint of The Orion Publishing Group Ltd
Carmelite House, 50 Victoria Embankment
London EC4Y 0DZ

An Hachette UK Company

SRD

A CIP catalogue record for this book is
available from the British Library.

ISBN (Hardback) 978 1 3996 0343 0
ISBN (Export Trade Paperback) 978 1 3996 0344 7
ISBN (eBook) 978 1 3996 0346 1
ISBN (Audio) 978 1 3996 0347 8

Typeset by Input Data Services Ltd, Bridgwater, Somerset

Printed and bound in India by Manipal Technologies Limited, Manipal

MIX
Paper | Supporting
responsible forestry
FSC
www.fsc.org   FSC™ C104740

www.weidenfeldandnicolson.co.uk
www.orionbooks.co.uk

For Holly

Dreams do come true

CONTENTS

KEY PERSONALITIES

Jane Archer née Sissmore (1898–1982): An expert in communism and Soviet espionage who became the first female MI5 officer in 1929, later serving in MI6 during the Second World War.

Vera Atkins (1908–2000): Deputy head of Special Operations Executive (SOE) F Section.

Milicent Bagot (1907–2006): The first woman to reach the rank of MI5 assistant director in 1953.

Agnes Blake (1858–1950): The first woman employed as an MI6 agent on 17 December 1909.

Joan Bright (1910–2008): MI6 Section D secretary who worked in MI(R) before heading the Special Information Centre in the War Cabinet Rooms during the Second World War.

Joyce Cameron (1911–2006): Secretary to Director of Naval Intelligence Admiral John Godfrey and his successor Rear Admiral Edmund Rushbrooke during the Second World War.

Christine Chilver (1920–2007): SOE agent FIFI who tested agents' resolve and skills before being assigned overseas work.

Dorothy Dimmock (1895–1981): MI5 Registry clerk during the First World War.

Margaret 'Teddy' Dunlop (1906–1969): MI6 officer in Tangier, Morocco.

Dorothy Furse (1907–1999): SOE Personnel Officer for Women's Staff.

Olga Gray (1906–1990): MI5 agent who infiltrated the Communist Party of Great Britain during the 1930s and uncovered the Woolwich Arsenal spy ring.

Lois Hamilton (1908–2001): MI6 Section D 'secretary' who later worked in SOE.

Dorothy Henslowe (1897–1993): MI6 'secretary' who served under Mansfield Cumming and Hugh Sinclair.

Muriel Jones (1903–1973): MI6 'secretary' who worked with Kathleen Pettigrew at 54 Broadway, London headquarters.

Gladys Lincoln (1906–1922): The youngest woman (fourteen years old) to work for MI6.

Edith Lomax (1870–1953): MI5 Controller of Women's Staff during the First World War.

Edith Lunn (later Rothstein) (1887–1970): MI6 'secretary' who briefly worked in Helsinki in 1919.

Helen Lunn (1895–1948): GC&CS translator from the early 1920s, later stationed at Bletchley Park during the Second World War.

Lucy Lunn (1891–1982): MI6 'secretary' who worked in Constantinople, Rome, Bletchley Park and London headquarters.

Marjorie 'Peggy' Lunn (1898–1977): GC&CS translator during the early 1920s.

Dorothy McCarthy (1922–2022): MI6 messenger at Bletchley Park and 54 Broadway, London headquarters.

Eileen McCarthy (1920–2005): MI6 teleprinter operator at Bletchley Park and 54 Broadway, London headquarters.

Phyllis 'Phyl' Mackenzie (1906–1991): SOE 'secretary' in charge of F Section's agent clothing department.

Georgina 'Ena' Molesworth (1901–1990): MI6 'secretary' who served in Berlin, Geneva, Bletchley Park and Lisbon.

Olive Montgomery (1888–1968): MI6 'secretary' who began her career working under Mansfield Cumming. She later worked in the Mansion and Hut 10 (MI6 Codes) at Bletchley Park.

Daphne Park (1921–2010): MI6 officer appointed Controller Western Hemisphere in 1975, the highest post ever occupied by a woman.

Beatrice Peters née Mortimer (1900–1979): MI6 messenger and telephonist.

Kathleen Pettigrew (1898–1990): MI6 'secretary' who served under five MI6 chiefs and inspired Ian Fleming's Miss Moneypenny character in the James Bond novels.

Margaret Priestley (1920–2005): The only woman and civilian to work in Ian Fleming's secret naval commando unit, 30 Assault Unit (30 AU).

Stella Rimington (1935–): First female Director General of MI5 from 1992 to 1996.

Maud Russell (1891–1982): A close friend of Ian Fleming who worked in the propaganda section of the Admiralty's Naval Intelligence Division (NID) during the Second World War.

Ruth Sebag Montefiore (1916–2015): MI6 codist at Bletchley Park.

Nathalie 'Lily' Sergueiew (1912–1950): Double Cross agent TREASURE handled by Mary Sherer during the Second World War.

Mary Sherer (1914–1988): MI5 sabotage expert and first woman to serve as an agent handler.

Evelyn Sinclair (1886–1971): Sister and personal assistant to MI6 chief Hugh Sinclair, who worked temporarily in GC&CS.

Winifred 'Winnie' Spink (1885–1973): The first female MI6 officer sent to Russia in 1916.

Margaret Stewart (1907–1986): The first woman to lead a team in naval intelligence during the Second World War.

Eva 'Hope' Symons (1877–1966): Worked in Special Branch's Secret Service Registry.

Maud Symons (1868–1951): Worked in Special Branch's Secret Service Registry.

Isabel 'Lesley' Wauchope (1912–1988): MI6 Section D 'secretary', who later worked in SOE.

Kathleen Weeks (1902–1975): Personal assistant to Jane Sissmore (Archer) during the 1930s.

Dorothy Westmacott (1892–1976): The first woman employed by MI5. The typist took up her position on 16 January 1911.

Marguerite 'Rita' Winsor (1909–1986): MI6 officer who worked in Zurich, London and Lisbon.

Claire Woolf (1904–1984): Assistant in SOE F Section's agent clothing department.

PROLOGUE

Sidmouth, Devon, 1978

Having retired from a lifetime of service in London to the quiet solitude of Sidmouth, a grey-haired woman sat on the balcony of her flat 'watching the waves as they tried to engulf the thatched houses that straggled up the hill ahead'.[1]

Like the handful of retired spies who had flocked to the seaside town, Kathleen Pettigrew had been drawn to its timeless charm and its Georgian-era buildings. Before leaving the Secret Intelligence Service, more commonly known as MI6, Kathleen had known Sidmouth and its narrow winding streets for years. She had decided long ago to spend her final years in Devon, a county from which her Pettigrew ancestors hailed.[2]

Yet, as she was a former servant of the secret state, tacit limitations defined her retirement: she would never be entirely free from her former employer. Despite her departure from London in 1958, the office still occasionally called upon her services and sent a car to Sidmouth for her.[3] To the younger generation of intelligence officers, Kathleen was a walking, talking history book. Her knowledge of the organisation's history was invaluable and perhaps surpassed that of 'C' himself, the head of MI6.

Quietly revered within the secret service, the legendary Miss Pettigrew had loyally served her country for four decades. Secretary to three consecutive Cs, Kathleen had assumed an all-powerful position behind her typewriter as the service's all-knowing and ever-present sentinel, and MI6 relied upon her knowledge and insight of past events and people.

From the surprise apprehension of First World War courtesan spy Mata Hari to the unmasking of MI6 officer Kim Philby, the 'Third Man' of the Cambridge spy ring, Kathleen had created, organised and archived an empire of secrets. As an MI6 super-secretary, she had worked in complete secrecy at the very heart of the British establishment.

While retirement suited Kathleen, she envied the youth of the next generation of intelligence recruits. Compared to the cohort of new 'Friends' serving in a modern and professional intelligence organisation, she was a relic of a time and world that no longer existed.[4] Kathleen was born in the reign of Queen Victoria and her working career had begun when pens and inkwells were still widely used. Over time, the tools of her trade evolved. Electric typewriters, encryption devices and Xerox machines were just some of the challenges she overcame and mastered.

However, the gradual rise and fall of hemlines during the first half of the twentieth century reflected the slow progress of women's fight for equality in all areas of life. Like most females working in intelligence, Kathleen had entered her profession at the clerical level. She began work during the First World War but found herself in a paradoxical position: she was trusted to keep the government's top secrets, but she was not deemed deserving of the vote. Some women were granted suffrage at the war's end, but Kathleen would have to wait until 1928 before registering and marking her first ballot paper.

Like many disenfranchised women in intelligence, Kathleen spent her youth perfecting a range of skills that fell under the loose job title 'secretary'. Despite deriving from the Latin *secretarius*, meaning a person entrusted with keeping records and thus secrets, this occupational label provided the perfect cover for women working in misleadingly low-status intelligence positions. In reality, they fulfilled a challenging range of complex clerical, technical and operational roles. From encoding, decoding and translating enemy messages, to writing propaganda and running agents, women were not beyond outsmarting older and better-paid male intelligence officers. Their duties varied over time and were transformed during both world wars, with women providing the majority of labour.

Still, only a tiny minority of women managed to tap the glass ceiling and become fully fledged intelligence officers before 1945. Women would have to wait until the 1970s before they were regularly recruited at the officer level. Such progress came far too late for Kathleen. Motivated by a steadfast belief in the state's legitimacy, she had worked tirelessly without any expectation of recognition. Unsurprisingly, she never committed anything to paper about her life in the shadows, and MI6 remains forever tight-lipped about the identity of former personnel.

Much of what the world knows about MI6 and spying comes from the writings of Ian Fleming. The Bond film franchise has immortalised James Bond and cemented Fleming's fictional representation of MI6 in the collective public memory. Fleming drew many of his ideas from his service in naval intelligence during the Second World War. Some of the audacious wartime operations he devised, oversaw and supported, working alongside several notable real-life personalities such as the Director of the Naval Intelligence Division, Admiral John Godfrey, informed the characters and storylines of his post-war storytelling. Fleming found inspiration for characters such as James Bond, 'M', 'Q' and the ever-dependable secretary Miss Moneypenny in naval intelligence and MI6.

One can only imagine Kathleen Pettigrew's possible bemusement on watching the iconic film scene in *Dr No* (1962), where Bond enters M's office and, with cool precision, tosses his trilby hat on the stand. A voracious womaniser, he then proceeds to flirt with Miss Moneypenny. While enjoying the attention, the prim and proper secretary quickly makes it known that flattery will get Bond nowhere.

Fleming never revealed the identities of the individuals he drew upon. The 007 creator would undoubtedly have incurred the displeasure of MI6, had he not changed the name originally given to M's devoted secretary, Miss Pettavel, who appeared in the initial draft of his first Bond novel *Casino Royale*, published in 1953.[5] Fortunately for MI6, Fleming realised that his blend of fact and fiction was far too close to reality. The name was crossed out in pencil, and a new name was inserted: Miss Moneypenny.

Kathleen Pettigrew's story has, until now, remained invisible to the public. Like many career MI6 women, she never married and had no children. Her wider family 'knew that she worked for the Secret Service, but beyond that, she was an unknown entity'.[6] At some point, Kathleen made a conscious choice to distance herself from her family. Alienation must have seemed to her essential to not breaking cover. For those like her working in clandestine intelligence roles, any connection to real life could pose significant problems.

With Kathleen having abandoned her own, MI6 became her substitute family. In retirement at her home in Sidmouth, she hosted many of her 'Foreign Office' friends.[7] Nevertheless, she would also occasionally receive visits from select family members who had been loosely 'in the know' regarding the nature of her former employment in 'the Foreign

Office'. For instance, Kathleen had kept in touch with a cousin, the composer Ken Warner of BBC Light Orchestra fame, to whom she had been close since childhood.[8] His two sons, Richard and Tim, would visit from time to time, and Kathleen would regale them with stories of the Pettigrew family.

Sometime in 1978, the eldest of these two cousins, Richard, paid an unannounced visit with his wife and two-year-old daughter. Richard is the only living member of the Pettigrew family to have known Kathleen. He recalls how she had looked uncomfortable as they walked through the door on arrival. Richard had a very strong feeling that his distant relation disapproved of his beard and long hair.[9] The flat was untidy, with books and papers piled everywhere.[10] Consequently, as if embarrassed, Kathleen promptly directed them outside into the garden.

The conversation gradually turned to the politics of the day, when Kathleen warned Richard that he could not repeat anything she said. She advised him that he should keep such matters to himself. Kathleen knew things about people she had worked with that were not safe to know. She informed Richard that certain politicians in office had questionable pasts. To his annoyance, no names were forthcoming.[11]

Towards the end of the conversation, Richard half-joked about Kathleen being 'Miss Moneypenny'. Without hesitation, she responded: 'I was Miss Moneypenny, but with more power.'[12]

1

The Real Miss Moneypenny

The woman behind the typewriter was a loyal keeper of secrets. Her appearance gave 'an immediate impression of being exceptionally well-bred'.[1] A striking woman of middle years, she occupied a unique position in the secret world of British intelligence. A silent witness who helped shape historical events, she was no ordinary secretary.

As personal assistant to the MI6 chief, Kathleen Pettigrew had been privy to a lifetime of state secrets. She served her country unseen and unnoticed but was never invisible to the men and women she worked alongside. An indispensable linchpin, she was a source of both stability and security. This was no more apparent than during the Second World War when all secret intelligence distributed by the MI6 chief went through Kathleen: 'Consequently, she enjoyed great power.'[2]

Although she was a commanding presence in the wartime office, no job was beneath her, not even the mundane daily tasks that required her attention, such as maintaining her typewriter. As she set about changing the ribbon on her machine one autumn day in 1943, she instinctively paused, resting her fingers upon the spools. The sound of approaching footsteps had momentarily broken her concentration. A young messenger turned the office door handle and entered, closing it immediately behind her.

With several important documents to deliver to a tight deadline, the courier had run the short distance from the secret underground Cabinet War Rooms to the MI6 headquarters located at 54 Broadway. Kathleen finished feeding the typewriter ribbon through the small guides at the sides of the spools and looked over at the awkward visitor from Britain's wartime command centre. Her gaze was 'cool and direct and quizzical'.[3] She motioned for the special despatch box to be placed on her desk. The messenger quickly disappeared, leaving the special delivery 'for her eyes only'.

The experienced secretary opened the box and reviewed the solitary secret report and accompanying cover note. On 2 July 1943, she had sent a 'Most Secret Document' to Prime Minister Winston Churchill. The document never made it to the desk of the wartime leader. It had been kept in a sealed envelope under lock and key for the past three months.[4] Taking a memo-sized piece of blue foolscap from a writing pad stored in her desk drawer, Kathleen typed a short, perfunctory acknowledgement of receipt. She signed her name in blue ink and used a red 'Most Secret' stamp, leaving an impression in the top left-hand corner.[5] She then placed the note in a tray bursting with private papers.

Women like Kathleen have always had confidential information at their fingertips. From the seventeenth-century laundry women who smuggled King Charles's letters out of Carisbrooke Castle following his surrender during the English Civil War to the women of Britain's first secret service established in 1909, women have been present in all aspects of intelligence work.[6] They stood shoulder to shoulder with men. Yet their achievements and contributions to the organisations they worked for remain largely undocumented.

Unlike the famous fictional character Miss Moneypenny of the James Bond novels and films, the names of real women in intelligence remain mostly unknown. Stories of bold and daring female spies have cast a long shadow over a multitude of unnamed women. The infamous and tragic story of Mata Hari, the Dutch exotic dancer convicted of being a German spy and executed by a French firing squad in 1917, has captivated writers and filmmakers for over a century.[7]

Mata Hari dared to challenge the social conventions of her day. She weaponised sex to obtain secrets from army officers and diplomats, leading those at the time to judge her actions as deceitful and immoral. Interestingly, Mata Hari was only ever a stage name. Few are aware that her real name was Margaretha Geertruida Zelle. Orphaned at a young age, she was a woman who survived an abusive husband and overcame the tragic loss of her children, who died very young due to their being treated for congenital syphilis with a high dose of poisonous mercury. Far too trusting and out of money, she ultimately turned to the oldest profession in the world.

The name 'Mata Hari' has become synonymous with the image of the femme fatale, a double agent who danced her way into the beds of unsuspecting men. Arrested in February 1917 on the charge that she had allegedly shared secret information with the German enemy, Mata Hari provided the perfect scapegoat at a time when the war was going badly for the French, who had incurred heavy losses on the Western Front. It was easy to blame a foreign woman with questionable morals. After a sham military trial, Margaretha bravely faced death. She refused to be blindfolded and told her executioners, 'I am ready', and famously blew a kiss to the French firing squad. The legend of Mata Hari was born.[8]

The legacy of the femme fatale has fuelled sexist depictions of women spies in fiction and film ever since. Ian Fleming's stereotypical and clichéd 'Bond girl' fulfils common male sexual fantasies.[9] Most of his female characters are scantily dressed young women who quickly fall into bed with the suave and sophisticated 007 agent, James Bond. Fleming's chauvinism shines through in *Casino Royale* when Bond's attitude to women is summed up in the misogynistic statement: 'Women were for recreation.'[10] The reality of women working in British intelligence could not have been more different.

From the founding of the Secret Service Bureau in 1909, women worked in every area of the home and foreign departments that later became the counterespionage agency MI5 and the espionage agency MI6 respectively. From cleaning to codebreaking, women performed various roles to meet ever-changing operational demands. Most of the work was carried out by women who rarely left the back offices of British intelligence, whether at home or abroad. Women were the cornerstone of intelligence work. However, their names remain largely missing from history today, raising the question: where are they?[11]

The secret world of British intelligence has been and still is portrayed as a man's world. A number of women are recognised within the pages of the authorised histories of Britain's secret services: MI5 (the Security Service), MI6 (the Secret Intelligence Service) and GCHQ (Government Communications Headquarters), but they represent only a fraction of the actual numbers involved.[12] In many ways, these master narratives reflect *the* missing dimension within intelligence history – women. Other histories focus heavily on particular groups of women, such as the courageous female agents of the Special Operations Executive (SOE), whose well-researched operational stories have recently become popular reading fare.[13] However, a good deal of work remains to be done by researchers and writers to ensure that all women's voices are heard, recognised and represented in the histories of secret intelligence.

This book sheds light on the untold history of women who worked in British intelligence and security during the first half of the twentieth century. From the working-class housekeeper to the wealthy socialite, women in intelligence came from all walks of life. Some were career-driven and served loyally for decades; others worked only until they married. For the thousands of women who stepped forward during the world wars and contributed directly to the secret war effort there were greater opportunities. Manpower shortages during the Second World War saw women working at officer level, a promotion usually only open to men. Unsurprisingly, these women worked without the position titles and for less pay than their male colleagues. Unusual career prospects such as these ended abruptly in 1945. What then followed was a Cold War freeze on post-war opportunities for women, which remained in place until the 1970s.

While most never wore a uniform, generations of civilian women shared an unwavering belief in government service. The British state capitalised on the gendered and class-based notion of duty and loyalty, mainly targeting women with good connections, a proper education and a man of stature who could vouch for them. Ultimately, the primary qualification that all women working in the secret services had to possess and demonstrate was the ability to hold one's tongue and maintain secrecy.

Most of these career women took their secrets to the grave. In many ways, this book could not have been written while they were alive. Some might have quietly approved of a written history of women in intelligence but would have remained silent, bound by the Official Secrets Act. Most women never wavered in their duty as public servants, not even when they watched in disbelief as former male colleagues were permitted to disclose secret information in published memoirs. Of those whose service was limited to one of the world wars, a number of elderly women recorded their recollections of secret service work. But their reminiscences remained unpublished: safe with family or donated to archives and museums.

Historians of espionage traditionally rely on documents produced by clandestine organisations. These records present a top-down history of British intelligence, reinforcing the image of intelligence work being a solely masculine enterprise. For historians working this way, it is far easier to research men than women. Women certainly feature in organisational records such as correspondence and reports, but not as often as their male colleagues who were largely responsible for making decisions. Evidence of women's use and handling of paperwork survives in the form of chits and cover notes. Such practices are remnants of a bureaucratic culture that no longer exists in the digital era of the modern office. It is deeply ironic that the histories of secret intelligence organisations could only be written by consulting organisational documents created, organised and archived by women.

Women's records typically lie outside the archives, in private family collections. They are rarely complete and can, like any intelligence records, be a den of misinformation and mystery. To unlock and interpret them, historians must adopt a forensic approach, employing the skills and methods used by counterintelligence officers, leaving no stone unturned. By broadening the search, historians can hunt down and track women's individual and collective endeavours in modern intelligence. The chase is addictive, demanding and exhilarating. It can take years to make connections between sources and individuals. Researching intelligence history is by no means a speedy process to undertake.

MI6 women are perhaps the most difficult to research. They worked for the most secretive of all the services. They never married; they shied away from having their photographs taken; and in the years leading up to their deaths, they destroyed all personal evidence that linked them to their secret employers. Tracking down these women can be like trying to summon ghosts. However, the impossible becomes possible through meticulous research, proving that history is a prismatic kaleidoscope of interconnected stories.

This book traces the lives and careers of several women whose paths crossed in interesting ways. One woman's career in particular spanned the history of the emerging secret state and its intelligence and security apparatus. The legendary MI6 secretary Kathleen Pettigrew began her career in secret intelligence during the First World War. As a secretary in the Special Branch of the London Metropolitan Police, she witnessed key events in history, many of which thrust her into the path of foreign spies and double agents.

In 1916, Kathleen was the youngest woman working under the ambitious head of Special Branch, Basil Thomson. At eighteen years of age, she was an apprentice learning the trade that would set her on the way to becoming history's most famous unsung secretary. Already equipped with various secretarial skills, Kathleen quickly became adept at handling secret files and privileged paperwork. Privy to all kinds of secrets, she first captured them in shorthand while taking dictation of letters, several of which concerned suspected German agents.

In November that same year, a woman identified as the German spy Clara Benedix was removed from the Dutch steamer *Hollandia* when it docked at Falmouth. Travelling with an extensive wardrobe packed in numerous trunks and boxes, she was escorted from the Cornish port to New Scotland Yard on Victoria Embankment in London, where Basil Thomson was waiting to question her. In fact, the woman arrested turned out to be not Benedix but Mata Hari, who had been en route from Spain to neutral Holland. And so, a case of mistaken identity and prevailing historical circumstances threw two women together – an infamous double agent and an unassuming spy-catcher's young secretary.

On 16 November 1916, Mata Hari and Kathleen Pettigrew sat rooms apart in a labyrinthine building originally intended to serve as an opera house. Kathleen had intimate knowledge of Scotland Yard's Norman Shaw Buildings complex, with its 'ramification of floors, corridors, rooms, staircases, lifts, [and] baffling nooks and corners'.[14] Here her experience of working in the shadows was one of order and anonymity. It could not have been more different than that of Mata Hari, the famous performer known across Europe for her lavish lifestyle.

Mata Hari was interrogated at length in a long room overlooking the Embankment. Basil Thomson, her main inquisitor, was seated at his desk in an elevated position designed to intimidate a suspect and get to the truth.[15] He was flanked on both sides by the silent Major Reginald Drake of MI5 and Lord Herschell, assistant to the Director of Naval Intelligence. When she entered the room, Mata Hari was greeted with a deathly silence. Seated in a padded leather armchair, she found her face in full light. Thomson's cross-examination was a master class in how to deploy the art of abrupt questioning to full effect.[16] But Mata Hari was a consummate actress, surprising him by being 'ready with an answer to every question'.[17]

Eventually, however, the dancer spy broke down and confessed to being a French espionage agent, although not a German one. Thomson remained unconvinced of her innocence but had no evidence with which to detain her further. He had no choice but to send her back to Spain, where she had begun her journey. Mata Hari eventually returned to Paris, where she was identified as a German spy codenamed H-21. Arrested on 13 February 1917, she was thrown into a filthy cell at Saint-Lazare prison. She languished for several months in the rat-infested women's prison before being tried in July and found guilty. The merciless sentence was death by firing squad.

Historians remain obsessed with Mata Hari's sensational story. With their attention firmly fixed on one woman, they have neglected to ask who the other women were in this lurid tale. During Mata Hari's interrogation in London, we know that an unnamed woman sat behind a screen in the interview room, recording every question and response.[18] This anonymous shorthand writer, forgotten by history, was probably Kathleen Pettigrew. Skilled in stenography, Kathleen used a range of alien symbols to record the exchange between Basil Thomson and Mata Hari. In fact, as Thomson and his secret committee interviewed a series of suspected German spies during the course of the war, Kathleen would regularly sit in on interviews and produce transcripts.[19] The long days and endless nights of hard work prepared her for a career that did not follow a nine-to-five routine.

On the same day that Mata Hari was a guest of the pince-nez-wearing Basil Thomson, Kathleen sat at her desk and rolled a piece of paper into her typewriter, a copy of which may be found in the National Archives at Kew.[20] Addressed to the Dutch ambassador, the confidential letter dictated by Basil Thomson informed the Dutch diplomat that Mata Hari had been detained pending further investigation. For security purposes, Kathleen typed her initials 'K.P.' at the top left-hand corner of the letter. We will never know for certain from whom this office practice originated, nor the context in which it was introduced. This security custom of initialling files hints at a possible universal distrust of people that all those who worked in counterintelligence roles strove to uphold.

Kathleen's career trajectory could not have been less like Mata Hari's, the double agent who threatened the patriarchal system of the day and paid a heavy price with her life. Like so many professional women working in intelligence roles, Kathleen conformed to a system designed to favour the career advancement of men. In the Edwardian era, the occupational culture associated with spying and spy-catching was no different from that of any other workplace. Women in intelligence faced barriers and met resistance. They all encountered sexism. Yet women had the power to shape the matriarchal hierarchy within the intelligence world. Their work had real value and, over time, there was a gradual change in how they saw themselves and their place in the various secret services, as they faced an uphill battle for recognition.

After the First World War, Kathleen left Scotland Yard and went to work for MI6. During the interwar period, she became an important member of the MI6 chief's trusted inner sanctum, occupying a unique proximity to power. An unwritten special relationship between the second MI6 chief, Hugh 'Quex' Sinclair, and his personal assistant allowed Kathleen to operate as an extension of C himself. She was devoted, loyal and completely trustworthy. Much later, during the Second World War, her power increased to a level that saw her handling papers on C's behalf. However, several male officers viewed this achievement with suspicion.

Typically, women who crossed into male-dominated roles were viewed as not being 'real women'. Social attitudes of the time dictated that any demonstration of female strength had to be associated with something being wrong. Women were labelled 'lesbians' to explain their challenge to the gendered division of intelligence duties. Some male colleagues even attacked the outward appearance of successful women. Robert Cecil, MI6's Foreign Office adviser during the Second World War, described Kathleen as a 'formidable grey-haired lady with a square jaw of the battleship type'.[21] As has been pointed out recently by the *Financial Times* defence and security correspondent, Helen Warrell, 'If there is to be any real equality for the women who [spied] for their country, then they must wrest it from the past.'[22]

The extraordinary story of Kathleen Pettigrew and the remarkable women who worked in Britain's secret services is told here for the first time. This accomplished woman who inspired Ian Fleming's character Miss Moneypenny came from humble beginnings, unlike most Whitehall women who were drawn from middle-class backgrounds or the landed gentry. Driven by the ideals of the Edwardian 'New Woman', Kathleen's inspirational life began south of the River Thames close to the iconic Tower Bridge in Bermondsey, a poor area of London immortalised by Charles Dickens in his 1837 novel *Oliver Twist* and a part of South London that was home to thousands of unskilled and casual workers, many of whom lived in dreadful slums.[23]

Kathleen made her entrance into the world on 27 February 1898. Almost all babies were born at home during the Victorian era, and Kathleen's birth was no different. The Pettigrew family home at that time was 60 Bolina Road, located in the borough of Deptford in South

Bermondsey.[24] Described as being a 'quiet and respectable' street in 1899, the family lived either upstairs or downstairs in a two-storey workers' terrace house. There was no bathroom, and they shared an outside toilet with another family.[25] Lined by a scattering of trees, the street was set back from the Grand Surrey Canal, escaping the worst noise and smells generated by the factories, workshops and warehouses that occupied the nearby canal bank. Thanks to the philanthropic deeds of the wealthy, living conditions had improved considerably by the turn of the century compared to the grime and squalor of the earlier industrial period.

Throughout the nineteenth century, Bermondsey was a busy centre of trade and industry. Leather production was a vital driver of the British economy, providing shoes for workers and drive belts for machinery.[26] By the time of Kathleen's birth, her father, William Joseph Pettigrew, had worked for several years as a sealskin dresser. Exotic skins were fashionable, and the softest and warmest sealskin pelts were in high demand. Kathleen's father was one of many men charged with unpacking barges laden with seal carcasses from Alaska and Canada, and who then engaged in an unpleasant preparation process. The work was casual and poorly paid. Regular lay-offs when trade was slack or because of delayed shipments placed a tremendous strain on the family, who, as a direct consequence, lived a nomadic existence during the first few years of Kathleen's life.

For the working classes, Victorian life was a precarious state of affairs. No wages meant no rent money. During periods of hardship, some called upon the services of the nearest pawnbroker. Others turned to crime. Kathleen's own maternal grandfather, John Mackman, was convicted of theft at the age of seventeen. He served six months in prison and received several strokes of the whip.[27] At the turn of the century, living conditions in Bermondsey were still challenging. Overcrowding, poor air quality and severe poverty made it difficult for residents to break free. Nevertheless, it appears that the Pettigrews acted decisively to alter their lives and those of their two daughters.

In 1902, the family moved across the Thames to 1 George Court, located in Westminster, just off the Strand. Life in George Court must have felt very different from the Bermondsey slums. The narrow alley with its three-storey buildings and Victorian street lamps was approached by a flight of steps between numbers 50 and 51 Strand.[28] Despite its confined proportions, the short alleyway was no slum, but a bustling trade channel with a greengrocer, a tailoress, a Lyons tea-shop, and a popular public house. The passage led to the Adelphi the-atre and was often used as a cut-through by those wishing to see one of the modern dramas in the newly rebuilt theatre. Sir Arthur Conan Doyle may have ventured through George Court to oversee the pro-duction of his theatrical play *The Speckled Band*, performed in June 1910.[29] Watching from their window, a four-year-old Kathleen and her older sister, Ellen, aged eleven, must surely have been entertained by the constant foot traffic of shoppers and theatregoers in their fine clothes.

Confined to just three rooms, the family shared one floor over a ground-floor shop. Other residents were restricted to just one room, reflecting their out-of-work status or meagre wages. Some men may have succumbed to drowning their sorrows in The George pub conven-iently located next door at number 4. Built in 1675, the building had always been used as an inn (and remains the only surviving business in the alley today). Customers were treated to an aviary of live foreign birds.[30] In an attempt to invite custom and offer amusement, some pubs devised such peculiar features. These birds offered a welcome diversion from the chaos of urban London. Kathleen was captivated by the green and blue parakeets, which triggered a lifelong love of the birds.[31]

William and Ellen Pettigrew were determined to ensure that their daughters had a more comfortable and prosperous life. Sometime after their relocation to central London, an opportunity arose. In 1905, William was listed in the London directory as the owner of the chandler's shop beneath their home.[32] By 1911, it was clear that Ellen was the driving force behind this business venture and responsible for running the general wares store. A strong and resourceful woman, she completed the census return that year on behalf of her husband, proudly stating her occupation (not his) as 'general dealer'. Sadly, she also recorded the loss of a third child.[33] No doubt the business pro-vided Ellen with a timely distraction from her grief.

For more than twenty years, Kathleen's mother worked tirelessly in the shop. The additional income helped the family climb the economic ladder and provided a much-needed lifeline after William's unexpected death in 1915. While her mother was an important role model, her father lacked 'an ounce of ambition'.[34] Kathleen's comments on her father and the other members of the Pettigrew family survive in a rare letter she penned to her cousin, Ken Warner, in 1964.[35] She described her father as 'a kind, gentle and clever man, who spent most of his life reclining on a sofa, reading political history and arguing with his many man friends, who adored him. While all his friends and brothers were Tory, he was a Liberal or "Radical", as they called him.'[36]

Kathleen's father was one of twelve children. His father, also named William, had worked as a schoolmaster until he found himself out of work. He had managed to earn a small living working for the Royal Navy as a cork cutter. The family lived in a rambling, shabby old house in Portsmouth, and every day was a struggle. It is clear from Kathleen's 1964 letter that she did not look favourably on the Pettigrew men, whom she collectively described as being 'clever and interesting, but with one besetting sin – indolence!'[37]

She was particularly fond of one uncle, Harry, a dashing artist who had joined the army but deserted. He then changed his name to Harry Davies and joined the navy. Uncle Harry was a great adventurer and knew all the celebrities of the day in artistic and literary circles. Kathleen recalled how Oscar Wilde had apparently 'tried it on' with Uncle Harry but got a 'sock in the jaw' for his pains. As a result of the scuffle, one of the brooches the flamboyant Irish playwright and poet wore in his hair got painfully lodged in her uncle's hand.

Kathleen and her wayward uncle shared a keen interest in the family's origin. Harry had unearthed an old book in a church near Looe in Cornwall. The book contained a fascinating account from the time of the Norman Conquest about 'a band of sea pirates-cum-fishermen who were led by a small red-headed man'.[38] When William the Conqueror had his ships dotted around the coast, this little man used to take his fellow pirates out in small boats and, for sheer nuisance value, burn bits of the Conqueror's ships. This annoyed the French sailors, but they admired his courage and christened him either 'Petit-Grand' or 'Petit-Gros', meaning 'little but great'.[39] Over the years, the name became 'Pettigrew', and the family's auburn hair defined subsequent generations, including Kathleen.

The sudden death of Grandfather Pettigrew in 1877 left his wife, Harriet, penniless. She managed to support the family by taking on fine needlework, at which she was very accomplished. But this was not enough to feed all her children. Four years after his father's death, Kathleen's father, William, and her Uncle Alfred, aged twenty and twenty-two, left Portsmouth for London, where they took lodgings in

Bermondsey and began their work as cork cutters. The oldest of her father's siblings, Uncle Charles, remained in Portsmouth but could not help his mother in any meaningful way. A talented artist with a fiery temper, he barely managed to earn a decent living. However, it was a chance visit from his art master that changed the lives of his mother and his three younger sisters, Hattie, Lily and Rose, who would become models for the most celebrated painters of the Victorian age.

After calling at the tiny house in Portsmouth to leave a small commission for his aspiring student Charles, the art master was rendered speechless by the girls' beauty when their mother opened the door to him. Aware that the family had fallen on hard times, he advised Grandmother Pettigrew that she should take the girls to London. Artists would pay a small fortune to paint the distinctive Pre-Raphaelite-looking girls. This was a scandalous suggestion to make to a poor but respectable woman as, at the time, artist's models were looked on as no different from prostitutes.

However, Grandmother Pettigrew was an intelligent woman and did not dismiss the idea. Instead, she gave it serious consideration. Realising that she had two choices – remain poor in Portsmouth or gamble on brighter prospects in London – she wisely chose the latter. Armed with letters of recommendation supplied by the art master, the three girls, aged between twelve and seventeen, travelled around London boldly without a chaperone, seeking work from such famous artists as the gifted John Everett Millais.

In 1947, Kathleen's Aunt Rose, the youngest of the three sisters, took to her typewriter and wrote about her youth working as an artist's model.[40] In 1884, she had been scared to death and was almost on the point of tears when she and her sisters had been ushered into the hall of John Millais's custom-built studio house at 2 Palace Gate in Kensington. A twelve-year-old Rose instantly fell in love with the handsome and charming artist, who spoilt the three girls with chocolate and cakes before painting them in his studio. Millais constantly roared at them to stand still as he sketched what would become *An Idyll of 1745*.[41] With each brushstroke he captured the intense gaze of the novice models and transformed them into three forlorn Scottish peasant girls listening to music played by a young British fifer during the Jacobite Rising of 1745.

To their mother's astonishment, Millais paid them each a golden sovereign. They continued to pose for several weeks, earning hundreds of pounds alongside a bonus payment of £20 each when the painting was completed.[42] The sisters then took London by storm and posed for 'every great artist in the land'.[43] Their story was a true tale of rags to riches. The 'beautiful Pettigrew sisters' were scandalous trailblazers who ignored the rules of conduct expected of Victorian women. Known for their wit and their lively free spirits, the sisters caused quite a stir, broke many hearts, and made lots of money, proving that women could survive without men.

Kathleen's famous aunts made bold choices at a time when women were often faceless and nameless. They were proud of their bodies and had no reservations about posing nude. Hetty, the most famous of the three sisters, regularly sat for Théodore Roussel and featured in his celebrated yet controversial painting *The Reading Girl* (1886–7).[44] The life-size nude depicts a relaxed Hetty seated in a wooden folding chair, absorbed in her book. However, she was no mere 'girl' as described in the title. She was in fact nineteen years old and an independent wage earner.

Interestingly, Edwardian women who could read were still considered dangerous and a threat to patriarchy. Hetty shook off the shackles of societal expectations and lived her life the way she chose. A married Roussel quickly fell in love with his fearless model. They had a daughter, Iris, in 1902, but when his wife died, and he unexpectedly married someone else, a distraught and unforgiving Hetty cut all ties. Iris in her turn did not let the scandal surrounding her parents jeopardise her future. She was just as headstrong and determined as her mother and managed to carve out a successful career as an actress, making her debut in the 1920 film *Wuthering Heights*. She later moved to Germany, working under the stage name Colette Brettel, where she found further fame starring alongside Marlene Dietrich in *The Imaginary Baron* (1927).

Something in the Pettigrew genes helped produce ambitious and strong women. Like her trailblazing aunts, the self-effacing Kathleen had inherited the same instinct for self-determination. The extra income generated by the family shop allowed Kathleen's parents to send her to one of the oldest girls' schools in Britain, St Martin-in-the-Fields School for Girls, founded in 1700.[45] Kathleen attended the preparatory class, not far from George Court on Charing Cross Road. The school was a charitable enterprise aimed at providing Christian (Anglican) teaching for the female children of the poor – a radical notion at the time of its establishment, when there were almost no schools for girls – but the schooling was not free. Kathleen's parents paid an annual fee of between £3 and £5. Admitted at age five, 'Katie', as her father affectionately registered her, studied various subjects including French, German, Latin and mathematics, as well as drawing, cookery and dressmaking.

For three years, Kathleen walked the short distance from her home at George Court to the school. It took her less than ten minutes to reach the iron gates at the school entrance. She would have then taken her place in one of the six classrooms and would have exercised in the large drill hall.[46] The school was presided over by an accomplished headmistress, Miss Mary Pullee. Much loved and admired by her students, she was an inspirational role model to a young, impressionable Kathleen. A charismatic leader, Miss Pullee offered bracing words of encouragement and rejoiced in her pupils' successes.[47]

Kathleen attended St Martin-in-the-Fields until 22 February 1906. It remains a mystery as to which school she then attended. However, from age fourteen, she likely learnt her technical skills in typing and stenography at the nearby Pitman Metropolitan School on Southampton Row.[48] The world's largest and most successful business college prepared students for well-paid positions in London's banks, merchants, brokers and the Civil Service.[49] The founder, Sir Isaac Pitman, created his globally adopted shorthand system and established the first Pitman school in 1870.[50] In 1904, a young Winston Churchill declared the school was 'without equal in the world'.[51] After a student's graduation, Pitman's could be relied upon to provide an introduction, and their recommendation carried colossal influence. Many positions were offered exclusively to Pitman students, offering one explanation as to how Kathleen and her sister, Ellen, came to work for Special Branch. They likely took elocution lessons to rid themselves of any lingering cockney accent. Manners, speech and dress were of enormous importance to aspiring office workers.

Kathleen worked hard to achieve the coveted role of secretary. The office was a desirable destination for women seeking economic independence and a fulfilling career. Her education and training opened doors to her that had previously been closed to earlier generations of women. Miss Moneypenny, Fleming's fictional long-serving secretary, shares many traits with her real-life counterpart. Kathleen was clever, confident and possessed capabilities far exceeding her qualifications.

Dedicated to her work, she made a lasting impression on Ian Fleming, who undoubtedly passed through her office on his way to meet Stewart Menzies, the head of MI6 during the Second World War.

Miss Kathleen Pettigrew was just one of many women who have worked since the Edwardian era in the secret world of intelligence and counterintelligence. Their fascinating stories are full of twists and turns, reflecting the secrecy surrounding their entangled histories. Like the ever-changing, intricate mosaics formed in the cylinder of a kaleidoscope, the narratives of individual women can be pieced together to tell the shared history of women in British intelligence. After all, intelligence work has always been a woman's game.

2

Licence to Type

Click-click-click . . . Ding!

On 15 January 1952, a determined Ian Fleming sat at his large
roll-top desk and placed his fingers on the keys of a twenty-year-old
Imperial portable typewriter.[1] The quiet solitude of his Jamaican
retreat, Goldeneye, provided the perfect refuge in which he could con-
jure up the imaginary world of 007 complete with fast cars, deadly
gadgets and beautiful women. A curl of cigarette smoke drifted up
from an ashtray as he contemplated the opening sentence of what
would become his first Bond novel, *Casino Royale*. When he finally
sprang into action, the clatter of a typewriter drowned out the sound
of waves crashing onto the beach in his private bay below.

The character of Miss Moneypenny was born on the machine
that defined her role and the career of her real-life counterpart, Miss
Kathleen Pettigrew. The typewriter opened the office door for women
like Kathleen and her elder sister, Ellen, who began their careers at
Scotland Yard's Special Branch. The sisters joined an amazing cast
of women whose history in secret intelligence began in 1909 with the
creation of the Secret Service Bureau. Such early recruits were part of
a growing movement of women who were happy to relinquish traditional domestic arrangements and serve their country.

During the late Victorian and early Edwardian period, women
flocked to cities in search of new opportunities. The rise of the secretarial class saw women employed as bookkeepers, typists, secretaries,
stenographers and telephonists. Some 'lady-clerks' chose to lodge with
respectable families or professional landladies, while others resided in
new women's hostels with small bedrooms but generous living rooms,
offering an empowering haven of female fellowship. In many ways,
the typist or 'lady type-writer' became the face of the 'New Woman',
a feminist ideal that spoke to a growing number of free-spirited educated women who sought self-fulfilment and legal and sexual equality.

The typewriter was an invention that revolutionised the office. Male clerks sitting on tall stools at high sloping desks writing with pen and ink became a thing of the past. Female typists' work was defined by a writing machine whose origins dated back to the Industrial Revolution, when there was a desire to produce a device that could create inexpensive and legible letters faster than the process of handwriting. With very few moving parts, typewriters were simple and cheap to produce. Consequently, hundreds of inventors across Europe and America built machines of all shapes and sizes that could make an impression on paper, using many methods 'based on pushing, pressing, dropping, lifting, spinning, sliding, striking, and hammering'.[2]

Women were thought best suited to being typists due to their 'quickness of eye and ear, and delicacy of touch'.[3] The 'White Blouse Revolution' saw thousands of women employed in clerical roles.[4] In 1901, over 5,190 women listed their occupations as typists on the national census. Within ten years, this had increased to 13,809 female typists. At the start of the interwar period, the 1921 census recorded an explosion of 122,269 women employed as typists.[5] During this period, women redefined the world of work and their place within it, but they would have to fight long and hard for their seat at the table of power.

The arrival of independent and free-thinking secretaries, typists and filing clerks had an adverse effect on some men, who were troubled by the army of women invading the office. Male discontent became evident in sexualised images of the typist that appeared in newspapers, popular novels, music halls and film. This misogynistic response bore many similarities to that inflicted on Mata Hari. Office typists were presented as the object of man's erotic gaze. Driven wild by the desperate desire to claim a husband, they were portrayed as dangerous flirts who schemed and seduced their office bosses.

Society quickly became hostile to women who sought freedom outside the home. Suffragette marches organised under occupational banners such as those of office workers, together with picketing outside the House of Commons and Downing Street, only led to heightened tension.[6] Gendered behaviour had been turned upside down. Unwritten social codes were being challenged and people were genuinely fearful that society was degenerating.

The Liberal government faced unprecedented challenges; accelerated social change was just one of many. While some saw the expanding roles of women as a threat, others would seek their assistance to rid the country of the German spy menace. This occurred when a secret government department staffed by retired military officers and women typists was established in 1909. During the pre-war years, imperial breakdown and fears of invasion gripped politicians and the broader public. As Britain mobilised its warships, imaginary tales of German espionage and sabotage operations were cooked up by writers who should have known better, such as E. Phillips Oppenheim and members of the press.[7] If the government were to stand any chance of ridding the country of the Kaiser's legions of spies, it would have to collect sufficient evidence to prove that the imagined enemies were real, and it did so with the aid of a prolific spy writer.

The war-scaremonger William Le Queux published a number of fictional invasion stories that fed anti-German feelings and heightened public and government anxieties over an imaginary spy threat. Building on the success of his previous masterpiece, *The Invasion of 1910* (published in 1906), Le Queux published fourteen short stories under the title *Spies of the Kaiser* in 1909.[8] Despite appearing in print at the height of spy mania, Le Queux had initially struggled to find a publisher. He eventually convinced his friend D.C. Thomson, owner of the *Weekly News*, to serialise his stories. Quickly capitalising on the spy paranoia and the desire to sell more newspapers, the *Weekly News* invited its readers in February 1909 to submit letters about suspicious foreign spying activity. They were rewarded with a crisp £10 note for their efforts.

Le Queux received so many letters that some reports of suspected German spies made their way into the short stories that finally hit the bookstands in May 1909. Presenting his theories as being grounded in fact, Le Queux claimed that around 5,000 German spies were present in Britain, and that they all reported to a head agent in London.[9] His sensationalist work of fiction helped to convince the British that thousands of fifth columnists were actively targeting naval ports. The public wanted answers from the government on how it intended to solve the spy problem. In what became his most influential work, Le Queux made an urgent plea for 'some sort of contraespionage'.[10]

The Liberal prime minister, Herbert Asquith, ordered the Committee of Imperial Defence to investigate whether there was any truth to the invasion and spy stories. Colonel James Edmonds, the Director of Military Operations Counterintelligence, was commissioned to investigate; in a twist of irony, he consulted Le Queux. Edmonds used letters sent to the writer by scared members of the public as hard evidence that Germany was actively targeting Britain.[11] As a direct result of Edmonds's recommendation that the spy menace posed a significant threat, the Committee sanctioned the establishment of a Secret Service Bureau. The fledgling organisation officially began operating on 1 October 1909. It set about chasing down imaginary German spies with a staff of just two men, who each headed up one of the Bureau's two sections: a naval foreign-espionage section (MI6) and an army counterespionage section (MI5).[12]

The first head of MI6 was a fifty-year-old retired Royal Navy officer. Commander Mansfield Smith-Cumming was a grey-haired man with a prominent Punch-like nose and chin. He was short in stature and his somewhat stern appearance was made less threatening by his kindly demeanour and bright, curious eyes.[13] Born on April Fool's Day 1859, Cumming attended the Royal Naval College, Dartmouth. His service record reveals that he began his career in 1878 patrolling the East Indies and later served aboard the Royal Yacht, the *Victoria and Albert*. However, his time at sea was cut short when, in 1885, he was deemed 'unfit for service' and placed on the retired list.[14] It is thought that chronic seasickness got the better of him, but this seems unlikely given he later owned and sailed a number of small boats.[15]

Cumming's activities over the next decade remain undocumented. What is known for certain is that he married twice. His first wife, the South African Dora Cloete, sadly passed away after only four years of marriage. Cumming then married for a second time, and as part of the marriage settlement with the Scottish heiress Leslie Valiant 'May' Cumming, he changed his name to Smith-Cumming.[16] With a preference for 'Cumming', he later adopted the practice of signing secret memoranda with a solitary 'C' in green ink, a colour that was not uncommon at the time. His successors adopted the practice in homage to the legendary first spymaster, and the current head of MI6 is still known as 'C'.[17]

As suggested by the current doyen of British intelligence history, Professor Christopher Andrew, Cumming most likely conducted 'occasional intelligence forays' for naval intelligence sometime before the end of the century.[18] After this, he took charge of building up the Southampton boom defences to protect the port from waterborne attacks. The defensive measure of laying nets, otherwise known as 'booms', was experimental at the time. Cumming was a man who embraced change and innovation. He possessed a creative mindset and had a passion for technology. He loved to race his many yachts, motorboats and cars, and later took to the skies after gaining his Royal Aero Club certificate in 1913.[19] With minimal spying experience, Cumming was in many ways an unlikely candidate to head up the new espionage section. Still, his bold leadership skills and enterprising eccentricities made him the perfect man for the job.

On the army side, the head of the Bureau's home section, Vernon Kell, could not have been more different to the flamboyant sailor turned spy.[20] The 36-year-old army captain had had a glittering career as an army interpreter. Fluent in seven languages, which included Russian and Cantonese, Kell was a gifted linguist and arguably a better candidate than Cumming for heading foreign espionage. A well-travelled Kell returned from overseas duty to London in 1902, where he worked on analysing German intelligence for the War Office. As head of MI5, he would become the all-time longest serving head of any British intelligence organisation. With an army work ethic and a penchant for proper procedures and processes, he was diplomatic and tactful to the point where he was laughingly called 'the man with the golden tongue'.[21]

Cumming and Kell ran their sections singlehandedly from the same office premises at 64 Victoria Street, a short walk from Westminster Abbey. Rented under the cover of a retired Special Branch police officer, the office set-up and position proved to be problematic. Also, neither Cumming nor Kell was informed who was in charge, nor how the Bureau should be managed: 'The War Office thought it controlled the Bureau, the Admiralty thought it controlled Cumming, while the Foreign Office, which paid for it, did not at this stage want too much to do with it.'[22]

Initially, Cumming was convinced that Kell was the preferred option to lead the Bureau. Compared to Kell, who had previously worked in the War Office, Cumming was an outsider. However, he did not react well to the news that all War Office matters would be handed over directly to Kell. Working in such close proximity to each other only exacerbated the situation. Both men had a room, a telephone and an all-important safe for keeping secrets secret, but the impracticalities of conducting espionage and counterespionage from the same headquarters quickly became apparent.[23] Their visible arrival and departure from the office with its imposing stately facade, alongside the large number of visitors they received, made it impossible for them to operate under the cloak of secrecy. The office was also directly across Victoria Street from the Army & Navy department store, popular with naval and military officers, which 'led on more than one occasion to awkward meetings with inquisitive friends'.[24]

After two months of such proximity and adversity, an insecure Cumming jumped ship and rented a flat at Ashley Mansions on Vauxhall Bridge Road. With the Bureau operating on a shoestring budget, Cumming had to use his own money to cover its considerable costs, which included laying a telephone line. In many ways, this may be seen as the first headquarters of MI6, given that Victoria Street never functioned as a truly secret base.[25] Operating under the cover address of Messrs Rasen, Falcon Ltd, a bogus shipping and export firm, the new independent headquarters also served as Cumming's home, as he took up residence in an adjacent flat.[26]

At first, the new MI6 office was a lonely set-up with only a safe and a typewriter to keep Cumming company. Costing the princely sum of £18 8s, which was the equivalent of two months' wages in 1910, the machine, most likely a Caligraph, was deemed a cheaper option than employing a clerk.[27,28] However, Cumming soon found keeping up with the paperwork intolerable. Therefore, Miss Josephine Barnwell, a 32-year-old Foreign Office typist and shorthand writer, was drafted in to assist him.[29] Born and raised in London, Josephine was the daughter of a retired civil servant who had spent his career in the War Office.[30] Following in her father's footsteps, Josephine opted for the Foreign Office and was one of the sixteen women who worked in the FO typing pool before 1914.[31] Given that she was entrusted with confidential papers at Ashley Mansions, it is hard to imagine that she would have been kept at a distance from the balding Cumming and banished behind a curtain, as was the practice of gender segregation in the Foreign Office.[32]

Other than Cumming's wife, Josephine was not the first woman to enter the secret headquarters. A witness to all Cumming's mysterious goings-on was his trusted blue-eyed housekeeper Fanny 'Louie' Limburn.[33] Before her employment at 15–16 Ashley Mansions, Louie had worked as a domestic servant for two elderly sisters in Southampton.[34] Born and raised in the same city where Cumming oversaw the boom defences, it is likely that Louie's London appointment with the first

head of MI6 came about via a recommendation from one of the sisters
or some unknown link to Cumming himself.

For a woman only in her early twenties, the new position must have
seemed a world apart from the young housekeeper's previous domestic
duties for the aged spinster and her widowed sister. Cumming relished
disguise and surprised Louie regularly. After experimenting with a
wig and moustache for a covert meeting in Paris during the summer of
1910, Cumming sought the advice and assistance of the famous theatrical costumier William Berry Clarkson. With links to the criminal
underworld, Clarkson was a dubious character, but his services proved
very useful. In January 1911, Cumming visited Clarkson's costume
shop on Wardour Street in Soho. He required a convincing disguise,
complete with makeup, for a rendezvous with an engineer who had
offered his services to travel to Trieste and report on Austrian ship-
building there. Cumming's disguise was so successful that he kept a
photographic record in case he would find future use for it.[35]

An element of theatrical amateurism defined the early years of the
secret service. For Cumming, secret service work was 'capital sport',
an adventure pulled straight from the pages of one of Le Queux's
spy novels. Agents received obvious codenames, such as the case of
Mr Strange, a businessman allocated the codename QUEER.[36] The
MI6 spymaster devised and managed operations that saw Royal Navy
officers despatched to German dockyards under the simple cover of
'being on holiday'. His recruits were quickly arrested, convicted and
imprisoned before collecting any valuable intelligence.

With no handbook on conducting espionage, it would take time for
Cumming to master tradecraft and navigate inter-departmental rival-
ries.[37] The spy chief appreciated the importance of cover and the value
of agents possessing the necessary linguistic and technical skills.[38] For
agents to travel to Germany, their cover stories had to be believable,
and businessmen, journalists and writers proved ideal candidates.
Cumming used personal acquaintances to grow a network of agents
and sub-agents. During the first few years, he employed only a handful
of permanent agents and had no problem employing women.

A Foreign Office file concerning secret staffing matters contains
correspondence that sheds light on the identity of the first female MI6
agent. Mrs Agnes Blake, known as 'Agent A', was a fifty-year-old widowed literary translator.[39] The youngest child of Frederick Garraway,
a wealthy West Indies merchant, Agnes had been home-tutored by a

capable governess.[40] The Garraway family wealth was accumulated primarily by her grandfather Frederick, who, in the 1820s, had made his fortune in Dominica, where he owned a sugar plantation and the enslaved Africans who worked there.[41]

Like so many children of Victorian gentlemen whose wealth derived from the blood-stained colonial plantation trade, Agnes benefited from the opportunities and privileges such money brought to a woman of her station. As an accomplished and educated young woman with the right connections, she established herself as a translator, playwright and inventor. She adapted German plays for the British stage and translated German literary works into English during the interwar period.[42]

She even designed and patented a puzzle.[43] Agnes was a clever, ambitious and driven young woman. With such impressive credentials, any future husband would have to entertain and support her modern mindset.

Very little is known about Agnes's husband other than that his surname was Blake, and that they were married for eleven years before he died.[44] Who was he? How did he fit into her life? With no children and no surviving Garraways today to remember Agnes, answers to such questions remain an enigma. However, her status as a middle-aged widowed translator with family links to Germany gave her the perfect cover story, enabling her to travel to Germany without raising suspicion.

On 17 December 1909, Agnes made history as the first woman employed as an MI6 agent.[45] Agnes's connections with the literati of the day saw her adviser of many years, the *Punch* political satirist Charles Larcom Graves, recommend her to the Foreign Office's Permanent Under-Secretary and MI6 paymaster, Sir Charles Hardinge.[46] She was perfectly placed to provide early information regarding a possible German invasion and declaration of war.[47] Her older sister, Mary Jane, had married into the aristocratic Falkenstein family in 1869, and it was through her German brother-in-law's military connections as equerry to the Crown Prince and future Kaiser Wilhelm that made Agnes such an important asset to Mansfield Cumming and the War Office.

Agnes met her chief for the first time on 8 March 1910.[48] Cumming made a note of the meeting in his diary, a remarkable document that is kept in an MI6 safe at their present-day headquarters in Vauxhall,

London. The diary provides a unique record of the early history of MI6, an organisation that has yet to release any records into the public domain. Luckily, a handful of vetted historians and writers have been granted exclusive access to the diary. These include Cumming's biographer, Alan Judd, a former MI6 officer, who highlighted a diary excerpt relating to the first meeting between Cumming and 'Agent A'. The MI6 chief found Agnes disappointing and noted that she had 'a very slight grasp of what is required and very little power of obtaining any news of importance'.[49]

Such a frank assessment could have resulted from Cumming's resentment towards the War Office's haphazard meddling in the supervision of some Bureau agents such as Agnes. He was seeking results and needed a steady flow of information to achieve success. As a relatively inactive agent, Agnes could not help him achieve this goal. The Foreign Office ruthlessly monitored the spymaster's spending on agents and their travel, as they provided funds from what was known as 'the secret vote', a mechanism that permitted secret intelligence organisations to be financed with minimal oversight. Charles Hardinge, the man overseeing Secret Service Bureau expenditure, sharpened his pencil and began assessing the cost-effectiveness of Cumming's agents.[50]

Hardinge's financial review resulted in the dismissal of two agents. Agnes managed to survive the cull with a reduced annual salary, set at the revised rate of £100 (equivalent to £8,000 today).[51] From the end of March 1910, however, she really began to prove her worth. Taking on a more proactive role, Agnes provided Cumming with a long list of active and retired German officers, noting 'the degree of intimacy' with which she knew them. Upon a return trip from Germany, the new MI6 agent provided information concerning the movements of one particular 'Staff Corps man' on whom she had previously reported. She also assisted Cumming in the office, writing letters and telegrams in German.[52]

However, working for less money did not sit well with Agnes, who became quite unhappy. She shared her concerns with her personal adviser, Charles Graves, uncle of the famous war poet Robert Graves. Somehow news of their conversation reached Hardinge, who took serious issue with what he saw as a breach of trust. To Agnes's total shock and surprise, she was dismissed by Cumming, who bid her farewell with a derisory sum of ten pounds. Understandably, Agnes was not pleased, noting several months later that the cash did not cover her 'out-of-pocket expenses'.[53]

On 9 November 1910, Agnes wrote a statement of what had occurred concerning her unfair dismissal. Sitting in Charles Graves's home, a splendid ground-floor apartment in the Victorian mansion block of Iverna Gardens in fashionable Kensington, she took several sheets of Graves's personalised writing paper and used pen and ink to scrawl her account. She began by outlining her visit to Cumming where she had pleaded her case. Agnes saw no issue with entrusting Graves with information about her salary, since he had been the one who had originally put her name forward to Hardinge and was therefore fully aware of her hush-hush work.[54]

In response, Cumming sought to reinstate Agnes. At a later meeting he told her that 'the authorities took back what they said' and offered her a position for work abroad, though at a reduced annual rate.[55] Agnes quickly realised that the offer, if ever really intended, was not financially viable. She proposed an alternative: 'that I might possibly be of use here, and that I would willingly continue in their service with shorter spells of work abroad, as required, and at a lower salary'.[56] But the matter was then left unresolved for several months while Cumming recovered from ill health.

Unhappy at what had transpired, Graves wrote to his brother-in-law, the Foreign Secretary Sir Edward Grey, informing him that he should know what had happened and enclosing a copy of Agnes's statement.[57] After Foreign Office intervention, Agnes was discharged from the Secret Service Bureau on 16 November 1910 with a final settlement payment of £58 10s.[58] According to Graves, Agnes was 'most grateful and quite content with the settlement'.[59]

Had it not been for Agnes's dismissal and her refusal to go quietly, the identity of 'Agent A' would have been lost to history. The settlement suited both sides. Agnes emerged from the ordeal unscathed, partly thanks to Cumming, who she believed had 'always been so kind in the matter'.[60] Perhaps Cumming was secretly relieved to be rid of a woman with a keen intellect who questioned and challenged decisions. It may have been the plan all along to make a token offer of reinstatement with less pay in the hope that 'Agent A' would decline. There was also great concern that all agents discharged from duties should have any pay claims dealt with amicably so that they remained quiet about their work.[61] If the cloak-and-dagger enterprise were to stay secret, it was imperative that both Cumming and Kell should remain on friendly terms with any departing employees.

The following year, Home Secretary Winston Churchill pushed a defining piece of legislation through Parliament: the Official Secrets Act. Trials of incompetent German spies had continued to fuel public anxiety, and the presence of German gunboats in British and French spheres of influence had added to the alarming situation. Germany's military leaders were sending an unmistakable message that they advocated European war. Unsurprisingly, the legislation encountered little opposition and was passed within a day.

The 1911 Act was a significant moment in the history of official secrecy. For the first time, the state defined in law how it should manage its information and stipulated the penalties for spying. Building on the original 1889 Official Secrets Act, the 1911 Act recognised the need for greater government secrecy and tighter controls on the flow of information.[62] It no longer merely targeted foreign spies and corrupt civil servants but also whistle-blowers and the press. It affected everyone. Secret Service Bureau employees were prohibited from disclosing and publishing secret information, even though this did not deter some from later writing books about their espionage escapades. Upon signing a version of the Official Secrets Act, generations were, and still are, legally bound not to disclose state secrets. But this early legislation and subsequent amendments were written by men for men. Legal secrecy did not recognise women. They were trusted to keep secrets at a time when the state did not trust them to vote.

Vernon Kell, head of the Bureau's home section, was silently pleased with the Act's passing.[63] Asquith's Liberal government attacked the very civil liberties it had lobbied for decades earlier, while at the same time aiding Kell's campaign to unmask German agents.[64] With a small London-based staff of only seventeen by the time war broke out in August 1914, Kell used his resources wisely and focused on working with the police. This was a shrewd move on the spy-catcher's part, as Kell was able to tap in to existing police resources and utilise their powers of arrest. Chief constables rallied local bobbies up and down the country to carry out surveillance and investigate suspected German agents. With the support of the Home Secretary, Winston Churchill, wider mail interception also became possible.

It was not long before Kell's investigations generated a tsunami of paperwork. The London headquarters stored every piece of information received in what became known as the 'Registry', an ever-expanding emporium of colour-coded cards and dossiers that lay at the heart of Kell's fledgling counterintelligence enterprise. But, to defend the realm, Kell required the assistance of a dedicated team of trustworthy men and women to manage the use of this prototypical card-index filing system of suspects, which would eventually transform British counterintelligence into a serious outfit that hunted real German spies.

Such an endeavour fell to those men and women behind the scenes who did not hold officer rank, and whose efforts have remained unrecognised for far too long. The recruitment of a 'Chief Clerk' on 14 March 1910 signalled the first steps of an information revolution that would take hold during the First World War.[65] Working under Kell at the Victoria Street office, James Westmacott, a former soldier-clerk at the War Office, was the second employee after Kell to work in what would become MI5. Allocated his own small office, which contained a bell so that he could be summoned at will, the retired Superintending Clerk of the Royal Engineers played a crucial role in managing the volume of information during the first year of the Bureau's operation.[66] As more demands were placed on him, the experienced administrator hired more staff, personally vetting his only child, Dorothy, the first woman to work in MI5, and his two nephews, the Strong brothers.[67]

James Westmacott arrived in London at age fifteen to serve an apprenticeship in the wine trade, but in 1882 he ran away to pursue his dream of serving in the army. He cut a fine figure in his army uniform, with his pale grey-blue eyes and dark brown hair.[68] The young soldier excelled in clerical duties of every kind, including confidential work. Exemplary conduct earned him several promotions, which led to a transfer to the intelligence section of the War Office, where Kell was employed. After Westmacott's retirement from the army, it seems that Kell invited him to work for the Bureau. At fifty-five and having reached the rank of warrant officer, he retired in 1920 and was awarded the MBE for his decade-long secret service.[69]

Nine months after Kell had headhunted her father, Dorothy Westmacott took up her MI5 position as a typist on 16 January 1911.[70] A quiet and unassuming person, MI5's first woman proved a competent assistant to her father. Dressed in the simplest of cotton frocks, and covered from neck to hem by a sensible and businesslike overall, Dorothy served dutifully in what became the secretariat during the war. When her father retired, she too bid farewell to the secret service.

During her time with MI5, she had experienced four office moves, reflecting the increased staff and ever-expanding Registry. The first move came only a month after her employment with her father began, when Kell decided to move to cheaper and larger chambers at 3 Paper Buildings in the Temple.[71]

On 18 September 1911, Dorothy's cousin, the handsome Frank Seymour Strong, walked through the new office door. The former solicitor's clerk had been living with his family in Reading when his uncle offered him the secret appointment.[72] A larger-than-life character, Frank could not resist the mysterious offer. He worked for Kell until 26 July 1916, when he enlisted in the Royal Garrison Artillery and served as a gunner with the Mesopotamian Expeditionary Force.[73] After the war, he went on to have a long career with the Prudential insurance company. He became a community pillar, playing a prominent role in the local Conservative Club, where he enjoyed playing snooker.[74]

A month after Frank was initiated into Kell's circle of trust, Miss Helen Newport was appointed the first female secretary. The forty-year-old was the cousin of Captain Frederick Stanley Clarke, who served as Kell's first assistant until December 1912, when he left and became deputy chief constable of Kent Police. The Newport and Clarke families hailed from India, where generations of their men served in the Bengal Civil Service and the Indian Army. Helen's appointment was the first of many by MI5, who drew heavily from the daughters of Indian Army officers. They included Jane Sissmore, MI5's first female officer, who followed in Helen's footsteps, and Mary Sherer, MI5's first female agent handler.

Helen Newport made MI5 history. Alongside opening and acknowledging all letters addressed to Kell and overseeing the security of all secret and confidential documents, she was responsible for 'the formation of a card index to the records of the Bureau'.[75] The outdated ledger-based system was discarded in favour of the Roneo carding system, a modern information management system at the forefront of records administration. MI5's first secretary set to work on indexing vital information.

'Special Cards' marked the beginning of MI5's card index.[76] Using data collected by the 1911 census, a national count of all households, MI5 compiled a secret Register of Aliens. The list was then circulated to local police to collect information on enemy aliens. For those Germans and Austrians deemed a possible or actual danger, their

Roneo card quickly became a montage of text and various coloured seals, and symbols. Those judged the most significant threat had their cards marked with a red wafer seal and a double X, signalling that the individual was to be arrested when war was declared.[77]

Over the year, the piles of paper and card indexes generated by the monitoring of suspicious aliens led to a severe strain on storage space. In September 1912, the MI5 workforce relocated for a third time to Watergate House, York Buildings, on the Strand. At 'Watertight House', as it was known to those within its walls, Helen was joined by two secretaries, Miss Holmes and Miss Bowie, and another Strong cousin, Stanley Cecil Strong, who had been working as a coal merchant's clerk when his uncle recruited him.[78] The Strong family remember Stanley as being very secretive with an air of self-importance, undoubtedly imbued in him by his close professional relationships with MI5 gentlemen officers throughout his career.[79]

However, unlike the Strong brothers, who were deemed part of the 'establishment staff', the team of four women were categorised as 'temporary staff'.[80] There was a strong and enduring belief that women's work would only be an interim before marriage. This view was used to justify paying women lower wages, and it provided a rationale for why women were rarely promoted to higher positions, which were normally held by men. Despite these challenges, the first carefully selected women managed to successfully carve out their positions in an organisation unlike any other at the time, and helped lay the foundation for the Security Service that exists today.

As part of Kell's small team, these pioneering female record-keepers played a significant role in curbing German espionage efforts. Through registry information they had acquired by means of mail interception, Kell's spy-catching organisation unmasked Adolf Frederick Schroeder (aka Frederick Gould), the final German spy convicted before war broke out. At his trial on 4 April 1914, it was revealed to a packed courthouse that the 63-year-old moustachioed major in the Kaiser's army had attempted for six years to 'induce British soldiers and sailors to betray their country'.[81] Schroeder was found in possession of battleship designs and gunnery drill books, and his wife, also on trial, had been set to sail for Ostend to share them with German intelligence.[82]

A month before the trial, Kell drew upon the Schroeder file to demonstrate the importance of record-keeping in building cases against hostile enemy agents such as Schroeder. On 3 March 1914, Kell made his way to 2 Whitehall Gardens, a short taxi ride from Downing Street. With the aid of his deputy, Captain Eric Holt-Wilson, he presented an assortment of maps, charts, registers, forms, lists and index cards to the select members of the Committee of Imperial Defence.[83] With a captive audience consisting of Prime Minister Herbert Asquith, Winston Churchill and a handful of other notables, Kell reinforced the importance of counterintelligence work to war planning.

The imaginary enemy agents that MI5 had begun to hunt in 1909 were now very real in 1914, but the scale of the threat they posed remained grossly exaggerated. After Britain declared war on Germany on 4 August 1914, spy fever reached new heights. Whether the enemy was real or not made no difference to Kell and his spy-tracking department. As the perceived threat grew in size, so too did his workforce. The sound of clacking keys and the percussive ding of the typewriter's bell was soon magnified by the hundreds of young women who stepped forward to serve their country during the war.

3

The Nameless

On 15 May 1915, a small funeral party stood under the shade of mature woodland in the far northeast corner of Nunhead Cemetery in Southwark, London. As those in attendance stepped away from the graveside and made their way to the nearest path, young Kathleen Pettigrew was left to say a private farewell to her father, who, only days before, had died at Charing Cross Hospital.[1] The 53-year-old William Pettigrew had succumbed to Bright's disease, an inflammatory disease of the kidneys, no doubt partly caused by years of breathing in toxic fumes generated by the Bermondsey tanneries.

Despite several years of running the shop in George Court, Kathleen's mother, Ellen, lacked the funds to pay for private interment. The widow had no choice but to bury her husband in a common grave shared with several other departed souls.[2] William's humble resting place stood in stark contrast to the imposing Victorian memorials of the wealthy, whose tombstones were adorned with lions' heads and weeping angels. While Kathleen's father left no lasting mark on the world, the decisions he made during his life changed the lives of his two daughters.

For seventeen-year-old Kathleen, her father's death presented a turning point. She would soon have to seek work and contribute to the financial stability of the now all-female Pettigrew household. Her older sister, Ellen, had previously secured employment as a Registry clerk in the Special Branch of the London Metropolitan Police.[3] Following her sister's lead, Kathleen took a position in the office of Basil Thomson, the tireless head of Special Branch.[4] Eager to learn and serve her country, she got off to a successful start and adapted to the ever-changing demands of her wartime job.

Kathleen was one of the many thousands of nameless women who helped turn the cogs of the wartime counterintelligence machine, but her work came at the end of the spy-catching process. As a trained stenographer, she produced a verbatim record of police-suspect interviews conducted by Basil Thomson. These documents would serve as important first drafts of a history that hinted at the inner workings of the emerging bureaucratic intelligence industry.

When Kathleen took up her position at New Scotland Yard in 1916, the country faced unprecedented anti-German hysteria. During the first few days of the war in August 1914, the government rushed through a series of laws. The Defence of the Realm Act (DORA) was a draconian attempt to regulate public safety and security, providing the government with powers just short of martial law. It was amended six times throughout the war and saw police powers widened to the point where anyone causing alarm could be arrested. The lives of non-British-born men and women were defined, restricted and monitored under the Aliens Restriction Act, which saw men of military age interned for the duration of the war.[5]

Anybody who sounded, had the appearance of, or actually was a foreign national was viewed with suspicion, so much so that in July 1917, the Royal family abandoned their German surname, Saxe-Coburg-Gotha, in favour of the quintessential English surname, Windsor. The British people were convinced that hidden armies of foreign enemy nationals were busy gathering key strategic information on British defensive capabilities or lying in wait to commit acts of sabotage. As a direct consequence, Special Branch officers worked past midnight each day to tackle huge sacks of mail sent by scared members of the public who were convinced that a Swiss waiter was a German agent or a neighbour's homing pigeon was carrying enemy messages.[6] Outpourings of public support resulted in a ton of paperwork for Basil Thomson and his team, who worked around the clock to identify who was a threat and eliminate who was not, no matter how absurd the complaint may have been.[7]

Special Branch did not operate alone. It worked alongside various War Office departments, the Home Office and police forces across the country. However, the task of co-ordinating this wartime security apparatus fell to the workaholic head of MI5, Vernon Kell, known as 'K' to his staff. Before the outbreak of war, Kell had carefully made plans to cripple the German intelligence network. Working around the clock, he slept at the office with his bed surrounded by telephones.[8] On 4 August 1914, Kell used a secret telephone exchange and telegraph system to launch one of the greatest spy hunts in history.

As Big Ben chimed the eleventh hour that fateful day, the country found itself at war with Imperial Germany. Crowds quickly formed outside Buckingham Palace, cheering and waving to King George V and Queen Mary as they stepped onto the balcony. Men raised their straw boaters, some tossing their hats high into the air in a show of patriotic support.[9] Little did they know that twelve hours earlier, Kell had sent secret instructions to the police to apprehend those marked for arrest on the outbreak of war. In the months leading up to August 1914, the capable spymaster and his enterprising team had spent months compiling a secret register known as the 'Special War List'. Over two hundred foreign residents, mostly Germans and Austrians, had been identified across the country as posing a danger to the state, though the majority had never actually committed any offence.

Before the day ended, plain clothes undercover Special Branch officers sprang into action. However, this was not the great round-up of a twenty-strong German spy ring as some historians claim.[10] Rather, it marked the beginnings of a carefully choreographed partnership between MI5 and the police, who arrested nine or ten known German agents.[11] Kell was only too happy for Special Branch to take the credit for the arrests, as it drew attention away from his covert organisation. However, as the war progressed, he became displeased with Thomson's monopolisation of suspect questionings.

While their relationship became fraught at times, the success of both men's combined counterespionage efforts rested on the accuracy of the intelligence gathered. Information was, and still is, the main currency of counterintelligence work. Several secret civilian and military intelligence branches fed into the spy-catching machine to detect and prevent espionage, sabotage and subversive activity on home soil. A small number of secret services were staffed by brilliant and capable women who joined the workforce during the war, replacing the men who had left to fight on the frontline.[12]

Scores of women identified suspicious mail and telegrams intercepted by the postal and cable censorship administrations.[13] Of the two branches, postal censorship was usually the first to determine that something was amiss. One censor, Freya Stark, who went on to become a famous writer and explorer of the Arab world, wrote to her mother describing the thrill of identifying suspicious mail after reading hundreds of dull letters each day:

The suspicious letters were, of course, interesting: some one could make sure of – the Morse code cut round stamp edges, the lining of envelopes, and the flourishes and underlinings used as guides to key words.[14]

Propaganda, translation and press censorship departments also filled increasing numbers of filing cabinets with snippets of information relating to shady individuals and unusual activity. Civilian women were recruited for similar roles by the military. The soft-spoken Mary Jenkin studied German at Oxford before the war. One of the first jobs assigned to her in Room 40, the centre of naval intelligence, was the translation of Franz von Papen's private correspondence. To her surprise, she found that the German military attaché in Washington, who would later become Chancellor of Germany, had preserved all his chequebook stubs, providing a perfect record of all monies paid to spies during his time at the embassy.[15] Papen was subsequently expelled from the United States for espionage and sabotage activities.[16]

All this information, including police surveillance reports, civilian passenger travel records, and much more, was handed over to MI5 for investigation. Responsible for co-ordinating all intelligence information and tracking suspicious activity, MI5 relied on women as a cheap and trustworthy source of labour. From the four women in post at the outbreak of war in 1914, the service's female workforce grew exponentially to 161 by December 1916. It peaked in June 1918, with 296 women working at its London headquarters, domestic ports and overseas offices.[17]

During the course of the war, MI5 employed more than 650 women.[18] It was no different to any other wartime employer in seeing women as emergency workers.[19] However, a particular type of woman was sought. Headmistresses of such exclusive girls' schools as Cheltenham Ladies' College were asked to recommend suitable alums, and candidates were sought from the Oxford University women's colleges, St Hugh's and Somerville.[20] Recruits had to be intelligent, hardworking and discreet. Knowledge of foreign languages was also sought. Many recruits were the daughters or nieces of army officers who worked in MI5 or knew someone who did, and through such associations and family ties, it was assumed the women had 'inherited a code of honour'.[21]

Unsurprisingly, MI5 was full of privately educated, bright young women under thirty who outsmarted male officers on many occasions. They excelled in their work, and a few managed to rise to positions normally held by men. For instance, the daughter of a Scottish carriage maker living with her family in Lambeth became the first woman to be appointed head of a government finance department.[22] Having previously worked as a secretary for Maldwyn Makgill Haldane, the MI5 officer in charge of Administration and the Registry, Agnes Masterton had not yet turned twenty when she took on the new, highly responsible role. Women also went on to head the photographic department, and at the start of 1917 'lady chauffeurs' were found behind the wheel for the first time.[23]

Yet such opportunities were rare. While the war provided possibilities for women working in intelligence roles, they were generally time-limited. Most of MI5's female staff were employed in administrative and clerical roles, where they excelled in designing and running spy-tracking records systems.[24] However, success was a double-edged sword. The temporary nature of women's wartime work as low-paid office workers saw future generations confined to desk roles, making it almost impossible to break the cycle and climb the career ladder to positions held by men.

One woman did manage to tap at the glass ceiling and achieve officer status, but this did not happen until 1929. Kathleen 'Jane' Sissmore joined MI5 on 24 August 1916 as an eighteen-year-old straight from Princess Helena College in Ealing, where she had been head girl.[25] Her imposing and fiercely patriotic headmistress, Miss Mary England Parker, had been asked to send suitable school leavers along to MI5, an endeavour she would continue with after the war had ended. Like other fellow students who joined MI5 at the same time, Jane most likely went for an interview straight from the exclusive public school, still wearing its distinctive green serge uniform.[26] The school had a long tradition of educating the daughters of military officers and Anglican clergy. It produced resilient young women who embodied the school motto: *Fortis qui se vincit* – 'strong is she who conquers herself'.[27]

Given that Princess Helena College was so close to the Sissmore family home in Ealing, it was an obvious choice for Jane's parents to send their only daughter there as a day girl. However, the grandeur of the Sissmore home, 21 King's Avenue, an impressive red-bricked Victorian–Gothic style mansion, was in stark contrast to the modesty of George Court, the bustling alley located off the Strand where

Kathleen Pettigrew resided with her family in just three rooms. The two women – Jane and Kathleen – who began their work in secret intelligence during the same year came from entirely different worlds, but both succeeded in carving out long, contrasting careers in MI5 and MI6.

Born months apart in 1898, Kathleen Pettigrew hailed from a working-class Bermondsey background, whereas Jane was born into privilege. Her father, Colonel John Edmund Angelo Sissmore, was stationed with the Bengal Army in the malaria-ridden military fort at Barrackpore, near Calcutta.[28] For many military families living in India at that time, child mortality due to disease was a constant worry. For this reason, a concerned Colonel Sissmore resigned his commission and moved his young family back to England, where he earned a living as a tea merchant.[29]

Described as 'one of MI5's most remarkable wartime recruits', Jane Sissmore began her MI5 career working in the Registry.[30] There was no better place to start learning her spy-catching trade than the service's beating heart, a secret emporium staffed entirely by women. The ever-expanding Registry known as 'H.2' sat within 'H' Branch, a section of MI5 responsible for administration, records and managing the office and staff. MI5 was very much a 'living organism', and the eleven sections of 'H' Branch were continuously reorganised to meet new demands.[31] Chief Clerk James Westmacott and his daughter Dorothy, the first woman ever employed by MI5, worked together in 'H.7' despatching overwhelming volumes of correspondence and managing office equipment, furniture and stationery.[32]

The Registry was one of the seven wonders of the secret world. It had more people than any other branch, with its staff outnumbering secretaries by two to one.[33] Industrious and eternally busy cardists recorded, indexed, filed and retrieved all information passed to them, ranging from the ludicrous to the serious. As one MI5 officer smugly remarked in 1917, the Registry's filing system was 'our great standby and cornerstone': all government departments, including security services in the Empire and allied countries, came to the Registry for information.[34] Resembling a 'bee hive' by the end of 1918, its 130-strong workforce retrieved over 10,000 documents a month and managed a card index of nearly a million entries.[35]

Filing, classifying suspects and sharing files were key to laying the foundations of an emerging information-based system enacted through a disciplined female workforce. Standardised Registry practices and procedures saw intelligence on potential enemies help to shape a new way of knowing and remembering. Through the detection and processing of information, MI5 women sparked the beginnings of what would later become an information revolution. All this took place within the walls of its London wartime headquarters.

From August 1916 until the war's end, MI5 ran its organisation from Waterloo House, 16 Charles Street, Haymarket.[36] The service's first woman secretary, Helen Newport, recalled how security was paramount. All staff were issued with strict instructions that under no circumstances should they reveal the address of where they worked.[37] As a precaution, all visitors were directed to the enquiry office on the ground floor in nearby Adelphi Court.[38] Staff were provided with a special pass that was known by sight to the doorkeeper, and internal security was just as rigorous. If rooms were to be left vacant for more than a few minutes, staff had to ensure that doors were locked, and women were expressly told that keys should not be carried in handbags.[39]

The Registry was a spacious and airy room that occupied the entire second floor.[40] It housed an enormous card index that stretched around the room like a snake.[41] Table upon table was covered in specially designed wooden boxes full of cards.[42] The cards had previously been stored in tall Roneo filing cabinets with partitioned drawers, but this proved problematic, as the women were prone to cracking their heads on the sharp edges of the open cabinet drawers.[43] The 'Queen Bee' of the Registry, Edith Lomax, made the wise decision to place the drawers on tables. This was one of several changes she made when she joined MI5 as Lady Superintendent on 21 February 1915, bringing with her as her assistant Elsie Harrison.[44]

Edith Lomax was considered a reliable pair of hands. At forty-five, her hair was beginning to grey, but the twinkle in her distinctive green eyes was still very much present.[45] She was born and raised in Hereford, where her father, the Reverend John Lomax, was a schoolmaster. Edith pursued a career in teaching and worked as an assistant teacher before moving to London, where she was employed as a secretary at a publishing house.[46] Edith's loyal and capable assistant, Elsie Harrison, was in her early thirties when she took up her post with MI5. As a former employee of *Encyclopaedia Britannica*, she was a trained shorthand writer and typist. In fact, the entire Harrison family worked with typewriters in some capacity or other. Her father, Frederick Harrison, was a bookkeeper for the Smith Premier Typewriter Company, and both her sisters worked for Remington: one as a shorthand writer and typist, and the other as manageress of the copy department.[47]

The arrival of the administrative dream team marked a 'new epoch in the history of the Registry'.[48] As the work increased, the number of staff was doubled. Edith made several necessary improvements to the running of the central clearing house, such as abolishing the time book and the night shift due to frequent air raids. She also instituted periods of regular leave for the women employees to help alleviate the growing strain.[49] As the female workforce expanded, it became clear that better co-ordination between the secretaries and the Registry was needed. In 1917 Edith Lomax was appointed Controller of Women's Staff, and Elsie was promoted to Superintendent of the Registry. Edith was now responsible for the hundreds of women employed by MI5. Good productivity levels depended on well-rested young women who dressed sensibly and were generally healthy. While a lady doctor was not appointed until 1918, the Lady Controller scored a small victory by dealing head-on with one 'problem' of intimate importance to female staff.

The social taboo of rubber menstrual aprons and belted girdles was a subject that remained a mystery to most men in the office, but Edith Lomax ensured that charwomen cleaned the ladies' lavatories and emptied the sanitary bins daily.[50] At the time, attitudes emphasised the importance of keeping periods hidden, to preserve idealised notions of femininity. Sanitary towels had been available since the 1890s, but it was not until after the war, during the 1920s, that the Cellucotton Company finally solved women's oldest problem by introducing its more comfortable and disposable Kotex sanitary pads to the market.[51] During the war, the company had discovered that nurses were using its wood-fibre field bandages to manage their 'monthlies' and had immediately recognised the urgent need for a better method.[52]

It was thanks to Edith Lomax's caring oversight that MI5 met this particular womanly requirement. Her motherly approach provided an important 'personal touch' that began the very moment her ladies were recruited and had pledged to remain silent about their work. After completing the interview process, a young Scottish teacher from Edinburgh, Margaret MacGregor, remembered being directed to sign the Official Secrets Act, which she described as 'a special oath'. Many

years later, she reflected that the whole process seemed extraordinary. Her mother had suggested an office job in London, and it was through a family relation, Maldwyn Makgill Haldane, the officer in overall charge of MI5 Administration and the Registry, that she was offered a position with the War Office department, MI5.[53]

On 5 May 1916, the third newest recruit that month was directed towards a typewriter. Maldwyn Haldane's young cousin began her work in the typing pool before progressing to the Registry, where she worked in indexing. Every document received in the Registry was given a serial number and filed using a number system to retrieve it quickly. The sole purpose of recording every incoming paper was to know its later whereabouts, as most were sent to other branches after an officer or their secretary had requested a trace, but all papers had to be returned to the Registry so that it could function efficiently. All names, places and subjects mentioned in papers were indexed, so that any new information received could be connected with that already recorded. By 1917, the indexing of names was so 'gigantic' that seventeen typewriters were needed for this purpose alone.[54] The Registry was a hive of activity with over 600,000 name and place cards corresponding to 27,000 personal dossiers. Subject files contained several hundred thousand entries and occupied 360 feet of shelves, amounting to the same height as the Big Ben clock tower.[55]

The card indexes sat alongside several other files, finding aids and reference materials. Women clerks could call upon dictionaries and atlases to help with unknown place names.[56] Florence Caswell worked briefly on subject files and quickly concluded that though an enemy could change his/her name, there would always be a contact address.[57] Books could be consulted that contained handwriting specimens and copies of every photograph received by MI5.[58] There was also an important file on invisible inks.[59] Perhaps the most useful aid were the numerous printed volumes of countless biographical references to individuals under suspicion, known as the 'Black List'.

While the index served as the 'life-blood of MI5', the work of the 'look-up' supplied vitality to all the branches.[60] The process of 'looking-up' began when an officer sent down a chitty to the Registry to see whether any information could be found on a particular individual. As the experienced Registry Superintendent Elsie Harrison pointed out, all investigations depended on tracing a connection between isolated scraps of scant information that was sometimes dubious.[61]

An MI5 staff report on women's war work noted that good 'look-ups' had to be intelligent, knowledgeable, proficient in foreign languages and in possession of a good memory. The Registry women were known by the officers for their clairvoyant powers, for on many an occasion it was a woman's memory that saved the situation. However, the most prized quality noted was the 'peculiarly feminine gift of intuition'.[62] The same report also described organisational and decision-making skills as being 'more masculine qualities', which some women like Edith Lomax were deemed to display.[63]

However, it would be wrong to assume that these skills are gender-specific, when in reality they are person-specific. Intuition is in fact a key skill for any man or woman working in secret intelligence. Women's clandestine work has historically been limited to roles defined by managing paperwork, and those females assigned to MI5's Registry oversaw huge amounts of information. They sorted, classified and retrieved documents logically and analytically. They repeated such processes for weeks, months and even years on end, creating the ideal systemic framework within which intuition could thrive.

The author of the MI5's women's war work report noted one particular occasion when instinct and second sight prevailed. A German-American who had visited England several times had convinced the authorities that he was a 'harmless commercial traveller'. However, a conscientious Registry clerk suspected the name might be similar to a sea captain whom MI5 had on their watch list. The female clerk offered her thoughts on the subject to an officer, but her suggestion that the visitor and the sea captain were the same person was initially disregarded, as it was considered too 'far-fetched'. It turned out that she was entirely correct, and her excellent work led to the arrest of yet another spy.[64]

Through the daily consultation of card indexes and dossiers, the women trained their minds to be more critical and hence became more intuitively alert to any changes or connections. This process produced one of the best counterintelligence officers in MI5's history: a woman called Jane Sissmore. After the war, the 'tough-minded and rough-tongued' Jane spent decades working on Soviet and communist activity, sniffing out Soviet moles.[65] As a skilled interrogator and lawyer, MI5's first female officer ruthlessly pursued the devil in the details. Understandably, failure to find information in the Registry weighed heavily on those who worked as 'look-ups' or 'searchers'. Dorothy

Dimmock was all too familiar with the pressures of running a trace in the Registry and finding nothing. She would constantly ask herself: 'Have I missed something?'[66] The daughter of a retired surgeon in the Indian Medical Service, Dorothy worked at MI5 headquarters for just over a year until she married in 1917.[67]

After refusing a place at Somerville College, Oxford, because of her father's poor financial position at the time, Dorothy worked as a house mistress at Bridgenorth High School in Shropshire. One day she received a surprise letter from the War Office inviting her for an interview. The letter informed her that 'Miss Lomax of MI5' had recommended her as a suitable applicant for work in her department. Dorothy later learnt from her mother that 'Miss Lomax' was an old friend of her aunt, Constance Harvey-Kelly, who, unbeknown to her niece, had put her name forward.

At the end of the 1916 summer term, Dorothy packed her treasured 1792 Klotz violin and left for the capital, excited for what lay ahead. The vibrant cosmopolitan city was now hardly recognisable to anyone who had visited it before the war. Conscription had been introduced at the start of the year, turning London streets green with khaki-clad soldiers on their way to the front. The documentary *The Battle of the Somme* appeared in picture houses for the first time in August.[68] The British people were brought face to face with the grim realities of trench warfare. Audiences could not even drown their sorrows after screenings due to severe alcohol restrictions, and many could not sleep properly at night for fear of Zeppelins dropping their bomb loads on the city.

Despite such challenging times on the home front, the people of London stood resolute and daily life continued. As soon as she arrived from Shropshire, Dorothy headed for the nearest department store and purchased a smart new coat, skirt and hat in preparation for her interview. Possessing the 'Dimmock persistence' and the 'Dunsterville observance', Dorothy was an ideal candidate.[69] Her famous uncle had these qualities in abundance. Later, at the end of January 1918, the middle-aged but intrepid Lionel Dunsterville led 'Dunsterforce', a mobile expeditionary force, across present-day Iran, to hold the Perso-Russian frontier and safeguard Baku oil.[70] While the expedition did not succeed, Dunsterville and his men demonstrated tenacity, grit and spirit.

The general's niece impressed MI5's Edith Lomax, who saw

potential in the young woman. The unassuming Lady Superintendent arranged for the quiet and serious recruit to take a room off Baker Street at Bedford College for Women. Founded in 1849, the University of London college was the country's first higher-education institution for women. It also served as a hostel for women undertaking war work in the city during the war. Dorothy ate her meals in the college hall, where she made several friends, including an accomplished pianist named Violet. They spent many evenings together playing morale-boosting violin and piano sonatas until it was lights-out.

Dorothy's violin never left her side. The music devotee took her prized instrument everywhere, which included the college basement during Zeppelin raids. On the night of 1 October 1916, Dorothy and Violet discovered a trap door, and tentatively decided to venture onto the flat college roof. Together they climbed along the top of Baker Street, with all of London opening up before them. The brilliant flare of searchlights captured the outline of an airship in the night sky above them. That night, the famous L31 Zeppelin airship was shot down, and the two women watched it plummet to the ground in flames somewhere near Potters Bar.[71] The following morning at breakfast, Dorothy and Violet could not wait to share their midnight tale with the other female residents. Unfortunately, the news got back to the college warden, who was not pleased. She threatened the women with eviction should they attempt to go onto the roof again, which was subsequently placed out of bounds to all residents.[72]

Having to explain any future moves to her parents would have been problematic, but nowhere near as difficult when her family and friends asked her where she worked. Dorothy always provided the same enigmatic response: 'Where Nelson looks like Mephistopheles.'[73] The explanation was simple. Dorothy and many other MI5 women took the opportunity after lunch in the canteen to escape to the headquarters roof for a few minutes of fresh air and relaxation. As Dorothy inhaled the invigorating cold autumnal air, she looked directly at Nelson's Column, but she did so from such a strange angle that the admiral's tricorne hat looked like a pair of Faustus devil horns, and his officer's sword strongly resembled the trickster's tail.[74]

There was no chance of the devil finding work for idle hands either in the Registry or the rest of MI5. British Summer Time was introduced in May 1916 to maximise working hours during the day. Registry staff worked late if required, taking their lead from their manager, the clean-shaven and nervous-looking Scot, Maldwyn Haldane, who, at the start of the war, rarely found his bed before 2.30 a.m. and would be back at work again by half past nine the same morning.[75] Nicknamed 'Muldoon' or 'Marmaduke', Haldane ran a tight ship.[76] As the first graduate recruit of MI5, he was an accomplished linguist with as keen an intellect as any of the women working for him. There was no time for amusement, with men and women kept apart to avoid unnecessary distractions. A few Registry women stole a glance through the sash windows to see what was currently playing at the Haymarket theatre. A handful of bolder young women made signs at the window to the people below, but this remained their only connection to the outside world.[77]

The Registry was a spectacle wilder than anything Alice could have dreamt of in Wonderland. It was 'a Sanctum Sanctorum of filing cabinets' containing secret dossiers that comically classified suspects as 'Absolutely Anglicised' (AA) or 'Bad Boche' (BB). Rosy-cheeked women carried cardboard folders to and from the safe, while a troop of Girl Guides ran errands and messages between floors at great speed.[78] The teenage girls were put on their honour that they would not read the papers they carried.[79] They were also charged with filling ink pots, disinfecting telephones and dusting tables and bookshelves.[80]

Everyday files were received from other sub-departments that shed light on those suspected of being in league with the enemy. As searchers, Dorothy and her colleagues were responsible for looking up these people in the card index and determining whether any of the information contained in the files was connected with that on the card. They had to be patient and physically fit. A sturdy short-block shoe heel was essential for the women, who would be on their feet all day. Most of the time, the searchers would find nothing, leading them to initial and return the file to the respective sub-department whence it came. Their work was made more challenging by the problems with phonetic spelling and with secretaries from other branches rushing in to request files and then forgetting to sign the documents out.[81]

Another difficulty arose when the women had a short tea break, as the British staple hot drink was freely supplied to the entire women's staff.[82] Helen Cribb recalled how:

Tea in the Registry was a daily excitement, but a cause of heartache for some of us, as owing to the eagerness for the few minutes welcome break – to say nothing of the refreshment – buns and cakes were eaten over the card boxes with total disregard of the currants which were dropped amongst the cards causing some to stick!![83]

Such whimsical working conditions did not deter Dorothy from her work, especially when she happened to unravel an exciting trail of information within the cards that left her with a great sense of job satisfaction.

However, nothing could prepare Dorothy for the day she came across her aunt's name, Constance Harvey-Kelly, in the card index. Horrified, she read the following statement on the card: 'harbouring the accomplice of a well-known spy'. She sought expert advice straight away from Edith Lomax, whose immediate response was: 'I will tell the Chief – your aunt herself is unimpeachable.'[84] Constance Harvey-Kelly took in paying guests to supplement her small Indian Army widow's pension. Edith Lomax determined that her old friend must have taken on the suspect as a boarder and been utterly ignorant of her lodger's shady connections.

Somehow Edith discreetly got word to Dorothy's aunt, and the suspicious house guest was sent packing. However, the woman's departure was wrapped in mystery. Before she left, the suspect cryptically gifted her aunt a white coral necklace, stating that it was 'for your niece who works in London', suggesting that Dorothy should visit a certain hairdresser. Intrigued by the gift and the mysterious recommendation, Dorothy dutifully made an appointment and wore the coral necklace, but nothing unusual happened except a haircut.

Dorothy later learnt that the woman had subsequently attempted to flee the country. MI5 had flagged her passport application during the verification process. It was decided that the woman should be issued a passport to see what would happen next. Unsurprisingly, she made her way to the port and was stopped. Nothing more of her story is known. When Dorothy next saw her aunt, she appeared to know more than her niece, declaring, 'our contra-espionage department seems to be on the spot after all!'[85]

The work of looking-up was relentless. It was intense and tiring. Dorothy could not manage it for too long a stretch, so arrangements were made for 'look-ups' to specialise in some other work to alternate between the two jobs.[86] Dorothy was put in charge of the 'Museum', a strange collection of spy paraphernalia found on or used by arrested enemy agents. Items such as bootlaces impregnated with secret ink and a piece of hollow chocolate used to convey a written message were exhibited to entertain VIPs who visited MI5 headquarters to see what kind of work was being undertaken.[87] Brigadiers were entertained by the intriguing objects that appealed to a schoolboy interest.[88]

A Browning revolver and ammunition caught many a visitor's eye. The objects belonged to Augustos Alfredo Roggen, a German spy from Latin America who had been arrested in June 1915 at the Tarbet Hotel on the shores of Loch Lomond. The immaculate city-dressed Roggen raised suspicions when he tried to convince the hotel owner that he was staying at the remote Scottish loch to fish, for he had no fishing gear and only maps of Loch Lomond, a restricted area used to test new torpedoes.[89] MI5 was alerted to Roggen's espionage activities when they intercepted two of his postcards sent from Edinburgh to a Rotterdam resident named on the MI5 Black List.[90] After Roggen's arrest, he was turned over to Special Branch in London, where Basil Thomson was waiting to question him. Convicted and sentenced to death, Roggen refused to be blindfolded and boldly faced the firing squad in the Tower of London on 17 September 1915.[91] The failed spy was one of eleven enemy agents executed during the war.

The work of MI5 Registry 'look-ups' was vital if suspects such as Roggen were to be apprehended and brought to justice. The key to MI5's success depended (and still does) on the accuracy of its files and the people whose job it was to extract what was required. The information was then passed to Special Branch, which had the power to arrest, detain and interrogate suspected spies, domestic dissenters and foreign subversives.[92] Those arrested found themselves sitting in Basil Thomson's office, Room 40B at Scotland Yard, an imposing building located less than a hundred yards away from the cells of Cannon Row Police Station. Thomson's office was an Edwardian ensemble of mahogany bookcases and austere chairs covered in red leather. A large polished desk was positioned opposite a low padded armchair that had 'felt the impress of practically every captured spy, male or female'.[93]

A smaller table was positioned in front of the window next to Thomson's desk so that his stenographer, Kathleen Pettigrew, could capture every exchange. The young apprentice secretary bore witness to every grunt, nod, bluff, sob and monosyllabic reply from those questioned in one of Scotland Yard's most notable heirlooms – a chair now lost to history. According to one Special Branch officer, the average weekly number of suspected agents who sat in the famous 'spy arm-chair' was thirty, with over a hundred a month.[94]

Kathleen, the competent secretary, sat poised, holding her quill pen aloft, foolscap pad at hand, and her ink pot filled to the brim. Dressed in the typical Edwardian business dress of the day and sporting a full pompadour hairstyle that saw her coiffure perfectly shaped and curved away from her head with a distinctive decorative top bun, she was perhaps one of the most efficient and trusted women in the building.[95] As tension crackled in the air, Kathleen remained expressionless during interrogations. Basil Thomson spoke gently as he manoeuvred the suspect in what resembled a game of chess, with him the master and the suspect a novice.[96] She rarely paused from her note-taking, even when those questioned squirmed, shouted, or sobbed. Not even when Mata Hari had vigorously gripped the arms of the chair during a hailstorm of probing questions did Kathleen let her body language betray any thoughts she may have had.[97]

Nothing could prepare Kathleen for one particular suspect who caused much astonishment wherever he went. MI5 and Thomson's spy-catching team kept a close eye on people who worked for travelling circuses, as they believed the German espionage service had taken to using performers as spies based on the notion that they would invite less suspicion. On one particular day during the war, postal censorship intercepted a telegram to a world-famous American showman. The sender said he was about to book his passage to New York.[98]

The English-born Fred Walters had once served in the 17th Lancers before performing in *Buffalo Bill's Wild West* shows and then travelling with the famous Barnum & Bailey's Circus, founded in 1871 by the greatest showman, Phineas Taylor Barnum. Before Walters set sail for America, Scotland Yard summoned him for questioning. In his post-war memoir, Thomson described what happened next: 'The stage was set, the chair was ready – and there walked into the room a blue man! His face was a sort of light indigo set off with a bristling red moustache. He was a really terrifying spectacle.'[99] Kathleen glanced at the 'blue man' seated beside her and leapt a foot from her chair, expelling a little sob. This shade of blue proved far too much even for the woman who had witnessed so many colourful persons of interest being questioned.

Walters had been working as a circus 'freak' since 1891. Described as a theatrical extravaganza, he wore a negligee costume of ultramarine to enhance his peculiar blue colour and shock audiences around the world.[100] After his death in 1923, an autopsy revealed that Walters's brain, heart and tissues were just as blue as his skin due to silver poisoning.[101] He first began taking silver nitrate to treat locomotor ataxia, a degenerative disease of the nervous system that affects muscular co-ordination. Once he realised the connection between the nitrate and turning a deeper shade of blue, the more he ingested until his heart finally stopped beating.

Kathleen found herself confronted with extraordinary and odd figures such as the 'blue man'. While his death was widely reported around the world, the facts behind his visit to Scotland Yard remained out of print until Basil Thomson published his memoir in 1923.[102] The Official Secrets Act ensured that most autobiographical authors kept a lid on classified information, but it proved difficult to deter former intelligence officers and government ministers from securing lucrative publishing deals and spilling the beans during the interwar period.[103]

Vernon Kell made every effort to keep the work of his 'Hush-Hush Men' – and women – out of the newspapers. Instead, Special Branch was presented as *the* British secret service, and Basil Thomson revelled in the attention. As a leading figure, he had pursued an impressive public service career that not only equipped him with special knowledge and insight into criminals and how to deal with them, but that also taught him how to negotiate, persuade and communicate with the British press.[104]

Before being appointed Assistant Commissioner at Scotland Yard in 1913, the son of William Thomson, Archbishop of York, began his diplomatic career working in the Colonial Service in the South Pacific, where he became a magistrate in Fiji during the 1880s. He worked closely with the Prime Minister of Tonga before taking on the role himself. He eventually returned to England, bidding farewell to the land of volcanoes, cannibals, pirates and malaria. Once home, he served as Governor of Dartmoor Prison and later of Wormwood Scrubs, before securing the position of Secretary to the Prison Commission in 1908.[105]

Thomson was used to working in the limelight and wearing several different masks, one of which enabled him to operate under a cloud of secrecy. As a servant of the Crown and keeper of official secrets, he was stringent in his assessment of all who worked for him.[106] Evidence has even survived that sheds light on the nature of his working relationship with Kathleen Pettigrew. After the war, Thomson took to writing crime novels where his imagined plots had a touch of realism about them. In July 1934, he sent a copy of the second instalment of PC Richardson's murder mystery series entitled *Richardson Scores Again* to Kathleen. Thomson inscribed a personal message to his former secretary: 'From a friend who values her opinion'.[107]

Gracefully impressionable, Kathleen worked closely with Thomson for five years, and they remained friends until he died in 1939. A man considered above reproach, the head of Special Branch appreciated a woman with intelligence. While some of Thomson's colleagues were doctrinaire misogynists who believed that a woman's place was in the typing pool, he firmly believed that 'every man and woman is potentially an intelligence officer if he or she uses the brains that God has given to us all'.[108] Kathleen never abused Thomson's confidence, and she may well have been on his mind when he wrote the following: 'Among the clerical staff of all police offices, there are persons of both sexes who show marked ability in appraising the qualities of persons with whom they come into contact; these are naturally the material from which intelligence officers were recruited.'[109]

Given that they were operating within the shadowy fringe of public and secret service, we will never know the extent to which Thomson mentored Kathleen during her early career. However, we do know that she remained calm and collected when sitting in the witness box. As Thomson's trusted shorthand writer, Kathleen sometimes found herself thrust into the spotlight when called upon to testify on the accuracy and content of her notes taken during suspect questionings.[110] The head of Special Branch did an almost impeccable job of keeping her name out of the newspapers, but on a few rare occasions, it was noted by an eagle-eyed court reporter.

In 1917, Kathleen was catapulted into public view as a witness in a sensational murder case. On the morning of 14 August, the dashing Douglas Malcolm of the Royal Artillery entered a boarding house at 3 Porchester Place and fatally shot a naked Anton Baumberg. The murdered man, who went by the self-styled name 'Count de Borch', had been having an affair with Malcolm's wife, who had written to her husband informing him that she could not give her lover up and intended to divorce Malcolm. While at home on leave from the Western Front, Malcolm had purchased a riding crop to give Baumberg a good thrashing; however, driven wild by jealousy, he called upon the services of a revolver to finish the blackguard off.[111] The guilty man then gave himself up to the police.

The case captivated the British people, who followed the story as it unfolded. On Monday, 20 August 1917, the *Evening Standard* ran a front-page story covering the coroner's inquest held earlier that day. Intriguing questions remained unanswered. Malcolm had provided the police with a statement in which he claimed Baumberg was a white-slave trafficker and a spy and, more importantly, revealed that Scotland Yard knew all about him.[112]

The London evening newspaper was the only tabloid that named the Special Branch shorthand writer called as a witness.[113] Kathleen informed the coroner that she had been present on 30 March that year when the man who called himself 'Count de Borch' had appeared at Scotland Yard for questioning over his identity. The well-dressed impersonator confirmed his true identity as Anton Baumberg. The Russian Jew was educated in Warsaw and had served in the Russian Army for a year when he decided to take his father's surname of Borch to escape prejudice. However, as his mother was Jewish, the marriage was not considered legal. She later married a man named Baumberg, who permitted her illegitimate son to take his name.[114]

Anton Baumberg decided to leave Russia for England, and after short stays in Geneva, he obtained employment with Waring and Gillow, the well-known Oxford Street furniture store. When war broke out, he attempted to obtain a position as an interpreter in the Royal Horse Artillery but was rejected. He admitted to the police that his friends knew him as 'Count', and due to his self-confessed vanity, he let them believe this to be true. Basil Thomson cast further light on Baumberg's questioning in his post-war memoir. He declared that the 'Count' had made a bad impression on him.[115] The shrewd spymaster remained unconvinced by Baumberg's tall tales and grew concerned by the Russian's influence with a wide circle of London hostesses from whom he was believed to be drawing large sums of money.[116]

Thomson confirmed that Malcolm had called at Scotland Yard to determine Baumberg's address, but no information had been given to the distressed soldier. However, during the emotionally charged trial that followed, a witness testified that he had accompanied Malcolm to Scotland Yard where an unnamed police officer had informed Malcolm that his wife's lover 'was a man of very bad character'.[117] Like so many cases at the time, the suspected spy was placed under surveillance until his death, when his name was brought before the public.

In a crowded courtroom at the Old Bailey, an all-male jury returned a verdict of not guilty that was met with a long and continued applause.[118] For five minutes, pandemonium reigned in the courtroom and outside on the street. On the advice of his lawyer, a lucky Malcolm left the court without making a statement, and drove away in a taxi-cab alone.[119] Despite everything they had endured, Malcolm and his wife remained together for the rest of their lives.[120]

The jury's judgment was clearly affected by the patriotic image of a chivalrous gentleman in uniform who defended his foolish wife's honour against a foreign sexual predator who had led a weak and innocent woman astray. Alongside Malcolm's defence lawyer, Sir John Simon, who derogatorily referred to Baumberg as a 'Russian noble-man', the British press were happy to paint the dead man guilty by stressing his foreignness and feeding public xenophobia. The Times newspaper ran simple but effective headlines such as 'Russian Pole's Death'[121] and 'Russian "Count" Shooting Case'.[122]

As readers turned the pages of their daily news rags, they found detailed coverage of the growing crisis in Russia running alongside coverage of the Malcolm trial. From the autumn of 1916, the fragile Russian Empire had been drifting towards revolution. News of the Bolshevik rising in November 1917 generated further fears around the spread of Bolshevism across Europe. As a result, the final phase of the war saw Kell and Thomson's attention focused on domestic subversion; Mansfield Cumming, head of MI6, shared the same concerns as Vernon Kell, his MI5 counterpart. He frequently met with Basil Thomson, and no doubt would have been introduced to Kathleen Pettigrew during one of his visits to Scotland Yard.[123] At the start of the war, Cumming noted in his diary that 'Russia will be the most important country for us in future and we should sow seed and strike roots now'.[124] The prophetic spymaster saw his intelligence mission located in Petrograd, the capital port city formerly known as Saint Petersburg. MI6, like MI5, had a shared need for talented women, and so Cumming placed his trust in Winifred Spink, the lone woman to serve where only men had gone before: Russia.[125]

4

From Petrograd with Love

There was an air of mystery in the darkened room. Filing cupboards and side tables were littered with books and intricate drawings. A regimented row of candlestick telephones stood on a large desk covered in secret papers. Model aeroplanes, submarines and intriguing mechanical devices were dotted around the room. The walls were adorned with strange charts and maps, and several seascapes hinted at C's passion for sailing. A large safe was placed against one wall, and glass bottles containing chemicals used to make invisible inks were proudly placed on the shelves that lined the walls of Mansfield Cumming's office at 2 Whitehall Court.[1]

The MI6 headquarters in London was located at the very top of an impressive nineteenth-century French Renaissance-style building.[2] The famous playwright George Bernard Shaw was just one of many neighbours oblivious to the secret work conducted in the top-floor flats. One day in June 1916, a fashionably dressed woman sporting a loosely fitted jacket belted at the waist entered the building, passing the commissionaires. These two burly men were in fact Special Branch policemen. Following her guide, Miss Winifred Spink struggled to match his long strides and was thankful for the momentary pause when they stepped into the private lift. As she ascended seven floors, she remained unperturbed by the loud creaking of wheels and pulleys in action. After disembarking, she acknowledged the liftman with a gracious nod of thanks and accompanied her guide up a narrow flight of stairs that took them to the roof. There, they crossed a short iron bridge and entered a maze of anonymous passages before arriving in a small chamber that resembled a waiting room.[3]

After a short time, a pleasant looking, dark-haired secretary appeared and pressed a secret bell that set in motion invisible clunking machinery which revealed a hidden staircase.[4] One can only imagine the thoughts racing through Miss Spink's mind as she climbed the winding stairs and made a dramatic appearance through a hole in the floor. An ageing man with a peculiar disposition looked on and motioned her to a chair in front of his desk. Dressed in naval uniform, Mansfield Cumming sat with his shoulders hunched, signing several urgent letters in his distinctive trademark green ink. Eventually he turned his attention to the young woman before him and explained how she had been recommended for special service. She listened intently to the eccentric head of MI6, never betraying her thoughts when he outlined the nature of the work on offer and the exact location of the post.

On 16 June 1916, MI6's newest recruit was inducted into the shadowy world of espionage.[5] The 31-year-old secretary entered the service history books as the first female officer ever sent to Russia.[6] Winifred Spink was bright, bold and brave. She was a gifted young woman whose life was full of surprising twists and turns. Like the famous Russian matryoshka dolls that open to reveal ever smaller hollow wooden dolls nested within them until a solid tiny doll is unveiled at the centre, Winifred possessed a quiet kind of courage and endurance at her core that enabled her to overcome the various challenges that marked her life. Cumming had chosen wisely. Freezing temperatures, growing food shortages and mounting paperwork awaited Winifred in Petrograd. Yet nothing prepared her for finding love, which, like the revolution, came without invitation.

Many decades later, in 1963, Winifred came to reflect on her Russian adventure. Then an elderly resident of San Francisco, she had enrolled on a creative writing course at the University of California delivered by the author Lloyd Eric Reeve.[7] Having witnessed the turmoil of revolution first-hand on one continent, she watched as history appeared to repeat itself on another. The Cuban revolution of the late 1950s triggered memories of her past secret work. Inspired by the novelists and poets Maurice Baring and Hilaire Belloc, for whom she had worked as a private secretary during the early 1920s, the miniskirt-wearing septuagenarian began to prepare an account entitled 'Russian Reminiscence'.[8] Initially intended for *Reader's Digest* as a human interest story, the article was never published.

After returning to Britain, days before her death in July 1973, Winifred received a visit from her great-nephew David, who was studying at Oxford University. He was extremely fond of his open-minded aunt, who loved a good, friendly but hard-fought argument.[9]

He looked forward to visiting her tiny book-filled flat in Reading.[10] Throughout her life, Winnie or 'Win', as she was known to family, had lived in cities across the globe, and every time she moved, she travelled with a hundred packing cases filled with her beloved collection of books.[11] During her nephew's final visit, she handed him a thick bundle of assorted papers labelled 'Personal Reminiscences'. With the aid of her much-loved diary and random newspaper clippings that only made sense to their owner, Winnie had planned to write her memoir that summer with the assistance of her nephew, but serious illness prevented the 87-year-old from preserving a lifetime of memories.[12]

When looking at the magpie assemblage of treasured ephemera today, one cannot help but appreciate the spectral power of the past attempting to assert its place in the present. The Russian passes, date-stamped 1917, or the rouble banknote safely stored within an old brown envelope and placed within her St Petersburg travel guide, are much more than souvenirs. These objects paint a colourful portrait of Winnie's life, covering everything from good to bad to undisclosed. As the late great Hilary Mantel wisely pointed out in her memoir: 'History's what people are trying to hide from you, not what they're trying to show you. You search for it in the same way you sift through a landfill: for evidence of what people want to bury.'[13]

It is evident from reading Winnie's diary that her Russian experiences were just as compelling and cryptic as the items she left behind. On the last page of her diary, she listed significant dates and individuals: the first date related to her lifelong support of women's suffrage and association with the Pankhurst family. She noted 1918 and 1928 as important milestones for women achieving the vote. Below that, a curious addition was written in pencil: the name, home address and favourite restaurant of Grigori Rasputin, the murdered mystic and adviser to the Russian royal family. The circumstances surrounding Rasputin's death are full of mystery. It is an intriguing story that involved MI6 officers assigned to the Petrograd office.[14] Winnie recollected how she had been 'destined to witness world-shaking events' and that 'Rasputin's murder seemed to be the overt act which triggered the long threatened Russian Revolution'.[15] Her diary and papers cast further light on the extent of MI6's knowledge and involvement in the assassination of the mad, meddling monk.

From a young age, it was clear that Winnie was different. Intellectually driven, she was a free spirit born perhaps a century early.

As a young woman, she broke rules that she did not make and failed to conform to societal norms of the time. Born on 6 December 1885, Winnie came from a large family with money. Her father, Samuel Spink, ran the London-based business Spink & Son, famous for valuing and purchasing collectable coins and medals. Despite his wealth, however, the family home in Sevenoaks had no central heating, as the unsmiling patriarch believed in the benefit of fresh air. During the winter, the windows of Zurich Lodge were left wide open, subjecting Winnie and her siblings to painful chilblains. Samuel Spink was every inch the stern Victorian father. If Winnie or one of her four brothers and sisters misbehaved at the dinner table, they would feel the sting of their father's whip.[16] When her Swiss-born mother, Elise Höfer, died in 1899, Samuel despatched his children to a separate residence in Bromley.[17] In what must have been viewed by his children as a cold and detached decision, the head of the family wasted no time and took the 24-year-old family nursemaid, Grace Hitchcock, as his second wife and had further children.

As a committed member of the Plymouth Brethren, a strict and secretive evangelical Christian movement, Samuel valued the importance of marriage and children. Like most past and present Brethren, Winnie was born into fellowship. She had no choice and struggled within the confines of an unyielding patriarchal religion that mirrored Victorian conventions when it was established in 1831. Samuel vehemently believed his daughters should follow Brethren teachings, marry, and have a family – and a teenage Winnie soon rebelled. One day, she was caught passing a note to a boy during a meeting and was promptly packed off to a finishing school in Zurich, where her mother's Swiss family closely chaperoned her.[18] After this, Winnie was free to pursue her dreams and to live her life as she chose, and she did this surrounded by like-minded women.

Unsurprisingly, Winnie was drawn to the suffragette struggle. She shared the same strong convictions as Emmeline Pankhurst, founder of the Women's Social and Political Union (WSPU). This militant organisation championed equality for women in all areas of life and work, and campaigned for female suffrage.[19] Winnie was determined to achieve something with her life and 'cast off the shackles of yesterday' to put herself through university, studying French at the University of Lausanne.[20] Then, during the winters of 1911 and 1912, she studied French at the world-renowned Sorbonne in Paris. After welcoming the

New Year of 1913 in the French capital, the headstrong student called on her friends Emmeline Pankhurst and her daughter Christabel, the WSPU's main strategist.[21] Predicting the outcome of the proposed women's suffrage amendments to the Manhood Suffrage Bill, the Pankhursts suspended militant action while the bill was debated in Parliament and headed to Paris for a short break. The two suffragettes did not trust the Liberal government, which, in their eyes, was always looking to pin the blame on the troublesome women who favoured 'deeds not words'.[22]

At the end of January 1913, the government withdrew the bill, sending a clear message that they never intended to give women the vote. The suffragettes responded by immediately resuming their campaign of violence and arson. Having completed her studies on the continent and returned to London, Winnie attended a WSPU meeting on 27 January 1913 and listened to an impassioned speech by Emmeline. Disgusted by the government's betrayal, Winnie recorded in her diary that she was 'committed to militancy once and for all'.[23] While the conscientious suffragette never spent time in a police or prison cell, Winnie remained committed to female suffrage. On 18 March 1913, she joined large numbers of men and women convened at Kingsway Hall.[24] The crowd were united in their strong disapproval of the cruel and degrading method of forcible feeding practised by the government on the imprisoned hunger-striking suffragettes. This form of protest was perhaps the most radical and disturbing aspect of the women's suffrage campaign, but it ended abruptly when war unexpectedly broke out in August 1914. The pragmatic leader Emmeline suspended militant action once again and tasked the WSPU with supporting the war effort, rebranding its membership as patriotic feminists.

As battalions of suffragettes rolled up their sleeves to operate factory machines while the men were away fighting on the Western Front, Winnie spent the first eighteen months of the war working as private secretary to a number of interesting men such as Sir Henry Simpson Lunn, the head of a growing travel business. She also worked for Charles Hobhouse during his term of office as Postmaster General, before taking a position in 1916 with the dapper Colonel Walter Bersey of the White Cross Assurance Company, where she was also in charge of supervising the shorthand typing staff.[25] Bersey, like Mansfield Cumming, was a passionate motorist and early member of the Automobile Club of Great Britain (later to become the Royal

Automobile Club), founded in 1897.[26] As an electrical engineer, Bersey developed electrically propelled carriages at the turn of the twentieth century and later designed and sold car engines. His latest venture, car insurance, promised a more stable and lucrative enterprise.[27]

Bersey was duly impressed by Winnie's credentials: university educated, well-travelled, full secretarial training completed at the respected Pitman's Secretarial School on Southampton Row, where she came second out of 700 candidates across the country for advanced French and achieved a medal for advanced German, and since September 1914 had been studying Economics at the London School of Economics.[28] She had even found time to begin training as a car mechanic.[29] Armed with a recommendation from Bersey, Winnie left one employer fascinated with motoring for another equally obsessed, but with one significant difference: Mansfield Cumming's driving licence was under the name 'Captain Spencer', an alias known only to those who worked in MI6.[30]

Women were an important part of Cumming's secret workforce. By the summer of 1915, head office staff numbered over thirty people, including seven officers, eight clerks and twelve female typists, of whom some were married.[31] An inspirational leader, Cumming invested in his workforce, developing talent and trust. We will never know whether the MI6 chief was aware of Winnie's suffragette activity, but what is clear is that he definitely appreciated her many gifts and showed excellent judgement in assigning her to the British Intelligence Mission in Petrograd, where she was paid the same as her male colleagues.[32]

On 8 July 1916, Winnie boarded the two o'clock train bound for Newcastle at King's Cross Station.[33] It would be a year until she saw the square Italianate clock tower again. She travelled with the newly appointed Mission head, Sir Samuel Hoare, and his wife, Lady Maud Hoare. The 36-year-old Oxford graduate and former Conservative politician was at the time serving as a yeomanry colonel with no previous intelligence experience.[34] While acting as an army recruiting officer, the future foreign secretary had learnt Russian, hoping it would open exciting doors for him, since illness had prevented him from being deployed to the front. Hoare's gamble paid off when he was recommended by a fellow politician to Cumming, who subjected him to a crash course in spy tradecraft and then despatched him to Petrograd on a special assignment. On his return, Hoare submitted his detailed review of the intelligence mission and found himself appointed the new Mission head, replacing the silent but capable Cudbert Thornhill, whom Cumming had never warmed to.[35]

Hoare's posting to the Russian imperial city was a challenging assignment that required great diplomatic skill. The Mission operated both overtly and behind closed doors, and co-operation was vital to maintaining its cover and keeping some of its more nefarious activities away from prying eyes. Hoare had to work hard to avoid stepping on the toes of the many other British departments represented in Petrograd and to avoid any trouble with the Russians. The Mission's role was to liaise with the Russian secret service, provide accurate information about German troop movements on the Eastern Front, and report on enemy shipping and trading. More routine work included flagging suspicious individuals via the passport control system, transmitting agents' reports to London, and exchanging departmental memoranda.[36] Before Hoare's return to Petrograd to take up his appointment, Cumming stressed the importance to him of using his diplomatic assignment to mask his 'real' work, as well as keeping on good terms with the ambassador, George Buchanan, who did not look kindly on Cumming's officers, over whom he had no control.[37]

Setting sail from Newcastle, Hoare's small entourage took eight days to reach Petrograd. After spending a night at the Grand Hotel in Stockholm, Winnie and her travelling companions reached their final destination on 15 July 1916.[38] Visitors could not fail to be impressed by the grand facade of the Winter Palace and impressive brick-red stucco-fronted buildings. But, beneath the beautiful veneer, there was growing political discontent and economic hardship. Tsar Nicholas II had assumed army leadership at the Eastern Front, leaving his German-born wife, Alexandra, alone to conduct government affairs. Susceptible to the wiles of the debauched Rasputin, Russia's last Tsarina remained convinced of his ability to 'heal' her young haemophiliac son, Alexei, the heir to the Romanov throne. Rumours were rife about the nature of the relationship between Rasputin and the 'German woman'. Stories quickly spread about the gifts Alexandra gave to her 'favourite', such as a bracelet engraved with her name.[39]

Winnie had arrived in a country aggravated by court intrigue and anti-German sentiment. Petrograd was recovering from riots and strikes, and with nearly 2 million lives lost at the fighting front, the country was on the verge of collapse. It was only a matter of time before Russian troops and police would join protesters in overthrowing the autocratic Tsar. As a result of the deteriorating situation, Russia's allies grew concerned about the developing crisis. Russia could not be permitted to withdraw from the war. Consequently, there was a growing mix of American, British and French diplomats in the city, who all struggled to navigate the bureaucratic chaos of the Tsarist regime. The influx of foreign visitors meant that hotels and guest houses were bursting at the seams, making it nearly impossible for Winnie to find lodgings.[40]

On 17 July 1916, an eager Winnie arrived at the British Intelligence Mission for her first work day.[41] The office was housed in the west wing of the imposing four-storey-high General Staff Building. With its endless offices and baroque central arch, the British Mission was located next to the office of the French Intelligence Mission. From their office windows Sir Samuel Hoare's staff of ten were treated to views of the Winter Palace and the Great Square. Surrounded by buildings with unimaginable facades of exquisite architecture, Winnie quickly learnt that the back of the General Staff Building stood in stark contrast with its foul-smelling yards and muddy passages.[42] As the only woman to work in the British Mission, Winnie did not record how her male colleagues received her or how long it took her and the new Mission head to settle in.

Hoare had to work particularly hard to win over Stephen Alley, who had been second in command under Thornhill. Alley was a competent and talented officer. Born outside Moscow in 1876, this son of a wealthy businessman had returned to England when he was fifteen years of age to work for the family business in mechanical engineering. A family argument forced his return to Russia, where he found work with the Maikop & General Petroleum Trust. The company was busy building a new oil pipeline from the Maikop oilfields in southern Russia to the Black Sea.[43] When war broke out, he was recruited for secret service. He had passed through stormy times under Thornhill's leadership and was glad to be rid of him. However, after Hoare's appointment, the experienced deputy was demoted and assigned to the Naval and Military Control sections. This kept him extremely busy, as managing all passenger travel between Russia and England was no small task. The Romanov Empire was vast, stretching from Petrograd in the west to Vladivostok in the east. All traveller details were stored in a card index, which was regularly updated and used to create unique lists of suspicious individuals, which were then shared with interested parties.[44]

The Coding, Typewriting and Secretariat section busily managed the card indexes, alongside encoding and decoding messages and typing reports, some of which ran to 30,000 words. After two weeks on the job, Winnie began feeling the strain from days of endless typing.[45] She could type up to ninety words a minute and was the fastest in the office.[46] However, the volume of work became too much for her to handle. The Mission had taken on considerable military work and struggled to keep up with all the paperwork generated from 'investigating, classifying and controlling every passenger from Russia to the United Kingdom'.[47] The solitary office typewriter did not fare well under the constant hammering of its keys. With little hope of quickly acquiring a new machine in Russia, Hoare made an urgent request to London headquarters for a Remington typewriter with a paper carriage eighteen inches wide to cope with paper of any width and a complete supply of much-needed accessories. He also pleaded the case for an additional typist and shorthand writer, male or female, stressing that they should be fluent in Russian.[48]

Cumming was very fortunate in appointing Winnie, a non-native Russian speaker, as most of the Mission staff, like Stephen Alley, had been born and raised in Russia or had worked in the country before the war. They were fluent in Russian or had a good command of the language, and they were accustomed to the capital's oppressive summers and severe winters that began when the Neva river froze over at the beginning of November and lasted until the end of April, with residents enduring months of plummeting temperatures. At the very end of summer and the beginning of autumn, the streets quickly became a sea of mud, and Winnie and her new colleagues relied heavily on their galoshes to protect their shoes and boots. Not long after the new Head of Mission had been in post, one of his waterproof overshoes mysteriously went missing. Whether Hoare was subject to a welcome prank or the act of a disgruntled colleague, the seasoned saboteur chose to hide the shoe cover in the samovar, thereby also impeding the making of tea with complaints received en masse concerning the unpleasant taste.[49]

With vodka prohibited by the Tsar at the start of the war, the daily ritual of drinking glasses of hot steaming black tea became a much-needed substitute, especially for older Russian generals in the General Staff Building, who regularly overcompensated by building towers of sugar cubes that forced the tea to cascade down the sides of their glasses.[50] While the sword-carrying Mission officers of the military, naval and war trade sections entertained their Russian counterparts elsewhere in the city, Winnie and the secretariat staff remained within the confines of the walls of the British Intelligence Mission. They worked long hours, sometimes through the night, and it was not unusual to find them in the office on Sundays and Christmas Day.[51] Nevertheless Winnie enjoyed the company of several colleagues, with whom she spent many evenings going to the cinema or the theatre.[52] Sir Samuel and his wife regularly took the office staff out to dinner before they returned to their coding and typing in the late evening hours.[53]

The intensity of the work suited Winnie. When she wasn't at the office or busy socialising, she volunteered her time in the soup kitchen at the Anglo-Russian Hospital.[54] However, the constant hours of hard work began to affect her health. Suffering from an ulcerated throat for several weeks, Winnie had her tonsils removed on 18 September 1916. After a brief recovery, she was back in the office by the beginning of October. Sadly, such distractions offered her no relief from nursing a broken heart. At the end of 1915, she received news that her fiancé, the 27-year-old French poet Georges Pancol, had been killed in action on the Western Front.[55] The two had met while studying in Paris in 1911. Pancol had advertised for an English tutor, and Winnie, ever in need of money, had responded. Both had enjoyed long walks together in the capital, and Pancol looked forward to romantic boat trips on the Seine with his 'adorable small Englishwoman'.[56]

Later in life, one of Winnie's greatest regrets remained not marrying her true love, Pancol, before the outbreak of war. She found brief solace in the occult and called upon her tarot cards, carefully stored in a silk handkerchief, to connect with the spiritual world.[57] Pancol was constantly on her mind while she immersed herself in work. On 7 October 1916, she received an unexpected package. It contained extracts from Pancol's diary that his grieving mother had carefully copied for the woman who would have been her daughter-in-law.[58] After reading her betrothed's diary entries, one can only imagine Winnie's emotions. After the war, his diary and a collection of his love letters were published for the first time in 1923.[59] Pancol never referred to his fiancée by her full name; consequently, Winnie's true identity has remained a mystery until now.

Winnie consoled herself with sightseeing for the next two months and attended weekly concerts and parties. She found several willing escorts among her bachelor work colleagues, and on a few occasions, companionship led to desire. As a feminist, Winnie had discarded prudish Victorian taboos concerning sex before marriage, despite not having easy access to safe birth control. Like some suffragettes, she was a sexual revolutionary. Her body was her own, and she was free to choose her sexual partners, as recorded in her diary with the phrase 'another scalp'![60] However, it was not long before she found true romance again. Fellow officer Lionel Reid shared an uncanny resemblance to Georges Pancol. Both men were tall, dark and handsome with thoughtful eyes. They possessed a wistful intelligence that matched Winnie's keen intellect and her natural curiosity for the unknown.

However, Reid was somewhat of an anomaly within MI6. Born and raised in Newcastle, he did not attend a public school, nor was he university educated. Despite being from a respectable middle-class family, Reid's father was a philanderer who deserted his wife and two sons, bringing shame and poverty to the family. Lionel worked as a secretary with various firms on the bustling Newcastle quayside to make ends meet. At some point during the years before 1914, he made a life-changing decision, chose to escape his career trap, and travelled to Russia, where he worked in the oilfields. In the process, he became fluent in several languages.[61] Reid served as a civilian alongside other Petrograd MI6 officers such as Stephen Alley, Maurice Mansfield and Ernest Boyce, who had all worked in the Maikop oilfields before the war.[62]

Reid began his career in MI6 during the war when Mansfield Cumming tapped into the British community living in Russia to recruit linguists. By January 1917, Reid had worked his way up in the Mission and now supervised the office and its staff consisting of Winnie, Frank Hayes, Lawrence Webster, Harry Anderson and Herbert Grant.[63] Severely understaffed, the team somehow managed to keep up with the work. Even Sir Samuel occasionally rolled up his sleeves and helped with coding and typing. Towards the end of the year, the Mission workforce increased to seventeen, and the room at the General Staff Building suddenly grew smaller.[64] Additional rooms were secured on the Moika Embankment, but further space was needed.[65] On 8 December, the office moved to a flat at 28 Mokhovaya, an elegant building close to the Summer Garden established by Peter the Great. Winnie often walked down the avenue of lime trees, admiring the white marble statues pillaged long ago from Warsaw.[66] On occasion, it felt good to escape. Working and living at the new office became overwhelming at times. Hoare had decided that Winnie and two others would reside at the flat for security purposes. At considerable expense, he also ordered the removal of a heavy safe from the Moika office and its transportation to the new premises.[67]

When Winnie started working closely with Reid, it was not long before the two became romantically involved. Throughout November and December 1916, the office manager accompanied Winnie on walks and joined her and others at genteel dinner parties.[68] Their courtship reached starry heights on 19 December when the pair took a glorious sleigh ride together. With winters lasting for six months, Petrograd was a place of ethereal beauty. Beautifully adorned sleighs lined the Nevsky Prospect, the city's central thoroughfare. The broad snow-covered boulevard was lined with magnificent hotels and palaces, tempting cafés and restaurants, high-end boutiques, and churches of every denomination, making it the perfect backdrop for a romantic sleigh ride. The sound of tinkling silver bells accompanied the gentle movement of steel runners and horses' hooves on the packed snow as the sleigh made its way up and down the street, a journey that lasted for some miles.

Petrograd's social scene flourished. From endless official dinners to the dashing men in military uniforms accompanying bejewelled women to the Mariinsky theatre, it appeared that the war had not touched the diplomatic community or Russian high society. The timeless luxuries of the Old World lingered, but trouble loomed on the horizon. Winnie recalled how 'the Russian people were hungry, cold and thoroughly war-weary. Long bread lines waited patiently in the killing cold, day and night. Those that stepped out of line fell dead from exposure and undernourishment.'[69] Her boss, Sir Samuel Hoare, held a gloomy view of the state of affairs in Russia, but he never predicted a revolution. At the time, he remained convinced that Rasputin was spearheading pro-German 'Dark Forces' to undermine the Russian war effort, and that if he were removed, so would be the problem.[70]

Hoare had been approached as early as November 1916 about a plot 'to liquidate' Rasputin, but as he later claimed in his memoir: 'My friend's tone was so casual that I thought his words were symptomatic of what everyone was thinking and saying rather than the expression of a definitely thought-out plan.'[71] Trained in espionage, he would never have admitted to knowing about the plot or playing a part in 'one of the most brutal and ruthless incidents in the history of Britain's secret service'.[72] Hoare's deputy, Stephen Alley, along with John Scale and the six-foot-four barrister, Oswald Rayner, are all believed to have conspired with a group of disaffected Russian aristocrats to remove the promiscuous, power-hungry 'holy man'. Rayner, who loved to smoke good Turkish or Egyptian cigarettes, had attended Oxford with one of the leading Russian plotters, Prince Felix Yusupov, and the two remained good friends for the rest of their lives.[73] It was for this reason that Rayner was posted to Petrograd. His friendship with Yusupov provided Cumming with the connection he needed to the wealthiest man in Russia, who was determined to save the Russian monarchy from certain catastrophe.[74]

On the night of 29 December 1916, Yusupov lured Rasputin to his palace on the banks of the River Moika with the tempting promise of sex with his shy and modest wife, Princess Irina, who was also the Tsar's niece. The plotters plied the self-proclaimed mystic with drink and brutally tortured him to uncover his links with Germany. During the early hours of the ensuing morning, he was beaten with a rubber cosh, and his testicles crushed.[75] Rasputin was shot several times, with Rayner firing the fatal bullet from his Webley revolver.[76] The body was driven to the city's outskirts and tossed into an ice hole on the River Neva. At this time, Winnie went on a joyride in the Mission motor car.[77] Going for a spin with an unnamed driver was undoubtedly out of character for the conscientious young woman, but it did provide the British Intelligence Mission with an alibi. If witnesses saw the Mission car driving around the city, it could not have been the car that drove Rasputin to the palace and was then used to dispose of his body.

After arriving at work on 30 December, Sir Samuel told Winnie: 'No work today because the telegraph is closed, no wires are going in or out of the country, and we are shut off from the outside world.' He lowered his voice to add, 'Rasputin has been killed – but it is not publicly known.'[78] Interestingly, Hoare was offered the chance to view Rasputin's corpse. He was the only foreigner to be extended this courtesy, and he declined. Recovering from a severe chill, the Mission chief had no intention of leaving the warmth of his apartment on that particular black and cruel morning.[79] However, he was well enough to ensure that Cumming was the first outside Russia to receive news of Rasputin's death. As Hoare predicted, his team came under suspicion, and the cautious ambassador George Buchanan had to work hard to convince the Tsar and his grief-stricken wife that the British had nothing to do with Rasputin's death.[80] Hoare later admitted, 'It would have been better if the murder had never taken place.'[81]

Hoare kept Cumming updated with detailed reports sent via the King's Messenger, Charlie Burn, on account of their 'exceptional importance'.[82] After ensuring all secret papers on the death of Rasputin were in the diplomatic bag, Winnie handed it over to Burn on 2 January 1917.[83] Hoare had given express instructions that his confidential account was only to be shown to a trusted few in London, as the Petrograd Mission head was worried that the Foreign Office would accuse him of going behind the back of the ambassador. Hoare advised Cumming that he might want to share his report on Rasputin's assassination with the King and Queen, who were interested in seeing their Russian relations rid of the malign influence.[84]

Murder soon led to revolution. However, not all in the Mission would have a front seat for the final act of the drama: the fall of the Romanov dynasty. Suffering from constant chills and exhaustion, Sir Samuel Hoare had grown tired of the bitter Russian cold and never-ending work. On 21 February 1917, he returned to London with his wife, leaving his deputy, Stephen Alley, in charge for the remainder of the war.[85] Understandably, without the welcome company of Hoare and his wife, Winnie felt very alone. The situation in Petrograd was becoming untenable. Famine and severe fuel shortages affected everyone, including foreigners, who felt pangs of hunger as they shivered in their hotel rooms.

At the beginning of March, Winnie left for Moscow on the evening train, but she could not escape the collapse of the failing Tsarist state.[86] Like Hoare, she had endured months of intense work, and it was beginning to take a toll on her health.[87] Granted two weeks' leave to recover, Winnie enjoyed her stay at the luxury, art nouveau Hotel Metropol. She made good use of her time to meet with friends and take in the famous sights of Moscow, a city that, in her view, was 'older and more interesting than St Petersburg'.[88] In those days, one could walk freely in and out of the Kremlin, a building now heavily fortified. Standing on the cobblestones of Red Square, Winnie was in awe of the history and surrounding beauty on show, which included the breathtaking architecture of St Basil's Cathedral.[89]

While Winnie enjoyed the hospitality offered by an elderly bachelor one afternoon, hungry workers downed their tools in Petrograd and took to the streets to protest against hyperinflation and starvation. The gentleman had just invited her to stay for a couple of days at his country dacha outside Moscow when he was called to the telephone. On returning to the table, his voice had disappeared. He looked worried. He informed his young guest that rioting had broken out in Petrograd. After which, he quickly apologised and asked for her understanding as he retreated to pack.[90] The February Revolution (so-called as the Russian Gregorian calendar was thirteen days behind the Julian calendar) saw hundreds and thousands of men and women take to the streets in Petrograd. They had just two demands: the replacement of Nicholas II and an end to the war. When the Tsar ordered the Petrograd garrison to fire on the rioters, they refused and joined the protesters. The die was cast. The Romanov Empire would fall within days.

Winnie returned to her hotel. She recollected years later how 'all seemed quiet, but huge crowds were beginning to mill about the streets. The next day, no newspapers appeared, the police had disappeared, and the shops were closed. Looking out of the hotel windows, I was astonished to see soldiers of the local garrison parading the streets with small red rags tied to their fixed bayonets. "So it's really come" was my unspoken thought, for it seemed excitingly serious if the Army was mixed up in it.'[91] To her great relief, Lionel Reid arrived in Moscow, having returned from Kyiv. Both were determined to return to Petrograd, but no trains were running. The anxious couple contacted the British consul, the young and colourful Bruce Lockhart, who promised them tickets on the first train out of the city, and he kept his word.[92]

The couple left Moscow at midnight on 15 March 1917.[93] The train was full of people prepared to sit upright for the twelve-hour journey to Petrograd. The last three days had been a whirlwind experience for Winnie and Reid, but somehow, during the revolution, they had managed to get engaged. Perhaps the ominous sense of 'the end' encouraged Reid to propose and Winnie to accept.[94] Sitting happily in the railway carriage, she clutched her bag containing a mix of revolutionary newspapers thrown to the crowd from passing motor cars. She had collected them to send to Hoare in London.[95] As the wood-burning locomotive pulled out of the station, an old professor smiled sadly at Winnie, misinterpreting her relief as enthusiasm. 'Ah, young lady,' he said, 'I cannot be as happy as you. I have lived through three revolutions and, believe me, they all began with liberty, fraternity and love, but, alas, they all ended in terror and bloodshed, and so it will be now.' Winnie refused to believe him at the time, but she reflected years later 'how right he was!'[96]

The train arrived in Petrograd at noon the following day. With none of the usual sleighs to be found anywhere, Winnie and Reid managed to find a peasant sleigh to take them and their luggage to the Mission flat. The revolution had not been entirely bloodless as it had been in Moscow. The Mission staff recalled how 'even the Tsar's most loyal and privileged henchmen, the mounted Cossacks, refused to bring down their dreaded whips on the backs of fellow Russians and shook hands with them instead'. The hungry mob tore down all royal emblems from shop frontages, razed the Central Law Court, and released prisoners. In a bid to regain control, the police strategically established machine-gun nests in house attics and opened fire on the people. Angry gangs retaliated by systematically killing all police officers. A few escaped in disguise, but others were not so lucky. One policeman was hurled to his death from the top floor of the house opposite the Mission office.[97]

Following the Tsar's abdication and the detainment of his family, a Provisional Government was formed under Prince Georgy Lvov, whom the liberal-socialist Alexander Kerensky later replaced. Gradually, life settled down, but the city soon became dirty and neglected. As the newly engaged couple walked around the streets to survey the damage and attend the cinema to watch films about the revolution, they stepped on small mountains of sunflower seed husks, the Russian peasant and working man's chewing gum.[98] Meanwhile their work continued at the Mission and Russia remained in the war, which pleased the Allies, but failed to address one of the causes of the February Revolution, ensuring that a second revolution would follow months later, in October 1917. As 'the days grew longer and the nights whiter until the sunset show never left the night sky', Petrograd became a den of marauding thieves who began to call at private houses, hoping to steal anything they could find.[99] The Mission flat had a lucky escape, thanks to the quick thinking of one of the officers, whose name and actions were never recorded.[100] Food became ever scarcer, and like so many, Winnie survived on bowls of *mannaya kasha* (cream of wheat).[101]

Despite the goods shortages and the daily threat of trouble, Winnie found life strangely normal. She met friends, dined out and attended the opera and ballet, but she could not shake the foreboding sense that the worst was yet to come.[102] A month after the February Revolution, Winnie heard news of the arrival of the exiled revolutionary Vladimir Lenin. She happened to see him one day lecturing his followers from the balcony of the villa of the ballet dancer and former mistress of the Tsar, Matilda Kshesinskaya, which he had made the headquarters of the Bolshevik Party. He warned the captive audience below that they should not believe the promises made by the Provisional Government. While she could hear the future leader of the Soviet regime, she was not close enough to make out his features. However, she found herself close to George Buchanan when he received a letter from the Bolshevik Party. She was at the British Embassy as Buchanan opened a letter that addressed him as 'Dear Comrade': 'To anyone who had met the courtly ambassador, this was electrifying, as it probably was to him!'[103]

On 2 June 1917, Winnie heard confidentially that the ambassador, George Buchanan, was leaving Russia. She remarked in her diary that 'it seems to be the beginning of the end'.[104] Three days later, she was seconded to work for Buchanan's intended replacement, the Labour politician Arthur Henderson.[105] While Henderson found his feet, Buchanan took leave in Finland, where he caught up on his sleep. Before he left, the disgruntled ambassador chose not to offer his embassy residence to Henderson, who faced no other option than to conduct embassy business from the lavish Grand Hotel d'Europe off Nevsky Prospect. Here, Winnie worked as his private secretary, sitting in on Henderson's many meetings with the delegations. She likely served as a translator, for the new ambassador could not converse in any language other than English, putting him at a considerable disadvantage. Despite sharing socialist beliefs perhaps similar to those in the new Russian government, Henderson made little progress with the Bolsheviks, as they viewed him as too bourgeois.

Back in London, Mansfield Cumming and Whitehall ministers had lost confidence in Russia's ability to remain in the war. The new prime minister, Lloyd George, welcomed Emmeline Pankhurst's request to visit Russia. The indomitable leader of the suffragette movement was nearly sixty years of age but was keen to do all she could to ensure that Russia remained in the war despite her daughter, Sylvia, being committed to British and Russian withdrawal. Emmeline arrived in Petrograd in June and spent several months furthering her feminist agenda.

Accompanied by fellow suffragette Jessie Kenney, the two emissaries met with Russian women's societies and visited the barracks of the Women's Battalion of Death, an all-female combat unit established by an uneducated patriotic peasant woman, Maria Bochkareva.[106] These two thousand courageous female volunteers saw action on the Eastern Front and suffered casualties, but their primary purpose was to shame men into serving in the army.

Winnie admired these gun-carrying women when she attended their review in the Summer Garden.[107] At the beginning of July 1917, she managed to tear herself away from work and attend a reception hosted by Emmeline at the elegant Hotel Astoria.[108] With food becoming hard to find and unsafe to eat, Winnie was thankful for the invite to partake in delicious French pastries and cakes. However, such occasions masked the daily reality faced by ordinary Russian people. With rationing enforced, Winnie navigated the troublesome cobblestones across the city to take Emmeline one or two loaves baked from the small government ration of white flour. Suffering from gastric issues, the militant campaigner struggled to digest the heavy Russian black rye bread.[109] It was not an easy journey, as street demonstrations had become a daily occurrence. Lenin and his Bolsheviks were working hard to stoke the flames of discontent and cause as much trouble as possible.

The city was on the brink of destruction. Henderson had proven he was not up to the job of ambassador. After his hotel room was ransacked and papers stolen, the despondent dignitary decided enough was enough. He wrote to Lloyd George, informing him that no good would come of removing Buchanan.[110] On 12 July 1917, Henderson departed from Petrograd, leaving the seasoned diplomat Buchanan to continue as ambassador and manage the growing crisis.[111] Winnie returned to her work at the intelligence mission, where Stephen Alley was consolidating agent networks. London headquarters had been closely monitoring the volatile situation and had received reports from its Berne and Geneva bureaus that the Bolsheviks were receiving funds from the Germans. Lenin's constant scheming to orchestrate unruly and fierce anti-government street protests helped undermine the Provisional Government's attempt to escalate the war effort, and, as a result, it lost the support of the Russian people. It was now only a matter of time before Lenin and his party found themselves in government, and they were not afraid to use force to achieve a transfer of power.[112]

One stifling hot day in mid-July, Winnie and her fiancé, Lionel Reid, were returning home on foot after enjoying a Beethoven concert. Dressed in naval uniform, Reid had been awarded a commission in the Royal Naval Volunteer Reserve (RNVR), but like most Mission staff with service commissions, he knew absolutely nothing of naval or military matters.[113] The handsome couple found the Nevsky Prospect more crowded than usual, with groups of people huddled around stump orators. Lorries filled with rifle-carrying soldiers tore up and down the street, and workers brandished banners. Reid listened intently to one animated speaker as they stood at the corner of Nevsky Prospect and Sadovaya Street. Winnie's Russian was not as good as Reid's, and she struggled to follow the passionate orator. She soon became bored.[114] Years later, she put pen to paper and recorded the moment her sixth sense saved her:

> I got the strongest feeling: 'I must get away from here.' It persisted, so I plucked my escort by the sleeve and said, 'I'm sorry, but I want to go *now*.' Reluctantly, he came away, demurring, ' . . . it was so interesting . . .'. The next day, we heard that the soldiers had begun shooting into the crowds at just about the hour at which we left and, much later, I was to see the well-known photograph taken at the very crossroads of the Nevsky where we had been standing.[115]

She continued:

> This shooting incident inaugurated days of street fighting between the Bolsheviks and the Government troops and was Lenin's first open bid for power. I got bored with staying indoors and finally ventured out, alone, to take the air. It was a disconcerting experience; bursts of machine gun fire seemed to be coming from all sides. I had not realised that, in a city, sound is deflected and distorted, so it is impossible to gauge the direction. I soon scuttled back again, although I am sure I had been in no danger.[116]

Eventually, the Provisional Government restored order, and Lenin fled to Finland while other key Bolsheviks were arrested. The July rising had failed, but the revolutionary barometer would reach new soaring temperatures months later in October when Lenin and the Bolsheviks finally assumed control. Until that time, Winnie spent anxious days working at the Mission office. She was no longer able to survive on the starvation diet and her health declined. Diagnosed with beriberi, a thiamine deficiency, she was at risk of heart failure or muscle paralysis if left untreated. By now feeling ill and completely useless, she asked for permission to return home to England. When this was duly granted, she sold all her Russian clothes and gathered the necessary permits and passport for travel. On 12 August 1917, the Mission's only female staff member said her goodbyes to Stephen Alley and the rest of her colleagues.[117]

The following day, Winnie left Petrograd for good.[118] Russia's once beautiful imperial city was now unrecognisable. An eyewitness to the turning tides of history, Winnie worked at the heart of the British Intelligence Mission, which was 'an integral and essential part of a complex and far-reaching system'.[119] She was accompanied by her fiancé for part of the return journey. Lionel Reid travelled to Moscow, where he took up the new role of Passport Control Officer (PCO), a cover role for MI6 work collecting naval and military intelligence.[120] Winnie travelled the rest of her passage home in the company of the Scottish Women's Hospital Unit, which had suffered a gruelling experience in Serbia. Thin and frail, she took immense joy in hearing a cockney voice among the ship's crew as they sailed across the choppy waters of the North Sea.[121] With her Russian odyssey at an end, she reported to Cumming on 31 August 1917.[122] It took her several months to recover and regain her health and strength.

On 20 October, she met Sir Samuel Hoare in London and agreed to work for him in Rome, where Cumming had appointed him head of the British Military Mission, representing both MI6 and MI5.[123] As she emerged from her meeting at the War Office, she was a vision of feminine independence. Wearing a brimmed cloche hat tied with a ribbon under her chin, she carried a bunch of red carnations in one hand and her coat in the other.[124] With facial adornments only just gaining popularity, the former suffragette's red lipstick signalled her self-dependence and fortitude.[125] This young woman possessed an undeniable presence and inner strength, which served her well throughout her life.

Sadly, Winnie and Lionel Reid's long-distance engagement was not destined to last, with the couple's courtship confined to their time in Russia. During the summer of 1918, Winnie grew very concerned at having heard nothing from her fiancé since the end of 1917.[126] Due to the secret nature of Reid's work in Russia, he could not correspond. Sitting at her desk in Rome, she finally received news that Reid had reached London headquarters on 2 June.[127] She had hoped that they would marry before he returned to Vladivostok at the beginning of August.[128] An ardent believer in the need for planning due to the abnormal war conditions faced by the two sweethearts, Winnie had successfully secured a special dispensation from the Foreign Office to marry abroad without the customary three-month notice period.[129]

Having received only one letter from Reid, on 11 June, she descended into despair after hearing from him on 6 August and learning of the date of his departure for the Russian Far East, set for just two days later.[130] While suffering from Spanish flu the following year, nothing could prepare Winnie at the end of February 1919 for the news that, while working in Vladivostok, Reid had married his neighbour, a woman named Maria Klok.[131] Unlucky in love, Winnie eventually married the quiet and gentle Lieutenant Commander William Ramplee-Smith (Royal Naval Reserve) in 1926 and gave birth to a son the following year. However, in 1935, her heart was again broken when her husband died in Mombasa, Kenya, after his appendix ruptured while he was at sea somewhere in the Indian Ocean.[132] Faced with the daunting task of supporting herself and her young son, Winnie thankfully found work as Lady Maud Hoare's private secretary until the outbreak of a second world war, when she would once again briefly engage in secret intelligence work.[133]

Yet it was Winnie's clandestine wartime work during the Great War that left an indelible imprint on her memory. In 1919, Samuel Hoare wrote to his former secretary to thank Winnie for her service in the British Intelligence Mission in Petrograd. He stressed how 'the work was of a difficult and exacting character, particularly at the end of your connection with the Mission when the Revolution was already in full swing and conditions of life had become almost intolerable'.[134] Had Winnie known in advance what the posting entailed and all that she would endure in an unstable foreign country, there is no doubt that she would have still accepted Cumming's offer of work. Decades later, she declared to Hoare: 'I miss my work for you and always shall.'[135] MI6's first woman in Russia had found adventure and love at a time when the world seemed hopelessly upside down and inside out. While she missed the infamous 'ten days that shook the world', two sisters stepped forward after the Bolsheviks took power in October 1917. Working at the centre of a Russian storm, Lucy and Marjorie Lunn assisted MI6 officers in Moscow, and they did so at great personal risk.

5

The Lunn Sisters

The October Revolution changed everything. While the Bolsheviks claimed to offer a new world vision, they upset the political order in Europe. To its former allies, Russia was now an ideological enemy that threatened the very foundations of Western civilisation. By December 1917, Lenin had signed an armistice with Germany and had moved the Bolshevik government from Petrograd to Moscow. When a bitter civil war broke out in 1918, Mansfield Cumming's secret staff struggled alongside the few British consular staff who remained to look after the hundreds of British subjects who had not yet fled. As the Bolsheviks consolidated their power with the aid of their feared secret police, the Cheka, the country became a dangerous place for foreigners. Cumming relied on a motley group of adventurers, swindlers and covert agents who spied, subverted and supported various anti-Bolshevik coups. They were joined in their clandestine endeavours by several lion-hearted young women who assisted British intelligence efforts in a challenging and constantly changing field of operations.

As the great drama played out in Moscow, the sword-stick carrying Captain George Hill survived several swashbuckling escapades. This larger-than-life officer, codenamed I.K.8, had enjoyed several months of success gathering intelligence and evading the German secret service, who relentlessly tried to stop him. One assassination attempt saw a bomb dropped at the MI6 agent's feet, but the device failed to explode. Like a cat with nine lives, Hill took off with the bomber snapping at his heels. The former British Army officer dived into a shed, where he grabbed a brick. As the German agent came through the door, Hill struck him on the head. The agent instantly fell to the ground, and the British intelligence officer delivered a final, fatal blow to his fallen foe.[1] Spying was and still is a deadly game. With every covert action, there was an element of risk, and this applied to the extensive courier system established by Hill. As one of Cumming's most effective officers, Hill was responsible for getting important information to the right people in a timely fashion. His messengers faced long, hazardous round trips that tested their steely nerves and pushed them to their physical limit. After travelling for weeks, the weary secret envoys could rest in one of eight safe houses dotted across the city.[2]

A small number of brave British subjects put their homes at the MI6 officer's disposal. Two fearless sisters, Lucy and Marjorie (known as Peggy) Lunn, who were twenty-five and eighteen years of age respectively, offered their family's flat in Moscow. These Russian-born women came from an English expatriate family whose father ran a prosperous cotton mill in the small town of Balashikha, on the eastern outskirts of the new Soviet capital. Both risked their lives when they concealed British officers from arrest. They also kept papers and money hidden in their rooms and travelled daily to bring parcels of clothing and various comforts such as cigarettes to imprisoned officers.[3] However, by the end of August 1918, Hill's clandestine exploits began to suffer, as the Cheka unleashed a wave of violence against political opponents in response to the assassination of its Petrograd head and to an unconnected attempt on Lenin's life. The two sisters and their family grew fearful as terrifying events unfolded around them.

Eighteen of Hill's agents and couriers were caught and executed during what became known as the 'Red Terror'. The Cheka raided the British Embassy in Petrograd and threw most of the staff in prison. Sadly, there was one fatality: a naval attaché, Captain Cromie, was shot after he bravely offered resistance.[4] Lunn family members residing in Moscow quickly realised that they had no option but to leave. One particular incident expedited their departure. The Bolsheviks had called at their neighbours' flat and wrongly arrested the couple's sixteen-year-old son, who was taken away and shot. The murderers unashamedly returned the next day to apologise to his grief-stricken parents. The youngest Lunn daughter, Peggy, never forgot the Bolsheviks' brutal act. In what could have been a case of mistaken identity, Peggy most certainly felt guilt-stricken that her work for Captain Hill had led to the death of an innocent. However, the incident arguably saved her own life. She bore the emotional scars of the boy's death for the rest of her life, and understandably she remained utterly opposed to the Soviet system.[5]

Concerned that the Bolsheviks might return and arrest Lucy and Peggy at any moment, their parents took decisive action. Their mother,

Clara, a former governess, held her nerve. She took her two daughters by the hand and calmly walked them out of the flat. Accompanied by her son John, the family took no luggage, only holding what they could carry.[6] As the flat door closed, so too did their lives in Russia. The three children were the first Lunns to escape the country. At the beginning of September 1918, Lucy, Peggy and John took the same route to England as Winnie Spink, MI6's first woman to serve in Russia, a year before. The Lunn children travelled together by boat to England, joining their other siblings there.[7] Finally, on 11 September, their mother escaped with seventy-eight other women, children and men (the last being over the age of forty-eight). Under the protection of a member of the Swedish Consulate General, she joined the other desperate souls as they boarded the 3 a.m. train bound for the Finnish border.[8]

As the train pulled out of the station, its passengers breathed deep sighs of relief. Elsewhere in the Russian capital, the British Consul-General, Oliver Wardrop, sat in his smoke-filled office and wrote an urgent letter to the Foreign Office. He relit his pipe as he enclosed a long list of evacuees. The letter informed London that thirty British subjects remained under arrest, and that many others had gone into hiding. Earnestly exercising his diplomatic duty of care, Wardrop closed his letter pledging: 'I shall do my best to take them with me if I should be able to depart.'[9] However, two members of the Lunn family remained behind in Russia. The steadfast patriarch, Edwin, and his eldest son, Richard, were languishing in a Moscow jail.[10] Lucy later returned and secured their release, and so the family was eventually reunited in England.[11]

The Lunn family's story was a two-act drama, with the first act resembling scenes from Anton Chekhov's final play, *The Cherry Orchard* (1904). The Lunns were a wealthy business-owning family in Russia who faced an existential crisis in 1917. However, unlike Chekhov's tragic ending, the family's second act saw the Lunn children taking control of their destinies after their arrival in England. British intelligence first took an interest in the family in 1925, when MI5 and MI6 launched a joint investigation into four of the eight children: Edith and her three younger sisters, Lucy, Helen and Peggy.[12] The initial request for an inquiry came from Desmond Morton, an MI6 officer who worked on counter-Bolshevism.[13] Sporting a toothbrush moustache, the workaholic bachelor and close confidant of Winston

Churchill spent the 1920s gathering intelligence on the 'Red Menace'. The Bolsheviks had launched a hostile crusade to spread the revolution to the rest of the world, and they did so by using foreign business interests to support growing industrial unrest in Britain.[14] Morton suspected that Edith, who had previously worked for MI6, might be working for Moscow. By association, he also questioned the loyalty of the other Lunn sisters, two of whom were working for British intelligence at the time.

By 1921, Edith was employed as a secretary at the All-Russian Co-operative Society (ARCOS), located in the heart of the 'Bolshevik colony of Hampstead', an area of London populated by British communists and Soviet agents. Established after the signing of an Anglo-Soviet trade agreement that year, ARCOS provided the principal means by which the Russian government could promote trade with Britain. It also served as the perfect smokescreen behind which to conduct espionage operations in Britain. With her Russian background and earlier work for British intelligence, it was not long before Edith became a person of interest. MI5, MI6 and Special Branch investigated the British–Russian émigrée and shared their information. However, suffering from a depleted workforce and lack of funding, MI5 and MI6 struggled to cope with the mounting Bolshevik incursion. As a result, the 1925 investigation produced reports riddled with mistakes and misunderstandings concerning the women's identities and their previous work for the British secret services.

Without a shred of credible evidence, several historians have suggested that all four sisters, unwittingly or not, aided the Bolsheviks by providing them with helpful intelligence.[15] Others have placed their blind trust in the agencies that carried out the investigation, simply repeating the findings and failing to question the accuracy of the information recorded.[16] A closer look at the case reveals a very different narrative that speaks to the impact of the Russian Revolution on a household that lost everything because of it. As a direct result of the revolution, an ideological fault line ran through the family, separating Edith from the rest of her kin. She struggled to make sense of her experiences in Russia and the new post-war world she lived in. Communism offered those like Edith a new way of seeing the world, one that transcended class, gender and nationality. Untainted by later Stalinism, the early 1920s were halcyon days for British communists who were fashionably open about their left-wing leanings.

Before Edith committed wholly to the communist cause, she worked for British intelligence in censorship. With rich chestnut-brown hair and an oval-shaped face with heavy eyelids, she had the distinct look of a noble-born woman as captured in the many portraits from Jane Austen's era. Like so many women let go from work at the war's end, Edith briefly worked for MI6 in 1919 before being dismissed for taking a stand against British intervention in Russia.[17] However, her younger sisters chose an entirely different path. From 1919, Lucy and Helen devoted their lives to working for MI6 and the newly founded Government Code and Cypher School (GC&CS), which later fell under the administrative remit of Britain's foreign secret service. From July 1921, the youngest sister, Peggy, was employed as a 'Lady Translator' by GC&CS.[18] Several years later, after saving enough money, she commenced her studies to become a medical doctor, supported financially by her sisters.

What we know of the Lunn family history before they left Russia comes from the private memoir of the sisters' niece, Natalie Rothstein, who combined stories handed down through the generations with her own archival research on the sisters' grandfather Michael Lunn, the founder of the family's short-lived wealth. That memoir sheds an important light on the distinctive role Michael Lunn played in driving Russia's textile revolution during the second half of the nineteenth century. He was one of many Lancashire cotton men, foreign capitalists and entrepreneurs who benefited from the opportunities available in Imperial Russia. Born in 1820 in Slaithwaite, West Yorkshire, Michael Lunn came from humble beginnings. He was the first Lunn to make something of his life, ensuring a wealthy and meaningful legacy for his children and grandchildren. From the age of eight, Michael worked long, back-breaking hours in a Manchester cotton mill. Driven by a desire to climb the social ladder and improve the living and working conditions of the labouring poor, the ambitious young man learnt all he could about the cotton-spinning business.

He was determined to better himself and secured a position with Mather & Platts, a textile engineering firm that sold all kinds of ingenious machinery designed to spin cotton. His big chance came during the 1840s when he was sent overseas to visit a newly built cotton mill in Balashikha on the banks of the River Pekhorka outside Moscow. The recently widowed mill owner had ordered a steam engine, but she refused to pay for an engineer to install it. Predictably, the machine

soon stopped working, and with no skilled workmen on the premises, it was not long before the furious woman contacted the firm in
England, who quickly despatched Michael to investigate. Recognising
his specialised knowledge and engineering expertise, the inexperienced but savvy owner lost no time in offering Michael permanent
employment as manager.[19]

The eager young man did not hesitate to accept and moved his wife
and children to Russia. They joined scores of other English families
who soon established a thriving community in Moscow. The expatriates introduced football to Russian factory workers, and several
founded an Anglican church in Moscow. Eager to succeed, Michael
helped steer the cotton mill through troubled times, such as the disastrous impact caused by the American Civil War, which interrupted
cotton imports. Not wishing to find himself in such a dire supply situation again, he planted cotton in the Crimean Peninsula.[20] Two decades later, in 1874, Michael became a shareholder in the Balashikha
mill. He had successfully transformed his life from that of a poor
factory worker to a middle-class mill owner who could afford to wear
a diamond and pearl tiepin.[21] The self-made businessman ensured that
his sons received a proper education in England, with one son, Edwin,
studying engineering at Owens College in Manchester.[22]

By the time of Michael's death in 1895, the 75-year-old owned one
of the largest cotton-spinning mills in Russia.[23] Well respected by his
thousand-strong workforce, he remained true to his roots and made
sure that all his employees were well cared for. The Lunn enterprise
boasted workers' housing and a school. Gifted factory children were
sent to England, where they trained in accounting, engineering and
weaving. Michael's Owenite approach contrasted starkly with how his
Russian counterparts ran their factories. Yet the British industrialist's
investment in his Russian workers ensured the factory's survival after
the revolution, when the Bolsheviks nationalised the factory. When
Edith visited the factory in 1935, Russian workers candidly informed
her that they preferred the Lunns to industrial employment under
Stalin. Michael's legacy was continued by his fourth son, Edwin,
who took the helm until 1918. Together with his wife, Clara, Edwin
extended his father's pioneering philanthropic work, establishing a
hospital for the workers in 1902, which the family also used.[24]

Edwin and Clara were 'sincere liberals – with and without a capital letter'.[25] They read the *Manchester Guardian* newspaper and

encouraged their children to extend their intellectual horizons. The parents invested in their children's education, focusing on languages. Initially, the children had Russian, French and German governesses to ensure that they spoke good Russian, could converse in German for business purposes, and, with the aid of French, could engage in polite conversation when out in society circles. The children then attended a gymnasium in Moscow before being schooled in England. They enjoyed a carefree childhood, living in a large country house that looked out onto a lake with a view of the factory. Long summer afternoons were spent cycling and picnicking with their pet dogs. They even had a pet bear, which 'inadvertently killed one of the dogs with a friendly hug'.[26] The children swam naked in the lake, while their mother organised weekend house parties for as many as thirty guests, who sometimes included the English spy and writer Arthur Ransome, well known later for his series of children's books set in the English Lake District and entitled *Swallows and Amazons*.[27]

The Lunn children were very much a product of their liberal-bourgeois upbringing. As caring individuals, they understood class interests but were indifferent to the privileges they enjoyed. The eldest child, Catherine, known as Katya, was born in 1884. Musically gifted, she was a delicate, asthmatic child. Her musical training stopped once she became engaged to John C. Ford-Smith in 1907.[28] Edwin and Clara's second child, Edwin, died before his first birthday in 1886.[29] Clara never got over the loss. Overwhelmed with grief, she paid little attention to Edith, who was born a year later. In 1888, the couple welcomed a second son, Richard (known as Dick), who became his father's right-hand man, managing the factory until 1918. Known to be a difficult individual, Richard then returned to England before moving to Poland, where he managed a cotton mill until the Germans invaded in 1939. This unlucky Lunn immediately returned to England, and spent the rest of his life working for the Milk Marketing Board in Kent.[30]

A third son arrived in 1890. Walter, known by his middle name, Stanley, was a keen photographer as a young boy. He captured the evocative images of the Lunn siblings' childhood that survive today in family albums held by the University of Leeds.[31] Walter was commissioned in the Royal Artillery in the First World War and was awarded the Military Cross. After the war, he settled in South Africa and became Cape Town's chief engineer until his retirement in 1950.[32]

His sister Lucy, born in 1891, regularly visited her brother and his family. Shocked by apartheid, she held her tongue when her sister-in-law refused to sit at the same table as her black servant. Sensible and practical, with a pleasant smile, Lucy worked for MI6 for over fifty years. During the Second World War, she was based at Bletchley Park, where her younger brother John, born in 1894, and her younger sister Helen, born in 1895, also worked.

John Lunn was the black sheep of the family. Known as 'Jack', he was disliked by some of his siblings. Before 1914, he worked alongside his brother Richard, managing the factory. During the First World War, he served in the White Army that was formed to fight the Bolshevik Red Army, and was wounded in the knee. After the war, Jack struggled to find employment in England before eventually securing a job as a vacuum cleaner salesman.[33] He worked in censorship at the start of the Second World War, before joining Lucy and Helen at Bletchley Park.[34] Helen, known as 'Nellie', was 'probably the most brilliant in the family'.[35] Tall and slim with dark hair, she studied Modern Languages at the University of Liverpool, achieving a first-class degree in 1919.[36] After considering a university lectureship in Bordeaux, Helen chose to work for the fledgling GC&CS.[37] This secret cryptanalytical unit consisted of Russian defectors, talented linguists and extraordinary geniuses. The youngest child, Peggy, was born in 1898. Extremely fair with striking pale blonde hair, Peggy worked for GC&CS before studying Medicine at the University of London. She trained throughout the 1920s and worked in Chelsea as a general practitioner from the 1930s, treating everyone from the police to prostitutes.[38] While she was excellent at diagnosis and caring for others, she sadly did not give her own health the same attention, although she still managed to live well into her seventies.[39]

The surviving children possessed the same dash of temerity as their parents and grandparents but with one significant difference. They were the first generation born entirely in Russia, an important detail that would be later used against them by untrusting British counter-intelligence officers.[40] Educated to an excellent standard and fluent in four languages, they made ideal recruits for the British secret services, who did not initially view their place of birth as a problem. It was only when red flags were raised over Edith that it became an issue. After the October Revolution in 1917, the family found themselves dispersed. With most of the family remaining in Moscow, Edith and Helen lived

in England with their older sister Catherine and her husband, James
Ford-Smith, a teacher at the Market Bosworth Grammar School in
Leicestershire. Helen was busy studying at university, while thirty-
year-old Edith needed work. She would have loved the opportunity
to study at university too. After all, she had already passed her Senior
Cambridge examination at the turn of the century, but her parents had
refused to entertain the idea of sending their daughter to university.
At that time, they did not consider it an option for 'nice girls'.[41] Edith
deeply resented their decision and ensured that her younger sisters had
the same options as their brothers.

While her sister was at university, Edith secured a wartime position
in postal censorship. However, when MI5 ran their security checks,
they determined that the older Lunn sister was a 'very doubtful candidate'.[42] MI5 based their assessment on an intercepted letter that Edith
had written to Cyril Marsh Roberts on 15 November 1917.[43] Marsh
Roberts had returned from Russia to enlist at the start of the war.
Wounded at Ypres, he then became 'an out-and-out anti-war socialist' who proudly claimed to have shaken hands with Lenin himself.[44]
Edith closed her letter to Marsh Roberts: 'I am looking forward to
seeing you soon and hearing the truth about England and the war in
France.[45] The final part of her closing remark was enough to rouse the
suspicions of the secret service, but not enough to see her released from
work in the Censor Office. Thanks to the chief constable of Cheshire,
who vouched for her respectability and lack of known hostile associations, she continued in her position until 1918.[46]

However, it was during her formative years that Edith developed
a strong social conscience. As a privileged adolescent, she regularly
accompanied her mother, who visited the poor and sick of Moscow
and its surrounding villages. While the Lunn family always complied
with the factory acts, most Russian owners did not. Edith witnessed
at first hand the terrible poverty endured by those factory workers
not lucky enough to work for her family. Certain visits left a lasting
impression on Edith, such as a newborn baby placed under an icon by
its starving mother, who prayed her child would die and go straight
to heaven rather than endure a slow and painful death from hunger.
On another occasion, Edith overruled her father and brother Richard,
when they were about to give a workman his marching orders during
a particularly harsh winter. Edith was old enough to realise that, if the
man were dismissed, he would freeze to death. In what became her

first act of political protest, Edith convinced her father and brother to postpone the worker's dismissal until the spring.

At eighteen, Edith experienced the first Russian Revolution of 1905. Discontented workers attacked the mill, sending shock waves through the family. Edith's mother, Clara, was an astute woman who read the dangers ahead. Consequently, she pleaded with her husband to make investments in England. An indecisive man at times, Edwin refused to safeguard the family's wealth, believing that all would be well in Russia. Life continued for the Lunns, and Edith resumed her stewardship of a dozen English children, including her younger brothers, who attended school in England. She herded the gaggle of lively and energetic youths between trains on their journeys from Moscow to England. 'Sensible and calm', Edith never lost a child or the gold roubles carefully sewn into her belt.[47] While her brothers attended Owens College, Edith looked after the family home in the idyllic village of Bowdon, located on the outskirts of Manchester. She also kept up with her friends, including the handsome playboy Harry Gordon Selfridge Jr, who later succeeded his father as chairman of the famous London department store.[48]

By 1914, Edith had returned to Russia, and the family, like many others, had mobilised for war. Walter and John served on the Eastern Front, while Edith and Lucy joined medical students at a casualty evacuation station. The two sisters 'had a horrifying glimpse of the reality of life for the Russian poor' conscripted to fight.[49] Edith later recalled to her children how two peasant soldiers, who were lovers, were severely wounded and near death. In an act of kindness, Edith ensured that the two men were placed together in the same bed to share their final moments.[50] After 1917, the Bolshevik revolutionary leaders scrapped strict Tsarist religious policies and, in a progressive move, decriminalised same-sex relationships.[51] The revolutionaries' rethinking about the rights of their citizens struck a chord with Edith, as it did with Sylvia Pankhurst, daughter of the famous Emmeline and one of a few suffragettes who joined the communist cause following the revolution. Early Soviet ideas on marriage aligned with the modern thinking of women like Edith and Pankhurst, who saw matrimony as based on love, respect and economic independence, not official ratification. However, unlike Pankhurst, Edith and her future partner Andrew Rothstein, a founding member of the British communist movement and journalist for the Russian Telegraph Agency (ROSTA), eventually conceded out of necessity to ensure the legal rights of their son born in June 1926 and their future daughter, and wed officially in July 1926.[52]

The revolution was a defining event in Edith's life. Remembered as being 'so natural and friendly', Edith was an intelligent, tolerant and unmaterialistic woman, who became receptive to communist ideology.[53] Following her work in wartime censorship, she was briefly employed in 1919 as an MI6 secretary at the British Consulate in Helsinki.[54] Wrongly identified as 'Margaret Lunn' by MI5 and MI6, Edith's employment with MI6 was terminated after just one month because she had 'turned red'.[55] At the time, the British Legation in the Finnish capital was considered by some consulate staff to 'be getting redder and redder'.[56] The ambassador, Lord Acton, and the head of the Naval Mission, Captain Harold Grenfell, who worked alongside Edith on intelligence matters, were in close contact with the communist Finns. Both men socialised with well-known revolutionary socialists and left-wing journalists such as Arthur Ransome at the infamous 'Red Salon' run by Hella Wuolijoki, the wife of a Finnish socialist. Her sister, Salme Pekkala-Dutt, was later considered by Scotland Yard to be 'the centre of perhaps the cleverest communist group in this country'.[57]

After learning that the British intended to use Helsinki as a base for extending its intervention into Russia, Captain Grenfell stepped away from his secret intelligence duties.[58] Whitehall baulked at how far Bolshevik sympathies had spread within official British circles. In an effort to rid the Helsinki embassy of any staff that showed an ounce of radical thinking, Edith was given her marching orders. A year later, in 1920, Lord Acton, a liberal at heart, retired as ambassador. He was replaced by the more conservative George Kidston. Clearly, one could not be a socialist in the diplomatic or the secret world. The British government simply failed to grasp that the Russian people overwhelmingly supported Lenin's Bolshevik government. They had no desire to be led by former Tsarist generals or anyone appointed by foreign powers. While it slowly dawned on Whitehall that they could not turn back the clock, Captain Grenfell returned to England, and after thirty-five years of loyal service, he retired from the Royal Navy. As he was now considered a pure Bolshevik and traitor to his country, Grenfell's letters were regularly intercepted.[59] He continued to oppose British intervention and was joined in his efforts by Salme Pekkala-Dutt, who arrived in England in early 1920.[60]

Full of revolutionary spirit and well versed in the covert arts, Pekkala-Dutt established a secret information bureau for the Soviet delegation.[61] As the eyes of Moscow, she made contact with the British left and set about collecting information from local sources. The early Comintern, a Soviet-led organisation that advocated world communism, threw all its resources at establishing an information-gathering apparatus that, once wholly developed, provided the Soviets with a vital control mechanism. Pekkala-Dutt recruited several agents to gather information for the Soviets, including the Russian-born polyglot Lydia Stahl. An expert photographer, Stahl copied secret documents at her studio in Paris.[62] As Pekkala-Dutt's network grew, she soon needed help managing her mounting correspondence. She hired an exceptional, trustworthy young woman as her secretary: Edith.[63] The elder Lunn sister was a perfect choice. It is quite possible that the two women's paths may have crossed earlier while in Finland; alternatively, Pekkala-Dutt may at some point have sought a recommendation from Captain Grenfell. At any rate, on accepting the appointment, Edith had firmly chosen her side, but it proved to be a lonely one. While she entertained hopes of one day returning to Russia, her parents remained confirmed anti-Bolsheviks.[64]

As secretary to a Comintern agent, it was only a matter of time before Edith's name appeared on a Home Office warrant issued on 25 March 1921.[65] The investigation that followed called upon the resources of Special Branch, MI5 and MI6, who together generated a flurry of internal memos, surveillance reports and copies of intercepted postal correspondence addressed to the Lunn family residence at 85 York Mansions, an impressive Victorian block of flats on Prince of Wales Drive in Battersea. Every aspect of the family's life was put under the microscope and scrutinised. MI5 suspected Salme Pekkala-Dutt of using Edith's home address as her own. While none of the Comintern agent's correspondence was intercepted at York Mansions, Special Branch noted that ARCOS had written to Edith inviting her to call at their office to discuss her application for a position on their staff.[66]

Yet it was Edith's association with Andrew Rothstein, a known Soviet agent, that caused the greatest concern for MI6. The two had met at the Fabian Society, where they engaged in stimulating intellectual conversation, debating how to advance the socialist cause best and transform British society. The courtship blossomed while they worked at the ARCOS offices in Bush House, which today forms part of King's College London. Edith and Andrew enjoyed a modern partnership, with the pair choosing to pass as 'Mr and Mrs Lunn' until they married in 1926. However, a year before they wed, Edith fell pregnant. On hearing the news that his daughter was with child out of wedlock, Edwin threw Edith out of the family's new home at 67 York Mansions. He had tolerated her political affiliations, but her being unmarried and pregnant was a scandal that he simply could not entertain. As much as he loved Edith, he could not escape the censure of the times, nor could his daughter. A resolute Edith took a flat at Parliament Hill Mansions in Hampstead, known as the 'Bolshevik colony'. For a brief while, she was completely cut off from her family, having no communication with any of her siblings or her parents.[67]

From the late summer of 1925 to the beginning of 1926, Edith and Andrew's movements were monitored by MI5 and Special Branch. Surveillance was carried out on Edith's new flat, but the watchers recorded nothing more than the comings and goings of an unsuspecting charwoman and a middle-aged woman walking a large Airedale terrier around the gardens.[68] The couple were observed at home and when they travelled overseas, with MI5 reading all their mail. Such intrusive surveillance techniques recorded every intimate and private detail, including Edith's tragic miscarriage. At the end of August 1925, the Devon Constabulary reported to the head of MI5, Vernon Kell, that the four-month-pregnant Edith had lost her baby and was recovering at the comfortable Kingsbridge Cottage Hospital.[69] Supported by her Russian friends, the 37-year-old grieving mother longed to have Andrew by her side. She wrote to him in London, informing him of the sad event.[70] He later rushed to console Edith, unaware, or perhaps not, that he was being watched.

The Lunn family were oblivious to the secret campaign waged against them. MI5 stressed the need to proceed cautiously and discreetly with their inquiries. The intelligence community were on guard after the 1923 general election result that saw the first Labour government formed. The British secret services, which mirrored the establishment's old boys' network, were horrified that the very people they had been surveilling were in power. However, Ramsay MacDonald's

Labour premiership was short-lived. By the end of October 1924, the Tories had returned to power after eradicating their internal party disagreements. After a vote of no confidence in the Labour government was taken, just days before a snap general election was called, 'the Zinoviev letter', named after the leader of the Comintern, was leaked to the British press. Addressed to the Communist Party of Great Britain (CPGB), the letter called on workers to strike, but it failed to damage the Labour vote as intended. Whether or not the letter was genuine or a forgery is still debated.[71] What is clear is MI6's hand in the whole affair. After receiving the letter from the MI6 station in Riga, the SIS officer Desmond Morton evaluated it and confirmed its authenticity.[72] Whatever its true origin, Morton remains a key suspect in the distribution and use of the letter to throw doubt on the Labour government's credibility at a time when relations with Russia were tense.

In many ways, MI6 had an unhealthy obsession with the Bolsheviks. Its counterintelligence officers remained focused on the single target, and men like Morton were required to be patient and persistent in their work. While MI5 and Special Branch commenced their investigation of the Lunn sisters, Morton waited patiently for a verdict on current MI6 employees Lucy and Helen. Intercepted mail revealed that, after Edith moved to Hampstead, Helen returned to the family flat. Because of her distinctive mole on the left side of her nose and being the only dark-haired sister, MI5 correctly identified Helen. Family correspondence during the 1920s revealed how the family constantly teetered on a financial tightrope. Even after Lucy, Helen and John had contributed some of their wages to their parents and helped out when they could to fund Peggy through university, it was still not enough initially. However, their mother, Clara, remained hopeful, remarking, 'never mind, the sun will shine on our side someday'.[73]

Lucy and Helen shared their mother's optimism. Both had secured good jobs with GC&CS and MI6. Helen received £200 a year for her work as a translator, which was unsurprisingly less than her male colleagues received.[74] Handpicked by Alastair Denniston, the head of GC&CS, the brilliant linguist joined a workforce of seventy-five other men and women at Watergate House, located on the Thames Embankment.[75] At the GC&CS headquarters, Helen worked alongside the organisation's only female codebreaker, the gifted Emily Anderson.[76] Both women were meticulous in their approach to translation, learning additional languages such as Hungarian, which the eccentric cryptographer Dilly Knox much appreciated. Knox was known for his unusual wartime codebreaking methods, which included taking hot, steamy baths in his Admiralty office.

With their fluency in Russian, Helen and Peggy worked as 'Lady Translators' on diplomatic decrypts. While Peggy was employed for only a few years, Helen embarked on a nearly thirty-year career with GC&CS. She worked gruelling hours with veteran codebreakers who faced the prospect of retraining during the first few years of the organisation's existence. After the war, 'the methods of recypherment were very different, and staff had to learn a great deal about cryptography in its more complicated forms'.[77] The highly stressful working conditions caused the death of at least one member of staff, Sydney Fryer, who jumped in front of a moving train at Sloane Square tube station in 1924.[78] Hugh Sinclair, the new chief of MI6 and director of GC&CS, was greatly alarmed by the suicide and quickly set about making the necessary improvements for his workforce, many of whom had not enjoyed a break since 1914.

In 1925, Sinclair moved MI6 and GC&CS to the more spacious 54 Broadway Buildings, where both organisations occupied the third and fourth floors. Helen's work set-up improved significantly. Staff had a short walk from St James's Park underground station to the office, entering 54 Broadway via an unassuming door at 21 Queen Anne's Gate, home to the Passport Control Office (PCO). Shortly after the move, Helen was promoted to Junior Assistant in July 1925.[79] Sinclair invested heavily in GC&CS personnel, ensuring 'it was the largest and best codebreaking agency in the world'.[80] The peacetime signals-intelligence (SIGINT) agency remained at Broadway until 1939, when it moved to Bletchley Park. Helen was part of the second wave of staff billeted at 'Station X'.[81] She worked in the Diplomatic section housed in the requisitioned Elmers Grammar School near the main entrance.[82]

Helen's niece remembered her aunt as an elegant and stylish woman whose wages paid for her father's accommodation at a nursing home until he died in 1936. There was enough money left over each month to enjoy membership of the Roehampton Club, to shop for fashionable clothes, and to take skiing holidays.[83] Life was good for Helen, and in January 1940 she was promoted to Senior Assistant.[84] Unfortunately, while she found love, Helen could not entertain notions of marriage and keep her job. The Foreign Office's marriage bar prevented married women from working. Sadly, Helen did not get the chance to enjoy retirement with the unnamed love of her life, as the 53-year-old lost her battle with bowel cancer during the late 1940s and died on the operating table in December 1948.[85]

Helen never received recognition for her long years of service with GC&CS, nor did she expect it. Her sister Lucy lived the longest of all the Lunn siblings and was awarded an MBE in June 1969 for fifty years of service in MI6.[86] Her colleagues sent numerous congratulatory letters commending her skill and devotion to duty at a time when most would have expected the 77-year-old to be in an armchair.[87] Ironically, Desmond Morton, the MI6 officer who initiated an investigation into Lucy and her sisters in 1925, had shaken off all suspicion. In a short perfunctory note written in his hand, a retired Morton noted his delight on hearing the news of her award, writing, 'I can not think of anyone who deserves it more.'[88] In 1969, Lucy worked in the unknown 'L Section' at Century House, a dreary 22-storey tower block on Westminster Bridge Road in Lambeth. Very little is known about the personnel who worked at this headquarters, or the Cold War operations hatched and launched from the now transformed and glamorous apartment block.

A few records survive that shed light on Lucy's early MI6 career. In 1919, Lucy worked overseas in Constantinople (Istanbul).[89] The 'secretary' performed her MI6 duties under the cover of the PCO, which by 1921 formed one of twenty-eight such offices located around the world.[90] Despite the lack of post-war funding, the passport control system enabled MI6 to adapt accordingly and be flexible when needed. After the Great War, the Constantinople office was 'one of the most important, if not the most important' of all Cumming's overseas stations.[91] At the time, the Turkish nationalists were determined to remove the Sultan and establish an independent republic, thereby directly challenging British imperial interests in the region. MI6 and Whitehall equated all nationalist movements with communism. They chose to counter the perceived threat by recruiting former Tsarist officers and Russian émigrés to run a network of Russian anti-communist agents charged with gathering intelligence on the nationalist movement. The MI6 station was well staffed compared to other PCOs, which usually had what amounted to no more than a handful of staff. Lucy was most likely the only woman working alongside eight male officers. These included Harold Gibson, who had worked in Petrograd with Winnie Spink, Wilfred 'Biffy' Dunderdale, who had grown up in Constantinople, and Valentine Vivian, known as 'Vee-Vee', who rose to become the deputy head of MI6. All three had long careers in British intelligence. The MI6 station was highly effective, with one colleague at London headquarters declaring 'a better service of information has never been organised regarding events in the Near East'.[92]

After Turkey, Lucy worked at the MI6 station in Rome. She also assisted Charles 'C.K.' Scott Moncrieff to earn a little more money. The Scottish-born writer and prolific translator had moved to Italy in 1923, hoping it might improve his ailing health. His cousin, Louis Christie, was the Passport Control Officer in the Rome office, having taken over from Philip Rapinet Mackenzie.[93] The latter's daughter, Phyllis ('Phyl') Mackenzie, worked at the Rome embassy from 1926 to 1940 before serving in the covert British Security Coordination (BSC) and Special Operations Executive (SOE) during the Second World War.[94] Lucy and Phyl likely knew each other in Rome, as Philip Mackenzie dined regularly with his successor, Louis Christie.

Sporting an assertive auburn bob that accentuated a mischievous twinkle in her hazel eyes, Lucy was described by Charles as having 'a touch of strangeness' due to her Russian upbringing.[95] The secretary spent all day at the PCO, often concluding with evenings spent in the company of Louis and Charles. When the writer was not pontificating about his translation efforts, Charles engaged in intelligence work, reporting all he learnt from his travels around the country. He was fond of his part-time secretary, but Lucy initially misread his affection as a romantic interest. In 1925, MI5 intercepted one of Lucy's letters to her sister Helen. With remarkable honesty, she revealed, 'I am beginning to think I must have imagined a lot of things formerly because now that I look back, I don't think he ever did like me any more than he does now, but I used to think he did.'[96] In fact, as a promiscuous gay man, Charles was never attracted to women. However, during the last year of his life, he apparently considered marriage to Lucy and asked his fellow translator and friend Vyvyan Beresford Holland, the son of Oscar Wilde, for his thoughts on the matter.[97] Lucy never subsequently received a marriage proposal from the translator turned spy.

The petite and loyal secretary stayed with Charles until the forty-year-old drew his final breath on 28 February 1930. Lucy never married and remained in the secret world of British intelligence for the rest of her life. She had signed the Official Secrets Act in 1919 and kept silent about the true nature of her work for the 'Foreign Office'. Only once did Lucy let slip to her niece that she had known George Blake, a convicted Soviet agent who escaped from Wormwood Scrubs prison in 1966 and fled to the Soviet Union.[98] Towards the end of her life, Lucy 'tore up many family photographs and letters which she regarded as purely personal, not seeing that they had a much wider interest'.[99] Lucy 'lived for the present and could see no point in looking at the past', a trait that most who lived their entire lives in the shadows exhibited.[100] However, glimpses of Lucy's past survive in a few photographs that show her imbibing gin and tonics at cocktail parties and smiling at the camera while taking a break on the ski slopes during the 1930s.

A sisterhood of secrets and love bound Lucy and her female siblings together throughout their lives. Their Russian heritage made them women of two worlds. While Edith chose to commit her life to the country of her birth, Lucy, Helen and Peggy served the country from which their family originally hailed. As loyal servants of the British secret state, they learnt to live with the torment of secrecy, which, over the years, led to an even greater sense of distance between themselves and their communist sister. The unusual circumstances surrounding the Lunn sisters were unique in the history of MI6; it was only a matter of time before Desmond Morton or some other officer questioned the women's allegiance. Suspicion and paranoia were, and still are, inevitable by-products of keeping secrets and telling lies, but the sisters proved ultimately to be beyond reproach.

The investigation could find nothing on Lucy, Helen or Peggy that suggested they were guilty of passing secret information to their older sister.[101] After trawling through Edith's correspondence, MI5 concluded she knew nothing about Lucy's work for MI6 or Helen's position at GC&CS.[102] In March 1926, MI6 chief Hugh Sinclair 'decided that he desired no further action to be taken in this case' as he was satisfied that Lucy and Helen were 'quite sound from a security standpoint'.[103] However, MI5 and Special Branch kept Edith and Andrew Rothstein under surveillance for the rest of their lives. While Edith enjoyed being a mother to their two children, Andrew continued his work as a journalist for the Russian ROSTA news agency, providing suitable cover for his Soviet espionage work. He later recruited Melita Norwood into the NKVD, the Russian secret service, in 1935.[104] As

Russia's longest-serving British spy, Norwood (codenamed HOLA) worked as a typist and secretary at the British Non-Ferrous Metals Research Association (BNF) in London, where she accessed scientific secrets.[105] The 'grandma' spy 'who came in from the Co-op' was finally exposed in 1999 at eighty-seven years of age.[106]

Those who worked in the British and Russian secret services were mere chess pieces in a game of intrigue between East and West that continues today.[107] For the Lunn sisters, their shadowy roles finally ended in 1992. Lucy's death marked 'the close of a story which had started in Lancashire in 1822'.[108] The sisters were extraordinary women whose lives were woven together in a rich tapestry of courage, resilience and ideological differences that saw Edith discover a different path, one that led her to stand with the CPGB, 'into which she unquestionably put part of her soul'.[109] From the 1920s onwards, Soviet intelligence launched an offensive that saw British intelligence target working-class institutions to identify and stop the 'enemy within'. As a result, Britain's secret services were utterly blind to the Soviet Union's successful recruitment of privileged, high-flying students at Cambridge University during the 1930s. As the chess pieces moved around the board, the Soviets successfully wrong-footed British intelligence, who never thought to question the loyalty of the British ruling class and its gentlemen spies.

However, MI6 were quick to question Lucy and Helen's loyalty, choosing to see them as foreigners in that instant rather than as British subjects. They were not born in England and had no connections with the ruling classes. They did not know the 'right people' and did not move in society circles. Had they been born and raised in England with the necessary social standing, and had they attended finishing school as many 'well-bred' young women were required to do, one wonders whether MI6 would have ever pointed the finger of suspicion at them. Within MI6, there was a strong element of paternalistic separatism that countless female employees bought into. They enjoyed the intellectualism of their work, but were seduced by the empowering knowledge of being privy to secret information that the rest of society remained in the dark about. While the Lunn sisters were not a natural fit, Lucy and Helen became respected members of the MI6 family. They worked alongside many talented men and women who loyally served a succession of MI6 chiefs. As the secret staff worked tirelessly to combat communism during the interwar period, Mansfield Cumming welcomed a new addition to the family, someone well versed in the peculiarities of the covert world of His Majesty's Secret Intelligence Service. Her name was Miss Kathleen Pettigrew.

6

Through the Looking Glass

A self-effacing woman left her family flat and walked down the busy Strand in London. As she passed a shop, she glanced at her reflection in the window. The person she saw staring back was the version she presented to the world. Those she worked with knew her, or so they assumed. Perhaps her mother and older sister were the only ones to know who Kathleen Pettigrew truly was. She possessed a clandestine mentality, which the average person does not usually have to develop and call upon. The young secretary tried hard to conceal the cloak-and-dagger nature of her work, but this became an even greater task sometime after October 1921, when Kathleen left the familiarity of Special Branch and stepped through the looking glass into the secret world of MI6. She was not disappointed with what she found on the other side: a topsy-turvy world, complete with a unique staff for whom the word impossible did not exist. Intentionally obscured by smoke and mirrors, MI6 is one of the oldest and most secretive of all the intelligence services. It operates behind the looking glass, making it extremely challenging for historians to follow those who live and work in the shadows. However, 'cover is neither absolute nor permanent'.[1]

Many early MI6 recruits such as Kathleen spent their entire careers in the employ of the secret service. They devoted their lives to serving king, queen and country. Yet they also enjoyed moments outside 'spyland', allowing historians a brief insight into their lives and clandestine activities. An unspoken fraternity bound the eclectic mix of secret personnel, drawn from all walks of life. Even so, it was social class and gender that defined who was at the top and bottom of the organisational ladder. British intelligence was a dysfunctional family where men were bound by old-boy networks connected with schools and universities, the armed forces and police, and the smoked-filled private member clubs of London. As male personnel united in their shadowy pursuits, competent women were left to pursue their work in the back rooms of British intelligence, confirming the existence of a tangible division between the gentleman spy and his secretary.

MI6 took the safest route, primarily recruiting women who were the daughters and nieces of military men, politicians and diplomats who were somehow 'in the know'. However, the woman who inspired the creation of one of history's most famous literary and on-screen secretaries – Ian Fleming's Miss Moneypenny – never attended finishing school nor had the benefit of being waited on by servants. Kathleen Pettigrew had grown up living and sleeping in a tiny flat above the family shop in George Court. Without any social connections, she was recruited by MI6 purely on merit. However, had Basil Thomson not been dismissed at the end of 1921, she might still have been working for the ambitious Assistant Commissioner of Special Branch.

In the spring of 1919, Thomson and his secret staff left their wartime rooms in Scotland Yard and moved everything, including the famous leather 'spy armchair', to nearby Scotland House. As Thomson's trusted aide, Kathleen remained at the centre of the secret world, constantly observing and learning all she could from her seniors, like the 57-year-old Mary Bidwell.[2] After the move, such skilled female assistants now worked for a post-war organisation that served as a co-ordinated domestic intelligence agency, created to stem the growing tide of civil unrest that would ultimately culminate in the General Strike of 1926. Kathleen's dynamic and determined boss reported directly to the Home Secretary rather than to the commissioner of the Metropolitan Police.

Facing a considerable increase in work, Thomson called upon the talents of the veteran intelligence officer Colonel John Carter, who brought to the job a wealth of experience when he joined as assistant director in 1919. The bespectacled officer, who walked with the aid of a stick, had previously carried out a range of MI5 counterintelligence operations in wartime London. Previously, in 1918, he had worked with Thomson's close friend Sir Samuel Hoare in Rome, where he developed a pioneering method of dropping men and equipment into enemy territory using parachutes.[3] The men and women of the Special Operations Executive (SOE) would carry out similar aerial-insertion missions during the Second World War. During the early interwar period, Thomson and Carter accumulated a staggering amount of information on subversive activity at home and abroad, rivalling MI5 efforts and encroaching on MI6's terrain. As an experienced civil servant, Thomson delivered regular weekly summaries on revolutionary organisations to the Cabinet that were just as useful as anything produced by MI5.[4]

Unlike Vernon Kell and Mansfield Cumming, who kept all secret paperwork locked away in the vaults of MI5 and MI6, Thomson made attempts to archive key documents for future generations. In 1919, the 'invaluable sleuth hound' conducted a detailed inquiry into the brutal murder of Tsar Nicholas II and his family that had occurred in July 1918.[5] Thomson shared his findings with the King, who understandably had taken a keen interest in his cousin's death.[6] A year later, though Thomson was now dealing with militant Irish nationalists, the Romanov murder findings still preoccupied his thoughts. On 3 July 1920, Thomson called his secretary into his office and dictated a confidential letter informing the Keeper of the Records that he wished to deposit materials relating to the investigation in the Public Records Office. After Kathleen had noted the final sentence in shorthand, she promptly returned to her desk. The rapid 'dings' of her typewriter bell signalled the speed at which she converted her scrawling script into legible text. While the words belonged to Thomson, the finished correspondence bore all the hallmarks of its creator: characters mechanically struck with trained precision, identical spacing visible between each word, and uniformly straight lines. Like a great artist, she always signed her work 'K.P.' in the top left-hand corner.[7] Only after reviewing the typed letter for imperfections did she relax the unnaturally rigid body posture demanded of all good operators.

Kathleen was not the only woman to handle highly sensitive documents within the Directorate of Intelligence.[8] Women played an essential role in both branches of the directorate known as SS1 (Foreign Branch) and SS2 (Home Branch). The Foreign Branch worked closely with MI6, and in an attempt to keep secret documents away from the prying eyes of police officers who had not signed the Official Secrets Act, a highly confidential registry was established and staffed solely by two sisters, Maud and Eva (known as Hope) Symons. Together, they maintained the Secret Service (SS) Registry of MI6 materials, such as Home Office warrants and confidential correspondence. To ensure maximum security, the two women slaved away in complete isolation and adopted the same office practices and registry system used by MI6. In their efforts to safeguard information, the two sisters quickly encountered problems when sharing files with SS1 and SS2, as the latter followed Special Branch procedures. Over the years, the MI6 practices came to be considered by the Symons' colleagues as 'peculiar' and 'impossible to deal with'.[9]

The elder of the two sisters, Maud, was the first to join the service on 15 May 1920, when she took up the post of Assistant to the Foreign Section (SS1) and independently ran the SS Registry. Her sister Hope joined her on 19 July 1924, and the two worked together until 1928.[10] Born in Lancashire in 1868 and 1877, the two Symons were related to one of the first female officers at Scotland Yard, Lilian Wyles, who was later appointed chief inspector in 1932, becoming the first woman to achieve such a promotion.[11] The Symons sisters and their seven siblings benefited from a wealthy upbringing, courtesy of their parents, Frederick and Delfina Symons. Frederick originally came from Falmouth, where his family owned several lucrative shipyards, but after working as a merchant for some time in the tropical climate of Rio de Janeiro, the hardworking businessman moved to the outskirts of Manchester, and raised his growing family. Alongside his work representing several Brazilian firms in the city, the senior Symons found time to engage in various philanthropic efforts and served as a magistrate for the county of Chester.[12] The children attended good boarding schools, and Maud and Hope received schooling in various languages, which served them well in their future secret roles. In fact, the sisters proved so good at their jobs in the SS Registry that men never replaced them.

Unfortunately, Basil Thomson's time in power did not last as long as the Symons sisters'. The Director of Intelligence came under attack from a small number of powerful men. The commissioner of the Metropolitan Police, General Sir William Horwood, resented his deputy's success and the directorate's independence. Vernon Kell was less inclined to support Thomson after the government slashed MI5's funding. Thomson's directorate had certainly muddied the water, causing confusion and jealousy among the other heads of services. Thomson's enemies seized their chance to get rid of him when four young Irishmen broke into the grounds of the prime minister's official country residence at Chequers and chalked the slogan 'Up, Sinn Féin' on the walls of a summerhouse. Severely shaken by the event, David Lloyd George blamed Thomson for the breach and threat to his personal safety.[13] Summoned to the House of Commons for a ticking off, a sixty-year-old Thomson found himself in the difficult position of having no choice but to accept retirement with a favourable pension before being unceremoniously dismissed in October 1921.[14] The Directorate of Intelligence ceased to exist, and Special Branch inherited SS1, SS2 and the SS Registry. While Maud Symons continued her secret MI6 liaison work, others who had served Thomson loyally since the war faced a difficult choice: should they stay or leave?

As Thomson's personal assistant, Kathleen Pettigrew had experienced much danger and excitement. One wonders how she felt when her mentor walked out of the great gates of Scotland Yard for the final time. Perhaps she shared the same concerns as Thomson, who remained convinced that he was ousted because he knew too much and could jeopardise the prime minister's plan to recognise the Soviet government.[15] While Thomson's supporters debated his sacking in the House of Commons, Kathleen left Special Branch. At twenty-three years of age, the young secretary represented the growing number of professional women who refused to leave the factories and offices at the war's end and return to home duties. Kathleen and her older sister, Ellen, had no option but to work. Along with the money brought in by their mother's shop, the Pettigrew women saved enough cash to move from the cramped conditions in George Court to a more spacious and upmarket flat across the road at 19 York Buildings. While Ellen continued in her role as a Registry clerk in Special Branch, her younger sister took a new position that utilised her unrivalled skill set.

Though the exact date remains a mystery, Kathleen joined MI6 sometime after the winter of 1921. By then, Mansfield Cumming had moved his wartime headquarters from Whitehall Court to a large Victorian villa in Holland Park.[16] Perfectly camouflaged by the residential surroundings, 1 Melbury Road also served as the workaholic MI6 chief's home.[17] The noticeable increase in footfall from staff and visitors soon led to the extension of standings for hackney carriages in the surrounding streets, with spaces for a further seventeen cabs added to service Melbury Road.[18] As a security precaution, visitors were required to report first to an office at 1 Adam Street, off the Strand. A stone's throw from the luxury Savoy Hotel, the 'visitors' office was strategically located on the other side of London, far from the new secret headquarters. Upon arrival at the Adam Street office, staff revealed the actual headquarters address to visitors, who left grumbling at the inconvenience of additional travel to the other side of London.[19] The Pettigrew family flat was just a short walk from the Adam Street office and a half-hour underground ride to Melbury Road. Kathleen joined a workforce of sixty-five staff based at headquarters. A total of 132 men and women were posted overseas, and with 484 agents on the books, MI6 generated the astonishing total of roughly 13,000 intelligence reports each year.[20]

C did not subscribe to Foreign Office practice, which forced women to resign from their posts once married. By all accounts, Cumming and his male officers were, for the most part, courteous gentlemen with impeccable manners, accustomed to treating women with respect, and C's own manner and tone were impeccable. His business and social etiquette were the same for good reason. During the war, he ensured that his 'lady drivers' had appropriate uniforms, and he occasionally took his female typists out for lunch.[21] An inspirational leader, Cumming invested in his workforce, deliberately developing trust, which was essential if intelligence work was to be kept out of public view. As he argued, secrecy was 'the first, last and most necessary essential of a Secret Service'.[22]

As a professionally trained confidential secretary and former personal assistant to the Director of Intelligence, Kathleen worked alongside several interesting women who had come, like herself, from humble beginnings. Beatrice Mortimer began her MI6 career as a messenger.[23] In 1921, she was based at the Adam Street office, which served as the MI6 Registry, 'a clearing house for a great deal of intelligence work'.[24] Born at the turn of the century, Beatrice came from a single-parent family. Her mother, a widow, had made ends meet by taking a boarder on at the family home and cleaning at a local London school. By 1921, Beatrice was living with her mother and older sister at their aunt's house. The three women had cut all ties with Beatrice's brother, Alfred, who walked a dangerous path. In 1920, the crooked postman was found guilty of stealing letters and parcels that he should have delivered. This was far from being his first misdemeanour, as Alfred had stolen an entire bedroom suite months before.[25] Having such a wayward brother did not affect Beatrice's work for MI6; by 1925, she had taken on the respectable role of 'Lady Telephonist', a position she continued to hold after she married until retirement.[26]

Though telephone operators played a vital role in MI6 and the other secret services, with security a key concern, only a few women held the job for long periods. Patching calls through manually, operators had to be utterly trustworthy, given that they could easily listen in to conversations. Rather than going through the local exchange run by the General Post Office (GPO), Britain's secret services had private telephone exchanges. Beatrice would have been an expert at recognising callers' voices and knowing further particulars about individuals. With her hair fixed perfectly to accommodate the headset and mouthpiece strapped around her neck, Beatrice possessed an excellent speaking voice and was tall enough to reach the top sockets on the vast switchboard of competing plugs and wires. Typically, when calling MI5 regarding the Lunn sisters in 1925, MI6 officer Desmond Morton would pick up the telephone in his office, to be greeted by Beatrice's voice asking him for the number. The telephonist would then promptly ask Morton to 'hold the line please' while she connected the call by removing and inserting the necessary jack plugs on the switchboard.

The ability to converse on the telephone revolutionised intelligence work, speeding up the process of collation and dissemination and providing necessary alerts and warnings as situations arose. However, both the British secret services and their enemies benefited equally from the ability to intercept conversations as a source of intelligence. This meant that there was still a need to courier information in printed form across the city by service messenger, and even further afield via diplomatic bag and the use of King's Messengers. At just fourteen years old in 1921, Gladys Lincoln was perhaps the youngest woman ever to work for MI6.[27] As a messenger, she joined several other women who, like Beatrice Mortimer, have remained entirely anonymous until now and deserve recognition. They were Agnes Bell, Ethel Cory, Lilian Doolan, May Harrison, Dorothy Henslowe, Edna Hill, Gertrude McKay, Olive Montgomery, Gwendolen Rogers, Oohna Stewart, Catherine Tims, Margaret Churcher, Bridget Battye and Nina Vertier.[28] And so Mansfield Cumming's female personnel grew to become an excellent mix of professionally trained women such as Kathleen Pettigrew, who worked alongside affluent women previously schooled in how to hold a champagne glass.

Take, for example, the case of Dorothy Henslowe. After attending finishing school in Geneva, the pretty, dark-haired seventeen-year-old worked for an eccentric, ageing admiral during the First World War.[29] Dorothy had been born in 1897 at Fort Sandeman, Baluchistan, where her father, Lieutenant Colonel Francis Henslowe, commanded the 22nd Sam Browne's Cavalry (Frontier Force), an elite Indian Army regiment stationed near the Khyber Pass.[30] With a lack of medical facilities and a high child-mortality rate in India, Dorothy's parents wisely sent their two young children back to England, where they lived securely with two devoted elderly aunts.[31] Unfortunately, the separation from her parents at such a young age was unbearable for Dorothy; as a result, she felt she never truly knew her father.[32] She soon came to see her MI6 boss as a surrogate parent. She quickly became a part of the Cumming family, enjoying summer holidays with C and his wife, May, who both enjoyed the company of young people.

As one of Cumming's first secretaries, Dorothy helped the spymaster manage the service's ever-expanding paperwork, while he recovered from a nearly fatal accident. Early in the Great War, Cumming had met up with his son, Alastair, who was serving as a staff officer at General Headquarters on the Western Front, to take him to Paris for a few days' leave. With the young officer behind the wheel, father and son travelled through the night but unfortunately crashed into a tree. Alastair was flung from the car as it overturned and killed instantly. His father was severely injured and taken to the nearest hospital, where his lower right leg was amputated.[33] On his return to London, Cumming was fitted with an artificial leg, and legend has it that he used to stab his prosthesis with a penknife during the interview process to unnerve potential recruits. Dorothy and her peers were not deterred, and slowly established office procedures and practices that set the organisation on the path to becoming a modern intelligence agency. Working with her cousin, Catherine Tims, Dorothy proved to be a formidable character in the office, taking no nonsense from the male employees. Accomplished and full of life, she enjoyed attending parties hosted by her colleagues and, many years later, told her granddaughter that she had once danced with Sidney Reilly, one of the service's more colourful spies, renowned for his courageous exploits in revolutionary Russia.[34]

Cumming's death on 14 June 1923 had a profound impact on his devoted secretary and the rest of the secret service staff. That day, C had spent the afternoon chatting with a journalist friend from the war, Valentine Williams, who recorded in his autobiography that he had left Cumming at 6 p.m. that evening. The old man was 'comfortably installed in a corner of the sofa. When his secretary went to him soon after, she found him dead. He had died in harness, as he would have wished.'[35] For Dorothy, Cumming 'was a friend such as one does not expect to meet again'.[36] The first MI6 chief's reign ended before he could enjoy retirement, and his successor, Hugh Sinclair, would also suffer the same fate.[37] Dorothy, on the other hand, continued to work for MI6 until leaving in 1926 to nurse her dying mother, after which she married and started a family before it was too late to do so. When she left the service, Sinclair wrote his confidential secretary a glowing reference stating that he could not 'speak too highly of her tact, discretion and judgement'.[38]

Thanks to his predecessor, the newly appointed C inherited a secret service with a worldwide intelligence-gathering network. Hugh Sinclair, the former Director of Naval Intelligence, was just as unorthodox as Cumming, and had even grander plans for MI6. He challenged the need for a separate MI5, arguing that domestic security should merge with MI6, but just as Thomson failed to create a single intelligence service, so too did Sinclair.[39] However, the debonair chief had more success with the 'Z' Organisation, a covert network that relied on British contacts working in foreign cities across Europe. Run by Claude Dansey, the Z Organisation gathered vital information on Nazi Germany and Fascist Italy during the 1930s. In case MI6 should ever become compromised, Dansey's organisation worked independently of the service's established, more conventional Passport Control Office (PCO) network.

Despite having to operate MI6 on a shoestring budget, Sinclair accomplished more than was possible during the interwar period. He rarely buckled under pressure, and 'no emergency ever saw him "rattled"'.[40] Sinclair was a seasoned naval man, having entered the Britannia Naval College in Dartmouth as a cadet at the age of thirteen. MI6's future chief quickly rose through the commissioned ranks, earning recognition for his intolerance of 'any sort of slackness or inefficiency, which he was likely to castigate with an astonishing flow of forcible language, such as was traditional in an earlier generation of sea officers, delivered without hurry or any change of expression'.[41] Sinclair's deceptive poker face served him well after adopting the spymaster mantle. When not at MI6 headquarters, the newly appointed C was to be found at the Army and Navy Club in Pall Mall, a distinguished London club whose membership included several other MI6 officers. London's club land provided the perfect setting where the city's spies could wine and dine agents and assets, and could socialise with those at the heart of government. Sinclair 'possessed a fund of caustic humour and entertaining anecdote' that left an unforgettable impression but also rendered him a dangerous opponent during a debate.[42]

As the son of Admiral Frederick Beauchamp Paget Seymour, Sinclair was one of seven children. His father, the first and last Lord Alcester, refused to marry but had several relationships with women. The woman who bore his seven children, Angus May, was left £1,000 in her so-called husband's will in 1895, but she could only draw upon it if she promised not to trouble the beneficiaries, her children. As the only two siblings to live beyond 1928, Sinclair and his younger sister, Lady Evelyn, lived aristocratic lives, benefiting from their late father's wealth. Never without servants, they always travelled first-class, but unlike some of their peers, they were not the sort of English gentry despised for their mindless pretensions. Those who served under them held the two in high esteem, and the siblings valued mutual loyalty above all else.

Assisted by his enigmatic sister, Sinclair kept his trusted inner circle small; he counted his personal secretary, Kathleen Pettigrew, as one of his closest confidantes. Like Evelyn, Kathleen would have known the exact locations of the 'dead letter boxes' used for communicating with agents.[43] She also had access to the safe in Sinclair's office, which contained top-secret papers and important personnel information. Evelyn Sinclair worked closely with Kathleen and several other long-serving MI6 women, such as Rita Winsor, Ena Molesworth and Frieda Moon. Evelyn was good friends with Nicholas Elliott, the MI6 officer who famously confronted his best friend and colleague Kim Philby with evidence that he was a Soviet spy, and she also counted Neville Chamberlain's cousin Pearl as a close friend.[44] A family member recalls being taken to Evelyn's Mayfair apartment for afternoon tea in 1960. The young man was impressed by the grandeur of his relation's flat, filled with family photographs and silverware passed down the generations. Evelyn was a clever woman who regaled her impressionable visitor with stories of her brother, Sir Hugh, but she did not suffer fools.[45] She had an excellent knowledge of politics and a shrewdness of observation that was not to be trifled with.

Sadly, very few family photographs survived after she died in 1971. Evelyn made great efforts to ensure her anonymity in history. She even made provisions in her will for her ashes to remain unclaimed, leaving no memorial or headstone. Luckily, a rare photograph of her is to be found in her brother's scrapbook, a remarkable artefact given that it has survived outside MI6 within the archive of the National Maritime Museum in Greenwich. It is a snapshot taken when, at the end of 1936, Sinclair and his sister travelled from Southampton to New York aboard the RMS *Berengaria*. While enjoying after-dinner drinks on the Cunard White Star luxury liner, 63-year-old Hugh Sinclair is smiling directly at the camera. However, his sister, Evelyn, sits beside him wearing a fashionable silk evening dress adorned with delicate shoulder feathers. With her head turned sideways while she converses with guests at the neighbouring table, Evelyn makes it difficult for later generations to discern any facial features beyond her short brown hair styled in a typical fashionable 1930s bob with elegant waves at the side.[46] Despite her attempts to evade the camera, the veil of secrecy surrounding her work and support for her brother extended to every facet of Evelyn's life. Evidence of her contribution to the secret world has survived in records relating to the women of the secretariat who managed the Government Code and Cipher School (GC&CS) records. In 1935, Evelyn was employed as one of three 'Special Temporary Clerks'. These women were brilliant, possessing 'a working knowledge of one or two foreign languages . . . and a capacity for critical analysis'.[47] This short-term offer of support was not the last time that Evelyn would step forward to help her brother and the service.

Masterful at connecting with the right people, Evelyn assisted her brother in proactively problem-solving various quandaries. Whether it was paranoia, enemy plots or everyday actions on the part of officers or their dependants that saw questions arise about the nature of their work, the service saw to it that those in the outside world could not peer through the looking glass. Throughout the interwar period, enemy agents tried their hardest to identify the chinks in British intelligence's armour. The Soviets threw as much money and manpower at its intelligence services as was required to complete the job. The Russian secret service was, and still is, relentless in its mission to crush opposition and penetrate enemy intelligence agencies. MI6 officers had their work cut out for them, monitoring the communist 'infection' both abroad and at home. As a committed anti-Bolshevik, Sinclair remained resolute in MI6's assessment of this chronic threat, which in many ways blinded him to the rising danger of fascism during the 1930s. However, the MI6 chief was right to remain vigilant.

Sometime after Sinclair was appointed C, a London-based Soviet spy ring targeted one of the MI6 offices in the City. Operating under the cover of the so-called Federated Press of America, the head of the spy ring, Norman Ewer, ordered one of his agents to watch 1 Adam Street. Given the activity level at the MI6 office, Ewer had grown very interested in those who came and went. His agent struck lucky one day when he shadowed an MI6 officer as he left the Adam Street office and the careless officer dropped one of the Arabic documents he was carrying home to translate, which was duly picked up by the Soviet agent.[48] Another attempt by the Soviets to turn MI6 employees came in June 1923. Rose Edwardes, a typist and courier who worked for Ewer, masqueraded as an American intelligence service member when she approached an MI6 secretary at the Melbury Road headquarters. The two women had several meetings, culminating in Edwardes offering Mrs Frieda Moon of MI6 £5 a week plus a good bonus should she provide useful information about the British secret service. Luckily for Sinclair, his secretary 'apparently got nervous and eventually refused to take up the work'.[49] Edwardes later ran a typing business in Holborn called the Featherstone Typewriting Bureau, which hosted regular meetings for Ewer's spy network. While the attempt to recruit Frieda Moon failed, Ewer eventually succeeded in employing an Indian known as Karandikar, who obtained information from two women, one in the India Office and the other at the Colonial Office.[50]

Of course, what the Soviets were really after was secret information. MI6 staff were at great risk, especially the women. Frieda Moon was completely unprepared for enemy approaches, for Cumming and Sinclair failed to adequately train and protect female personnel in their care, rendering them extremely vulnerable. Whether the chiefs neglected or discriminated against women, we shall never know, but their cover was certainly not good enough. Typists and secretaries were perfectly placed to gather information for intelligence services. Both the Soviets and the British put trained female agents under the cover of the typing pool. In some instances, they recruited typists for purely strategic reasons. They offered the women undercover roles with little training or preparation for the months or years they would endure living under an assumed identity. MI6's sister organisation, MI5, recruited several women during the 1930s to infiltrate and spy on members of the Communist Party of Great Britain (CPGB). One such secretary, Olga Gray, had no prior spying experience when Britain's domestic intelligence agency approached her in 1931. Her achievements were remarkable, given that she suffered badly at the hands of her handler, Maxwell Knight, a ruthlessly manipulative man who dismissed her once she had proven her worth.

Many women found themselves on the MI5 employment carousel. Vernon Kell's organisation effectively weaponised typists and secretaries, reinforcing the ugly side of clandestine service. Adopting a dispassionate, businesslike attitude, MI5 ruthlessly utilised clever and gifted women to achieve operational success. MI6, on the other hand, demonstrated a more family-orientated approach to its long-serving female employees. Perhaps this quality appealed to Kathleen Pettigrew when she joined the opaque world of British intelligence. Over the years, she certainly fared better than her MI5 counterparts. Having taken a vow of absolute secrecy, the uncelebrated MI6 'secretary' watched with great concern throughout the interwar period as her former boss, Basil Thomson, and several former intelligence officers published their wartime memoirs.[51] But the ego-inflating confessions of former male spies were not the only obstacle to maintaining cover, as politicians also regularly commented on intelligence. Fleet Street journalists too took an active interest in anything that might pique public interest in secret matters.

To the outside world, British intelligence was presented as a manly enterprise, but behind the looking glass, it could not have been more different. Newspaper headlines in early 1938 offered the public a rare glimpse of the vital role played by women undertaking secret service. The country became captivated by an Official Secrets Act case that saw MI5 agent Olga Gray testify as 'Miss X', but the attempt to protect her true identity ultimately failed.[52]

7

The Secretary Spy

It was cloudy and cold in London when Olga Gray arrived at Bow Street Magistrates' Court on Thursday, 3 February 1938. Smartly dressed in black with an accompanying hat that did not distract some male attendees from admiring her svelte figure, the fair-haired young woman appeared in court to give evidence against the four men charged under Section One of the Official Secrets Act. Percy Glading and his accomplices Albert Williams, George Whomack and Charles Munday all stood accused of supplying a foreign power with secret-weapon blueprints taken from Woolwich Arsenal. Known as 'Miss X', Olga's identity was kept confidential during the sensational trial that later took place at the Old Bailey. Over the next two months, newspapers across the country covered the case as the press took an active interest in the undercover MI5 agent, running headlines such as 'Story of Girl Who Foiled Plans'.[1] To the outside world, Olga was merely 'the blonde spy in the flat', but the evidence she provided behind closed doors emphasised for readers how central her role had been in uncovering a Soviet spy ring intent on getting its hands on plans for a top-secret naval gun.[2]

By this time, Olga had worked for MI5 as an undercover agent for six long years. Codenamed M/12, the trusted typist had infiltrated the Communist Party of Great Britain (CPGB), where she had worked as secretary to its leader, Harry Pollitt, and to Glading, the leader of the spy ring and a national organiser of the CPGB. Adopting a calm and dispassionate tone, the prosecution's star witness described the highly secret operation that had targeted Glading to uncover evidence of a link between the CPGB and Soviet espionage. Speaking in a 'low, cultured voice', Olga recounted her amazing story, pausing occasionally to adjust the long black fur stole covering one shoulder.[3] Through skilful deception, she had eventually unmasked the Soviet spy ring and delivered a timely victory to her handler, Maxwell Knight. While she provided a great service to her country by singlehandedly bringing down a Soviet spy ring, it came at a heavy price. Olga may have changed history, but as far as MI5 was concerned, she had served her purpose, and they washed their hands of her without any duty of care or concern for her future welfare. Olga lived for the rest of her life in fear, constantly looking over her shoulder should Soviet assassins strike her down. Sadly, she never knew the true importance of her covert work. The information she uncovered provided British cryptanalysts with the means to read CPGB communications with Moscow, thereby providing MI5 with definitive evidence that the closely surveilled party was indeed an instrument of the Kremlin.

The 'secretary spy' was one of the greatest undercover agents ever employed by MI5. Olga was brave, confident and daring. She was a woman with perspicacity. Strong and independent, she possessed an uncanny ability to connect with people and build relationships. Her story is one of strength, where, despite all odds, she pursued an opportunity and, through hard work and remarkable resilience, disabled the Woolwich Arsenal spy ring. Yet Olga had never worked for MI5 before being approached by one of their spotters at a garden party in Edgbaston during the summer of 1928. After a game of clock golf, Dolly Pyle, an MI5 secretary, sat chatting with Olga. Dolly passed a plate of cucumber sandwiches to Olga and asked the 23-year-old whether she would like to join the 'secret service'.[4] The two women had met at the Automobile Association in Birmingham, where Olga worked as a secretary. Dolly had to convince Olga that the job offer was genuine and not a joke. After much persuasion, Olga finally believed that the offer of work was sincere and expressed her interest. The spirited young woman craved a chance to do something different. To seize control of her life rather than conform to what society and her mother thought she should become: a housewife. Pragmatic and grounded, she knew the risk to herself. Despite waiting two years before she heard anything back from MI5, she did not hesitate when finally summoned to London in 1931.

MI5's newest recruit left home for the first time, determined and ready to take on whatever came her way. Ever since she had been a young girl, Olga had always challenged herself and others. Born in 1906, she was the daughter of Charles Gray, a subeditor of the *Daily Mail* in Manchester, and his wife, Ada. Olga's father was a domineering man who struggled with his headstrong and wilful daughter, who 'wished him dead' on more than one occasion.[5] Sadly, the two never got the chance to develop their volatile relationship for the better, as Charles died at Passchendaele in 1917. Ten-year-old Olga was left to look after her distraught mother, younger brothers and sister. She was fiercely protective of her family, a trait inherited from her mother, who managed to cover her children's boarding school fees by taking in lodgers and canvassing for the Conservative Party. Despite tragically losing her husband and her two sons – Edward, who died from meningitis at the age of five, and seventeen-year-old Victor, who fell from his bike after being hit by a car in 1928 – Ada never gave up. Her indomitable spirit ignited the same flame of courage and resilience in her eldest daughter.

Growing up, Olga was determined to do everything her way, which got her into trouble on a number of occasions, leading several schools to expel the wayward rule-breaker. Ada was insistent that Olga should receive a private education and, after issuing a final warning to behave herself, Ada despatched her daughter to St Dunstan's Abbey School in Plymouth, where stern but inspiring Anglican nuns educated the extremely bright but rebellious young woman.[6] Boarding-school life certainly suited the tomboy, who enjoyed the experience of forbidden midnight feasts and 'jolly hockey sticks' as portrayed by the children's author, Enid Blyton, in her renowned series of *Malory Towers* novels. Olga excelled in her studies, especially literature, and took great pride in captaining the hockey and netball teams. The wimple-wearing teachers encouraged their pupils' ambitions and developed their mental fortitude. Olga thrived and never looked back. Today, St Dunstan's boasts a long list of old girls, such as the brilliant comedian Dawn French, who, like Olga, stood out from the rest.[7]

Yet this is not the picture presented by historians, who have provided accounts of Olga's success from the perspective of the spymasters she worked for.[8] They have suggested that Olga grew up outspoken, hot-tempered and a bully to her siblings.[9] They claim that, as an MI5 agent, her flaws and insecurities defined her. Due to a 'wretched childhood', Olga was apparently 'crippled with insecurities'.[10] Some historians have even gone so far as to suggest that Olga and Harry Pollitt were lovers, despite there being no shred of credible evidence or proof of such rumours.[11] In reality, nothing could have been further from the truth. Olga actually smashed the MI5 myth that 'women do not make good agents', as claimed by the head of MI5, Vernon Kell, in 1934.[12]

She performed at the highest level, demonstrating tremendous strength of character and achieving great success for MI5 and her country. But there was one problem. She had proved that there was much more to women than just their looks: that they could be feminine and also smart. However, historians have adhered to the same old sexist clichés: they have presented Olga as a woman racked with self-doubt instead of emphasising her achievements. Had she been a man, perhaps Olga would have achieved the same revered status as her handler, Maxwell Knight, whose bizarre eccentricities have been embraced by historians as accepted behavioural differences.

Unsurprisingly, there was much more to the 'peroxide blonde' who was plucked from relative obscurity and offered the chance to defend the realm. In 1931, Olga and Knight met for the first time. The spymaster met his new agent at Euston Station. Known as 'M' to his agents, Knight headed MI5's 'M Section', to which he lent his name. Based at a flat in Dolphin Square, a short distance from MI5 headquarters, he was in the habit of recruiting men and women who, for all outward appearances, held rather ordinary jobs, such as secretaries and office clerks. As long-term penetration agents against the CPGB, their camouflage was perfect. Knight was convinced that the answer to learning more about Soviet skulduggery was to infiltrate the CPGB by placing an agent at the bottom of the organisation. Understaffed and under-resourced, MI5 monitored the growing Soviet threat as best it could. In 1929, communist moles were discovered hiding in plain sight within Special Branch. When a mutiny of naval ratings at the Scottish port of Invergordon broke out in September 1931, the Security Service, as MI5 is officially known, suspected the Comintern's involvement. As the mutineers loudly sang the communist song 'The Red Flag', politicians grew fearful that a violent outbreak might spark a revolution.

Knight's M Section offered MI5 the perfect means to combat espionage within the CPGB. The spymaster's approach to agent handling was a calculated gamble that paid off, thanks to his agents' work. Knight possessed a unique sixth sense for selecting talented individuals for undercover operations. He actively sought out women with secretarial abilities who, in his opinion, offered 'unique opportunities for exploitation'. He later committed his ideas to paper, declaring that 'no official or other single individual ever has the same opportunity for obtaining information covering a wide area as does a clerk or secretary. A woman so placed will have a much wider grasp of the day-to-day doings in a movement, than any of the officials of the movement will ever dream of.'[13] Olga was precisely the type of woman Knight was looking for: an intelligent middle-class secretary from the North who had no ties to London, and who was ready to leave her conventional conservative life and step into the unknown. Knight deemed Olga an ideal candidate to pretend to turn 'red'.

The master spook was impressed with his new charge. The two had long conversations. Knight listened to Olga while he puffed on his long, handmade cigarettes. When he spoke, his smooth, rich voice seemed to have a hypnotic effect on Olga, who hung on his every word. Her knowledge of secret service work had been shaped entirely by fiction books and films. Knight was conscious that he had to gain Olga's trust and determine what her interests were. He believed that an officer 'must at all costs make a friend of his agent: the agent must trust the officer as much [as] – if not more than – the officer trusts the agent; and that basis of firm confidence must be built up'.[14] Knight had to work quickly to assess Olga's capabilities and limits. More importantly, he had to ensure that she was up to the job. He was personally acquainted with the dangers of being an undercover operative from his own experience in the field during the 1920s when he penetrated the British Fascisti movement.

It took Knight only two days to understand how best he could exploit Olga. He was 'impressed by her intelligence and patriotism' and claimed to have no problem working with women.[15] Curiously and contrary to MI5's thinking at the time, Knight chose to champion the benefits of using women as agents, for he acknowledged 'that in the history of espionage and counterespionage a very high percentage of the greatest coups have been brought off by women'.[16] He stated that he firmly believed that 'female spies, if not "over-sexed", are more effective secret agents than men'.[17] He apparently could not 'imagine anything more terrifying than for an officer to become landed with a woman-agent who suffers from an overdose of Sex'.[18] It certainly needs to be recognised that Knight was a complex, ascetic man when it came to heterosexual relationships. It was extraordinary that, despite being wed three times, all his marriages remained unconsummated. He certainly saw no value in his female agents using 'Mata-Hari' type methods, which only achieved short-term gains. Instead, he favoured the long-game approach, with his agents establishing solid relationships based on friendship that aligned with the target's beliefs and values. Knight remained convinced 'that more information has been obtained by women-agents, by keeping out of the arms of the man, than ever was obtained by sinking too willingly into them'.[19]

Whatever his unusual traits and attitudes, MI5's chief agent handler transformed counterintelligence work by using female agents and establishing a precedent for their deployment during the Second World War. Alongside Olga Gray, Knight recruited two other extraordinary women: Kathleen Tesch and Mona Maund. Kathleen was another unlikely choice. The Buckinghamshire housewife, who was fond of dogs, infiltrated a pro-fascist group in Britain, intending to get close to Adolf Hitler. Just before the war, she met Hitler at his Eagle's Nest, high in the German Alps. While Agent M/T did not gather anything of value from the unplanned and fortuitous encounter, she did leave the Führer's home with a signed copy of *Mein Kampf*. Knight's other agent, Mona Maund (codenamed M/2), had previously worked as a policewoman during the 1920s before changing career paths to work as a secretary, when Knight coincidentally recruited her to infiltrate the CPGB. In one of her first reports submitted in 1932, Mona flagged Melita Norwood as the type of person suitable for underground activity. Knight passed her report up the MI5 chain of command to his superior, Jasper Harker, who chose to ignore Mona's report. Thus Norwood remained undetected for decades, entering the pages of history as the Soviet Union's longest-serving spy in Britain.[20]

Knight succeeded in proving to his MI5 superiors that women do make better spies than men. However, while he was wise enough to see the benefits of using women agents, he did so based on their operational value, not because he supported the feminist cause. Olga was exceptional because she received little training to operate in the shadows. Having never previously worked for MI5, her undertaking was a baptism by fire. Like all Knight's recruits, she possessed the drive and the key ingredients to live a double life – grace, courage and instinct. But Knight had to gain her trust for the partnership to succeed. Operating on a very fine line between persuasion and manipulation, the self-taught spymaster presented himself as a kind older family member, offering Olga reassuring candour and a 'guiding hand', but there was something decidedly cold-blooded about his manner.[21] Reflecting on her time working for MI5, Olga described Knight as 'very charming, very avuncular'.[22] Aware that she had been without a father figure from such a young age, Knight's adoption of a paternalistic role had won over his newest recruit despite there being only six years in age between the handler and agent.

Later in life, a whole generation of children would come to know Knight as 'Uncle Max'. The enthusiastic BBC natural-history broadcaster captivated audiences with his explorations of woodland and explanations of how to gain the trust of wild animals. Knight had always been fascinated by animals. Growing up, he cared for various injured wild animals, such as hedgehogs, tortoises, lizards and rats. He enjoyed studying the different behaviours and interactions of domestic and wild creatures; doubtless he would have made an attentive vet or zoologist. However, fate had something different in store for him. After leaving the Royal Navy in 1918, the soon-to-be spymaster lived with a menagerie of animals in his London flat. Dressed in shabby tweeds, he regularly walked Bessie the Bear in Chelsea. Ironically, his favourite pet was a rescued cuckoo called Goo, and just as the dove-sized bird lays its eggs in another's nest, Knight placed his agents inside British communist and fascist groups . . . and waited.

Olga was not the only egg laid in the CPGB nest. An obsession with the communist threat drove every decision that the M Section head made.[23] The clock of deception was ticking as to who of his agents would be the first to supply Knight with the most valuable information. He knew he would have to wait several years before reaping any potential rewards. Knight was learning on the job, tailoring his methods after various blunders and errors were made. His success rested on the skill and tenacity of his agents. In the end, it was agent M/12 who came through. Olga's double life began in the autumn of 1931, just days after meeting Knight for the first time. On her handler's instructions, she started to attend the meetings of the Friends of the Soviet Union, a communist front funded and run by the Comintern. Adopting the cover of a typist who was sympathetic to the cause, Olga transformed herself into a convincing candidate, who, after a year of voluntary work, was employed at the offices of the League against Imperialism in August 1932. There, Isobel Brown of the Communist Anti-War Movement approached Olga with an offer of part-time work as a typist.[24] During this time, MI5's newest agent became acquainted with leading communists Harry Pollitt and Percy Glading.

Glading, a highly placed member of the CPGB and leader of the Woolwich Arsenal spy ring, had worked as a grinder at the Royal Arsenal in Woolwich until the end of the First World War. As an engineer he took jobs when vacancies arose, but it was not long before he was recruited as a Comintern agent. In 1925, he travelled to India, where the Comintern hoped to overthrow British rule. Glading became implicated in the Meerhut Conspiracy led by the communist agitator Manandra Nath Roy. After the conspirators' arrests, Glading fled and returned to Woolwich Arsenal, where he took a position as an examiner in the naval department. Inside the high brick walls, he had access to classified documents and military equipment. However, MI5 soon identified Glading as a risk because of his known CPGB activities, so he was sacked in 1928.[25] He then spent a year in Moscow at the Lenin School, where he studied communism, the basics of espionage and subversive practices, all of which he would put to good use in Britain and further afield.[26]

Glading had been under MI5 surveillance since the mid-1920s, monitored by MI5's first and only female officer appointed before the 1950s, Jane Sissmore, who was responsible for Soviet intelligence. Kathleen Weeks, a former governess who was the daughter of a Treasury solicitor, assisted Jane. Tall with a piercing stare, Kathleen was fluent in French with a penchant for the *Times* crossword puzzle. She was a stickler for grammar and worked well with Jane, who also appreciated those who paid attention to the finer details of reports and correspondence.[27] Kathleen worked for MI5 until 1943, when she married. However, Jane Sissmore continued working after becoming Jane Archer, wife of the liaison officer between MI5 and the RAF, Wing Commander John Oliver 'Joe' Archer, in 1939. Jane was certainly an exceptional officer: a solitary example of a woman within MI5 who had been encouraged to train as a barrister by the head of MI5, Vernon Kell. After serving several years as head of Registry, Jane was admitted to the Honourable Society of Gray's Inn in 1921, personally recommended by Kell, who wrote his supporting statement in green ink, a choice of colour not only used by the chiefs of MI6. Kell stressed Jane's 'marked capabilities' and how she had 'proven herself capable of fulfilling highly confidential duties'.[28] The ambitious young woman was called to the Bar in 1924.[29]

Jane and her assistant Kathleen Weeks were unusual among the MI5 sections. In a workforce of nearly fifty in 1931, the all-female team provided a progressive contrast to the traditionally male-led departments.[30] Bound together by female camaraderie, the two conventionally dressed women puffed away on cigarettes as they sifted through phone taps, postal surveillance reports and MI6 memoranda on the overseas activities of Pollitt and Glading. In the summer of 1931, Jane wrote a short note stating that Glading was the 'recipient for military espionage reports compiled in this country and intended for Moscow', and that he was the paymaster for those reports.[31] Through Knight's patience and Olga Gray's masterful work as a covert operative, MI5 now had a source that could report directly on the two comrades and their associates, providing further information to Jane and Kathleen.

Knight worked hard at cultivating his star agent. He later wrote proudly how Olga 'had attained that very enviable position where an agent becomes a piece of furniture, so to speak: that is, when persons visiting an office do not consciously notice whether an agent is there or not'.[32] Olga reported everything of interest that happened at CPGB headquarters located on King Street in Covent Garden. With an exceptional memory, she recalled to her handler via telephone every conversation and described minutely her new colleagues' appearance. Unlike other agents, Olga did not need to take the notes prescribed by her MI5 training, partly because she had adjusted so well to life as 'the sympathetic socialist'. However, as years passed, undercover work slowly took its toll. The weekend commute from London to Edgbaston to see her mother only added to the strain of her job and to her fatigue, though in a small way it did help diminish her growing sense of loneliness.[33]

Olga's mother eventually moved to London, but the burden of secrecy weighed heavy on the agent's shoulders. Olga adopted a new persona, which entailed different behaviours and contrasting characteristics from those of her normal self. Understandably, she began suffering from daily paranoia while working at the King Street office. She once recalled how 'the most terrifying ordeal of my life in the early 'thirties was a popular song that was continuously played on the radio and used to obsess me to such an extent that I thought everyone at the CPGB headquarters was looking at me with growing suspicion. It was called "Olga Polovsky – the Beautiful Spy".[34] However, any worries that her new work colleagues harboured thoughts that she might be a mole disappeared on 8 May 1934, when Harry Pollitt, the General Secretary of the CPGB, asked Olga to undertake a special mission. Glading had cleared her for espionage work as a courier. To add credibility to her cover, she appeared to be not too keen on the proposal before finally accepting it.[35]

Excited, nervous and apprehensive, the former typist turned secret agent left England on 11 June 1934 bound for Paris. Her fellow travellers had no idea that she was smuggling large sums of sterling notes concealed within her sanitary pads.[36] Once in Paris, she met Glading, who exchanged the smuggled money for dollars and issued her further instructions before she boarded the ship to Bombay.[37] Supplied with invisible ink, Olga was instructed by Knight to note down the numbers of the original banknotes. She struggled to get the invisible ink to work and instead memorised the numbers. MI5 was over the moon at M Section's breakthrough. The Security Service now had eyes and ears within the CPGB and a chance to learn just how far the Comintern's reach was in India and beyond. From Glading's perspective, Olga might have been inexperienced, but she was unknown, and her anonymity provided the perfect cover. Unlike other CPGB members who typically had their visas refused, Olga had never been arrested for communist activity and, therefore, possessed a clean British passport.

However, the 'English Lenin' Pollitt made a mess of Olga's travel plans, and in an unusual move, Knight stepped in to devise a credible cover story for his agent that would explain why an unaccompanied young Englishwoman would be travelling alone to India during the monsoon season. According to Knight, 'this was no easy task but eventually a rather thin story of a sea trip under doctor's orders, combined with an invitation from a relative in India met the case'.[38] His scheming paid off, ensuring that Olga's journey was smooth sailing, apart from her receiving an offer of marriage from a male admirer en route. When she arrived in Bombay, the pretend Comintern courier made her way straight to the Taj Mahal Hotel to meet an MI5 contact, as directed by Knight. The luxurious upmarket hotel was a haven for British colonials and the rising professionals of the Indian middle class. The hotel hosted a jazz band; its conductor was the MI5 contact who found Olga a boarding house.[39] From there, she visited an address in the city and delivered the Comintern's money and messages. The Indian communists directed her to sit tight and await further instructions.

After receiving news that she was required to carry something back to England, Olga waited three long weeks before being told she would be returning empty-handed. Her nerves were in tatters. The realisation that espionage work was not the glamorous undertaking depicted in spy novels hit her hard. She was alone with no protection from her MI5 handler, who was thousands of miles away. Bombay's highly charged atmosphere did not help Olga's growing anxiety. The colonial city was alive with protests and strikes. Fuelled by anger and frustration, Indian workers opposed wage cuts and demanded general recognition for unions, including communist bodies. Olga dared not leave the safe confines of the boarding house in which she was staying. With days of endless rain, her mood did not improve as she coped with the intense humidity. The thrill of undercover work was now extinguished. Olga admitted 'this was the first time I had been really afraid', and that 'I wasn't playing spy games any longer'.[40]

Olga finally arrived back in London on 28 July 1934.[41] Her mission had been a great success. Pollitt and Glading remained convinced of her loyalty. She met with Knight and told him everything she had learnt about the Indian communists and the Comintern courier system. Knight was delighted. Now the MI5 spymaster needed Olga to provide evidence of the CPGB's covert links with the Soviets, as sought by Jane Sissmore. In a stroke of good fortune, Pollitt asked Olga to work full-time as his secretary at the CPGB headquarters. From February 1935, her deception work became relentless and unforgiving. At the King Street office, also known as 'the Kremlin', Olga looked after Pollitt's correspondence and typed up his letters. She sat in on meetings with key communists and took minutes, as well as 'stitching reports into the lining of Soviet sailors' greatcoats to carry home'.[42] She saw Glading regularly and found him to be 'a very nice man with a little daughter'.[43] The Londoner turned Soviet spy wore distinctive large, round spectacles that made him look like the owlish stereotype of a dreary schoolmaster ready for retirement. Olga remembered 'him being a very stimulating conversationalist and about the only person who could make an account of a film or play he'd seen absolutely riveting'.[44]

Still suffering from exhaustion and nervous strain endured during the India mission, Olga began feeling guilty as she grew close to those she was betraying. Conscious that not all was well with his agent, Knight ensured that he saw Olga as often as possible. Knight brought to one of their meetings a delightful bullfinch that he was teaching to sing.[45] The welcome distraction was not enough to stem the deterioration of Olga's health, and with the surprise appearance of an old boyfriend, she decided she had done enough for MI5. Knight pleaded with her to reconsider. He was so close to achieving victory and securing arrests. Olga had gathered the 'most valuable information', as well as the final proof that Pollitt was secretly communicating with Moscow and following every order. Unaware of the significance of the information she had delivered to Knight, Olga reported how ciphered messages were constructed with the aid of Robert Louis Stevenson's *Treasure Island*, with the senders and receivers at each end of the communication link having an exact copy of the adventure novel. Messages were formed with words selected from the book, which were then identified by numerical references to the page, line and specific word. As a result, British codebreakers possessed the ability to intercept and decrypt the wireless communications. Olga's breakthrough resulted in a staggering 14,000 messages being read.[46]

Oblivious to the magnitude of her contribution, Olga refused her handler's pleas to stay and resigned from her post as Pollitt's secretary in July 1935, informing the CPGB that her boyfriend no longer wanted her working for them.[47] Not long after, she was admitted to the National Hospital for Nervous Diseases in Queen Square, where she gradually recovered from the detrimental effect of leading a double life. The act of constantly deceiving others had taken a toll on her mental health. Olga was far from alone in experiencing such a breakdown, for many covert operatives, whether in the police or in the intelligence services, have since been diagnosed with post-traumatic stress disorder (PTSD). While it is impossible to offer a retrospective diagnosis, Olga suffered similar symptoms. She was undoubtedly in a bad way. Only her family and Knight knew that she had been hospitalised. Knight visited Olga every day in her private room filled with flowers. He was first and foremost an MI5 case officer, so he had to achieve results. Knight was determined not to lose his protégée. He deployed his toxic charm and persuaded his former agent to remain on friendly terms with Glading and Pollitt, and he encouraged Olga to rethink her decision. This she did while working from the end of 1936 for an advertising firm.[48]

Over a year later, in February 1937, Olga, now single after parting ways with her boyfriend, lunched with Glading. The Soviet spymaster had withdrawn from the CPGB to ensure his invisibility. Wishing to remain off MI5's radar, he asked Olga whether she would like to run a rent-free safe house, for he required a flat where he could meet and carry out his clandestine meetings and activities. Olga immediately telephoned Knight, who must have leapt for joy on hearing her news. After turning his hand to writing bad detective novels, the newly published author was thrust into the limelight at the end of 1935 after the death of his first wife, Gwladys, who mistakenly overdosed on prescribed barbiturates, thinking they were aspirins. Newspaper coverage of the coroner's inquest cast suspicion on the death, described as a 'riddle'.[49] After he'd lost his star agent and now faced questions about his hand in Gwladys's death, Knight's standing at MI5 came under scrutiny, especially by those who considered him a 'gung-ho operator'.[50]

Olga's return could not have been timed better for rehabilitating his stained reputation. With the MI5 agent–handler relationship reinstated, Knight advised Olga to accept Glading's offer, and so she took a ground-floor flat on Holland Road. Knowing Olga's fragile state of mind, Knight assessed the circumstances and callously deemed her expendable. He understood the need to be on the offensive once his agents had successfully penetrated an enemy organisation. His role as handler was to ensure the continuous flow of high-value information. Just as Glading had used Olga, Knight did too. Both men were masters of manipulation who readily engaged in the morally ambiguous part of counterintelligence work, making difficult decisions based on operational outcomes and inflated egos.

In February 1938, 'Miss X' stood in Bow Street Magistrates' Court and confidently recounted events as they had transpired after her return to MI5.[51] Glading refused to look at Olga. While living at Glading's safe house on Holland Road, Olga met many Comintern agents, including Glading's handler, Theodore Maly, who went by the names 'Mr Peters' and Paul Hardt. Maly, who had a memorable dark moustache and gold teeth, visited the flat on 21 April 1937 to assess Olga's suitability for espionage work.[52] Given the green light, Glading informed Olga she would receive instruction on how to photograph 'borrowed' secret documents with a miniature Leica camera. She purchased a long refectory table from Maple's furniture store to photograph everything, from naval-gun blueprints to drawings of antisubmarine bomb fuses and a 200-page manual on explosives. 'Mr and Mrs Stevens' collected the documents from Glading's accomplices at Woolwich Arsenal, photographed them at the flat, and returned them the following day. Olga tried to note down the serial numbers as the negatives dried in her bathroom, but it proved tricky.[53]

Glading and his accomplices grew emboldened as they smuggled more and more secret documents out of Woolwich Arsenal. Once Knight had identified all those involved in the spy ring, he set a trap for their arrest with the aid of Special Branch. Knight was too late to catch 'Mr and Mrs Stevens', who had already returned to Moscow with blueprints, but his spy-catcher's net fell on Glading and his co-conspirators Williams, an examiner at Woolwich Arsenal; Whomack, an assistant foreman in the gun section; and Munday, an assistant chemist. On the evening of 21 January 1938, Olga telephoned Knight and informed him that Glading had left the flat and was on his way to rendezvous with Williams at Charing Cross Station. A plain clothes Special Branch officer watched Glading hand a brown paper parcel to Williams in the station yard. The officer apprehended both men and escorted them to New Scotland Yard. The parcel contained four blueprints of a pressure-bar device for testing detonators. A diary was found in Glading's possession, and an assortment of photographic equipment, including a camera with his fingerprint on it, film negatives and notebooks, were all found by police at his home and at the Holland Road safe house. Whomack and Munday were later arrested and charged with obtaining information useful to an enemy.[54]

After the four men were remanded in custody before their trial at the Old Bailey, Olga was left feeling exposed. It would not be long before those she worked with at the CPGB headquarters figured out who 'Miss X' actually was. The press was driven wild by the thrill of not knowing her true identity, and in a strange twist of fate, her family soon realised the true nature of Olga's work. At the time of the trial, her younger brother Richard was a student at Hendon Police College. His daughter recalls how her father was at an assembly when it was announced that 'the glamorous Miss X' required a bodyguard. Much to the envy of his fellow students, Richard was selected for the task. One can only imagine his surprise when he walked into the hotel room to find that the woman in question was his older sister.[55] Olga's family couldn't quite believe it. Her sister Marjorie read every newspaper account and remarked, 'It was incredible.'[56]

A tired and relieved Olga returned to the Old Bailey on the day of sentencing. On Monday, 14 March 1938, she sat in a guarded room lost in thought as smoke from her cigarette drifted across the magazine resting on her lap. She waited patiently to hear news of Glading's sentencing. The spy ringleader received six years in prison, Williams and Whomack were sentenced to four and three years respectively, and Munday was acquitted. In his closing remarks, the judge paid homage to 'Miss X', stating, 'I think that this young woman is possessed of extraordinary courage, and I think she has done a great service to her country.'[57]

The secretary spy was a trailblazer in the field of undercover operations. During the Second World War, Knight took his recruits through the Woolwich Arsenal case to demonstrate the value of the work that they would be undertaking and the dedication that it would require. For instance, Joan Miller worked for Elizabeth Arden when Knight recruited her to infiltrate the Right Club, a pro-Nazi group. She remembered how Knight pulled the 'Top Secret' file on the Woolwich spy ring from the MI5 Registry and took Joan through the case, page by page. She recalled how impressed she was 'by the vigilance and perseverance shown by Olga Gray, who kept her wits about her through the whole dangerous course of the undertaking, and never lost credibility with the other side'.[58]

After the trial, Olga's time as an undercover agent came to an end. With no thought of how she might help train future recruits, MI5 summarily dismissed the amateur turned professional, though Knight didn't dare to sack her himself. He had used and abused Olga's trust in him, demonstrating no loyalty to the woman who had handed him a much-needed victory. Shamelessly, MI5 sent an unnamed colonel to thank Olga for her service over lunch at the Ritz, where he paid her off with a £500 severance cheque, albeit a princely sum at that time. Many years later, as an elderly woman living in Canada, still embittered by her experience with Knight and the Security Service, Olga told a writer: 'I was a 50 shillings a week spy. Then I was dumped. In those days the adrenalin really flowed but since then the excitement has never been rekindled. That's why I feel so restless – and my abilities remain so unfulfilled.'[59] There is no doubt that Olga would have made an excellent agent handler, but sadly she was never offered the chance to prove it.

Women who worked for MI5 had a limited shelf-life. Even the service's star female officer, Jane Sissmore, could not escape the unforeseen future firing that awaited her. Until then, she continued her important work at MI5 headquarters, poring over Glading's possessions, such as his petty-cash book, hoping to find clues that might relate to his handler, Maly, and the other Soviet agents not yet apprehended.[60] A year after MI5 had washed their hands of Olga, she contacted them in April 1939. The former agent believed she had seen Maly at Mount Royal Apartments, Marble Arch. As well as acting as a handler for Glading, unbeknown to MI5, Maly was the NKVD officer who was closely associated with the infamous Cambridge Five.[61] Maly was recalled to Moscow in the summer of 1937 to face Stalin's purges.[62] MI5 could not determine whether Maly was alive or dead, and bluntly concluded that Olga 'must have been mistaken'.[63] Perhaps she had seen him and this was a final attempt on her part to demonstrate her continued value to MI5.

Instead, when the Second World War broke out, Olga bravely drove an ambulance during the Blitz. She found love at the war's end and married Stanley Simons, a dashing Royal Canadian Air Force (RCAF) officer. The couple later emigrated to Canada with their young family and lived there happily. However, the shadow of deception remained with Olga, as she lived in fear of retribution from Soviet agents who had long memories. She rarely spoke about her MI5 work with her family as, her granddaughter recalls, 'she was worried someone would come after us'.[64] Several years before her death, Olga, then in her late seventies, begrudgingly spoke with Anthony Masters, Maxwell Knight's biographer, on the understanding that he should not disclose where she lived or reveal the names of her family.[65] Olga was horrified when the book was published in 1984. While Masters had not revealed her married name, he had disclosed that she was 'living in a suburb of Toronto'.[66] With her spirit greatly diminished, Olga spent her remaining years filled with a sense of trepidation.

Olga died in 1990. A year later, MI5 announced the appointment of Stella Rimington as their first female Director General. Neither woman ever expected to be thrust into the spotlight; both were content to have their achievements remain unrecorded. Fully aware of the dangers that awaited her, Olga stepped forward to make a difference for herself and her country. MI5's 'most valuable penetration agent in the CPGB' gave everything of herself and received very little in return.[67]

8

Station X

'Government Buy Park' was the front-page headline of the *Bletchley District Gazette* on 28 May 1938.[1] The innocuous statement in a local newspaper read only by Bletchley residents came months after national dailies had covered the Woolwich Arsenal spy-ring case. Located fifty miles northwest of London, not far from today's 'new city' of Milton Keynes, the country mansion estate with its extensive grounds had recently been the home of Sir Herbert Leon, a wealthy stockbroker whose monogram can still be seen today over the mansion entrance. After the death of Leon's widow in 1937, a local builder, Hubert Faulkner, bought Bletchley Park and planned to demolish the Victorian mansion and sell the land for housing. However, the announcement that the property developer had sold the estate to the government now caused great mystery and intrigue. A local reporter rushed to investigate the curious level of hush-hush activity generated by the new tenants. The small Buckinghamshire town was alive with workmen digging up the ground and laying a special telephone cable that provided the now fenced-off site with a direct line to Whitehall.[2] The mansion underwent a major refurbishment programme, with the installation of electricity cables and a new water main; meanwhile, telephone engineers busied themselves with running landlines into the house.[3]

The *Gazette* reporter hovered around the Park's gates, wondering what was happening. His perseverance and patience paid off when, by a stroke of luck, he happened across Hugh Sinclair and Arthur Peel. The head of MI6 and his assistant had travelled from London to view the estate. They informed the reporter that the house and land would form part of London's air defences. Anxious for confirmation, the persistent reporter contacted the Air Ministry 'who indignantly contradicted the story'.[4] After the write-up appeared in print, other Buckinghamshire newspapers picked up the story.[5] The coverage generated a lot of undesirable attention for the new owners. MI6 had not anticipated such curiosity, and to prevent local interest from growing any bigger, the government slapped the bewildered newspapers with D-notices, preventing them from printing anything further about Bletchley Park.[6]

Unbeknown to newspaper editors and their readers, Hugh Sinclair had purchased the country house estate for £6,000 using his own money.[7] Meanwhile, as Hitler's lust for territorial expansion grew throughout the 1930s, the head of MI6 watched the Czech crisis unfold. With dark clouds forming across Europe, Sinclair took preventive action to identify war stations for the relocation of his London operations should war break out and bombing begin. Bletchley Park would be the ideal location for MI6 and the Government Code and Cipher School (GC&CS), a dual organisation that consisted of two entirely separate staffs but with MI6 maintaining administrative control of GC&CS. Situated close to the main lines of communication and transport in Britain and to the Royal Air Force's main Leighton Buzzard radio station, Bletchley Park, now designated 'Station X', could be effectively wired into the heart of British strategic communications. Given the rapid evolution of modern communications technology, Sinclair rightly forecast that codebreaking would play a significant role in any future war. Bletchley Park would become the centre of Allied codebreaking efforts during the Second World War, and thus Sinclair's lasting legacy.

While the role and contribution made by those who worked at Bletchley Park remained shrouded in secrecy until the 1970s, the home of the wartime codebreaking operation has since become hallowed ground dedicated to the memory of those who held one of Britain's best-kept secrets.[8] The legendary achievements of Alan Turing and the team of mathematical geniuses who broke the supposedly impenetrable German ENIGMA cipher machine are well known. By the war's end, Bletchley Park had been transformed into an industrial-scale 'intelligence factory'.[9] The multi-skilled workforce of 9,000 employees did extraordinary, innovative scientific and technical work around the clock, significantly impacting the war's progress. Women accounted for almost 75 per cent of the total staff in 1944, and just over half wore military uniform.[10] From cleaner to codebreaker, women powered this very large military industrial complex, performing a wide range of divergent roles critical to achieving Allied victory. However, few held senior roles.

Female codebreakers used pencil and paper to decipher German ENIGMA messages, which looked like 'utter gibberish' on first appearance, according to Mavis Lever, who was only nineteen years old when she arrived at Bletchley from University College London, where she was studying for a degree in German when war broke out. Abandoning her university studies, Mavis then began work with one of Bletchley's leading cryptographers, Dilly Knox, in No. 3 Cottage. Using a method explained to her by Knox, Mavis decoded a message sent by the German secret service, the Abwehr, which was considered a notoriously difficult encryption to break. Her work allowed the British to understand the wiring of one of the ENIGMA machine variants and to read future messages. Mavis's contributions, alongside those of fellow female codebreakers Joan Clarke and Margaret Rock, have received far less attention than their better-known male colleagues.

Successful codebreaking did not rest solely on the inspiration of geniuses but rather on the mundane act of processing and managing vast amounts of information. Thousands of women worked in the mansion, in the brick-built blocks, and in the wooden huts that had sprung up like mushrooms across the Bletchley grounds as the numbers of staff increased exponentially.[11] Administrators, card-index compilers, machine operators and messengers were just some of the roles performed by women. Sworn to secrecy, young debutantes worked alongside women from much humbler backgrounds, while Wrens despaired when they found themselves operating electro-mechanical bombe machines designed by Alan Turing to speed up ENIGMA decryption, with no prospect of going to sea as some had expected when they signed up with the Women's Royal Naval Service (WRNS). The deafening clatter of the wired rotor wheels in action became the soundtrack of the constant conveyor belt of intelligence. As bombes operated night and day, the Wrens spent their entire shifts on their feet operating and checking the machines.

From 1942, Bletchley Park operated on an industrial scale. The presence of numerous women undertaking a variety of routine tasks was noticeable from the constant tapping of heeled shoes walking across echoing floors in huts that all had the same dark green internal doors and bulky radiators. The sound of 'clerks' and 'translators' processing enemy communications resonated across the intelligence factory. The distinctive 'whooshing' noise of pneumatic tubes known as 'spit and suck' could be heard carrying important information around the blocks. The clatter of Hollerith machines as they punched cards to record details about the decryption processes was so loud that those in Block C were unable to talk to each other. Outside, the distinct rumble of motorcycle engines permeated the air as despatch riders arrived at the mansion, carrying their precious cargoes of intercepted messages from Y listening stations dotted around the country. The scale of women's work taking place was immense, proving the importance of female labour in driving the economy of wartime intelligence.

Some of the women's stories have been told and continue to be shared, while others have yet to be celebrated.[12] Unfortunately, the presence of MI6 employees, as opposed to GC&CS staff, has been largely excluded from the telling of Bletchley's story. Referred to as 'the other side' by GC&CS, MI6 personnel were deemed imposters despite being present from 1938 to the war's end.[13] The small autonomous unit of MI6 officers and female staff at Bletchley worked separately from GC&CS staff, initially occupying the mansion's first floor. In early 1940, before the Blitz began and as the 'Phoney War' continued, some MI6 administrative staff returned to London. Later, most of those remaining at Bletchley returned to MI6 headquarters when MI6 handed over control of the Park in 1942 to GC&CS. However, Sinclair's MI6 organisation retained responsibility for site security.[14] Only the MI6 coding department remained, moving in 1942 from the mansion to Hut 10. Several career MI6 women, such as Kathleen Pettigrew, helped establish the 'codists' in the mansion, which fell under the purview of Section VIII, a group of talented individuals who dealt with all forms of MI6 communication. The work that these women undertook was of utmost importance as the lives of MI6 agents depended on timely and accurate communication. Kathleen never spoke about her MI6 work. However, a handful of her female colleagues shared their stories later on in life, making it possible to understand what was essentially an MI6 operation at the start, beginning with the arrival of what has become known as Captain William Ridley's 'shooting party' on 18 September 1938.[15]

Expecting war to soon break out, Sinclair sent about 150 MI6 and GC&CS men and women to Bletchley Park. As MI6's chief administrative officer, Ridley was responsible for organising the move from London. Chaos quickly ensued when staff realised that no filing cabinets or bookshelves were present in the makeshift offices. The sudden appearance of middle-aged men in suits with younger, unchaperoned women caused residents to ask unwanted questions.[16] Confusion spread further when staff were billeted in hotels and boarding houses in the surrounding villages and were then ferried between locations by a fleet of 'chauffeurs'. To ensure his secret workforce dined well, Sinclair brought his chef from London, a highly strung and volatile man who had previously worked at the Savoy Grill, one of the MI6 chief's favourite eating places. Disaster struck when, after a few days of preparing dinners, the chef collapsed in an attempt to take his own life.[17] 'Self-murder' was a crime under English law, so Ridley duly sent for the police. Sinclair's war station was under threat of exposure. Fortunately, the chef recovered and, with the help of the local chief constable, the matter remained secret.[18]

Remarkably, evidence of Bletchley Park's mobilisation for war survives in the form of a single photograph. Evelyn Sinclair, who was most likely in attendance, sent copies of the now famous snapshot attached to a sheet of blue paper expressing her 1938 Christmas greetings to those 'in the know'.[19] The picture captured the moment when ten or more suited men stood relaxed, conversing in front of the mansion. A handful of smartly dressed women appear to be entering the house. The gathering of faceless spies and codebreakers gave no hint as to what was really happening within the mansion. When Prime Minister Neville Chamberlain returned from meeting with Hitler in Munich at the end of September 1938 and famously declared 'peace for our time', Sinclair ordered his staff to return to London.

A year later, war was declared and the codebreakers and MI6 staff returned to the transformed war station. They joined the first wave of men and women who had been stationed at the site since the summer of 1939. As numerous Oxford and Cambridge dons arrived at Bletchley Station and took the five-minute walk to the estate, Dorothy McCarthy from Barking could hardly believe her luck when she stood before the mansion and gazed up at its turreted roof and ornate gables. She joined her older sister, Eileen, who had been at Bletchley since July, when the beautiful rose garden was in full bloom.[20] Excited by the prospect of being away from home for the first time, Eileen and Dorothy were just nineteen and seventeen years of age respectively. They had joined MI6 before the war on the recommendation of their aunt, who cleaned the big houses of several MI6 officers in London.[21] Their well-connected relation also found work for their cousin, Marjorie Goldsmith, who worked as a switchboard operator at one of the London offices.[22]

The sisters came from an interesting Anglo-Irish family. Their parents, Patrick and Phyllis 'Patty' McCarthy, had met in London during the First World War. After fighting for the British, Patrick chose to return home to Tralee with his wife and small daughter, Eileen, born in 1920. It was deeply ironic that, having served loyally in the British Army, Patrick should have joined the republican separatists (Sinn Féin) only to find himself facing the Black and Tans, former British soldiers sent to Ireland to reinforce the constabulary. At this time, Patty fell pregnant with Dorothy. During a raid on their home, the British soldiers did not lay a finger on the pregnant Englishwoman. However, unbeknown to the soldiers, Patty was lying on a bed that concealed hidden ammunition and guns.[23] After the civil war came to a halt in 1923, the family struggled, as harvests failed, leading to severe food shortages and starvation throughout Ireland. Patrick and his wife therefore decided to return to London, eventually settling in Barking. Far removed from the threat of daily violence occurring on the streets of Tralee, their daughters enjoyed a sheltered upbringing, attending Catholic school and dutifully setting time aside each evening to pray before they went to bed. Dorothy was reserved and shy, whereas her older sister, Eileen, was more outgoing. However, both possessed an innocent naivety regarding the ways of the world.

The sisters found their time at Bletchley to be a liberating experience. In particular, it was a turning point for Dorothy.[24] The youngest woman to work at Bletchley before September 1939, she quickly recognised her self-worth. Upon joining MI6, an officer stressed to Dorothy the importance of 'eyes open, ears open and mouth shut'.[25] As a confidential messenger, she performed the same work at Bletchley as at MI6 headquarters in London. She diligently delivered papers to secretaries and ran off multiple copies of documents on a Roneo machine before distributing them to the various offices in the mansion. For security purposes, the office doors only displayed tiny plaques with numbers on them, yet Dorothy knew intimately about the mansion's interior, and who worked where. Interviewed at Bletchley Park in 2017, the 95-year-old remembered the fumed-oak entrance hall and beautiful embossed ceilings. MI6 took up residence on the first floor, where Dorothy's 'cubbyhole' was located in a large broom cupboard. She recalled how some partitioned rooms formed smaller offices occupied by senior army, navy and air force officers.[26]

As Dorothy made her way energetically about the mansion, she delivered messages from the Head of Section VIII, Richard Gambier-Parry. Parry was educated at Eton and barely survived the First World War after being wounded three times before secondment to the Royal Flying Corps. He had previously worked as a wireless specialist for Philco, the American radio manufacturing company. Personally headhunted by Sinclair in 1938, Parry possessed all the necessary knowledge and skills needed to overhaul and modernise MI6 wartime communications. He assembled a clandestine wireless-transmission network that linked MI6 with its overseas stations and agents.[27] The quick-witted officer was a larger-than-life character who posed for the camera on the grounds of Bletchley Park with a cigarette in one hand and a feather duster in the other.[28] The section head also had a penchant for marrying his secretaries. After divorcing his first wife, Parry married his secretary, before divorcing a second time and finally marrying his wartime secretary and driver, Elizabeth 'Lisa' Towes, in 1944.[29] Loved by all his staff, Parry was affectionately known as 'Pop'.[30] Dorothy recalled how 'he was the nicest man you would ever want to meet'.[31]

As a confidential messenger, Dorothy McCarthy spent much of her time delivering messages to her sister, Eileen, in the first-floor coding room, one of the mansion's biggest spaces. Accessed by several steps up to what used to be one of the back bedrooms, the coding room had a polished wooden floor and decorative embossed ceiling. Wires ran up from the room below, a ballroom that then operated as a teleprinter room. The copper telephone wires were connected to three teleprinters in the coding room that linked with MI6 headquarters and the Central Telegraph Office in London, and Whaddon Hall, home to MI6's secret communications department.[32] The teletype produced rapid clicking sounds loud enough to be heard from the corridor. As Eileen McCarthy operated the machines, the codists dealt with numerous cipher messages received from MI6 agents and officers based overseas at various embassies. MI6 had installed Radio Station 'X' in the mansion's tower in early 1939 and attached an aerial to a large tree on the green in the front of the mansion. By the middle of 1939, the wireless station had moved to Hut 1. Charles Emary operated the radio station until he was transferred to nearby Whaddon Hall at the end of February 1940.

In December 2001, a white-haired Eileen, now in her eighties, climbed the steep steps to the mansion attic that had once housed the

MI6 radio station. Wearing a beige wool overcoat with a red scarf thrown casually around her neck, she sat on a vintage folding chair and contemplated the countless runs from the coding room to the radio station that she had made long ago at Bletchley.[33] The veteran MI6 teleprinter operator had worked alongside a handful of experienced codists such as sisters Elizabeth and Jane O'Shea; Ena Molesworth, who had recently returned from the Passport Control Office in Berlin; and Olive Montgomery, who had served under Mansfield Cumming, MI6's first chief.[34] These women were initially presided over by Kathleen Pettigrew, Sinclair's trusted assistant. Described as a 'very nice secretary' by one codist, Kathleen looked after her team and took a shine to the McCarthy sisters.[35] When Eileen wed in October 1939, Kathleen presented her with a small tablecloth and matching napkins, hand-embroidered with delicate pale pink and white flowers.[36] Considering it a treasured memento of her time in MI6, Eileen later stored the precious gift in tissue paper and shared the story of its provenance with her children.[37]

Kathleen first met the sisters at 54 Broadway, the London MI6 headquarters disguised as the offices of the 'Minimax Fire Extinguisher Company'. When the McCarthy sisters joined the mysterious cast of characters who worked within the warren of narrow passages and wooden partitioned walls, Kathleen had already spent nearly two decades in MI6. She had accrued enough money to live independently in a new, upscale, art deco apartment block in Chelsea. Daver Court stood on tree-lined Manor Street, just off King's Road and mere moments away from her mother and sister, who had chosen to move to a similar fashionable property at Forsyte House at the same time as Kathleen in 1938. Now with middle-class incomes, the Pettigrew women had charted and navigated a path to success. The senior MI6 'secretary' was now financially secure, an astounding achievement for a woman who had defied social barriers to acquire power and influence in British intelligence.

In 1939, Kathleen Pettigrew, now forty years old but not keen to admit her true age, temporarily relocated to Bletchley to oversee the move of Section VIII. Billeted with the section head, Richard Gambier-Parry, and others at nearby Whaddon Hall, she was waited on hand and foot by a team of resident servants.[38] Throughout the war, Kathleen was the guardian of all clandestine communications that crossed her desk at London headquarters, whether MI6 radio communications with agents abroad or the intelligence generated by GC&CS codebreaking at Bletchley. The latter was considered to be above 'Top Secret' and was designated 'Ultra'. Kathleen belonged to an elite group of very few officials privy to such vital, sensitive information. As a security precaution, she was chauffeured to Bletchley each day, where she joined Evelyn Sinclair and Stewart Menzies, who were residing ten miles away in another country mansion in the quaint village of Newport Pagnell.[39]

Bletchley was a hive of activity during the first few months of the war. In the mansion, black, green and red telephones rang above the din caused by multiple typewriters clacking away. Those on both floors looked forward to the daily ritual of lunch, which saw all staff sitting at a long dining table with silver cutlery, waiting for, among other treats, the delicious Bletchley rice pudding. Outside, in the grounds, garages and stables were transformed into workshops used by MI6's Section D (supposedly meaning 'D for Destruction'). Formed in 1938 and headed by Major Laurence Grand, this covert paramilitary group, which was the forerunner of the Special Operations Executive (SOE), used any means possible to carry out deadly sabotage and subversion operations designed to stop the enemy in its tracks. As Grand declared, 'We just want to blow off people's hats.'[40]

Lois Hamilton joined Section D on 1 February 1939.[41] As secretary to Commander Arthur Langley, who was in charge of devices, Lois's days were never dull. She was occasionally despatched to Bletchley Park for a few days to work with Dr Drane, a physicist specialising in explosives who conducted important research in one of the workshops. During one visit, Lois received orders to carry an orange-brown attaché case on the train journey to Bletchley. Under strict instructions, Lois took great care of the case and never opened it. When she arrived at Bletchley, two men from the Woolwich Arsenal were waiting for her. One was Dr Colin Meek, a scientific officer working on plastic explosives. Lois handed him the case and walked with Meek to the edge of the ornamental lake. As Lois recalled, Meek had apprehensively opened the attaché case. As he tentatively stepped back, the case 'immediately burst into flames and blazed fiercely for some minutes'.[42] The secretary had unknowingly carried experimental incendiaries that were highly unstable and could have caused real trouble on the train had the case been set alight. After the fire died, the rogue pyrotechnicians returned to the mansion for lunch, and the incident was never spoken of again.[43] Lois and her boss Langley were later temporarily based at Bletchley. They shared a small office on the mansion's ground floor, but Langley 'spent most of his time scouring the countryside for a suitable house to accommodate the "Devices" department' and its penchant for experimentation with what were aptly referred to at the time as 'bangs'.[44]

The codebreakers did not take long to complain about the irregular pursuits on the grounds. Section D moved out in November 1939, but theirs were not the only 'bangs' to be heard in Bletchley. Considered an unlucky day by some, Friday, 13 October 1939 saw Britain's first wartime-blackout train crash, which occurred at Bletchley Station. Eileen McCarthy remembered hearing the loud clash of metal on metal in the evening and rushed down the road to the railway station with MI6 and GC&CS bigwigs. The scene that greeted Eileen was one of devastation and death. The accident occurred after the Euston to Stranraer passenger train hit a shunting engine at speed, destroying the waiting room and damaging parts of the station roof. Forty people were injured, and four lost their lives, including one RAF airman.[45] The memory of seeing the young man's disfigured body stayed with Eileen for the rest of her life.[46]

Within weeks of the accident at Bletchley Station, news of the death of Hugh Sinclair on 4 November 1939 hit the secret world hard. Considered a prime mover, the chief's 'great intuitive wisdom' and 'selfless sincerity' would be greatly missed.[47] The 66-year-old's visits to the war station had become less frequent as his cancer took hold. On the day before his death, Sinclair had written to the permanent head of the Foreign Office, Sir Alexander Cadogan, proposing his deputy, Stewart Menzies, as his successor.[48] In what was perhaps the final time he signed in green ink, Sinclair had instructed Kathleen to deliver the letter in the event of his death.[49] With a heavy heart, she dutifully carried out his wishes. Sinclair's office at 54 Broadway remained untouched after his death. A pistol with a mother-of-pearl handle lay next to the chief's cigar box on a round table. Kathleen walked across the thick-pile Turkish carpet to reach the chief's handsome desk.[50] She knelt to enter the safe combination and retrieve the letter of recommendation. Clever, well-educated and socially well-connected, Stewart Menzies would prove an excellent but ruthless wartime chief.

Days after Sinclair's death, MI6 suffered another blow with the disaster at Venlo. On 9 November 1939, two MI6 officers were kidnapped by the SS Security Service (Sicherheitsdienst [SD]) on the Dutch–German border, sending shock waves through British intelligence.[51] On the day before MI6's spy games went horribly wrong, Kathleen Pettigrew joined a stellar cast of covert and overt personalities attending Sinclair's memorial service at St Martin-in-the-Fields. An array of admirals, naval captains and colonels joined Evelyn Sinclair, Vernon Kell (head of MI5) and many MI6 and GC&CS personnel, such as Alastair Denniston and Richard Gambier-Parry, who had made the journey from Bletchley to pay their respects.[52] Back at the mansion, staff were understandably gloomy but remained resolute to carry on as Sinclair would have wished.[53]

By early 1940, Bletchley had adopted the cover name 'Government Communications Headquarters', and much to Denniston's annoyance, William Ridley continued to oversee Bletchley's entire administration and management, a role he shared from October 1940 with Paymaster Commander Alan Bradshaw of GC&CS.[54] Much mystery remains around the man who was in charge of everything from building new huts to the canteen and the perennial loss of crockery, because staff regularly took mugs away. Ridley never spoke about his time at Bletchley and initially rejected the OBE awarded him after the war. The former chief administrative officer remained convinced that his acceptance of any award would contravene the Official Secrets Act.[55] Ridley eventually received the award after a flurry of persuasive letters from Downing Street.[56] The seasoned naval officer who never commanded his own ship, at least not at sea, had grown up in the Nicola Valley of British Columbia, where his father owned and ran a cattle ranch. With the rest of the family in England, Ridley attended boarding school in Reading, after which he joined Dartmouth as a cadet on HMS *Prince George*.[57] The fifteen-year-old never looked back. Seconded to the Royal Australian Navy during the First World War, Ridley was awarded several medals for his wartime service and was appointed Commander at the end of 1920.[58] At some point in the 1930s, he joined MI6. However, the circumstances surrounding his recruitment remain a mystery. Ridley took the need for secrecy in his stride and never uttered a word to any of his family, who remained in the dark about his wartime activities.[59]

With the aid of his wife, Vera, who worked as his secretary, Ridley co-ordinated and oversaw the huge logistical set-up of the war station. The couple lived nearby very comfortably in a charming thatched cottage.[60] The rest of Bletchley's staff were not quite so lucky and were billeted with locals or at boarding houses in the surrounding villages. With no bikes, the McCarthy sisters had a two-mile walk each day to Bletchley. Dorothy lodged with an elderly couple, while her sister lived down the street. Sometimes, the young MI6 chauffeur, John, would spot them as he drove past and offer them a lift, which was very welcome during the cold winter of 1939 to 1940. Initially, there was little to do in Bletchley; the two sisters rarely went out, but spent evenings at each other's billets, chatting.[61] Dorothy returned to London headquarters in the spring of 1940, working there until the end of 1942. She later joined the WRNS and married an American airman. Eileen left Bletchley with most of MI6 at the end of 1941 and worked in the London headquarters before giving birth to her son in 1942. After nine months, she returned to work and finally left MI6 in 1945.[62] When Eileen left the mansion, Denniston was pleased with the extra space generated by departing MI6 colleagues. He had long believed that the two organisations could not coexist at the same location.[63] However, Bletchley Park and the small railway town where it sat somehow managed to cope with the 9,000-strong secret workforce that would eventually invade the area.[64]

As Captain Ridley and his team departed Bletchley, a small contingent of MI6 women remained and moved from the mansion to Hut 10. Operating on a three-shift rota in 1942, nearly one hundred women worked as codists, typists, teleprinter operators and tea makers. The majority of codists were young wartime recruits drawn from the upper echelons of society. The work they carried out remained completely separate from the wider work going on at Bletchley. Located near the mansion, Hut 10 had initially housed the air intelligence section from 1940 onwards. After MI6 took over, two long tables ran on either side of the large rectangular room. Codists sat hunched over endless pages of messages from brave agents operating far away behind enemy lines. Unlike those working in other huts who had no idea how their tasks fitted into the bigger picture, the women of Hut 10 were completely aware of their contribution to the war.

Ruth Sebag-Montefiore was one such woman. Intelligent and with a prodigious memory, Ruth had worked as an MI6 codist at Bletchley since 1941. Her cousin's family, the Leons, had once owned Bletchley Park. Born during the First World War, Ruth 'was brought up in an environment of Victorian rigour and convictions'.[65] She was the youngest of five children, who had never lived in a London house with fewer than twenty rooms or four servants. After the war, Ruth became the matriarch of a prominent Anglo-Jewish family. In her seventies, she penned a candid memoir describing the full extent of her secret wartime work. The former MI6 codist explained how agents would send messages providing details of safe houses that could be used by new agents and escaping prisoners of war. An urgent telegram might arrive, alerting MI6 to the sudden disappearance of an agent, warning London that there was a leak in the chain. Messages such as this were marked with three Zs to indicate the degree of urgency.

Other incoming messages provided times and safe locations for dropping agents and supplies. The courageous MI6 men and women operating behind enemy lines also offered details of enemy troop movements, sightings of U-boats and vital information to assist the RAF with the bombing of enemy targets. According to Ruth, anything useful to London headquarters was sent and received.[66] Ruth described the complex coding process in her memoir, revealing how 'each agent and each codist were given two identical books, one a paperback novel, and the other filled with five-figure groups and numbers. To encode a telegram, you selected the first few words – which had to contain more than fifteen letters – of a line in the novel, indicating, in figure code, the page, line, and five consecutive letters – which represented numbers – chosen, and the five-figure group in the number book where one was starting the message. After turning the telegram into the appropriate figures, the agent and codist could then proceed by adding or deducting one group of figures from the other to encode or decode the telegram.'[67] The erudite young woman thrived on the unpredictable nature of the work, declaring 'one never knew from day to day what the In and Out tray would reveal'.[68]

A retired general, Leslie Rowley Hill, was in charge of Hut 10. Several wartime recruits received a visit from the MI6 officer, who seemed woefully ill at ease taking charge of a group of women.[69] Despite being in his fifties, Hill appeared like a man with 'one foot in the grave'.[70] The women of Hut 10 found him to be 'a kind and rather awe-inspiring man' with an excellent knowledge of languages.[71] Hill was born near Edinburgh and attended Wellington College and the Royal Military Academy at Woolwich. During the interwar period, he served as military attaché at the Tokyo embassy, where he became aware of Japanese attempts to break his telegram cipher.[72] Hill may have had the look of a lacklustre diplomat, but he was razor-sharp when it came to security issues. MI6 kept its circle small regarding wartime recruitment, exploiting personal relationships and social connections to employ the right 'kind of people'. Such practices resulted in a mix of fresh recruits of various ages, with numerous wealthy debutantes and those who were not but wished they were.

Joan Orchard had not yet turned eighteen when she attended an interview in the mansion at Bletchley and was then read the Official Secrets Act. General Hill had approached her father, a personal acquaintance, and had asked whether Joan would like to join his section. She received 30 shillings a week and began work in Hut 10, filing and making cups of tea for Hill and his team. Eager to learn, the former schoolgirl rose to be a typist for one of the senior codists, and after a year of performing that role, she became a codist herself, a position she held until January 1945.[73] Linguists were vital for communicating with French, Dutch and Norwegian agents. Charmain Prendergast possessed a good working knowledge of several languages. She worked in Hut 10 from June 1943 to October 1944. The Voluntary Aid Detachment (VAD) nurse had joined MI6 on the understanding that she could leave at a month's notice should her fiancé, an Australian naval officer, return to the UK, for they planned to wed. After the war, she suffered from 'nightmares thinking about those agents who had fallen into Gestapo hands'.[74]

Young recruits such as Charmain and Ruth found the few middle-aged MI6 spinsters of Hut 10 to be a prickly bunch who did not take well to the noisy but efficient newcomers. Outside Hut 10, the group of attractive young codists, with their austere manners and a tendency to keep to themselves, were known as 'the Babes'.[75] Angela Gandell remarked, 'for some reason we considered ourselves rather superior to the people in other huts'.[76] To the young debutantes, Bletchley's 'boffins' were odd men with peculiar looks and strange mannerisms. 'As they poured out of their huts for a breather or en route for the dining hall, with their gesticulating arms, unkempt hair, and short-sighted eyes peering through thick spectacles', Ruth commented, 'they looked like beings from another planet.'[77] Lady Cynthia Tothill was an entirely different creature. The Hut 10 deputy was well known as the 'face' of Pond's beauty products.[78] The glamorous socialite was an appropriately haughty and naughty figure with immense chic. As a 1930s divorcee, she was also a regular feature in the celebrity gossip columns. Her presence at Bletchley certainly cemented perceptions of Hut 10 as a nest of socialite snobbery. However, as a founding member of the Women's Committee established in 1942, Cynthia ensured that the MI6 women were kept abreast of matters and had their views represented.[79]

Suffering from ill health, Lady Tothill left Bletchley in June 1943.[80] Her successor could not have been more different. Known as 'Monty' to her MI6 colleagues, Olive Montgomery was a secret service careerist like Kathleen Pettigrew. Born in 1888, Olive came from a comfortable middle-class family in Deptford. Her father was a rate collector and earned enough to keep one servant. Olive attended Queen's College, London, and later worked as a governess before joining MI6 during the First World War. Leslie Hill's new deputy was a 'thin and angular', matronly woman, described by Ruth as being 'neatly dressed in well-cut coats and skirts so that the long paper cuffs she wore – a fresh pair every day – to protect her sleeves struck a bizarre note in so nondescript and conventional appearance'.[81] Olive possessed an 'agile mind hidden behind a deceptively gentle Miss-Marple-like exterior'.[82]

Olive resided at The Chase within the grounds of Whaddon Hall. Her job at Bletchley was considered 'so secret and important' that, like Kathleen Pettigrew, she was chauffeured to and from the codebreaking site each day with other staff billeted at Whaddon.[83] At the end of 1944, the MI6 'secretary' left Hut 10 and travelled to New York to take up undisclosed secret service work across the Atlantic. After the war, she was awarded an MBE for her clandestine wartime endeavours. However, she chose not to attend the investiture at Buckingham Palace, perhaps because she was still working overseas and received the honour through the post without any formalities.[84] Olive spent her retirement years with her pet poodle, Susie. Nicknamed 'Curly Pig' by family members, the well-fed dog disliked men and hid from Olive's nephew whenever he visited.[85] The former Hut 10 deputy spent the last few years of her life at Fairmount Care Home in Mottingham before she passed away in 1968.[86]

Olive belonged to a group of MI6 women who had been born during the reign of Queen Victoria, had made gains in certain professions, and had found new freedoms. But she was very different from most women in Hut 10, who were mainly born after women had won the right to vote. The codists, secretaries and messengers worked just metres away from the very spot where two suffragettes had chained themselves to a tree in the grounds of Bletchley Park in 1909. As Prime Minister Herbert Asquith began to deliver his speech at the mansion, which was then the home of the former Liberal MP Sir Herbert Leon, the two women yelled with all their might.[87] Of course, they had no idea that their chosen protest site would later see thousands of women come together to achieve something special at Station X, the creation of a new age of information.

While the isolation of the Hut 10 codists at Bletchley ended in early 1945, when the chief of MI6, Stewart Menzies, enquired about moving the coding department back to London, several other MI6 women had also been working elsewhere at various locations outside the capital besides Bletchley. The MI6 Registry, for example, had been evacuated to St Albans at the start of the war.[88] Staffed by sixty women, the card indexes then expanded at an alarming rate; however, they soon began to suffer from the inevitable transfer delays caused when responding to document requests from central London. As a result, MI6 headquarters came to rely heavily on MI5's more comprehensive registry for the remainder of the war.[89] Unfortunately, however, the secret head office was not immune to falling bombs.

From September 1940, the Luftwaffe had delivered its deadly cargoes for fifty-seven consecutive nights, leaving local office workers, primarily civil servants, regularly scurrying for shelter. Stewart Menzies had seriously contemplated a move to the countryside, but Winston Churchill had ordered government servants to remain at their posts.[90] During the Blitz that followed, Londoners experienced an extraordinary existence at the daily mercy of the air-raid sirens for over eight months. Even after the end of the Blitz in May 1941, German air raids continued for the duration of the war. Having returned to London headquarters at the end of 1941, Eileen McCarthy found herself on several occasions having to work through air raids instead of taking refuge in the emergency teleprinter room in the basement of 54 Broadway. Speaking in a soft cockney accent, she recalled decades later one particular bombing raid during a hot summer's evening. While she was working the night shift, the sirens sounded at midnight just as the teleprinter started up. The incoming message read: 'Tirpitz has been sighted.'[91] Eileen waited for the message from Bletchley Park to finish before running it through the duplicator machine. She grabbed the top copy and rushed upstairs to the duty officer, who had an hour earlier given her specific instructions on how to enter his room. Eileen cautiously entered the dark room and closed the window before pulling the blackout curtain. She then turned on the light. Laughing, the now much wiser Eileen revealed how she had 'found him lying on the floor all in the nude'.[92]

Passers-by occasionally attempted to take shelter in the sandbagged lobby of 54 Broadway, utterly oblivious to the men and women working on one of the four floors occupied by Britain's secret service. The commissionaire, Arthur Ackary, a retired army sergeant, was one of a handful of loyal 'front-of-house' watchmen who stood guard over the premises.[93] His sturdy frame cast a long shadow over the linoleum floor as he prevented unwanted guests from exploring beyond the lobby. However, trusted employees such as Menzies's secretary, Muriel Jones, passed through easily and with familiarity. On one occasion, she was beaten to the lift by another regular, Beatrice Peters, who rushed past Muriel and claimed her spot in the ancient cabin first. Beatrice had worked as a telephonist since after the First World War.[94] Married with no children, she had left her husband, Harry, sleeping at home that morning. Harry was a war reserve constable (WRC) in the Metropolitan Police, and he stoically worked night shifts, helping to maintain some semblance of law and order during the Blitz.[95]

Beatrice and Muriel rode the lift in comfortable silence, with Beatrice exiting first. Muriel checked the time on her watch. She was late. Walking at a fast pace, she began to remove her coat as she hurried down the corridor of the fourth floor. As she got nearer to her office, she could hear the continuous clacking of typewriters in action. Muriel slid furtively into her chair and fumbled with the papers on her desk. Elaine Miller, an expert and discreet typist, was typing at full speed and barely glanced at her colleague while drilling away at the machine keys.[96] However, Kathleen Pettigrew, surveying the room that was her domain, acknowledged Muriel's late entrance with a disapproving look. She was five years older than her assistant, her auburn hair was starting to show signs of middle age, and her overall appearance gave 'an immediate impression of being exceptionally well-bred'.[97] By comparison, Muriel was a 37-year-old attractive brunette with a softer, more feminine side.

Professional to the core, the three women operated on formal terms only, referring to each other as 'Miss'. They had worked together in the antechamber to C's office for several years and had grown accustomed to being summoned at ungodly hours. This included sleeping overnight at 54 Broadway. Kathleen regularly accompanied Menzies to 2 a.m. meetings with Winston Churchill, where she read through the decoded German ENIGMA messages from Bletchley.[98] The true extent of Kathleen's incredible wartime contribution will never be known. However, declassified files shed some light on her work, which hint at the power she wielded on C's behalf in facilitating the distribution of intelligence.[99] Nearly every kind of correspondence, from naval intelligence headlines to Bletchley decoded enemy messages, crossed Kathleen's desk.[100] In fact, C's executive assistant was one of the trusted few who knew that the German ENIGMA code had been broken. As the point-person at London headquarters, she communicated directly with the MI6 liaison officer in Hut 3 at Bletchley.[101] Hut 3 rewrote the decoded messages and presented them as originating from a British agent named BONIFACE.[102] However, those in Whitehall and the other services viewed the industrious fictional MI6 'agent' with scepticism and chose to disregard the material. In June 1941, Menzies dispensed with the cover and introduced a new security classification, 'Ultra Secret'.[103]

The sheer volume of such messages received and sent each day was staggering. ULTRA was of such overwhelming significance that Menzies sent a messenger with daily batches of raw translated decrypts to Churchill, satisfying the prime minister's consuming interest in reading messages directly from the enemy. The tenacious war leader held the key to the worn leather despatch box on his keyring. The contents of the box, carefully curated by Kathleen, presented Churchill with a clear, real-time picture of the war. The woman who inspired Ian Fleming's character Miss Moneypenny was perhaps one of the most powerful women in Whitehall, with the highest possible security clearance. MI6 chiefs were wise to keep Kathleen close, as she possessed an intimate knowledge of all secret and state affairs.

The number of letters sent by Menzies, most of which were to Churchill, was also high. Around eight thousand letters landed on Kathleen's desk.[104] The burgeoning amount of paperwork was not helped by the fact that the system for MI6 officers requiring an audience with Menzies was being abused and that 'recommendations from the staff to "C" tended to be full of slant, bias and prejudice'.[105] A solution in the form of a liaison officer was proposed by Alexander Cadogan at the Foreign Office, who wished to establish a closer relationship with MI6. Menzies accepted his idea, and Patrick Reilly arrived at Broadway in September 1942. Reilly quickly assessed that a radical overhaul of Menzies's decision-making process was needed if the Foreign Office were to advise on its needs in intelligence collection. The 33-year-old mandarin won over Kathleen with his diffident and fair-minded nature. The system that they devised together saw all those eager to see the MI6 chief submit their proposals and requests in writing with all relevant papers to Kathleen, who then forwarded the documents to Reilly. If the civil servant deemed the proposal important enough, it landed on Menzies's desk.[106] This change in practice was aimed at streamlining the decision-making process with an orderly appointment system, one that would avoid long queues forming outside his office.[107] However, in practice, the new procedure had the potential for creating huge logjams.

Unsurprisingly, C's old, less formal traffic-light system – the use of red and green lights above his office door to signal his availability – was never truly abandoned. Used to the late night and early morning on-demand meetings that C allowed, Kathleen sometimes found him engaged in informal ad-hoc meetings that had not been prearranged. On 11 December 1942, for instance, the red light above Menzies's door signalled that he was not to be disturbed. The elaborate use of such lights seems excessive, given that the possibility of anyone getting past his three secretaries and barging in was practically zero. Yet such measures were a fundamental part of the culture of secrecy in which C and others operated. After half an hour, the red light popped off and was replaced with a green one, indicating that it was clear to enter the chief's office if needed. Menzies's leather-quilted door opened, and a tall, well-tailored man wearing a grey pinstripe suit emerged. Guy Liddell, MI5's head of counterespionage, did not look particularly pleased as he gathered his coat from Miss Pettigrew.[108] Sadly, no trilby had been thrown on the hat stand to collect, nor was there any brief flirtation with 'Miss Moneypenny' as so often depicted in the James Bond films.

Yet something unusual did occur. Seconds before Menzies's office door closed, Muriel Jones caught a brief glimpse of her handsome boss: slim, sandy-haired and in his early fifties. Menzies looked up from his desk, and their eyes met for the briefest moment, neither revealing anything more than polite curiosity, yet his eyes softened just before the door closed.[109] An illicit office affair was being conducted right under Kathleen's nose. The relationship remained secret until the 1950s, when inevitable heartbreak led to tragedy and discovery.

9

The Ministry of Unwomanly Warfare

Exploding rats, incendiary suitcases and suicide pills are generally not associated with women and war. Yet the women of the Special Operations Executive (SOE) were all too familiar with the unorthodox nature of the organisation they worked for. Formed during the blazing hot summer of 1940, SOE was famously tasked by Prime Minister Winston Churchill 'to set Europe ablaze'.[1] His secret army, known for its big 'bangs', blew up communication and transport lines; carried out assassinations; and organised, trained and equipped resistance and partisan groups across occupied Europe and the Far East.[2] Unconventional to its core, SOE's business was sabotage and subversion, and it proved incredibly good at disrupting the German war machine. The dirty tricks carried out by the tough new secret service were a testament to the organisation's ability to think outside the box, devising creative and ingenious solutions to life and death problems. A key concern was keeping its secret agents alive and out of enemy hands.

From April 1942 onwards, women were formally recruited as special agents by SOE, breaking the taboo that women did not belong in combat.[3] Irregular warfare required irregular warriors, and women proved invaluable. Their gender provided the perfect camouflage. Female agents were sent behind enemy lines as wireless operators, who valiantly maintained communications with base stations to arrange vital supply drops. As couriers, women identified suitable locations for supply drops and carried messages and weapons to resistance groups. Unlike men, women were able to move more freely around the Nazi-occupied countryside under the cover of visiting relatives or friends and were rarely stopped at control points. Organised according to territories, four of SOE's country sections sent women into occupied Europe. France was unusual in that it had four sections rather than just one: RF worked with General de Gaulle's Free French networks,

EU/P worked with Poles in France, D/F's remit was escape lines and clandestine communications, and F was independent of De Gaulle and the largest of all SOE's country sections. F Section deployed 480 agents to France, 39 of whom were women.[4] RF Section sent eleven women to France, Section N sent three women to the Netherlands (Holland), and T Section sent two female agents to Belgium.[5] Dressed in civilian clothes, these women knew that they risked being shot as spies if caught, no less than male agents. Yet they still bravely volunteered. While stories of bold and daring female agents dominate SOE biographies, films and museum exhibitions, the endeavours of the many civilian women who were never deployed in the field, but who worked tirelessly in support roles overseeing the recruitment, training and equipping of agents, remain missing from history. Churchill called SOE his 'Ministry of Ungentlemanly Warfare', but it could easily have been named his 'Ministry of Unwomanly Warfare'.[6]

One woman occupied a unique position within SOE. From January 1941 to February 1946, Dorothy Furse, Personnel Officer for Women's Staff, looked after the nine hundred civilian women employed across the organisation. The 34-year-old was responsible for the recruitment, progress and welfare of female staff, and for discipline.[7] Her job was to identify talents among SOE's female employees and channel them into appropriate roles. Dorothy had previously worked for MI5 in London and Oxford as secretary to the head of the Investigations and Reports Section, where she supervised the Registry.[8] After moving to SOE's London headquarters at 64 Baker Street, she quickly advanced from assistant to manager.[9] The Marylebone headquarters of the organisation sat at the centre of a cluster of requisitioned offices and buildings on the same street or in nearby blocks of flats, which housed the various country sections, laboratories, workshops and clothing and equipment stores.

SOE personnel files that have survived at the National Archives bear testimony to the sheer scale of Dorothy's work with female staff.[10] Several of these records contain letters of recommendation, such as that for Alicia Grace, the daughter of a surgeon who co-founded an import–export company in Jamaica. Desperate to leave the Caribbean and serve her country, Alicia was vouched for by a friend who wrote to Dorothy on her behalf. Noting the 25-year-old's fluency in French and German, Dorothy immediately replied to Alicia and invited her for an interview. The young woman went on to serve in the RF Section.[11]

The tall and imposing personnel officer was perfectly placed to assess an applicant's language proficiency, as Dorothy had an excellent working knowledge of French and German.[12] However, during the war, she was occasionally asked to interview several unlikely applicants who happened to be men behind bars, such as Johnny Ramensky, who was released from prison after he agreed to instruct trainee agents in the art of cat burglary and safe-cracking.[13] Whatever their background, Dorothy always saw people's best qualities. She was never critical but always honest and supportive. Her boss, John Venner, SOE's director of finance and administration, commended Dorothy, disclosing that 'she has the most remarkable ability in handling staff and administrative problems which were for the most part of an extremely complicated nature in view of war time conditions'.[14] Dorothy's experience in working with capable women left her a lifelong supporter of gender parity in the workplace. She would regularly inform her family and close friends that she chose to have a female doctor, stockbroker, dentist and solicitor, as women were far more intelligent than men and, as a result of their sex, had to work hard to achieve such responsible positions.[15]

Growing up, Dorothy was not academically minded but excelled in sports at school. While her older brother Edmund (known as 'Niel') attended Cambridge University (1923 to 1926), Dorothy settled for finishing school. The two siblings had enjoyed a more than comfortable childhood at their maternal grandparents' house, a large country mansion in Surrey. Edmund senior was a lieutenant colonel in the Royal Horse Artillery, who fought and died during the First World War. Dorothy's mother, Emily, never remarried and, like her daughter, lived until her early nineties. During the Second World War, neither Dorothy's mother nor her brother knew the true nature of her work on the top two floors of 64 Baker Street.[16] Interestingly, Niel worked nearby as an accountant at Marks and Spencer's head office at Michael House, 82 Baker Street, which housed SOE's Codes and Ciphers team from 1943.[17] Perhaps he was aware of his sister's presence across the road and of the other 'Baker Street Irregulars' who entered via a mews at the back of the unassuming SOE headquarters.

Dorothy's younger cousin Aileen Furse also worked for Marks and Spencer as a 'staff manageress' at the Marble Arch branch.[18] Unlike Dorothy, Aileen had few memories of her father, who had died when she was four. Captain George Furse succumbed to his wounds at a casualty clearing station on the Western Front in September 1914. Aileen had a troubled childhood, causing her mother Hazel great concern. Unable to prevent her daughter from self-harming, Hazel placed Aileen in the care of Lord Horder, a renowned London physician whose patients included kings, queens and prime ministers.[19] Aileen also suffered from bouts of depression. Lord Horder advised that she should take a job. Worried that his cousin might slip into her self-destructive practices again, Niel Furse asked a colleague and friend, Flora Solomon, who had established the Marks and Spencer's staff welfare service, to find a position for Aileen and to keep an eye on her.[20]

Flora went out of her way to befriend the slim and attractive Aileen, whom she described as belonging 'to the class, now out of fashion, called "country"', and introduced her to some of her interesting friends.[21] As the daughter of a Russian Jewish banker, Flora had fled Russia after the revolution and had made London her new home. Widowed at a young age with a small son, Flora found solace in her social campaigning and support for the Zionist cause. The socialite used every opportunity to 'preach the justice of the Jewish cause in Palestine', but a number of her guests remained indifferent.[22] One of them, Harold 'Kim' Philby, had recently returned from Spain after covering the civil war for *The Times* newspaper. The tanned journalist enjoyed Flora's company but 'evinced not the slightest interest' in the Palestine conflict.[23] Flora had known Philby since he was a boy. The two would occasionally take luncheon together or encounter each other at dinner parties. On 3 September 1939 – the day that Britain declared war on Germany – the matchmaker hostess invited Philby to her Mayfair flat and introduced him to Aileen over afternoon tea.

Philby was charming and had impeccable manners, and his disarming stammer did not perturb Aileen. The two quickly fell in love and appeared to be well suited. However, Aileen's mother remained unimpressed at her daughter's choice of men. The conservative matriarch disapproved of Philby on account of his being a communist.[24] How Aileen's mother 'had established that fact, and what she did with the knowledge, is not known'.[25] To her and Flora's surprise, the young lovers soon moved in together, and lived a bohemian lifestyle for several years, producing three children before the end of the war. The couple told everyone that they were married but did not actually wed until 1946, when Philby divorced his first wife, Litzi Friedmann, an

Austrian communist. Whether Aileen was aware or not, her fate was now in the hands of a Soviet penetration agent, and there would be no happy ending for the second 'Mrs Philby'. As the years passed, Aileen came to suspect that her husband was a Soviet spy.[26] In 1952, she confronted Philby, who emphatically denied being a traitor, confirming her fear that he was lying.[27] At the end of 1957, she was found dead in her bedroom by her eldest daughter. The coroner ruled the 47-year-old had died from heart failure, but some within the Furse family believe Aileen was murdered.[28] Philby may have not fooled his wife, but he successfully managed to spin an elaborate web of lies, duping those in MI6 from the moment he was recruited in 1940.

After several months of 'phoney war', Germany invaded Norway in April 1940. Philby was conscious that his time was running out. His call-up papers could arrive any day. By design he connected with an old friend from his undergraduate days at Trinity College, Cambridge, where both men had developed communist sympathies. Guy Burgess secured Philby an interview with his employer, Section D of MI6 which specialised in sabotage and destruction. Britain's secret service was keen to boost its numbers and recruited Philby on the spot. He was precisely the type of candidate they were looking for – he knew German well and had travelled widely. He also had the right kind of 'connections': a senior MI6 officer, Valentine Vivian, knew Philby's father.[29] The Soviet agent left *The Times* in August 1940 and joined Section D's short-lived training centre for foreign agents based at Brickendonbury Hall in Hertfordshire.[30] There, Philby rubbed shoulders with the noted veteran intelligence officer George Hill, who had recruited Lucy and Peggy Lunn in 1918 to assist his clandestine couriers in Moscow. Now middle-aged, Hill no longer had the athletic look of a 'man of action'. Though in awe of Hill's achievements, Philby found him bald and 'immensely paunchy'.[31]

Before long, Section D staff found themselves working for SOE, as the new organisation absorbed the former MI6 paramilitary section. Consequently, Philby was transferred as a training officer to the new SOE field-agent school in the New Forest at Beaulieu. Soviet intelligence had achieved the unthinkable, with two of their agents, Burgess and Philby, both working in British intelligence just six months after the war began. Soviet intelligence had originally recruited Philby in 1934, having been introduced by his first wife, Litzi, and her friend Edith Tudor-Hart. In due course, the new Soviet agent then suggested like-minded friends from his days at Cambridge University as likely recruits. Although Philby, Guy Burgess, Donald Maclean and Anthony Blunt later became known as the 'Cambridge Spy Ring', they seldom co-operated as active Soviet agents, working instead very much in isolation. In 1941, Philby transferred from SOE to MI6's counter-intelligence department, Section V, where he took charge of the Iberian counterintelligence desk. The Soviet agent rose rapidly through the ranks of British intelligence, passing large amounts of classified information to the Soviets. As the most successful of the 'Cambridge Spies', Philby remained undetected until after the war, though a Russian defector did hint at his identity as early as 1940.

Unlike Philby, several Section D staff remained with SOE until the war's end. Lois Hamilton, the secretary who couriered an incendiary suitcase to Bletchley Park in 1939, was based at Aston House in the summer of 1940. The seventeenth-century, ivy-clad mansion with its 46-acre parkland estate near Stevenage was one of many remote country residences requisitioned during the war by SOE.[32] Known as Station XII, Aston House specialised in the production of 'special toys' for SOE agents, for the French Resistance, and for Britain's special forces. The secret weapons centre designed, tested and manufactured tailor-made plastic explosives, limpet mines, and over a million time-pencil fuses. The specialist equipment that Station XII produced was light enough to transport easily, strong enough to survive parachute drops, and so heavily camouflaged that agents could carry devices without arousing the suspicion of German troops or the feared Nazi secret police, the Gestapo.

Lois Hamilton was one of the first station staff to arrive at Aston House in late September 1939. Its secluded location kept prying eyes away from the top-secret work conducted in the mansion and its surrounding stables and outbuildings. The village of Aston consisted of just a few houses, a church and a row of cottages. Lois recalled years later in her unpublished memoir how 'the whole countryside was agog at our arrival'.[33] Initially, the staff was tiny, with only six men, all scientists and technicians, and four secretaries. Lois and the other women resided on the top floor of the house, where they had a small sitting room known as the 'boudoir'. This room served as a sanctuary where Lois could escape and gossip with the other women. For the first few months of the war, Lois enjoyed cycling and walking in the surrounding countryside. Life was good at the mansion, and

Lois found 'living in a community a novelty'.[34] The staff were well fed, despite the introduction of rationing in January 1940. It is difficult to believe, but the secret SOE workforce frequently dined on pheasant and grouse in the large dining room. By the summer of 1940, with the evacuation of British troops from Dunkirk and the subsequent Battle of Britain, the war had reached a crucial stage. From August 1940 onwards, Spitfires and Hurricanes took to the skies to fend off relentless waves of German bombers. One evening, Lois was abruptly woken and ordered to put on her dressing gown and assemble with the other station staff in the library. Slipping her feet into cold slippers, she made her way downstairs and joined her weary colleagues. Their commanding officer, Arthur Langley, informed the dishevelled group that a German invasion of the south coast could happen at any time.[35]

Langley ordered the women to cease office work immediately and to focus their attention on learning how to shoot with rifles and revolvers. They also received sabotage training. Lois recalled how 'we learnt how to cut a railway line. Under Colin Meek's guidance, we moulded a lump of plastic explosive, applied it to the correct place in a portion of railway line which had been obtained for training agents, attached the time fuse and released the catch. Then, we took cover behind a clump of trees. After a few minutes, the charge exploded, and any train coming along the line would have been derailed.'[36] Langley ensured that Station XII would not fall into enemy hands and issued orders to fortify the house. Soldiers carried a machine gun to Lois's bedroom and positioned it on her balcony, which looked out over miles of open countryside. The house and outbuildings were rigged with explosives, ready to be blown if the Germans arrived. The station evacuation plan stipulated that staff would leave by car at timed intervals. Lois noted with some misgiving that she was to join the last vehicle with Langley. Knowing her commanding officer's strong sense of patriotic duty, she predicted that he would not leave until the very last moment. But, as Lois revealed, 'days passed and there was no invasion. The opportunity had come and gone, and Hitler had lost his chance.'[37]

Aston House worked closely with Station IX, a large mansion known as The Frythe, near Welwyn Garden City.[38] The former private hotel was just a short drive from Aston House. Many of the boffins at Station IX resembled the fictional character Q, who equipped James Bond with various ingenious and deadly gadgets. In fact, these real-life SOE scientists devised everything from edible paper to exploding fruit and incendiary cigarettes. They also produced the single-shot Welrod silenced pistol, nicknamed 'the Bicycle Pump' by agents, because it resembled one. As the work increased, so too did the need for more secretaries. Barbara Keeley had begun war work in the Security Service (MI5) before being assigned to Station IX of SOE. Considered a challenging posting due to the highly technical nature of the work, Barbara excelled at her new job and received a pay rise on a par with junior officers.[39]

SOE was fortunate enough to employ many 'secretaries' who performed beyond expectations. However, unlike the luckless women of the Auxiliary Territorial Service (ATS) at Station XV (known as 'The Thatched Barn'), they were never required to handle dead rats. The 'Barn', home to SOE's Camouflage Section, was an enormous mock Tudor hotel previously owned by Billy Butlin, the holiday camp tycoon. Located north of London at Borehamwood, not far from Elstree film studios, which were then the centre of the British film industry, a team of industry experts commanded by a well-known film director equipped secret agents with booby traps and devised such unique items as 'the Striptease Suit', a camouflaged jumpsuit designed to protect an agent's clothing during parachute drops. Several ATS women worked here as technicians, carefully camouflaging explosives within everyday objects such as tins of peaches and hollow tree logs made of plaster. Joyce Couper was twenty years old when posted to Station XV in 1941. Before the war, Joyce had worked in a pottery firm. Her artistic skills proved helpful when painting plaster rocks and silk maps. However, she was less enthusiastic when it came to dealing with dead rats, as she explained in a post-war interview: 'They'd get dead mice and rats, scoop out the insides and send the skins over to us, and we had to fill them with plastic explosive and fasten them up again. The idea was that agents would drop them into the coal bunkers of steam engines, they would get shovelled into the furnace and blow the engine up. The girls didn't like doing that much because it was pretty messy, so the men took over, handling the dead rats and mice.'[40]

Generally, women rolled up their sleeves and were willing to do the work, no matter how unpalatable. However, such stomach-churning tasks as gutting rats were not normally assigned to civilian women with social pedigrees and family connections to the secret world of intelligence. For example, Phyllis Mackenzie, known to her friends as 'Phyl', was one such cosmopolitan SOE 'secretary' who took charge of agent clothing and personal equipment at the end of 1943.[41] She was a woman with a commanding presence, though it had little to do with her height of nearly six feet. Behind the confident veneer of class, Phyl possessed an inner wisdom. By the time she was recruited by SOE the young woman already possessed a wealth of intelligence experience and an endless list of exemplary skills.

As the daughter of a British diplomat and an American socialite, Phyl did not really need to work. Yet she preferred to follow the well-trodden path made by her father, Philip Rapinet Mackenzie, who as vice-consul at the British Consulate at Civitavecchia, the busy seaport of Rome, had also served (probably) as head of the MI6 Rome station from the end of the First World War.[42] Phyl's father enjoyed a passion for cars and regularly took his wife and three children out for drives in the Italian countryside. The Mackenzie family also enjoyed motoring holidays across Europe, which served as convenient cover for any active espionage Philip Mackenzie may have engaged in. They travelled everywhere in the latest cars and commemorated each vehicle's maiden voyage with a family photograph. But Phyl did not take her privileged upbringing for granted. Born in Rome in 1906, the gregarious youngster grew up speaking English with an American accent courtesy of her American mother, Angus, who was heiress to the wealthy Walsh family of Philadelphia, which owned a chain of department stores.[43] Fluent in French and Italian with a working knowledge of German and Spanish, Phyl was everything one would expect of a diplomat's daughter.

There was little that Phyl could not accomplish. Educated at convent schools in Ipswich and Stony Stratford in the early 1920s, she skied, mountaineered, cycled, competed in horse jumping, drove a car, sketched and loved to fence. She competed in major fencing competitions, including the first women's international sports meet in Italy in 1931.[44] Organisers had to seek support from Benito Mussolini, the leader of Italy, to ensure that the event took place, despite the fact that contemporary Fascist misogyny dictated that Italian women should not be engaging in male sports and damaging their precious bodies which were needed to reproduce the next generation of stronger and healthier Italians. Nevertheless, Phyl was able to join no fewer than 150 other athletes from eleven competing nations. Wearing a white skirt and jacket, with foil in hand, Phyl parried and lunged to a respectable third place, making fencing history in Florence.[45]

A woman of many talents, Phyl pursued her love of fencing along-side her work at the British Embassy in Rome, where she had worked since 1926. As a witness to the rise of Benito Mussolini and his Fascist Blackshirts, Phyl watched in horror as the Italian dictator established his reign of fear and forged an ill-fated alliance with Nazi Germany. However, it did not detract from her enduring love affair with the country that gave rise to the Renaissance. After Italy entered the war on 10 June 1940, Phyl realised that her family would have to leave. Chaos ensued at the embassy as staff began destroying important paperwork that could not be allowed to fall into Italian hands. As personal secretary to the air attaché, Phyl burnt ciphers and other intelligence documents. She was joined in this endeavour by Winnie Spink, the first MI6 woman sent to Russia in 1916, who had been working as a secretary to the naval attaché since January 1940. Phyl and Winnie finally left Rome under the cover of a blackout sometime after midnight on 11 June, before their diplomatic entourage embarked on the perilous sea voyage through submarine-infested waters to Britain.[46] Once in London, Phyl continued working for the Air Ministry until August 1942, when she was appointed to a clandestine role in New York.[47] During her time at the Manhattan headquarters of the British Security Coordination (BSC), a covert organisation run by MI6 to oversee all British intelligence activity in the Western hemisphere, Phyl met Mary Sherer, an MI5 sabotage expert seconded to advise the BSC head, William Stephenson.[48]

The two 'government officials' could not have been more different. Phyl was calm and charismatic, whereas Mary was prone to impulsive and reckless behaviour.[49] Both possessed an impish smile of devilment. Phyl's nephew remembers his aunt taking him to lunch at the Special Forces Club in London as a small boy. Left in total awe by the experience, he recalled Phyl's 'infectious and entirely mischievous smile'.[50] The two women formed a lasting friendship during the war that would endure until they died. It is unfortunate that some within MI5 misunderstood the true nature of Phyl and Mary's closeness, labelling them 'lesbians'. While some women in the secret services may indeed have formed enduring, romantic same-sex relationships, Phyl and Mary's remained completely asexual.[51] There was no stronger bond than sisterhood, and theirs was unbreakable.

In June 1943, the two women returned from the United States to England, travelling first-class aboard the *Esperance Bay*, a sizeable passenger-cargo ship.[52] Mary then became MI5's first female agent handler, while Phyl made her mark in SOE's French Section. Run by an officer who was a hopeless alcoholic, the F Section clothing department was in a terrible state by the end of 1943. Enormous piles of clothing lay strewn across the first-floor office at Orchard Court, a block of luxury flats near SOE's Baker Street headquarters. But all this was soon to change, beginning with the arrival of Claire Woolf in November 1943. The top brass at Baker Street hoped that the 29-year-old would bring order to the chaos caused by an officer not up to the job. When Claire first entered the department, she found one solitary tailor struggling in vain with the mountain of agent clothing. After a few days, the tiny brunette, who spoke fluent French and German, lost no time and marched over to the French Section headquarters at Norgeby House, 83 Baker Street.[53]

Claire was acutely aware of the danger her drunken boss posed to agents' lives. SOE's special agents were wholly dependent upon being able to 'pass' effectively without drawing enemy attention, and authentic cover clothing was an essential part of an agent's camouflage. Every design and style detail had to be authentic, from the stitching of seams and buttons to clothing labels, fasteners and zippers, not to mention the need to age unused clothes convincingly. Experienced tailors and seamstresses, many of them originally from all over continental Europe, reproduced French clothing from newspaper photographs and catalogues, and by studying minutely the design and manufacture of clothing obtained from recent refugees. Certain clothing items were adapted to conceal secret aids, such as maps sewn into silk underwear and a necktie designed to hide a small code printed on silk. Any mistake made in the clothing department put agents at risk.

Claire was determined to voice her concerns. Once inside Norgeby House, she passed the head of F Section, Colonel Maurice Buckmaster, shadowed by Misty, his pretty English bull terrier who sometimes accompanied him to work; that is, before she blew the section's entire London cover. Shortly before D-Day, Buckmaster's wife had been walking Misty along the street when the dog suddenly veered off into the secret F Section building, wagging her tail enthusiastically. Of course, neither Mrs Buckmaster nor Misty got any further than the duty commissionaire, but the section's secret was out.[54] At Norgeby House, Claire herself had no luck getting past the secretary to Buckmaster's second-in-command, Major Hugh Fraser.[55] Phyl

Mackenzie represented 'an impenetrable barrier'.[56] When it became clear that Claire would not be seeing Fraser that day, she decided to share her story and her concerns with Phyl. Several days passed before Phyl unexpectedly turned up at Orchard Court. To Claire's great surprise, Fraser's 'secretary' now replaced the 'deplorable predecessor'. Claire recalled later in life how 'Phyl had great energy and drive, was extremely efficient, and did an excellent job.'[57] However, the assistant did not exactly take to the younger and more glamorous Phyl, whose legs were nearly as long as Claire was tall. Perhaps Claire's dislike of her new boss amounted to jealousy, a clash of personality, or both. Either way, Claire maintained a civil and courteous working relationship with Phyl until the liberation.

Phyl and Claire saw agents daily, as all F Section meetings and briefings occurred regularly at Orchard Court, not Norgeby House. As a security measure, agents were kept in the dark regarding the location of F Section headquarters. However, after the flat address was broadcast on German radio, the clothing team was forced to move hastily to a house on Wimpole Street. In fact, the new ground-floor office served their needs far better. Walls adorned with cubby-holes held all the assembled dress items and accessories to be issued when an agent's departure date came through. Claire described how 'each cubby hole had an agent's number scribbled in white chalk, a wisely anonymous identification. Then, after the agent had left for the field, it was quite simple to erase the number and replace it with that of another agent as and when required.'[58] This effective system was the brainchild of Phyl.

Trainee agents often appeared at Wimpole Street in the early days of their enrolment, and Phyl and Claire made every effort to speak French in the office, so that British agents could perfect their fluency. Trainees attended various basic-training facilities that equipped them with survival skills, such as living off the land, before they joined the finishing school at Beaulieu, where they undertook a gruelling training regimen. Known as 'students', the volunteers were instructed on how to handle guns and explosives, to organise munitions and supply drops, to engage in unarmed combat, and to code and decode messages. SOE officers dressed in German uniforms replicated a taste of the harsh treatment agents would experience at the hands of the cruel and sadistic Gestapo, should they be captured and interrogated. Trainees were dragged from their beds in the middle of the night and were subjected to simulated interrogations. Those men and women who made it through advanced training faced one final test in broad daylight on home soil.

SOE despatched its secret weapon to ensnare selected trainee agents. Men and women were sent from Beaulieu on 96-hour exercises in cities around the country to see whether 'students' would fall prey to FIFI, an agent provocateur whose role was to learn everything about the trainee and his or her mission. Told to expect a man, trainees instead faced a glamorous and attractive woman who closely resembled the blonde seductress surrounded by captivated men in British service uniforms featured in the government's 'Careless talk costs lives' poster campaign.[59] Such scenes evoke images all too familiar to those acquainted with the spy-film genre. And yet the notion of a beautiful young woman in a luxurious lounge, sipping her cocktail while hanging on every word uttered by her unsuspecting target could not have been further from reality. FIFI actually met trainees in a dingy hotel bar in 'revolting' Wolverhampton, with all her expenditures scrutinised by SOE. The giraffe house at London Zoo was about as exotic a location as FIFI got to when meeting targets.[60]

Missing from SOE histories, the fictitious legend of agent FIFI has far surpassed the actual woman, Marie Christine Chilver, and has masked the true nature of her secret work designed to test agents' resolve. SOE described Christine as 'one of the expert liars in the world and extremely intelligent'.[61] She was an inspirational woman with 'unusual gifts of intelligence, courage, and assessment of character'.[62] SOE was truly fortunate to have found such an extraordinary young woman. Christine was the daughter of an English father and a Latvian mother. Born in London on 12 September 1920, she was educated at home in Latvia by English and French governesses, with some German acquired from a German maid. The sharp-witted polyglot spent her teenage years in England, Latvia and France before attending the Sorbonne in Paris in 1938. Her studies were interrupted by the death of her father and the lack of money to continue at university. Ever resourceful, Christine returned to the Sorbonne in January 1940.[63]

However, the fall of France later that year saw Christine interned in occupied France as a British citizen. Somehow, she escaped and made her way to Lyon in the *zone libre*. While nursing in a Lyon hospital, she met a downed airman who had lost the use of his hands and was suffering from severe burns. When the severely disabled serviceman was evacuated from France to England at the end of October 1941,

Christine accompanied him as his nurse. Initially, British authorities were suspicious that Christine might be a German agent.[64] The distrustful airman had expressed concerns over his nurse's excellent health, which, in his view, did not tally with Christine's story of being in a prison camp for some time.[65] Interrogated at the London Reception Centre, she was eventually cleared and managed to secure work at the press department of the Ministry of Information, compiling French and German translations. As it happened, an SOE officer read Christine's interrogation report, where she revealed that she spoke German, French and English, and that she had lived in France for over a year. The officer immediately placed Christine's name on a list of potential recruits for SOE's Security Section.

On 14 September 1942, Christine joined SOE on three months' probation.[66] Paid £300 a year, her experimental work was known only by a trusted few. After several months, the FIFI programme was deemed a success. SOE formally employed Christine, and she signed the Official Secrets Act on 31 January 1943.[67] She adopted the alias of Christine Collard, a French freelance journalist. Thought to be far 'too striking and foreign for English tastes' by her male superiors, Christine proved perfect for the continental European recruits.[68] She possessed a theatrical side to her nature, which enabled her to carry out her entrapment exercises with great ease. She approached the trainees by name to ascertain their reaction and response, a tactic used by the Gestapo, whose officers were well known for their ruthless extraction of names from captured SOE agents.[69]

Prue Willoughby, a secretary in SOE's Security Section, would normally contact the police to inform them of new SOE students' arrival in a chosen city or town.[70] Local police would be given agent descriptions by Prue, prompting the trainees to adopt disguises. If the police apprehended agents, the unlucky recruits had to stick to their cover story and secure release without any interference by SOE. As a final fallback, agents could call SOE to verify their identity, thereby securing their immediate release.[71] Of course, trainees had no idea that a professional predator would soon attempt to befriend them and learn their secrets. Christine received detailed physical descriptions of her targets and was told where to make her approaches. Her remit was not a licence to thrill but to determine whether the agents could survive the many operational risks and dangerous liaisons they would encounter in the field.

Christine's work reinforced how agents could trust no one, not even their own shadows. One male student, Jose Tinchant, quickly learnt this after his disastrous encounter with the agent provocateur. On Monday, 7 December 1942, Christine arrived in Liverpool with £10 in her pocket to cover expenses. She made her way to the State Café in Dale Street and kept watch for her target, alias 'Tas'. There were several students on this particular exercise, and FIFI had to ensure she got the right one. The 26-year-old and father of one had been serving in the Belgian Army and was about to divorce his wife when Germany invaded his country in May 1940. In civilian life, Tinchant had managed the Antwerp factory of the famous transatlantic cigar manufacturers José Tinchant y Gonzales & Cie. Captured by the Germans, the Belgian spent eight months in prison, and somehow managed to make his way to England via one of the escape lines. Upon arrival in England, he was interrogated at the Royal Victoria Patriotic School. Well-educated and intelligent, Tinchant provided useful information about conditions in Belgium that would aid Britain's secret services. SOE offered him the chance to fight the Germans, which he readily accepted. Tinchant showed great promise as a student, passing all the stages of SOE agent training with glowing reports. However, 'the fearless first-class man' fell prey to the striking Frenchwoman FIFI, who outsmarted the intellectual gentleman. Tinchant was subsequently deemed 'totally unsuitable' for special operations.[72]

When Christine returned to London from Liverpool, she submitted her report. In it, she described how 'Tas was seen passing through the bar of the State Café several times. It was not possible to contact him then, but as he lunched at the State, I went up to him after lunch and asked him whether he was Mr Tas. He looked surprised (and later told me his first impulse had been to reply "No") but I quickly said I had been looking forward to meeting him, to see whether I could be of any help. I sat down at his table and talked fast, explaining I was a journalist writing about War Transport and I had been asked to meet him and to be as useful as possible. I assumed a somewhat patronising tone and pretended to know everything about his job, as well as the whole training system – he later told me he was sure I was an instructor, particularly as I kept on giving him general advice.'[73]

Reflecting on her modus operandi, Christine declared: 'I am aware that there might be doubts as to whether my method of approaching him was quite fair; the fact that I knew his name obviously must have convinced him my story was true. On the other hand it is quite imaginable that an enemy agent would in a similar case have succeeded in getting the name of his victim. Besides, I understood Tas had been given a password, there was no mention of it. Indeed, it later appeared I had been talking so fast that he had not even noticed my introducing myself, so that, actually, he had been talking quite confidentially to a person whose only credentials were "I have been asked to help you . . .".'[74]

Christine spent the day with Tas, and by the evening, she had learnt practically all there was to know about him. The trainee revealed that he had almost completed his general training and would likely be sent to Belgium since he knew this country best. Tinchant explained how, in training, he specialised in sabotage and found this exercise challenging because it tested his mental fortitude. Christine extracted information about his family and how he came to England.[75] She discovered that foreign trainee agents tended to talk more than British male agents, who often refused to engage in role play, choosing to place a finger to their lips, citing the well-known wartime slogan 'careless talk costs lives'. Foreigners like Tinchant were lonely and isolated from friends and family, but this was the point of the exercise. SOE chose not to send the failed trainee to 'the Cooler', the name given to a handful of secure sites in Scotland that provided a temporary home and workplace for unsuitable candidates, who assisted in producing equipment for Britain's special forces. Tinchant went on to re-enlist in the Belgian Army, which had been his sole motivation for making his way to England in the first place.[76]

Agent FIFI's attentions were not solely directed to male trainee agents: just as many women were scrutinised. Of the thirty-nine women sent to France, SOE agent Cecily Lefort undertook her final test between 18 and 23 April 1943.[77] Christine received instructions to approach Cecily on the train from London to Sheffield, or at the luxurious nineteenth-century Royal Victoria Station Hotel in Sheffield, where the trainee would be staying. No record has survived showing whether Cecily passed the security test, but SOE superiors must have deemed her a suitable agent. Tragically, after several months of working as a courier in France, Cecily was arrested by the Gestapo and interrogated, and she gave no vital information away. In early 1945, she was murdered at Uckermark concentration camp near Ravensbrück.[78]

Francis Cammaerts, leader of the JOCKEY network, later claimed that Cecily should never have been sent to France.[79]

At a certain point, Christine's work had proved so successful that she felt confident enough to ask her superiors for a pay rise.[80] Rejecting her request, the Security Section chose to spend money on employing a small number of additional women as agents provocateurs.[81] However, the element of surprise in the Bond-like exercises had a limited shelf-life. Consequently, by the end of 1944, word had spread about Christine and her fellow FIFIs, rendering any future use pointless. Stories of a glamorous, tall, blonde honeytrap who bedded male trainee agents to extract information had spread like wildfire but were laughed off by those in the business of keeping secrets. In reality, the women were consummate professionals who never bedded any of their targets. Christine herself reported that she had made it to a hotel bedroom once, but she had spent her time hemming her target's silk scarves.[82] Some trainee male agents bragged about supposed conquests, claiming Christine had a mole on her inner thigh. They got a nasty shock when Christine attended the 'post-mortem' of trainee agents' exercises and challenged the boastful trainee to find the mole again.[83]

Christine Chilver was recognised as a 'woman of outstanding capacity' by her SOE superiors and by MI5 agent-runner Maxwell Knight, who knew only too well how to 'use' such capable women.[84] Christine was offered the chance to train as a high-grade agent herself. Despite her pleas to be sent to France, the opportunity never materialised. After the war, she worked as a translator in London and then retreated to a remote property in Gloucestershire with a close friend who had also been in SOE. She dedicated the rest of her life to animal welfare in Latvia.[85] At eighty-seven years of age, she quietly passed away in November 2007, seven years before her SOE personnel file was released into the public domain, and the world finally learnt of her significant wartime contribution. Christine had undoubtedly saved lives; without 'Special Agent FIFI', countless more could have been at risk.

Successful trainees were given a good report by FIFI and returned to London as accredited agents. While they waited for news from France that a reception committee was ready to meet them, they stayed in a converted hostel close to Wimpole Street. Phyl Mackenzie and her assistant Claire Woolf grew accustomed to SOE's latest graduates, who shut themselves away in the rooms above the clothing office. For hours, agents studied every aspect of their new identities, assigned trades and mission details. When the time for their deployment came, Phyl and Claire furnished the agents with money, clothing and accessories. They were also responsible for outfitting agents with special devices and equipment. Both women were constantly frustrated by the 'inordinately slow' delivery of weapons, but they did the best they could. Phyl regularly summoned two tailors, one from the East End and one from Savile Row, to demonstrate to Claire how buttons should be sewn onto men's suits in a particular French style.[86] All dress items needed to be exact replicas of items manufactured in France. Any mistakes risked detection, and ultimately death.

Claire would sometimes act as an escorting officer to male agents driven to premises in a mews off Queen's Gate in the Kensington museum district, where they would select items from the Station XV stores. After the depot received a direct hit during an air raid, it moved to a huge hall in the Natural History Museum. Meanwhile, female agents were usually whisked away to Golden Square in the Soho garment district, where an anonymous SOE officer, who was actually the managing director of a large textiles and tailoring firm, issued them with special equipment.[87] As agents left the flat for the final time, the two women would wish them luck by saying 'merde'. No one was to utter the words 'good luck' as it was considered bad luck.

Claire recalled how the agent Violette Szabó had visited the office one day with her young daughter:

A delightful and extremely beautiful young woman ... brought to the office her three-year-old little daughter who conjured up a picture of the prettiest doll in a toyshop. When Violette returned from her first Mission, she was wearing a beautiful dress and told me that she had bought it from one of the renowned couturiers in Paris – the first lovely dress she had ever possessed. Before she and her leader departed for their second Mission, she gave me her red cigarette lighter. I said that I would keep it against her return, but she insisted, 'No – it is a present.'[88]

Violette demonstrated huge moral and physical strength when she dropped into France, never to return. On 7 June 1944, the day after D-Day, SOE's courageous agent parachuted into southwest France, near Limoges. Sadly, after only a few days of working with local resistance groups to set up a new network, Violette was captured and sent to Ravensbrück concentration camp, where she was executed in early 1945.[89] The fearless war hero was the first woman to be awarded the George Cross for bravery. In January 1947, Violette's little daughter Tania, now five years old, was presented with her mother's medal by the King.[90]

The recruiting officer for F Section, Selwyn Jepson, believed 'women have a greater capacity for cool and lonely courage than men'.[91] Head of F Section Maurice Buckmaster's brilliant assistant, Vera Atkins, knew this only too well. SOE's rising star had joined the organisation as a secretary in 1941. The 33-year-old's talents were soon recognised, and she was promoted to intelligence officer.[92] Romanian-born Vera grew up speaking several languages, attending finishing school in Switzerland, and reading Modern Languages at the Sorbonne. She moved to London with her family during the 1930s, and, with anti-semitism rife in Europe, Vera dropped her German Jewish father's surname of Rosenberg and adopted her mother's maiden name, Atkins.[93]

In many ways, Vera was a no-nonsense type of woman, who some have suggested inspired the unflappable Miss Moneypenny character.[94] However, Vera was not the only woman in SOE who caught the attention of Ian Fleming. For instance, Britain's first female secret agent, Christine Granville, is thought to have been 'immortalised as the carelessly beautiful double agent Vesper Lynd'.[95] Yet the real lives of Vera and Christine were far more intricate and exciting than anything Fleming could have penned. Vera was the quintessential chain-smoking spymistress who spoke with a clipped, upper-class English accent, though her chilly demeanour masked the care and loyalty she actually felt towards the agents in her care. This fiercely intelligent officer worked closely with female agents who often confided in her. Vera helped the women prepare for their secret missions, ensuring that they received suitable cover stories and correct documentation. She also helped them prepare their wills, and gave 'communion', distributing a suicide pill to each woman. As the last person to see the agents before they stepped onto a Lysander aircraft at RAF Tempsford, Vera conducted the final security checks, instructing agents to turn out the contents of their pockets, in case they should be carrying with them any incriminating items.

In a rare post-war interview with the Imperial War Museum (IWM), Vera reflected on the considerable strain she felt when she saw agents off, knowing that they were going on perilous missions while she remained home. Drawing on a cigarette and exhaling through pursed lips, she added how 'some three hours later you'd be on the tarmac welcoming people who had returned. So, you turned yourself inside out and welcomed them back.'[96] Twelve of the women Vera sent into France did not return. At the war's end, she crisscrossed France and Germany searching for answers. Determined to learn of their fate, she spent several years seeking information about the missing agents whose doomed missions had led to concentration camps and execution.[97] One of the women, 29-year-old Noor Inayat Khan of Indian descent, was of particular concern to Vera. The wireless operator had been considered too frail, physically and emotionally, for special service.[98] Yet Noor demonstrated immeasurable courage when captured by the Germans. Tortured and beaten to near death at Dachau concentration camp in August 1944, she never revealed any information to her interrogators. As a camp officer placed his pistol against her head, Noor drew her final breath and uttered a single French word: 'Liberté.'[99]

10

Old Admiralty and the Citadel

On Tuesday, 18 May 1943, the fashionable society art patron Maud Russell had just completed a day's work in the Old Admiralty Building.[1] She tidied the papers on her desk and neatly rearranged the tools of her secret trade: a paper knife, scissors and a black cloth pincushion. Throwing a few scarlet sealing-wax sticks into a box, she grabbed her coat, her handbag and her gas mask, and made her way on foot to the Dorchester Hotel, just around the corner from her Mayfair flat. There she joined one of Lady Sibyl Colefax's small weekly dinner parties known as 'Ordinaries', named as such by the wealthy socialites and famous literati of the day who attended and paid a small token sum for their dinner.[2] Built of reinforced concrete, the Dorchester was a popular venue during the Blitz, when transport was almost impossible, and rations were frugal. With its impressive art deco interiors, the hotel was a suitable setting for Lady Colefax's distinguished coterie. Breaking away from friendly gossip and polite conversation, Sibyl quizzed Maud on the nature of her work: 'You doing something very secret?' To which Maud replied: 'No, ordinary stuff. Interesting, but not exciting.'[3]

In fact, her work was far from ordinary. As a woman of independent means, Maud worked six days a week as an unpaid assistant in the propaganda section of the Admiralty's Naval Intelligence Division (NID). Supervised by the former *Times* journalist Donald McLachlan, she helped produce subversive propaganda to undermine and deceive the German Navy. Maud was just one of many civilian women who worked at the very heart of naval intelligence, assisting in everything from tracking German U-boats to predicting the movement of great battleships such as the *Bismarck*.

Maud had been introduced to the secret world of intelligence by an intimate friend, the author and creator of James Bond, Ian Fleming.[4] Appointed shortly before the outbreak of war, Fleming served as personal assistant to the Director of Naval Intelligence (DNI), Admiral John Godfrey, who is credited with being the man behind 'M', the fictional head of MI6. Fluent in three languages, Commander Fleming (like his memorable character Bond) quickly assumed intelligence planning and liaison roles, making good use of his creative mind and ability to think outside the box.[5] Privy to all the Admiralty secrets, Fleming was the ultimate master of mind-blowing tricks. Many of the audacious operations he devised, oversaw and supported, working alongside several notable real-life personalities, informed the characters and storylines of his post-war storytelling. Within the dazzling world of wartime naval intelligence, Fleming found inspiration for characters such as James Bond, M and Miss Moneypenny.

In a nod to Fleming's wartime naval intelligence work, the Bond film *You Only Live Twice* (1967) features Miss Moneypenny wearing the uniform of the Women's Royal Naval Service (WRNS). While the wartime contribution of the Wrens has received attention from post-war writers,[6] civilian women generally remain faceless figures in a Lowry-like canvas.[7] Exactly who they were and what they did remains largely unknown. Women such as Joyce Cameron, loyal secretary to two wartime DNIs, or the clear-headed Margaret Stewart, the first woman to lead a naval intelligence department, or Fleming's ever-efficient assistant and only woman (and civilian) working with his crack team of secret commandos, Margaret Priestley, all deserve far greater recognition for their wartime contributions.

Within naval intelligence, information was ammunition. Women analysed, organised, managed and navigated a dangerous war of secret paperwork. They worked day and night, in every department, above and below ground, operating under continuous enemy air attack. Together with male naval officers, they extracted raw intelligence from decrypted enemy signals, captured documents and prisoner-of-war interrogations, transforming it into orders to ships at sea. This top-secret work took place within the confines of the Old Admiralty Building.

With petrol rationed and buses unreliable, Maud always enjoyed walking to work from her flat in fashionable Upper Grosvenor Street. It was a splendid twenty minutes, striding across Green Park, past Buckingham Palace, and down The Mall to Horse Guards Parade and the Old Admiralty Building. She had time to gather her thoughts and breathe fresh air, before being cooped up for twelve hours in a stuffy office where everyone smoked like a chimney. Maud loved the outdoors and, unless there was a 'flap' on at the office, she regularly spent her one day off a week at her Hampshire country estate, Mottisfont Abbey.

Crossing to the south side of The Mall, she passed the statue of Captain Cook, and successfully dodged the many cyclists, before finally making her way into the building. As she walked down a stark and echoing corridor, Maud overtook one of the indoor messenger girls, Pam Cuthbert, who was already doing her morning rounds, diligently carrying files from one office to another. Like a sailor's watches at sea, Pam's working day had begun at 0800 hrs and would not end until 2000 hrs.[8]

When Maud turned the door handle of Room 39, the office of NID 17, she was greeted by the sight of three tall west-facing windows. Through the main window, crisscrossed with tape, she could just make out the garden of 10 Downing Street on the far side of Horse Guards Parade. The window on the right offered a sombre view of the Foreign Office, St James's Park Lake and the Guards War Memorial, while through the left-hand window she had a perfect view of Horse Guards, the Treasury and Admiralty House.[9]

Room 39 was the bridge of the naval intelligence ship.[10] It was a large room with cream-painted walls and a big marble fireplace at one end. Desks were crammed in, with everyone in possession of at least one Bakelite telephone, which they all used 'incessantly and relentlessly – almost savagely'.[11] The hustle and bustle of the smoke-filled room resembled the hectic newsroom of a major newspaper.[12] Known as the 'Ideas Factory' by the men of naval intelligence, Room 39 was given quite a different name by the typists: 'the Zoo'. Working within this top-secret menagerie of Godfrey's central staff was an eclectic mix of several City stockbrokers, a schoolmaster, a journalist, an Oxford Classics don, an insurance agent, two regular naval officers, an artist, two female civilian officers, several female assistants and an army of typists.[13] With no one at the helm of this ragamuffin commune, there was little discipline and no routine.

All kinds of paper poured in and out of Room 39 – secret signals, staff papers, reports and maps.[14] 'Top Secret' dockets were filed using the prefix '00'.[15] While the brain work was intense and focus was essential, this was anything but a peaceful working environment. With people constantly coming and going, the slamming of filing cabinet drawers, the persistent ringing of telephones, and the loud clacking of many typewriters, the noise became so unbearable that Admiral Godfrey installed a green baize door between his office (Room 38) and Room 39. Ian Fleming's desk was closest to the baize door. He had earned this by loyally serving as personal assistant to Godfrey – his preferred boss of the two wartime directors. When Rear Admiral Edmund Rushbrooke replaced Godfrey as DNI in November 1942, Fleming thought him far too bureaucratic and conventional. Yet Joyce Cameron, trusted secretary to both directors, was perhaps the best placed of all those who worked for Godfrey and Rushbrooke, including Fleming, to assess the true qualities of both commanding officers.[16] Nothing happened in the world of naval intelligence that did not cross Joyce's desk, including memoranda from her counterpart in MI6 – the formidable Kathleen Pettigrew.

Joyce Cameron had joined the Admiralty as a typist in September 1931. From 1936 she worked in NID 14, which was responsible for the distribution and circulation of 'Most Secret' papers and telegrams.[17] Born in 1911, she came from a middle-class family in a naval town. Her father had worked for most of his life as a collector of water rents for the Portsmouth Water Company. After attending Chichester High School for Girls, where she learnt her secretarial skills, Joyce moved to the 'big smoke', sat the competitive exams for the Admiralty and passed.[18] She worked her way up from being a professional secretary during the war to a Higher Clerical Officer within the Admiralty's post-war Civil Establishment Branch, which dealt with the recruitment and management of civilian staff. In this capacity Joyce was responsible for posting the traitor John Vassall to the NID on his return from Moscow in the early 1950s.[19] Blackmailed into spying by the KGB, Vassall was eventually exposed, despite earlier warnings from an embassy typist which were ignored. He was sentenced to eighteen years' imprisonment.[20]

Throughout her career, Joyce preferred working as the private secretary to just one man, as she found attending meetings where people talked over each other to be a nightmare when trying to take notes.[21] Out of all the men she worked for, Joyce held Godfrey in greatest esteem. She maintained contact with him after the war, corresponding when the occasion arose, as well as taking on an administrative role on the post-war committee in charge of organising naval intelligence reunions.[22] Her professional relationship with the first wartime DNI began after an unorthodox interview. Early in 1939, Joyce had chosen to walk through Trafalgar Square to have lunch at the nearest Lyons' Corner House. As she was enjoying her genteel treat, she noticed Godfrey enter, and, to her surprise, he made his way to her table. Unbeknown to her at the time, Godfrey had personally selected Joyce to be his private secretary and had intentionally followed her that day. They chatted over lunch served by 'Nippy' waitresses in their neat caps and pinafores. Joyce asked Godfrey directly whether there would be a war. He confirmed that there was no doubt in his mind. After he departed, Joyce was left in stunned silence; she could not believe that she had dined with the new admiral in charge of her department.[23]

On 7 February 1939, the 'competent, discreet, and zealous private secretary' began work for Godfrey.[24] The senior naval taskmaster was considered by some working in Room 39 to be ruthless, relentless and remorseless, but he got results. He had a quick temper, probably due to the unknown fact that he suffered from piles and would not have them operated on until after the war had ended. On one occasion, Godfrey threw an inkpot across the room at Captain Joe Baker-Creswell, who managed to dodge out of its way successfully.[25] Ever discreet, Joyce was not perturbed by such behaviour and always treated Godfrey with great kindness.[26] Her relationship with Godfrey was built on mutual respect: respect that existed between the majority of uniformed naval officers and civilians working in the close confines of Old Admiralty.[27]

In the wartime secret world, Joyce was party to any number of classified conversations and secret matters. She organised and over-saw Godfrey's many visits to Bletchley Park, and had access to secret materials. Very much the eyes and ears of the office, she was often the first to arrive and the last to leave at the end of a working day. Every morning before 9 a.m., Joyce faithfully sat with the exacting Godfrey and reduced his notes and jottings to a series of actionable memoranda and instructions. As she left his office, Pauline Fenley would arrive with the previous evening's Special Intelligence summaries.[28] After which, the sound of a bell heralded the arrival of the admiral's next visitor.

Of the admiral's staff officers, Ian Fleming made good use of Joyce Cameron's skills. He would light one of his distinctive gold-banded cigarettes, handmade by Morland's of Grosvenor Street, and summon her over to his desk, dictating with an air of confidence and charm.[29]

Sitting with her legs crossed and her customary facial expression of a Mona Lisa half-smile, Joyce set to work with pencil and notepad.[30] A skilled stenographer, she used a range of alien symbols and short-form combinations to capture Fleming's monologue. Once he had finished dictating, Joyce would promptly leave to type up his report. Working with the grace of a concert pianist on a stand-up Imperial typewriter, she would return an hour later with a typed version. Fleming's censoring of certain paragraphs meant an edited version was taken away once more, and, from it, a good paper would finally emerge.[31] It is easy to appreciate why Joyce was credited with typing the best-looking memoranda in the Admiralty.[32]

The production of faultless paperwork was an all-important requisite of intelligence work. So much so that the pressures of having accurate and timely paperwork weighed heavily on Admiral Godfrey's shoulders. In his unpublished memoir, Godfrey commended Joyce, writing: 'To Miss Cameron I shall always feel deeply indebted. She dealt impeccably with all my personal typing and dictation and never failed to produce the right paper, however vague the clue. Moreover, she had a phenomenally good memory.'[33] When Godfrey left in 1942, she wrote: 'There must be few heads of department who had taken such an interest in the welfare of their staff as you have done.'[34]

Having signed the Official Secrets Act, Joyce remained true to her promise and revealed very little of her secret wartime work to her family. However, others have shared fleeting memories towards the end of their lives. In 2004, another secretary working in naval intelligence, Joyce Williams, wrote the following short statement on her secret wartime work:

> I was always very aware of the movement of ships due to my work and felt deeply upset when news came about the sinking of ships in the Royal Navy or Merchant Navy. I particularly remember the sinking of the *Hood* by the *Bismarck*.[35]

Real-time knowledge of such losses left a lasting imprint on the memory of those involved in reporting such events. Only three of the 1,418 crew survived when HMS 'Mighty' *Hood* was hit by the guns of Hitler's most formidable battleship on 24 May 1941.

After a high-speed chase from the Denmark Strait almost to the Bay of Biscay, the *Bismarck* was sunk four days later on 28 May

1941. Joyce Cameron did not think much of the 1960 film *Sink the Bismarck!* After taking her nephew to the cinema to see the film, she revealed to him afterwards that 'the film was not quite like how it really was'. During the search for the *Bismarck*, Joyce revealed that she had not been allowed to leave the building.[36] The role of intelligence in the pursuit, and the subsequent Atlantic campaign, gave birth to a flood of paperwork.[37] Consequently, from mid-1941 the Admiralty urgently sought additional support. By 1943 to 1944, there was a growing female representation within the 2,000-strong NID staff. Women were no longer restricted to traditional roles within the naval administration. Like Admiral 'Blinker' Hall during the First World War, Godfrey wanted only the best people. To fill the place of men serving at sea, he recruited well-educated women, who, in his opinion, possessed greater adaptability and staying power than those less educated.[38]

Godfrey's wife, Margaret Hope, a cousin of the former prime minister Neville Chamberlain, worked in the Inter-Services Topographical Department (ISTD), created in 1940 and based in Oxford. Margaret, a striking red-head, possessed a brilliant mind and would have graduated with a good Economics degree from Newnham College, Cambridge, had she not abandoned it in her second year to marry Godfrey in 1921.[39] She was not one to grumble, although her office working conditions at ISTD were far from ideal, as the only room available was the converted lavatory outside Room 39.[40] Understandably, Margaret was initially viewed with suspicion by her department head, the celebrated long-serving Royal Marines (RM) officer Sam Bassett, who suspected that Godfrey had sent her to spy on him. However, Bassett soon realised that he had been sent a real 'treasure'.[41] Consequently, Margaret quickly went from gluing photographs to serving as liaison officer with her husband's co-ordinating section.[42] One of her notable roles was working with Oxford University Press, which printed Admiralty handbooks, maps, operational orders and topographical reports.[43] ISTD went on to become one of the largest inter-service and inter-allied intelligence organisations, employing almost six thousand people, and having a major input into the planning of the war effort.[44]

Margaret was an extraordinarily calm person who believed in the ideal of a modern woman, a view shared by her husband. Godfrey believed that there should be no sex barrier in intelligence, stressing that 'a clever and knowledgeable woman will do every bit as well as a clever and knowledgeable man, and will probably be more discreet and security-conscious'.[45] In fact, Margaret was just one of many capable Admiralty women. Another, Joan Saunders, was a trained medical doctor who ran a nursing station during the Dunkirk evacuation. She was clever, highly organised and knew her mind. Her strong independence sometimes terrified those she worked with, who remembered the exotic, rather intimidating tiger-skin fur coat she wore during the cold winter months.[46]

Estranged from her first husband, Lyndall Urwick, a pioneer of British management theory, Joan lived alone in a Kensington flat. Rather fortuitously, a love affair soon blossomed with her next-door neighbour, the author Hilary St George Saunders, and the two wed in January 1940. A year later, Joan joined Ewen Montagu's 'war winning' team of Operation MINCEMEAT fame, which had relocated to a room in an adjoining corridor near Room 39.[47] Working alongside Montagu's secretary, Margery Boxall, Joan specialised in German agents' traffic and maintained indexes of enemy agents aboard neutral ships.[48] Within the Royal Navy, the content of decrypted enemy signals was always referred to as 'Special Intelligence'.[49] In July 1942, Montagu's team and that of Major Francis Lordon, RM combined to form a new Special Intelligence department, NID 12.[50] Godfrey had concluded that the Special Intelligence produced by Bletchley Park could be war-changing. Along with several other women, Joan extrapolated items of interest from Special Intelligence decrypts and transformed them into memoranda that were circulated via locked boxes within the Admiralty.

Printed on orange-coloured paper, the 'Orange Summaries' contained the cream of all Special Intelligence. Over the course of the war, 2,900 secret summaries were produced. By November 1941, the First Sea Lord, Sir Dudley Pound, was so impressed with them that he requested more. Additional female clerical staff and typists were employed to produce three to four summaries each day. To keep up with multiple productions throughout the day and ensure that the classified content remained usable, the duty editors and typists worked together on what became a 'running job', which resembled the production of the rush edition of a major newspaper.

The newly wed Pauline Fenley worked as a duty editor.[51] For a woman to take on such a role was undoubtedly a progressive step, one that had the full support of the director. Pauline proved that a woman could do the job as well as any man, if not better. Each morning, she arrived early to collect items of interest that the night watchkeeper had filtered out. Mimicking the newspaper production process, Pauline prepared a pre-press draft of the summary. Limited to just two sides of a sheet of foolscap during the final two years of the war, the draft was then passed on to one of the three carefully selected duty typists: Miss S. McCarthy, a veteran of Operation MINCEMEAT, Juliet Ponsonby and Patricia Hall, who joined the team in early 1944.[52] Together these three women covered the morning and evening summaries, banging out thick wads of orange tops and carbons on dreadful old Admiralty-issue typewriters.[53] Under tremendous pressure, they toiled for long hours with little hope of promotion. As a result of being worked harder than the male officers, a small number of women suffered mental breakdowns.[54]

Working conditions deteriorated even further when two German bombs hit the vicinity of Old Admiralty on the night of 16 to 17 April 1941. One struck the top of Admiralty Arch; another hit the Cambridge Enclosure (i.e. the Citadel).[55] As a direct result, the department was moved to Room 13, located in the basement. The rationale behind the move was that if the building received any future hits, Special Intelligence would be securely contained within the ship's belly and not scattered far and wide. On this occasion, paper proved more important than people.

Room 13 was small and stuffy, and not nearly big enough for the staff of twelve, who had to be mindful of the three load-bearing steel girders that ran across the ceiling. Later, the typists managed to escape the troglodyte existence and were relocated to the room next door, Room 14. This was an arrangement that their co-workers particularly welcomed.[56] Joan and Pauline were relieved to be able to check their Orange Summaries without the clatter of typewriters in the same room.

There was never a dull moment in the production of secret summaries. One evening, the duty sub-lieutenant attempted to retrieve a file from one of the many filing cabinets. Upon opening the drawer, he encountered one of the Admiralty's cats giving birth to the next generation of naval moggies. Without disturbing the process, the young officer managed to extract the correct file gently. For the rest of the night, every time he returned to the drawer to extract or return a file, another kitten had been welcomed into the world. By morning, six beautiful kittens had been born, yet the Orange Summary was as ever produced in time to reach the First Sea Lord before he left for the regular chiefs of staff meeting.[57]

The basement working conditions in Old Admiralty were little better than those endured by people working next door in the underground fortress known as the Citadel. Completed in 1941 on the site of a small park known as the Cambridge Enclosure, the now ivy-clad, bomb-proof bunker sits at the corner of The Mall and St James's Park, adjacent to Old Admiralty and unnoticed by the majority of tourists and other passers-by. Working across the parade ground in the subterranean War Rooms beneath Whitehall, Churchill famously described the hideous, brutalist building as 'that vast monstrosity which weighs upon the Horse Guards Parade'.[58] While this massive concrete iceberg may have been (and still remains) an eyesore to those above ground, it was a hive of industry below. Devoid of natural light and lacking fresh air, the bunker was a maze of narrow corridors and cramped rooms. As it was severely overcrowded, accommodating double the number of people it had been originally designed to hold, there was a distinct lack of cloakroom accommodation – a major challenge for any workforce, secret or not.

Isolated from the rest of the world, Gladys Mooge remembered how safe she felt in the primitive underground conditions. The twenty-year-old worked as a typist in the Citadel from 1942 to the end of the war. Living with her family in Islington, it took her half an hour to cycle to work each day. Gladys quickly became used to the fourteen-hour shifts and found the work exciting. However, at the end of her first night shift, Gladys fell victim to a heartless thief:

> We went to the restroom for a wash. I took off my engagement ring and put it on the side of the basin. When I'd finished washing, it had gone! I reported it to the Superintendent, but nothing was done. Lots of things were nicked, even the Supervisor's bright red coat.[59]

The Citadel was a microcosm of wartime life, with its occupants secretly beavering away in a miniature version of the Naval Intelligence Division. Home to the Operational Intelligence Centre (OIC), headed by Lieutenant Commander Norman 'Ned' Denning, it served as the eighth NID department (NID 8X). Over one hundred men and women worked in just one of its many subsections, each of which covered a particular sphere of activity, whether a specific geographical area or important functional role such as the Submarine Tracking Room (NID 8[S]).[60] In many ways, the OIC was more important than Room 39. If the latter was the bridge, then the OIC was the engine room of the Naval Intelligence Division.[61] Its job was to produce a snapshot of what the enemy was doing at any given moment, providing the First Sea Lord and the Commander-in-Chief of Western and Northern Approaches with an accurate picture of enemy activity and future intentions. It achieved this by sending and receiving information from all naval headquarters and naval wireless stations.

The flow of secret information began at Bletchley Park, where all enemy radio messages were decoded. The messages were then sent by teleprinter to Room 29 in the Citadel. Here 'teleprincesses' such as eighteen-year-old Beryl Embert worked around the clock, including bank holidays and Christmas.[62] The teleprints (or 'telexes') were then taken by one of the 'Secret Ladies' to be assessed by a naval officer watchkeeper, who made a quick decision on the importance of the decrypt.[63] If it was of operational significance, it would be placed in the relevant OIC subsection clip.

The OIC dealt with highly sensitive material under an open policy with Bletchley Park. Only those in the 'need-to-know' category were admitted passes.[64] Ned Denning drew heavily on talent from outside, recruiting men and women with first-class minds. What they lacked in naval training, they made up for by being hardworking, intelligent and proficient in shorthand typing.[65] However, working within such a pressure-cooker environment proved challenging for all involved. From 1943, a young archaeologist named Margaret Stewart was in charge of enemy activity from the River Elbe to the Spanish border. She had several heated exchanges with Denning over staff suffering from physical and mental exhaustion. He remained adamant that high-pressure situations yielded a heightened sense of intuition and greater clarity of thought. To Denning's frustration, sickness among the female staff was a big problem, with many suffering from anaemia brought on by wartime rationing.[66] As a direct result, some women left and did not return, proving Margaret's point.

Others grew tired of being sick and stressed, such as Gwen Clarke, who worked as a clerical officer under Denning. Gwen had joined naval intelligence in February 1938, but several years of suffering from catarrh and being plagued by flies, which thrived in the warm conditions experienced in the Citadel, finally took their toll. In August 1943, she left the OIC and became a radio mechanic in the WRNS. Perhaps it was the disconcerting sight of the grey and exhausted First Sea Lord, Sir Dudley Pound, walking past her office in his dressing gown that finally gave her the necessary push.[67]

With sleeping accommodation limited to the top brass, even Ned Denning had to resort to sleeping under his table during the hunting of the *Bismarck*. Margaret Stewart managed to find a 'hot bunk' and catch a few hours' sleep before returning to her desk and facing another flood of enemy signals. By 1943, the OIC had an insatiable appetite for intelligence production, with the most important source being decrypts of enemy wireless traffic. The Bletchley Park code-breakers had struggled to break the Atlantic U-boat Enigma key, yet by December 1942 they had successfully cracked it and were able to read scores of enemy naval messages.

Using these messages, Margaret plotted the movements of the German Navy and gave advance warning where necessary. As the first female section head, she advised and made recommendations, but she did not have the power to issue any operational orders. Predictably, a small number of naval officers disliked taking orders from a woman. On one occasion, Margaret phoned Portsmouth and forecast an enemy attack, which was subsequently intercepted by the Royal Navy with enemy losses. However, the naval officer on the other end of the scrambler phone remained unconvinced of Margaret's credentials and expressed this with several powerful expletives. After the war, she happened across him at a cocktail party, after which the unfortunate officer quickly revised his opinion of her.[68]

Born in 1907 in Trivandrum (Thiruvananthapuram), India, Margaret Stewart spent her early years in the remote Scottish Borders village of Eskdalemuir, where her father, Dr Alexander Crichton Mitchell, was the director of the local observatory.[69] From the age of five, she attended St George's High School for Girls in Edinburgh. Ahead of its time, the school adopted a liberal policy of female empowerment that nurtured a sense of sisterhood. Margaret was encouraged to excel in all areas, with the pressure of failure or losing removed. Her time in this pioneering school left a lasting impression on her outlook in life.

During the interwar years, she established her career and reputation as a renowned archaeologist, before marrying a Perth solicitor,

John Stewart, in 1936. Margaret was drawn to the early pre-history of Scotland. During her long and distinguished professional career, she was responsible for excavating many of the artefacts dug up near the imposing Croft Moraig stone circle near Aberfeldy. After the strain of an emotional crisis in 1939, Margaret travelled from Scotland to London seeking war work. She was initially sent to the Admiralty sorting department, where documents and files were processed, but she was later summoned to the Citadel for a role in the OIC.[70]

Confused by naval jargon and the use of acronyms, Margaret described her introduction to the OIC as a 'baptism by fire'. She arrived at a particularly low point. In early 1942, three major German warships (the *Gneisenau*, *Scharnhorst* and *Prinz Eugen*) had all made their way successfully through the English Channel to Germany. Everyone in the OIC was despondent. However, Margaret quickly threw herself into her work. She soon realised that she was on a very different footing from the 'teleprincesses' and 'Secret Ladies': 'It was quickly borne in on me that I had the qualities of mind and brain which were peculiar to me as a woman and which I did not share with the men who had equal status.'[71] As the U-boat war intensified, Margaret was given increased responsibility. Ena Shiers was brought in to assist her, allowing her more time to devote her attention to intelligence assessment. Later in life, Margaret reflected on the similarities of her intelligence work and her archaeological excavations, emphasising 'the laborious bringing together of detailed evidence, its arrangement, its interpretation, and its assessment'.[72]

Margaret Stewart summed up her pioneering experience of the war and what it meant for her as a woman in the following words:

> It was a unique experience and without boasting it was a unique experience for a woman and I was very lucky to have it come my way. For me personally it was total fulfilment. Physically and mentally I was stretched to the limit and one cannot ask for more than that. Of course it had emotional overtones and there were times when one felt hurt, wrongly blamed, and asked to do more than was within one's capacity. But the reward was immense. It proved that a woman could justify responsibility in what was not her normal sphere of activity.[73]

Guendolyn Boyle witnessed first-hand the complex work that Margaret and her team carried out. While running multiple errands, she sometimes found herself in Margaret's room, where she silently observed the changing symbols on a wall chart. As the wife of a serving naval captain, Guendolyn was acutely aware of the consequences of making a mistake – ships would be sunk, and lives would be lost. For two years, Guendolyn worked as Commander Rodger Winn's secretary in the Submarine Tracking Room. She was just one of many wives, sisters, daughters and nieces of serving naval personnel or intelligence officers who were recruited on the basis of being trustworthy.

Guendolyn navigated her newfound secret work alongside being a mother to two small children, with a third born during the war in 1944. Her work in naval intelligence offered a taste of temporary empowerment while fulfilling a patriotic duty. Born in the same year as Margaret Stewart, she spent much of her childhood sailing on the Norfolk Broads and playing croquet. With aspirations to become an actress, she trained at the Royal Academy of Dramatic Art (RADA), where she became good friends with Anthony Quayle, who would go on to serve with SOE as a liaison officer in Albania and would after the war perform many starring roles on stage, screen and television, leading to a knighthood in 1985.[74]

In 1936, Guendolyn married Lieutenant Commander Richard Courtenay Boyle, who would later command one of the destroyers sent to France as part of the naval evacuation of Dunkirk. Like so many other vessels during the rescue of the British Expeditionary Force (BEF) from northern France, Boyle's ship was bombed and sunk, along with the ship on which he was subsequently being evacuated. Both times Boyle ended up in the water, but he eventually made it home. He spent several months working alongside his wife in the Submarine Tracking Room before returning to sea in 1942.[75]

After completing her errands, Guendolyn returned to NID 8(S) and entered the top-secret room. Her boss, the brilliant peacetime barrister and judge Rodger Winn, would sit with his chin on his hand as he reviewed the large table in the centre of the room. Fluorescent lighting flooded the vast map of the North Atlantic stretched out on the oversized snooker table. A number of officers and civilians were busy plotting U-boat movements and measuring distances. Anything to do with U-boat activity was recorded, enabling Winn and his team to build up a picture of enemy submarines' movements and actions.

Guendolyn carried out a range of tasks, assisting the team of twelve in making sense of the barrage of information that arrived in the room on an hourly basis. She was well informed about what was happening at any given time – from the arrival of convoys to escort vessels making contact with U-boats. In many ways, it was the decisive convoy battles of January to May 1943 that provided Winn and his team with crucial insights into U-boat activity in the Atlantic. Yet the only way they could cope with this 'working fiction', where lives would sometimes be lost, was to view their work as a vast game of chess. On one occasion, this proved impossible.

In early 1943, Guendolyn's husband had assumed command of the destroyer HMS *Havelock*. With the help of three corvettes, HMS *Havelock* was escorting a convoy of nine oil tankers from Trinidad to the Mediterranean to supply Allied forces in North Africa. On 3 January, a U-boat spotted the convoy. Admiral Karl Dönitz lost no time in ordering a wolf pack of fourteen U-boats to attack. Over several weeks, Winn and his team tracked the wolf pack hunting the convoy. The situation was dire. Outmatched and outgunned, the small escort lacked adequate radar and radio direction finding gear.

During one encounter, a U-boat openly trailed the convoy on the surface during the day. As tensions grew among the crew of the *Havelock*, one officer ordered his signalman to flash a blinking light Morse code signal in plain English to the shadowing U-boat: 'Why don't you go away?'

The U-boat captain calmly replied, 'Sorry, we have our orders.'

The end result was a massacre. One by one the merchantmen were picked off by the hungry wolves. Only two of the nine tankers would survive. Ninety-seven officers and crew lost their lives.[76]

This gruelling ordeal was witnessed from beginning to end by Commander Boyle's wife, Guendolyn, who had watched every movement, sighting and sinking being plotted while working in the Submarine Tracking Room. One cannot imagine the complex mix of emotions she felt upon leaving the Citadel each day, unsure as to what she would return to the following morning: anxiety, worry, fear and finally relief when she received news that her husband had survived.

Like so many Admiralty women, Guendolyn experienced the full duality of war. For those working in the secret back rooms of naval intelligence, the war was both exhilarating and terrifying at the same time. The many air raids in London did nothing to alleviate their anxiety, yet somehow these women managed to endure such moments of crisis and to continue their clandestine work.

The typist Gladys McPhee was perhaps the most daring during an air raid, choosing a seat on the Citadel rooftop.[77] At the same time, others, such as the trio of Barbara Brice, Gwen Clarke and Doris Salmon, sought refuge in a luxury suite at the Savoy, paid for by a generous and wealthy naval officer working in the OIC. Unable to travel home during the Blitz, the three women took advantage of the very tempting offer to stay at a hotel that was usually beyond their reach. Writing in early 1976, Doris Salmon recalled their memorable stay in vivid detail:

> We used to go to Lyons' Corner House on our way there and buy our food. We could not possibly afford a meal at the Savoy, so we had a picnic in our beautiful sitting room. We never slept upstairs but in cubicles in the basement with very comfortable mattresses. The hotel was bombed one night while we were there. We hobnobbed with some very interesting people in the Lounge and some of the girls found partners and danced to the Savoy Band.[78]

The constant threat of air raids and the impending foreknowledge of a V1 doodlebug attack in June 1944 proved too much for some women. Eventually, Margaret Stewart's nerves gave up, and she returned home to Scotland on sick leave. Her boss, Ned Denning, had a devil of a time getting her back to work, which 'was not through lack of will power on her part'.[79]

Margaret greatly admired her boss and the kindness he had shown her, especially in the weeks building up to D-Day, when they were flooded with decrypted enemy messages. For several years, she had been preparing for this 'grand finale'. When it did come, and the first intimations on the signal traffic showed what a complete surprise it had all been, it was a sort of anticlimax: 'I don't know what we expected, but somehow it didn't measure up.'[80] Such disappointment was not universal.

For another Margaret, the opposite was the case: her work grew exponentially after the Normandy landings. Margaret Priestley had joined NID 30 in early 1944.[81] She was the only woman and civilian in the newly formed Coordination of Requirements department, which had been established in January of that year. Its main purpose was to assist Fleming's secret commando unit – 30 RM Commando (known from December 1943 onwards as 30 Assault Unit [30 AU]) – to seize enemy naval documents, equipment and weapons. Thought by some to be Fleming's greatest contribution to the war, with several of its men suggested as being the real-life inspiration for James Bond, the unit's intelligence-gathering commandos had undoubtedly already proven their value while rummaging around North Africa and Italy in search of enemy secrets.

Within Room 39, the forthcoming invasion of Normandy was a top priority. Fleming had personally interviewed Margaret Priestley for her post after she had been headhunted earlier by the Department of Naval Operational Research,[82] where she had worked as an assistant principal under the distinguished physicist Professor Patrick Blackett, a former career naval officer who would go on to win the Nobel Prize three years after the war.[83] As a history graduate of Newnham College, Cambridge, Margaret was recruited to this operational research role after a brief stint working in Hut 6 at Bletchley Park.[84] As a member of Blackett's department, often known as 'Blackett's Circus', she was tasked with the unique assignment of creating narrative accounts to complement the scientific data produced by the team of scientists and mathematicians.

Margaret played a vital role in the running and administration of Fleming's secret commandos, serving as their main link with the Admiralty. At one point, she was even singlehandedly responsible for the running of 'head office'. Yet she is rarely mentioned in any books on 30 AU or any biographies of Ian Fleming.[85] This is perhaps because she was extremely secretive and all too aware of the significance of her association with Fleming. Deeply conscious of a connection being made between her and the fictional Miss Moneypenny, she refused to be named in any post-war works and ensured that any reference to her real wartime role was instantly removed.[86]

Known as 'Peggy' to close friends and relatives, Margaret told her family very little about her secret war work other than that her boss had been Ian Fleming, leading her husband to occasionally joke that she was the real Miss Moneypenny. The truth is that Margaret may well have inspired some of the female characters that feature in Fleming's books. For instance, in his final short story *Octopussy* (written in 1962, two years before his death), a charming blonde Wren called 'Mary Parnell' features on the female staff of the 'Miscellaneous Objectives Bureau', otherwise referred to as 'MOB Force'. Working under a similar remit to that of 30 AU, 'MOB Force' was charged with locating secret information and reporting on concealed weapons dumps. The fictional Mary Parnell bears a striking resemblance to the petite and blonde Margaret Priestley. Both her initials and those of Moneypenny seem to be a homage to Fleming's brilliant and beautiful real-life assistant.

Margaret Priestley was an original blue stocking. Born in 1920, she came from humble beginnings. She grew up in the Lincolnshire coastal town of Cleethorpes, where her father worked as a butcher. Exceptionally clever as a child, Margaret gained a scholarship to Cleethorpes Secondary School for Girls. Astonishingly, in the sixth form, she won five higher-education scholarships in one year, including a major scholarship to study History at Newnham, which she entered in 1939.

Certain family members proved to be great sources of influence and support to Margaret. Her grandfather, a tradesman, was an enthusiastic reader and a skilled musician. Margaret was taught to play the violin as a child by her mother and would spend family evenings accompanying her grandfather as he played the flute.[87] One of her aunts, who had won a scholarship to study at Girton College, Cambridge, in 1914, also provided great encouragement. Margaret's headmistress too was a Newnham graduate and fully supported her university application. Surrounded and supported by such strong, like-minded women, Margaret eventually graduated with first-class honours. She later followed in the footsteps of other notable Newnham women who worked in British intelligence during the war, such as Joan Clark, the only female codebreaker to work alongside Alan Turing.

When she reached the Admiralty, Margaret quickly adjusted to her new naval intelligence role, though she found everything 'strange and confusing' at first.[88] However, with guidance from a 30 AU officer, Lieutenant Commander Robert Harling, she soon mastered the requirements of the job. Housed in the Citadel, Room 30 was extremely small and doubled as the night duty officer's bedroom. It was windowless and air-conditioned, and just about big enough to squeeze in two tables with telephones and a scrambler, several chairs, and two cupboards. The DNI used one cabinet for his spare uniform. The other was used to store special items brought back by officers from France, such as twelve Camembert cheeses. One can only imagine the reaction of the night duty officer to the pungent smell of warming cheese that filled the room as he bedded down for the night.

Margaret was kept busy with many different tasks, which ranged from increasing administrative efficiency by implementing a new filing system, to dealing with the many requests made by 30 AU officers. Quiet moments spent sitting at her typewriter in her underground chamber were constantly interrupted by the harsh ringing of the telephone. On one occasion, she picked up the receiver, and a voice alerted her to the arrival of a young marine at the entrance to the Citadel.

Marine Ron Guy had been ordered to deliver a sealed brown envelope to no one other than Commander Fleming. Without a special pass, he quickly realised he was going nowhere. After the guards confronting him had telephoned Margaret, he soon heard the sound of approaching heels on a hard floor. A smartly dressed woman with piercing blue eyes appeared carrying an armful of files. After signing the young man in, Margaret informed Guy of the long wait he had ahead of him.

Having made their way to Room 30, Margaret directed Guy to the small camp bed in the corner of the office and resumed her typing. A few minutes later, the telephone rang again, and she marched off to collect a newly arrived 30 AU officer, whom she instructed to sit and wait on the bed next to the marine. Margaret returned to her typing, and there the two men sat surrounded by mountains of files piled high. They spent considerable time silently studying the many maps and aerial-reconnaissance photographs that adorned the walls.

After completing her typing and answering yet another telephone call, Margaret directed the men to follow her. Walking in single-file formation, they made their way through the warren of Citadel and Old Admiralty corridors to Room 39. At the sound of Margaret's knocking, Ian Fleming appeared and smiled warmly.

'Ah, Miss Priestley, lovely to see you.'

'Commander Fleming, this is—' But Margaret did not have time to finish.

Such were the privileges of commissioned rank that the officer was instantly admitted by Fleming, whereas the poor young marine was forced to languish many hours in the corridor before delivering his vital letter ... much later that evening.[89]

The arrival of khaki-clad figures usually signalled a burst of activity. As D-Day approached, Margaret got to know all the officers she worked with, such as Lieutenant Commander Patrick Dalzel-Job, who described Room 30 as a 'silly little jack-in-office at Admiralty'.[90]

Margaret described the overcrowded office, with standing room only, as resembling the cabin scene from the Marx Brothers' film *A Night at the Opera*. The officers' excessive smoking quickly filled the claustrophobic room with smoke. In an age when everyone thought it normal to flick cigarette ash on the floor, whether carpeted or not, the poor night duty officer complained bitterly about the accumulation of such dusty detritus. Margaret had the perfect solution to this problem: 'There was a tiny hole in the floor into which I swept the ash before going home! Where it finally ended up remained a mystery.'[91]

Working alongside Dalzel-Job and others in the run-up to D-Day, Margaret busily collated 'all available information as to where the enemy's secret documents or installations were thought to be in France and Germany'.[92] Dalzel-Job revealed in his post-war memoir how the men of 30 AU knew almost everything about the plans for the D-Day landings, except for the date and precise landing locations. Such information was classified one stage higher than 'Top Secret' as BIGOT (British Invasion of German Occupied Territory). Margaret, however, worked with the highest level of security clearance and was therefore trusted with one of history's biggest secrets.

On D-Day itself, Tuesday, 6 June 1944, Room 39 had been locked for part of the morning. Maud Russell had taken advantage of this unusual occurrence to get a neck massage. The masseuse informed her at 0940 hrs that the invasion had been announced at 0800 hrs. Aware of the impending attack but not privy to the date, Maud immediately switched on the radio and listened to the broadcast, saying later, 'I felt deeply moved and very conscious of the great drama.'[93]

The men of 30 AU formed only a small part of the Normandy landings – the greatest amphibious operation in history. With no spectacular finds made by 30 AU in Normandy beyond a set of wheels from a Luftwaffe Enigma machine that was on their target wish list, Fleming scheduled a meeting to discuss priority targets for the commandos. The meeting was attended by several senior naval and military officers. Margaret took the minutes and recollected how at the end of the meeting Fleming had asked each officer if they wished to make any further comments. He then turned towards Margaret and made a point of soliciting her valued input with an unwavering and egalitarian: 'Miss Priestley?'

Margaret was later sent on a fact-finding mission, visiting other departments in the Admiralty:

> I particularly recall one occasion, after 'D Day', when targets had to
> be marked on a map of Paris as a 'rush job'. Lieutenant Commander
> Herbert Ward, who was then attached to NID 30, and I worked on
> it all day, finishing late at night. I arrived back at my digs in Ealing
> after 10 p.m.

The high-pressure working environment frequently yielded such long
days and even longer nights. Margaret Priestley responded to periods
of intense activity accordingly, working a seven-day week if necessary.
For most of her life, Margaret was subject to frequent and crippling
migraine attacks, which tended to strike when periods of stress were
ending.[94] As a result, she was granted brief respite on two occasions
when she visited Littlehampton, the headquarters of 30 AU.

The sleepy seaside town was a centre of covert operations. Allied
troops used its sand and shingle beach for mock D-Day landings, and
30 AU established its command centre at the Marine Hotel, with its
Royal Marines undertaking punishing commando training courses in
the surrounding countryside. Margaret remembered visiting the hotel
but revealed nothing more. After the war, she learnt of the astonishing
D-Day escapade of the troop mascot, a delightful fox terrier named Judy.
One of the men had inherited Judy from his landlady in Littlehampton.
Somehow, Judy made it to Utah Beach, 'digging her own slit trench
alongside [her owner] before the antipersonnel bombs were dropped on
[their] positions on the first night on French soil'.[95] However, the terrier
was soon seduced by a German police dog and gave birth to a number
of pups while the commandos were en route to Paris.

After the liberation of France, 'preparations were made for the
onslaught on intelligence targets in Germany'.[96] By November 1944,
the overall strength of 30 AU had increased to 310 officers and
men.[97] The tiny office of Room 30 could no longer accommodate
the increased numbers of officers and was relocated to a bigger room
above ground. Lieutenant Commander James Fawcett and two Wrens
joined Margaret. Together, they worked for months on compiling lists
of priority targets known as 'Black Books'. The successful seizure of
the German naval archive at Tambach in April 1945 kept Margaret
busy.[98] With the officers away for more extended periods, she took
many phone calls from them in Germany. The lines were terrible, and
Margaret constantly had to shout down the phone to make herself
heard. This resulted in a temporary loss of voice.[99]

Margaret's final assignment was 'to write a historical account of 30 AU using Admiralty files'.[100] As a trained historian, she did more than 'assist' Lieutenant Commander Trevor James 'Jim' Glanville, who is usually credited with being the author. She certainly did far more than merely type the 250-page history. By rights, Margaret Priestley should be fully acknowledged as at least a co-author of the unit history. Instead, her contribution was recast to suit the discrimination and gender bias of the time.

In the summer of 1945, Margaret was released from her duties, thus ending 'a challenging and fascinating job'.[101] Her work in Room 30 stimulated an interest in administrative history; consequently, in the autumn of 1945, she was awarded a doctoral scholarship to St Hugh's College, Oxford. She 'had a strong sense of duty, and in anything she set her hand to she would endeavour to achieve the highest standards'.[102] In April 1993, at the age of seventy-three, Margaret Priestley attended her first 30 AU reunion. After decades of silence and prompted by the 'happy occasion' of connecting with old wartime colleagues, she finally wrote a five-page account detailing her time in naval intelligence. This personal memoir, saved for posterity at the Imperial War Museum, serves as the only record of the key role Margaret played in the running of the unit.

Margaret was one of several women who worked with Ian Fleming in naval intelligence and recorded their wartime memories. The widowed socialite and long-time friend of Fleming, Maud Russell, preserved her contribution to the war in her diary. Fleming had been responsible for getting her a job in the Admiralty and the two would meet outside work for dinners at the Dorchester and the Savoy. Maud's war work provided her with a sense of purpose, but this came to an end on Thursday, 5 July 1945, when she handed in her two security passes at Old Admiralty and signed a declaration that she would never divulge in any form what she had learnt during her time there. Maud took one final nostalgic look at Room 39 and had a brief parting chat with Fleming. The two would remain close friends until Fleming's marriage to Ann Charteris in 1952. Maud confessed in her diary how difficult her departure was from the secret world of intelligence: 'I felt a pang at leaving as I loved working there.'[103]

However, far from closing the door on NID 17 with finality, Maud Russell and all the other able, versatile, gifted women who worked at Old Admiralty and the Citadel during the Second World War were,

without ever realising it perhaps, true pathfinders for subsequent
generations of young women who would carve out careers in post-
war intelligence, whether naval or not. They understood how to open
doors rather than close them.

Kathleen Pettigrew as a young girl with her cousin Onslow – later known as Ken – Warner, 1910.
(Courtesy of the Warner family)

Agnes Blake, MI6's first female agent (*third from the left*) with the Garraway family at their home in Finsbury Park, London, 1906. (Courtesy of Jackie Yates)

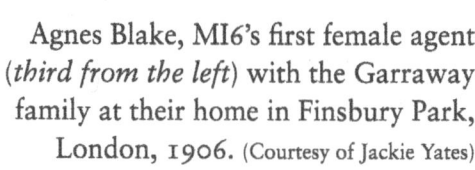

Dorothy Westmacott, the first woman employed by MI5 in 1911.
(Courtesy of Philip Strong)

Dorothy Dimmock, MI5 Registry clerk during the First World War.
(Courtesy of Felicia Line)

FRITZ ON THE RACK.
With Best Wishes for 1917 from New Scotland Yard.

Scotland Yard New Year's Card, 1917, depicting Basil Thomson sat behind his desk questioning 'Fritz', a suspected German agent. A young stenographer can be seen taking notes during the interview.
(Courtesy of the Military Intelligence Museum)

George Court, The Strand, London. Kathleen Pettigrew and her family lived in a small flat in the narrow alleyway until 1920.

(Courtesy of the Stapleton Collection / Bridgeman Images)

MI5 H Branch Staff (secretariat, Registry and administration) on the rooftop of Waterloo House, No. 16 Charles Street, Haymarket, 1918.

(Courtesy of Dr Nicholas Hiley)

Winnie Spink, Petrograd, 1916.

(Courtesy of Sarah Clark)

Dorothy Henslowe, MI6 secretary during the First World War and 1920s.

(Courtesy of Dr Emma Alexander)

The Lunn Sisters, Russia, 1910. Women seated left to right: Peggy, Helen and Lucy Lunn. Edith Lunn is seated third from the right. (Courtesy of Prof. Henry Rothstein)

Olga Gray, MI5 agent.
(Courtesy of the Gray family)

Dorothy McCarthy, MI6 messenger who worked at Bletchley Park and London headquarters.
(Courtesy of Jeani Tingle)

Eileen McCarthy, veteran MI6 teleprinter operator at Bletchley Park, who returned in December 2001 and visited the MI6 radio station housed in the mansion attic.
(Courtesy of Julie Salmon)

Dorothy Furse *c.*1949. SOE Personnel Officer for Women's Staff and cousin of Aileen Philby, wife of Soviet penetration agent Kim Philby.
(Courtesy of Nicholas Furse)

Ian Fleming at work in his home, Goldeneye, in Jamaica, February 1962.
(Courtesy of Masheter Movie Archive / Alamy)

Joyce Cameron with Edmund Rushbrooke, Director of Naval Intelligence, in his office at the Admiralty, 3 February 1944.
(Courtesy of Alamy)

Margaret Priestley, personal assistant in Ian Fleming's secret naval commando unit, 30 Assault Unit (30 AU).
(Courtesy of the Hunt family)

Jane Sissmore (later Archer) qualified as a barrister in 1924 while working at MI5. (Courtesy of Michael Curtis)

Mary Sherer, Rome,
c.1950s.
(Courtesy of Marcus Mussa)

Phyllis Mackenzie at the Ladies'
International Fencing Tournament,
Florence, Italy, May 1931.
(Courtesy of the Mackenzie family)

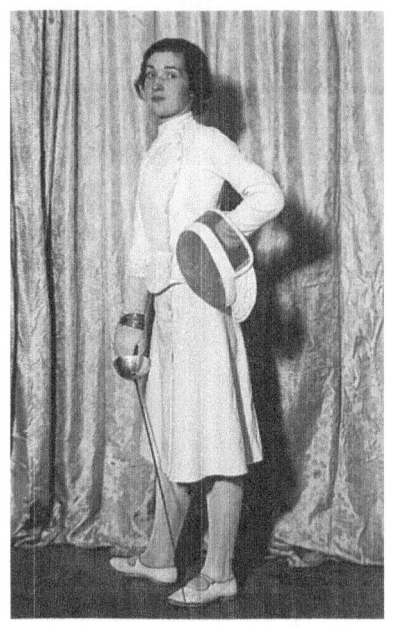

Ena Molesworth (*left*) and
Rita Winsor (*right*), London,
c.1950s. (Courtesy of the author)

Joan Bright, Special Information Centre, War Cabinet Rooms, London, c.1940–45.
(Courtesy of Richard Astley)

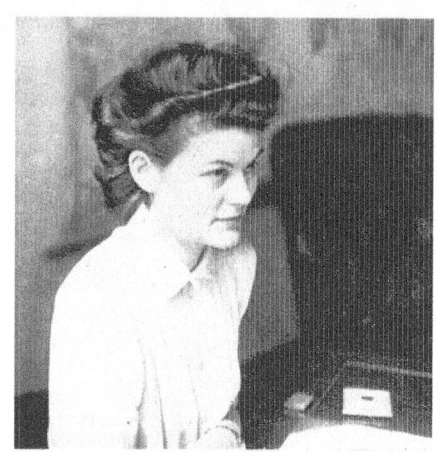

Teddy Dunlop with her husband, Harry, in Tangier, Morocco, 1937.
(Courtesy of Judy Shephard)

Milicent Bagot standing outside the gates of Buckingham Palace with her CBE, 1969.
(Courtesy of the Bagot family)

Stella Rimington, first female Director General of MI5, sitting at her desk, 16 July 1993.
(Courtesy of PA Images / Alamy)

A studio photograph of the woman believed to be Kathleen Pettigrew, 1950s.
(Courtesy of Dr Richard Warner)

11

MI5 Trailblazers

The joyous sound of a church organ signalled that a wedding was at hand. On 2 September 1939, the day before war broke out, MI5's first female officer, Jane Sissmore, became Jane Archer. Ten years her senior, Wing Commander Joe Archer served as the liaison officer between the Royal Air Force and MI5. The decorated officer was a quiet, practical man who loved the outdoors, a perfect match for the outspoken sport-loving Jane.[1] As the bride and groom emerged from the Sissmore family church of St Peter's in Ealing, they were met with a light rain shower. The wedding party was small, as the happy couple had planned to marry in October, but had decided to push the date forward due to the escalating situation in Europe.[2] It was a wise decision, as the following day the country mobilised for war. A forty-year-old Jane and her new husband spent their first few weeks of marriage living at the Carnarvon Hotel in Ealing.[3] Jane had previously lived with her parents and, until the newlyweds could find suitable accommodation, the hotel served as their temporary first home.

On becoming Mrs Archer, Jane had also taken on the role of stepmother to Joe's two grown children by his first wife, Esther, who had passed away in 1930. Jane had broken many formidable barriers in her MI5 career, but it was not a job that lent itself well to marital responsibilities. The undomesticated Jane still had to adjust to being a wife. As with everything she put her hand to, she succeeded. By now, the accomplished MI5 officer had tapped at the glass ceiling; yet she would fail in her subsequent efforts to progress further. The following year, Jane would learn first-hand how quickly women officers could fall when she happened to voice her opinion about a colleague's lack of professional ability. She was not a man speaking to another man, and her actions were perceived as those of a woman berating and belittling a male officer. Moreover, Jane did not quite meet the idealised contemporary stereotype of femininity. She was brash, confident and direct. To her detriment, Jane wrongly considered herself the equal of male officers. The repercussions of her lack of deference to male senior personnel would be felt throughout the organisation for the rest of the war. MI5's first female officer was a modern woman, but MI5 was far from becoming a leader in gender equality, and was simply not ready to accept her fully in an executive role.

In 1939, the Security Service expanded its numbers as it had in 1914. At the start of the Second World War, 133 women were employed in the Registry or in secretarial roles. By 1943, the female workforce had reached 939 compared to 332 male officers. Women effectively outnumbered men three to one.[4] But numbers can be deceptive. There was no revolutionary transformation in the role of women in MI5. Instead, the expanded wartime workforce magnified the lack of interest in championing change, reinforcing entrenched biases towards women that saw the majority relegated to backroom roles officially defined as clerical. During the war, the women of MI5 found themselves working from the cells of Wormwood Scrubs prison. Concerns had been raised that the Thames House MI5 headquarters was too well known to enemy agents. So, the decision was taken to move to 'The Scrubs'. At the end of August 1939, a fleet of prison vans arrived early one morning to collect prisoners. The following day, many more vans arrived, but this time they were filled with MI5 staff carrying top-secret files. The first women to arrive were told to stay away from the few remaining prisoners. Soundproof cells were transformed into offices, but left without telephones or inside door handles, some staff found themselves locked in for hours before it was realised that they were missing.[5]

Milicent Bagot, who had recently joined from Special Branch, was not impressed with the new surroundings. She complained that the dreary buildings 'appeared never to have been ventilated since their erection and their smell was appalling'.[6] Others, like Mary Grepe, found positives. When it came to the secretary's turn for night duty, Mary found the prison somewhat 'spooky', but as she got to sleep in the prison hospital, she took advantage of having 'the most wonderful hot bath' every night.[7] MI5 secretarial staff quickly adapted to wartime restrictions, such as conserving paper by recycling memos and reports that had only been typed on one side. The typists also accommodated such changes as setting their typewriters to single-spacing for the duration of the war.[8] One change that the women did not foresee was the radical removal of the restriction on having to wear dresses or skirts to work. After the prison move, it was soon discovered that female staff were unable to use the open-grating staircases. For the first time ever, MI5 women were to be seen wearing less revealing slacks.[9]

MI5 moved its headquarters once again in 1940, but this time to the grand stately home of Blenheim Palace, near Oxford. Barbara Price-Smith recalled her first impressions during a post-war interview, when she described how she came through the gate of the great mansion, and was transformed into Alice in Wonderland. As one of the first women to arrive, she enjoyed a lavish bedroom and bathroom with gold taps, while those who arrived later had to make do in makeshift huts on the grounds. In the main house, the Long Library was transformed into the typing pool, and the Great Hall was filled with endless rows of Registry filing cabinets. Barbara reflected how there was a cross-section of society who did not mix very often. Rather bitingly, the shorthand-typist described the Registry girls as tall, beautiful and statuesque, but with very little brain. Tongue-in-cheek, she added 'they knew their alphabet so they could be filing clerks in the Registry'.[10]

Unbeknown to wartime recruits, those who worked in the Registry before 1939 were held in high regard, as officers depended on the women's specialist knowledge and welcomed the personal service that they were rendered. After the original Director General, Vernon Kell, was sacked on 10 June 1940, the new Acting Director General, Jasper Harker, set about reorganising the service, modernising its antiquated filing system, and overhauling the Registry's ways of working. The changes saw Registry staff consigned to much simpler tasks such as filing and indexing.[11] It seemed as if women were no longer trusted to carry out specialist work.[12] Ironically, the downgrading of women's work in the Registry ensured far greater efficiency when it came to coping with greater volumes of information generated throughout the war.

Jane Archer possessed an intricate knowledge and understanding of the Registry's importance in supporting counterespionage work. After the First World War, she had herself managed the Registry, providing her with a useful window into how information was managed within MI5. She also learnt how to remain impervious to snippy lines of division within the female staff. While she never wore slacks, Jane adopted a masculine style of dress, favouring tweed suits and a tie, which served as a source of empowerment for a lone woman working alongside men with military rank.[13] In reality, Jane's appearance was very much a secondary concern, as her work came first.[14] Wearing round spectacles when needed, she tied her hair back in a simple low bun. While there was no application of makeup, Jane did devote ten minutes of each day to brushing her hair with soft-bristle ivory brushes that left her hair shiny and smooth. Unfortunately perhaps, her clothes smelt of cigarettes from years of chain-smoking, leaving her with a smoker's raspy voice, which did not, however, detract from her plummy upper-class accent and endearing lopsided smile.[15]

The MI5 trailblazer did not suffer fools kindly. Jane was tough, loud and famously blunt.[16] However, there was a softer side to the woman who had achieved so much. Her grandchildren remember her fondly as 'Granny Jane'. They looked forward to her Christmas boxes packed with presents that she had lovingly collected throughout the year, but they recognised that Jane was not 'a typical grandmother'.[17] The veteran intelligence officer was anything but domesticated. Jane would cook for her stepdaughter and young family when they visited her and Joe at Cornhill Cottage, a delightful chocolate-box thatched cottage in Melbury Abbas in Dorset. The grandchildren would hide behind the kitchen door, watching Jane battle with a variety of saucepans while skilfully balancing a cigarette on her lip. The children would wait patiently to see the ash grow so long that it eventually dropped off into a cooking pot.[18] Jane eventually gave up smoking ten years before her death in 1982.[19] The noxious habit had nevertheless sustained a career that had entailed high levels of stress and very long hours. After a lifetime of sniffing out Soviet agents, Jane was a walking history book of secrets. While she never disclosed anything of note to her family, it was known that she had worked with Kim Philby in MI6. When asked about him, Jane would remark in her usual brash manner, 'the way that man speaks you would think he was a communist'.[20]

Professionally, the Soviet specialist was a formidable force. With a ruthless forensic mind, Jane proved to be one of MI5's most skilled officers. To catch a spy, she would analyse every anomalous scrap of information, earnestly trying to identify characteristics and patterns of behaviour. It was slow work, as the enemy tried its best to mislead and confuse. Jane had only been married three days when news arrived from Washington that the Foreign Office had been penetrated by Soviet agents. Walter Krivitsky, a senior Soviet intelligence officer, had defected to the West in 1937. While in America, the Soviet spymaster teamed up with a journalist and produced a series of sensational magazine articles denouncing Stalin's methods. In them, he unmasked John Herbert King, a Foreign Office cipher clerk. Krivitsky also hinted at the identity of other Soviet agents working in government, leaving British intelligence guessing as to who they might be.

Jane devoured Krivitsky's articles and became convinced by his revelations. On 10 November 1939, she wrote to Valentine Vivian, MI6's head of counterintelligence, urging him that, 'if we wish to get to the bottom of Soviet military espionage activities in this country, we must contact Krivitsky'.[21] MI5's Deputy Director General, Jasper Harker, agreed with Jane. The following month, Krivitsky accepted an invitation to visit Britain. The joint MI5 and MI6 debriefing that would follow in London was the first of its kind. A small team consisting of MI5 and MI6 Soviet specialists was formed to take charge of the debriefing. Jane, Harker, Guy Liddell and Vivian set to work planning everything from Krivitsky's travel from Canada to London, to the actual debriefing, discussing the important matter of how they were going to extract as much information from him as possible. The steps that the team took determined the way in which defector debriefings were conducted throughout the rest of the war and beyond. The joint taskforce spent considerable time assessing suitable strategies that they could deploy during the debriefing, such as selecting the right physical environment, understanding how best to build rapport and trust, and knowing when to withhold certain information to elicit a particular response or reaction. They also explored the ways in which they could keep Krivitsky focused on the questions asked.

MI5 were notified of Krivitsky's departure on 10 January 1940, leaving Jane very little to prepare. The Soviet defector had stipulated that he wished to stay at the exclusive and rather expensive Langham Hotel, frequented by the rich and famous of the day. MI5 dug deep into its pockets and agreed to Krivitsky's demand.[22] Jane perhaps understood best how to deal with Krivitsky. American intelligence had tipped MI5 off that the Soviet officer was a vain man who would respond to flattery and the presence of high-ranking officers.[23] Krivitsky was also fearful of Soviet retribution. His visit to Britain was kept secret and his true identity concealed. Everything from his luggage tags to his travel bookings displayed the name 'Mr Thomas'.[24] Should they get wind of what was going on, the press were prevented from printing any stories about Krivitsky's arrival. To ensure maximum security, the circle of those in the know was kept to a minimum.[25]

From the moment he arrived in Britain, Krivitsky was part of a carefully devised plan. When he docked at Southampton, he was met by MI5 officer Stephen Alley, a Russian linguist who had worked in Petrograd during the First World War. Krivitsky was both surprised and suspicious to be greeted by someone who spoke such good Russian. However, when Alley took Krivitsky to tea, a minor mishap tested both men's resolve. With sugar in short supply, Alley offered Krivitsky a saccharine tablet. The defector 'sheered right off this, obviously thinking it was dope or poison'.[26] The team agreed to handle Krivitsky with care. He was naturally on edge, but he was also a seasoned professional with vast experience of running agents. He would therefore sense when he was being played or manipulated. Those conducting the debriefing would need the right temperament and intellectual tools to handle the questioning of a fellow professional intriguer who knew the rules of the spying game.

The decision was taken to conduct the debriefing in Krivitsky's hotel room, in the hope that it would put him at ease. On 19 January 1940, 'Mrs Moore', the name used by Jane during the debriefing, and Harker and Vivian began to question 'Mr Thomas'. It all went terribly wrong to start with, as Krivitsky proved not very helpful, fearing the consequences of revealing the part he played in Soviet operations against Britain. He also wanted assurances that anything he revealed would not lead to him being called to give evidence in court. Krivitsky's identity had to remain secret, otherwise the Soviet government would be able to trace the information back to him.[27] Once he felt reassured, the Soviet intelligence officer began to talk about the Foreign Office agent, John Herbert King, who had subsequently been arrested. But once he learnt King had been sentenced to ten years in prison, he was quickly deflated. However, as soon as Jane took the lead in questioning, Krivitsky began to open up and soon provided Jane with a detailed overview of Soviet military intelligence and the Soviet secret police.[28]

An expert on Soviet espionage and a trained barrister, Jane questioned Krivitsky as an equal, a fellow practitioner, albeit on the other side. From her years of scrutinising Soviet espionage operations and key players, she 'understood the Soviet threat as an international rather than simply local phenomenon'.[29] They spoke for hours each day, and four weeks soon passed. All Jane's instincts as a trained barrister surfaced, and the hotel room became her courtroom. She presented

Krivitsky with documents that he claimed to have seen in Moscow, skilfully leading the Soviet spymaster into revealing key information, which she confirmed by pulling the relevant Registry records. Krivitsky claimed that there was a Soviet agent at work in the Foreign Office, who was sharing secret files with Russia. He described the mole as a wealthy young Scot who was the son of one of the Foreign Office chiefs, and mistakenly said that he had been educated at Eton and Oxford.[30] At this point, the team and Jane of course had no idea that this vague description could have been of Donald Maclean, for it could equally have been any number of other likely candidates working in the Foreign Office.

Having gained Krivitsky's respect, the interrogators were advised by the Soviet defector on how best to counter the Soviet threat, which was in his words 'to grow up agents from the inside', and he cited the successful case of MI5 agent Olga Gray as an excellent example. Olga had spent seven years working undercover to penetrate the Communist Party of Great Britain, finally unmasking the Woolwich spy ring in 1937.[31] MI5 had deployed the same methods as the Soviets were using against them; however, unlike Russian intelligence, Britain's Security Service planned operations in years, not decades, and they did not 'dispose' of rogue agents. On 16 February 1940, Krivitsky left London and returned to the United States. The following year, he was found dead in a Washington hotel, but questions remain as to by whose hand. With a bullet in his head, Krivitsky's death was recorded as a suicide, but in reality, Soviet assassins had no doubt finally caught up with him.

In Jane's final debriefing report, she recorded that Krivitsky had revealed fragments about a third Soviet agent, a young British journalist who had travelled to Spain during the civil war.[32] Kim Philby recorded in his memoir that when he later read Jane's report, he instantly recognised himself.[33] Krivitsky had provided British intelligence with valuable information. Of course, Jane's work had only just begun, as the Soviet defector had thrown to MI5 a few tasty morsels of information that required further investigation. Consequently, Jane would now have to spend hours, days, weeks and months sifting through mountains of paper and interviewing suspects to uncover the extent of treachery among their own ranks. But, with a much smaller staff than MI5 has today, Jane struggled, as resources were funnelled to the fight against fascism. However, her work would soon come to an abrupt end.

On 18 November 1940, Jane attended a top-level meeting that was led by the Acting Director General, Jasper Harker. He was nothing compared to Vernon Kell, whom she had worked under for decades and greatly admired, a man who had recruited Jane straight from school and had supported her application to train as a barrister. During the meeting, a situation arose where Jane confronted Harker, outlining his inadequacies as a leader. An exasperated Harker did not take the criticism well. The two engaged in a heated exchange. Harker was furious. The service's only woman officer found herself sacked for insubordination. To her male colleagues, Jane's behaviour was seen as intolerable. Had she been a man, Jane would no doubt have been given a swift telling-off, but permitted to remain in post. Her male MI5 (and later MI6) colleagues survived many heated confrontations, yet they were never given their marching orders.[34] Having heard of Jane's dramatic dismissal, Guy Liddell recorded in his diary how it was 'a very serious blow to us all'. In his opinion, Jane was 'completely on the wrong leg', but he believed that 'the incident should not have happened'.[35]

Two days after Jane's shock departure, Liddell met with her outside Blenheim Palace, at The Bear Inn in Woodstock. He recorded how 'she seemed to be quite normal and in a fighting mood. She was determined to put her views in high quarters.'[36] Liddell was on Jane's side and asked her to do nothing while he attempted to smooth things over. However, besides resigning his post, which he was not prepared to risk, Liddell held little sway. He lobbied on Jane's behalf, arguing that she had a moral right to appeal given her twenty-four years of devoted service. He regarded Jane 'as far more efficient than most of the men', and thought that it was 'little short of a disaster that her services could no longer be utilised'.[37] But without the support of other high-ranking officers, some of whom Jane had personally trained, nothing could be done to change Harker's mind. When Jane issued an apology to Harker, it fell on deaf ears.

Jane's termination of service with MI5 may have proved detrimental to unmasking further Soviet agents working in British intelligence and the upper echelons of government. It was no longer her job. She had been promoted on account of her ability, whereas her male colleagues had been offered positions based on the colour of their tie. One wonders whether Philby and the other Cambridge spies could have been discovered much earlier, had Jane remained in post. Unfortunately, we will never know the answer to that question, but when Jane moved to MI6, she kept her eyes and ears open. Ironically, within weeks of her dismissal from MI5, Harker was deemed not up to the job and replaced.[38] As a direct result of Jane's apparently unfair dismissal, no further female officers were appointed for the remainder of the war. MI5 implemented a new regulation that prevented women from achieving officer rank in the future, sending a clear message that women were not wanted in positions of power.[39]

Several years later, in 1943, the Security Service appointed its first female agent handler, Mary Sherer, who did the same job as her male colleagues, but without the officer rank and for less pay. As one half of the only all-female agent–handler team in the Double Cross operation, Mary broke new ground. She was responsible for Nathalie 'Lily' Sergueiew, a French woman of Russian extraction codenamed TREASURE, who proved to be one of the most effective wartime double agents ever to serve. However, Lily was anything but a treasure to deal with. For the first time, MI5 had no control over whom it recruited as double agents, for these men, together with a handful of women, had already been selected by the Abwehr, the German military intelligence service. While Mary initially judged Lily 'to be a character well suited to becoming a double agent', their partnership would be fraught with problems. To begin with, MI5 seriously misjudged the value of Lily's beloved white terrier, Babs.[40] Despite Mary's pleas to find a solution to bring Babs from Gibraltar to London, she was ignored. As a result, Lily proved difficult to deal with and came close to blowing the entire D-Day deception operation.

As one of the most dramatic and masterly deception operations of the Second World War, the Double Cross system unmasked German agents in Britain and abroad. British intelligence learnt all they could about what the enemy was up to, before then turning the agents and using them to feed false information back to their German handlers. Established by MI5, Double Cross was overseen by John Cecil Masterman, who headed the Twenty Committee, so named for the Roman numerals 'XX' which form a double cross.[41] Thanks to the efforts of Bletchley Park codebreakers, British intelligence was privy to all wireless messages between Berlin and its Abwehr stations, which effectively meant that German intelligence operations could be tracked from start to end. One of the biggest and most ambitious deception plans of the war was Operation FORTITUDE, which was designed to divert the enemy from Normandy, fooling the Germans into thinking that the D-Day landings of June 1944 would take place elsewhere.[42] Mary and her agent Lily played an important part in the intricate web of deception designed to trick the enemy into wrongly believing that there was intense activity by Allied forces in southeast England, when in reality Allied troops were massing in the southwest, preparing for the invasion of Normandy. However, the women's partnership was far from a match made in heaven, although Mary demonstrated great skill in managing the temperamental and troublesome TREASURE.

The small team responsible for running the double agents was Section B1A run by a brilliant MI5 officer, T.A. 'Tar' Robertson. This son of a Scottish banker liked to party and adored women. He also had a penchant for wearing tartan army 'trews' (trousers), which earned him the nickname of 'Passion Pants'. Robertson had worked for MI5 since 1933 and possessed the very useful skill of being able to spot a lie, which proved essential in his deception work. Mary had joined MI5 in 1938, working as a secretary to Joe Archer, the future husband of Jane Sissmore.[43] The 23-year-old Mary was a no-nonsense type of character, cut from the same cloth as her peer, Jane. Both women were daughters of empire, born in West Bengal, with sixteen years separating them in age. Mary's father, Lieutenant Colonel John Corrie Sherer, was a severe man from a long line of medal-wearing army officers who were trained to show no emotion. When Mary was only a toddler, he despatched her to England with his eldest daughter, Catherine, who was twelve years older than Mary. Consequently, Mary became very close to her sister, while suffering a distant and strained relationship with her father and mother. Mary felt that she had been sent away at far too young an age and had had to grow up extremely quickly. As a result of her poor relationship with her father, she had very little time for men, with one of her favourite phrases being 'stupid man'. She tolerated a select few males in her family, along with one other man whom she never named.[44]

Mary's parents eventually returned to England, reclaimed their daughters, and settled in Bath, where, from January 1926 onwards, Mary attended the Royal School for Daughters of Officers of the Army.[45] With a love for organising and fixing, young Mary took charge of the library, which was in a poor state. She set to work completing catalogues and adding new books to the empty shelves.[46] Mary had great patience, which served her well when it came to running agent

TREASURE. Before her work as an agent handler, Mary had begun her career in the Security Service as a personal assistant in Malta. On the outbreak of war, she was assigned to assist Lord Rothschild, a leading authority on German and Italian sabotage methods. After this, Mary could not wait to be posted abroad again, as she complained to her friend Peggy Manisty in February 1940 that MI5 had grown enormous, 'being mainly filled with very stupid girls'.[47] In 1942, Mary was seconded to the MI6-run British Security Coordination headquarters at the Rockefeller Center in New York. Despite never seeing its enigmatic head, William Stephenson, she advised on the subject of sabotage. Mary was on the ball when it came to her salary and took action to ensure that she was paid accordingly for her work. On arrival at the New York office, Mary despaired when she learnt that her wages had been set at a secretary's salary of $35 a month. She refused to accept it and – remarkably – managed to secure an increase to $50 a month.[48]

As a sabotage specialist, Mary was a person of action. She was enterprising and far from risk-averse. When Mary returned to Britain in 1943, the ambitious MI5 'secretary' had proven herself worthy of taking on a case-officer role running agents. However, she was unlucky in the agent assigned her. Lily Sergueiew was high-maintenance and required a soft touch, something that did not come naturally to Mary, though, as mentioned before, she did have patience, a virtue she would have to call upon often when running her agent. Lily came from a Russian family who had fled the Russian Revolution in 1917. Brought up in France and educated in Paris, she later trained as a journalist. Following the fall of France in June 1940, the multilingual Lily was recruited by the Abwehr, and was trained in how to use a wireless and secret ink. Then, in November 1943, she decided to change sides. The pragmatic agent had all along sought to escape occupied France and had merely used the Abwehr as a means to achieve her goal. The Germans despatched Lily on a mission to Britain, travelling via Madrid, where she took the opportunity to contact the British Embassy, who arranged for her to be flown from Gibraltar to England on 6 November 1943.[49]

As Lily's case officer, Mary Sherer was conscious of how nervous Lily would be when she arrived at Bristol Airport. The agent still had family in Paris and feared reprisal action from her German handlers, should they learn of her betrayal. Mary sent instructions to those responsible for greeting Lily, advising that she should be dealt with in the normal manner, and that no mention should be made of her connections with the Germans.[50] When Lily met Mary for the first time on 7 November 1943, the agent took an instant dislike to her handler. Lily recorded the meeting in her diary, writing: 'A door is open, and I enter into a sparsely furnished room. The first thing that attracts my attention is two pairs of legs: the man's because he wears khaki socks with civilian trousers and shoes; the woman's because they are twisted one around the other like a corkscrew. Their owner is sitting on the edge of a chair, her arms folded, chin resting on a closed fist. She glances at me through slightly slanted greenish eyes; her gaze is not friendly. Her brown hair is soberly brushed up and fixed without art, and her features are icy. "She would be easy to hate," I reflect.'[51]

The initial vetting process was not designed to be an enjoyable experience, as MI5 had to determine whether Lily was trustworthy and credible in her wish to work for the British. After the meeting with Mary, the German agent was then escorted to the London Reception Centre (LRC) for further interrogation. Lily was subjected to repeat questioning to see whether she made any slips in her story. After several days being detained, Lily was released on 12 November 1943, but she was a nervous wreck. Her time in the Royal Victoria Patriotic Building in Wandsworth left an indelible mark, as she likened the non-physical interrogation methods to those used by the Gestapo on her several years earlier.[52] Despite her heightened emotional state, Lily was exactly the type of worldly, well-travelled woman whom British intelligence was seeking for its Double Cross operation.[53] But, as with any enemy agent taken on, the British were playing a high-risk game, as they had no real way of knowing who was truly working for which side.

Lily was one of 34,000 European refugees who entered Britain during the war, passing through the LRC doors. A young MI5 secretary by the name of Diana Wadeson was responsible for building up the invaluable information index that recorded all kinds of data gathered on individuals questioned at the LRC.[54] Diana had joined MI5 in 1938 straight from Princess Helena College, where she had been headhunted.[55] She later recalled one wartime story of how an enemy agent was discovered when he claimed to have reached England by swimming the English Channel. At the LRC they threw him in the swimming pool, where it quickly became evident that he could not swim, and so his cover was blown.[56] He would not be the first or the last enemy agent discovered at the reception centre.

Deemed sincere in her desire to work for the British, Lily was installed by MI5 in a flat in Rugby Mansions in Kensington, where she set to work writing letters in secret ink to her German handler, Emile Kliemann. Mary befriended her agent as best she could, such as accompanying Lily to the cinema. A handler had to gain an agent's trust, and Mary had to move quickly. On 17 November 1943, Mary wrote to her boss, 'Tar' Robertson, suggesting that arrangements should be made for Lily to correspond with her mother, and that the letters could be sent via diplomatic bag. Conscious that feelings of loneliness would soon set in, Mary rightly believed that establishing a line of communication between the agent and her family would help keep Lily 'in a happy state of mind'.[57] Mary took her duty of care to Lily seriously, but the overly passionate agent found her handler 'a sort of automaton', unable to express emotion.[58] The truth was that Mary was just British to the core and stereotypically stoic. Though far from being unfeeling, she was simply not the kind of woman to share her feelings. She maintained a suitable professional distance from Lily, and gradually, as the months passed, the two women came to understand each other. Lily would learn that beneath the reserved exterior, Mary had an extremely kind and tender side to her.[59]

The female MI5 case officer was an interesting and formidable character who did not conform to many things in life, including feminine ways of dressing or behaving. Mary had a distinct style when it came to fashion. She liked to wear a suit jacket with gold buttons that gave her the appearance of a general, enhanced even further when she swung her arms as if marching like a soldier on parade.[60] When the weather turned colder, Mary adopted a fur coat that led Lily to name her handler the 'panther woman'.[61] Neither the jacket nor the coat was made for blending in, so Mary was entirely conspicuous when walking in public. With her distinctive red lipstick and packet of Kent cigarettes always at hand, she stood out from the crowd.[62] She aspired to be someone, and she saw MI5 as a place to make her mark. Within a short period of time, she had risen from secretary to case officer, proving herself capable of working at officer level. All she needed now was the rank and pay associated with the role. And so, Mary worked hard in her new position, hopeful of further promotion that would never come her way. She had unknowingly hit the glass ceiling.

By the end of 1943, Lily began to feel unwell, and in Mary's words she had become 'very unreasonable about her dog'.[63] On 8 December 1943, Mary wrote to Robertson:

TREASURE is very upset about the absence of her dog, and has seriously threatened that if the dog does not arrive soon she will not work anymore. I think this can be dealt with but it will mean a scene. I do not know what we can do to help, because if we have the dog sent over here officially it will have to go into quarantine, which from TREASURE's point of view would be as bad as having it in Gibraltar. I am afraid that TREASURE's American boyfriend has let her down and has no intention of smuggling the dog over here for her. I am wondering whether we could get the Navy to help via Commander Montagu.[64]

Before a solution could be found, Lily was admitted to hospital with kidney stones and was informed that unless they were operated on, she would most likely die. Mary stayed by her agent's bedside until her recovery, and again at the start of 1944, when Lily was taken sick once more but refused to be operated on.[65]

Aware of how much the dog meant to Lily, Mary explored every possible means of getting the much-loved terrier from Gibraltar to her owner, but there was one problem: Lily did not want Babs suffering in quarantine. Mary concluded 'there is nothing we can do', and the matter was put to bed by MI5.[66] By March 1944, Lily was in reasonably good health and was despatched to Lisbon armed with a wireless transmitter and operating under Ministry of Information cover.[67] The capital of neutral Portugal was alive with both friendly and enemy spies. There Lily rendezvoused with her German handler, Kliemann, who was impressed that she had made it to Lisbon. He handed her a transmitter disguised as an ordinary radio set, so that she could send her reports to Germany via wireless. Lily's mission was deemed a success by her British masters, and she returned to England, where she began transmitting a constant stream of misinformation to the Germans on 13 April 1944.[68] In the run-up to D-Day, Lily's messages were considered 'so valuable' by Britain's codebreakers, who designated them 'high importance'.[69] However, disaster struck in May 1944 when Lily received news that her dog, who was staying with her sister in Algeria, had been run over and had died. Distraught and angry, she blamed MI5 for the death of her beloved Babs. She revealed to an alarmed Mary how she had planned to blow the operation by leaving out a secret code in her messages to Kliemann, thereby alerting her German handler that her cover was blown, and that someone other than herself was transmitting.[70]

MI5 pondered what to do with their untrustworthy star agent.[71] Despite her unexecuted sabotage plan, MI5 kept Lily in play, and Operation FORTITUDE was a success. When Allied troops landed in Normandy on 6 June 1944, the Allies took the Germans completely by surprise. However, several days later, Lily became ill and was hospitalised once more. After she was discharged for a third time, Mary helped her poor, suffering agent back to the flat. Now that Lily was considered a liability, MI5 took the decision to let her go. Several weeks after D-Day, Robertson visited Mary and her agent, informing a distraught Lily that her services were no longer required, and that MI5 would continue to transmit while imitating her style.[72] Robertson explained that MI5 would pay Lily a small monthly sum, and would cover the cost of her operation, as well as any outstanding doctors' bills. However, he made it clear that, should she be indiscreet or 'in any way act contrary to the interests of the Allied cause', MI5 would take severe action by imprisoning her or handing her to the French authorities.[73] Mary did her best to console Lily. As Mary left the flat, she turned as Lily called her back. Lily finally divulged the details of the secret Abwehr code to her loyal handler, at which Mary made her commit it straight to paper.[74] But the confession came too late to reverse decisions.

Mary's career was very much tied to that of her agent TREASURE. After Lily's dismissal, the two women found themselves adrift in different directions. Lily returned to France at the end of the war and married, but she would continue to cause MI5 anxiety as she attempted to publish her wartime memoir. Just months before the war ended, Mary travelled to Italy and decided to settle in Rome after 1945.[75] The energetic former MI5 case officer later took a job escorting British prisoners from Rome to the UK, travelling aboard aircraft, handcuffed to hardened criminals. Mary kept in touch with several friends in MI5, such as Diana Wadeson and Peggy Manisty, and maintained a lifelong friendship with Phyl Mackenzie, who had worked in the Special Operations Executive and had returned to her home in Rome before the end of the war. Both Mary and Phyl were extremely well connected in Rome, as their joint enterprise, the Lion Bookshop, operated as a centre for expatriates.[76] The two secret service veterans greatly enjoyed each other's company and eventually moved in together. However, Phyl was not so keen on Mary's neurotic Pekingese named Lilo or her succession of pugs and Boston terriers.[77]

As a dog lover, Mary had understood her agent TREASURE's devotion to Babs. She had tried her best to reunite Lily with her dog, but to no avail. MI5 had failed to appreciate just how important the dog was as a means of support to a lonely and unpredictable agent. Mary had been dealt a difficult hand when it came to running TREASURE, as Lily's planned sabotage of the Double Cross operation had called into question her ability as an agent handler. In many ways it had made no difference whether Mary succeeded or not as MI5's first female case officer, as she was damned either way. Both Mary Sherer and Jane Archer had hit the establishment brick wall. The failed pioneers had proven what clever and capable women could achieve, but while they had shown what women could bring to the table as officers, women in MI5 would ultimately have to bide their time while men decided when enduring change would happen, and they were in for a long wait.

12

Rita and Ena

MI6 was once described as 'the best travel agency in the world', and no one knew this better than Rita Winsor and Ena Molesworth.[1] Throughout their lives, these two MI6 women travelled the world. Operating under secretarial cover at various embassies and consulates across Europe, Rita and Ena were involved in several dramatic exploits. They found themselves thrown together in June 1940 when Germany invaded France, and concerns grew that Hitler's panzers might not stop at the Swiss border. Over the course of ten days, Rita and Ena left Geneva and cycled across France, trying hard to avoid advancing German forces. A friendship developed that saw the two women bonded for the rest of their lives. With a passion for life and a marked sense of vitality, Rita and Ena anchored each other in a world full of uncertainty and deception. From Berlin to Lisbon, they demonstrated that they had the capacity to transform their lives and to save those in need.

Like most men and women who worked for Britain's foreign intelligence service, Rita and Ena's names have never been officially disclosed, despite Rita being one of the first female MI6 officers to be appointed before 1945. During the war, she broke down barriers, proving that women were more than capable of stepping into leadership roles. Both women belonged to a breed of career MI6 women who killed the myth of Mata Hari, proving women's capacity for sheer brilliance in their respective fields of duty. Ena was a skilled linguist whose secret coding work saw her rarely leave the office. Rita was enterprising and resourceful. She exuded a lively enthusiasm for everything that she put her hand to, which included organising clandestine wartime travel and running agents. Not until retirement did Rita and Ena eventually share a few selected memories of their time working for the 'Foreign Office'. While they never gave interviews and were extremely guarded about their past, they could not hide in the shadows. Like everyone, they had a starting point and an end.

Born on 23 December 1909, Marguerite 'Rita' Winsor enjoyed a middle-class upbringing in Stoke Newington in the London Borough of Hackney. The Winsor family home conveyed an air of respectability. The three-storey terrace house with its pillared porch stood out, as Victorian architects favoured individuality rather than Georgian uniformity. As a successful photographer, Rita's father managed to earn a more than comfortable wage, amply providing for his wife and three children. Rita was academically bright and attended St Paul's Girls' School, a progressive private day school located in West London.[2]

Rita was 'prim, smart and elegant'.[3] In contrast, Ena resembled a Margaret Rutherford-type character, a shrewd and unpretentious battleaxe.[4] Forthright and serious, she had a lovely way of laughing with a snort that amused those in her company.[5] Ena came from a privileged background. Her father was a close relation of Lord Molesworth of Swords, an Irish peer. As befitted his family's station in life and his intended career as an artillery officer, Herbert Crofton St George Molesworth attended Cheltenham College and the Royal Military Academy Woolwich. As an infant, Ena travelled across the globe to Jamaica, where her father, now a major, served as Commander Royal Engineers (CRE) from 1903 to 1906. The retired soldier rejoined the army during the Great War and took charge of London's artillery defences. From 1916 to 1917, his experience saw him posted to the Western Front, where he commanded the 11th Heavy Battery of the 11th (Northern) Division.[6]

Several years older than Rita, Georgina 'Ena' Molesworth was born on 7 September 1901 in Wales. Widely travelled, she and her two older sisters, Adrienne and Vivienne, were tutored by governesses. Their famous aunt, Mrs Mary Molesworth, the prolific Victorian children's author, would often visit the young girls and take inspiration for her later stories aimed at children of the Edwardian era.[7] All three sisters excelled in languages, especially French and German. The three Molesworth sisters belonged to a group of women schooled in the codified but unspoken system of Edwardian social etiquette. Suitably refined, they came from a world where servants wore white gloves at dinner parties and young women adhered to such conversational conventions as always enquiring about the health of their guests' families as an opening gambit. Ena and Vivienne never married and enjoyed careers in MI6. During the war, Vivienne worked for MI6 in Turkey.[8] Adrienne wed late in life, only five years before she died in 1950.

Ena's clandestine calling came on 1 April 1929 when she began work in Special Branch's Secret Service (SS) Registry.[9] She joined Maud Symons, who had singlehandedly run the registry since its inception under the auspices of Basil Thomson's Directorate of Intelligence. A decade later, the arrival of Ena and 22-year-old Milicent Bagot alleviated the growing crisis unfolding in the Special Branch registry, now charged with overseeing the distribution of MI6 documents. Maud's sister, Eva, was on the verge of a nervous breakdown due to the relentless nature of the work. Initially, Ena and Milicent stated that they were happy to work for a short period on the promise of better terms once they had settled into the job.[10] Along with several other hand-picked women appointed that year, Ena and Milicent helped to transfer a mountain of secret papers from the Special Branch Registry to the SS Registry.[11] While they completed this mammoth task, the women continued to facilitate the sharing of MI6 materials with Special Branch, distributing secret papers to the police in distinct red dockets.[12]

Overseen by MI6's head of Registry, Bill Woodfield, the SS Registry operated as an independent entity within Special Branch, forming a 'common pool' of information on communism at home and abroad.[13] New recruits were well-educated women with excellent knowledge of languages. Like Ena's, Milicent's family also belonged to the landed gentry. Her father, Cecil Villiers Bagot, was a London solicitor and distant relation to the barons Bagot, of Bagot's Bromley. As befitting her father's station in life, Milicent benefited from the tutelage of a doting French governess at home. She then attended Putney High School before studying Classics at Lady Margaret Hall, Oxford. Ambitious and hardworking, Milicent followed in Jane Archer's footsteps and became a specialist in international communism, achieving officer status in 1949.[14] Both women spent their lives getting inside the heads of the enemy, but where the straight-talking Jane was underestimated and cast out by her male MI5 superiors, the more refined Milicent succeeded in breaking the glass ceiling, when she became the first woman to be appointed assistant director of MI5 in 1953.

Milicent's MI5 career began in 1931 when a group of Special Branch staff transferred to the Security Service. Ena, on the other hand, probably moved over to MI6 at this time, as by the mid-1930s, she was working in the MI6-run Passport Control Office (PCO) of the Berlin embassy.[15] Life in Germany's capital was a strangely surreal experience for the secret consulate staff. As the Nazis consolidated their power, democracy was eroded and replaced with terror and intimidation. In many ways, Berlin embodied Germany's two faces: one of heightened fear and the other of diminished pleasure. After Hitler restored economic prosperity, it was all enforced sunshine and swastikas for the majority of Germans, bamboozled and brainwashed by Nazi propaganda. On the other hand, for social democrats, communists and certain minorities, daily life became a struggle to accommodate escalating Nazi repression. Ena looked on in horror as Hitler's agents of terror regulated nearly every aspect of German life and imprisoned hundreds of thousands of Jews deemed 'enemies of the State'. Working in passport control, the MI6 'secretary' was in a unique position to help Germany's Jews, and she did so willingly.

The MI6 station head, Frank Foley, and his team risked their lives and careers to help those fleeing Nazi persecution in what has been described by Foley's biographer as 'a stupendous act of humanity, borne not out of political necessity but out of a moral imperative'.[16] Located on Tiergartenstrasse, the passport office was a fair distance from the British Embassy on Wilhelmstrasse. To camouflage its covert espionage work, the MI6 Berlin station operated an overt passport control department, which routinely processed visa applications. Foley used his official job as British PCO to bend the rules and help those in need. When Ena and her colleagues, the 'Misses Lloyd, de Fossard, and St Clair', arrived at the small office each day, they faced a growing queue of desperate Jews.[17] Together with their male colleagues, the women issued tens of thousands of visas and false papers for travel to Britain and British-ruled Palestine. However, their life-saving work was briefly interrupted in 1938.

On 12 March, the German Army invaded Austria, and troops encountered enthusiastic crowds thronging the streets. Three days later, Hitler officially annexed the country of his birth, declaring Austria a part of the German Empire. The Germans lost no time in plundering and seizing Jewish homes and expropriating Jewish businesses. The vast majority of Austria's Jews resided in its capital, Vienna. They had watched the Nazi dictatorship exclude Jews from everyday life in Germany, believing such persecution would never happen in their country. As the Nazis tightened their grip on Austria, Viennese Jews' initial shock and disbelief quickly turned to panic. All over the city, Jews were beaten and arrested, and suicides were reported.

Many attempted to flee and sought visas from the British PCO run by MI6 spymaster Thomas Kendrick. Nineteen-year-old George Weidenfeld stood in Kendrick's office and listened to his mother's pleas for help. With his father imprisoned, the young man found himself expelled from Vienna University on account of being a Jew. The MI6 officer took a significant risk and issued the student a three-month temporary visa, which the British government had counselled against using. Kendrick knew it would be difficult to send Weidenfeld back to Austria once in Britain.[18] At the end of July 1938, the future giant of British post-war publishing said goodbye to his mother and family at Vienna's train station, 'unsure if he would see any of them ever again'.[19]

Overwhelmed by the deluge of requests, the MI6 Vienna station head and his team became the subject of Gestapo attention. By August 1938, the situation remained highly volatile in both Austria and Germany, where arrests and harassment of German Jews had accelerated since Austria's annexation. German authorities arrested the 57-year-old Kendrick as he attempted to take a short break with his wife to recuperate from months of working fourteen-hour days. Escorted back to Vienna from the border town of Freilassing, the MI6 officer was immediately interrogated by the Gestapo about his espionage activity. Kendrick's arrest was reported in newspapers worldwide, blowing MI6's PCO cover. He was later released and expelled from the country.[20] Kendrick's networks and operations in Nazi-controlled Austria collapsed and threw the security of MI6's other European spy networks into question.

Fearing for the safety of his Berlin staff, the MI6 chief Hugh Sinclair immediately recalled Frank Foley and his team in August 1938. Ena and the other 'secretaries' were evacuated from Berlin.[21] After arriving in England, the women enjoyed a brief period of leave to recuperate before spending time at London headquarters.[22] By November 1938, Foley and his team had bravely returned to Berlin.[23] The number of staff soon doubled to keep pace with the ever-increasing work, which was made all the more difficult by Nazi restrictions placed on Jews and the harsh immigration rules imposed by the British government. However, nothing could have prepared Foley's staff for the brutal pogrom of co-ordinated death and destruction carried out across Germany on 9 to 10 November 1938. Sparked by the murder of a German diplomat in Paris by a Jewish teenager, *Kristallnacht* (as it became known) saw Jews targeted by rampaging mobs. Ena and others bore witness to the destruction of Jewish businesses and homes, the desecration of synagogues, and the murder of many Jews. As shards of broken glass filled the streets of Berlin, the message was clear: Jews had no future in Nazi Germany.

Nearly a month after the 'Night of Broken Glass', a 26-year-old graduate of Girton College, Cambridge, joined Frank Foley's team.[24] On 12 December 1938, Margaret Reid spent her first day filing, an overwhelming task that others before her had failed to prioritise. Foley faced no other option but to close the passport office two days a week so that his staff could catch up with the relentless processing of visas.[25] In a letter to her mother, the doctor's daughter from Nottingham described how she sat 'with two other new girls and a man who came over from London a few weeks ago'.[26] She had spent all day working on the card index with the phone constantly ringing. Margaret lamented how:

> There are of course pathetic tales of woe and people ring up from the aerodrome just before their plane leaves in a final attempt to get a visa to get out of the country. The big businessmen seem to have been preparing some of them for a long time and have the necessary capital in foreign banks, but more pathetic are the uneducated letters from wives whose husbands are in concentration camps (some of them have died there or are in hospital as a result of infection caught there and undernourishment). It is a panic stricken land.[27]

The mild-mannered Berlin station chief took action when others dared not. Foley looked nothing like a master spy when he bravely marched into concentration camps waving visas at the German guards. Dressed in a Harris Tweed jacket and wearing owlish glasses, he secured the release of many Jews who were already resigned to their inevitable, terrible fate in the camps. Foley and his team ultimately saved more people than the celebrated hero Oskar Schindler, whose story was immortalised in Steven Spielberg's 1993 Academy Award-winning film *Schindler's List*. As one of Britain's unsung heroes, Foley was honoured by Israel's world Holocaust remembrance centre, Yad Vashem, in 1999 as one of the 'Righteous among Nations'. Margaret Reid is the only MI6 'secretary' to date to have been posthumously awarded the title 'British Hero of the Holocaust' by the British government in 2018, an accolade she shares with her boss, Foley.

Other rule-breaking MI6 'secretaries' such as Ena remain unrecognised for their role in saving Jewish lives. After the war, Ena kept in touch with a dentist in Cambridge whom she helped escape from Nazi Germany.[28] However, those who remember the period will soon be gone, making it extremely difficult to provide the documentary evidence needed by Yad Vashem or other organisations to honour MI6 women such as Ena formally. Perhaps hope lies in the secret service she worked for, MI6, and its acknowledgement of the extraordinary endeavours of its past employees. Ena shared a few select stories of her secret work in 1930s Berlin, but the highly skilled MI6 retiree never revealed any secrets nor sought recognition.

Sitting in the car's passenger seat in the 1980s, Ena wore a distinctive French beret, as the actors playing French Resistance members did in her favourite television show, 'Allo 'Allo. Her driver, Philip Jeffries, was a friend from the village who often navigated the winding countryside roads to take Ena wherever she wanted. He remembers one particular journey when he listened intently to the veteran MI6 secretary as she recalled the story of her escape from Berlin in 1939.[29] The evacuation of the British Embassy and MI6 staff began after Germany concluded the Molotov–Ribbentrop Treaty of Non-aggression with the Soviet Union on 23 August 1939. The secret pact effectively sounded the death knell of the uneasy peace that had existed since 1918. News of the Hitler–Stalin alliance reached British ears courtesy of Hans Oster, the anti-Hitler deputy head of the German military intelligence service, the Abwehr.[30] Hugh Sinclair immediately ordered Foley and his team home for a second time. Ena, Margaret and the rest of the MI6 station set about burning papers that could not be taken with them, while Foley continued to issue British travel permits for German Jews right up until the moment he closed the office for the final time.[31]

As the countdown to war began, British diplomatic staff moved temporarily to the Hotel Adlon, just around the corner from the Berlin embassy.[32] Ena and her MI6 colleagues selected a few prized possessions and hastily drove to Rotterdam, where they boarded a ship bound for England. Ena recalled her three most treasured items: a typewriter, a fox fur and a silk negligee. While she had to dispose of the bulky typewriter en route, she hid the fur and her expensive underwear in the leather car seat. When the travelling party stopped at the German–Dutch border, the guards failed to check the car seat, ensuring that Ena's precious cargo remained undetected.[33]

After Ena's safe arrival back in England, MI6 despatched her to Bletchley Park. Working as a codist on the mansion's first floor, Ena communicated with agents and embassies across Europe, which remained on high alert as hostilities grew. On 3 September 1939, the entire war station's staff assembled in a large marquee in the grounds to hear a bitterly disappointed Neville Chamberlain address the nation.[34] Huddled around the wireless radio, they listened to the prime minister's sombre voice informing them that Britain was again at war with Germany. Ena spent several months at Bletchley before being posted to Geneva. The MI6 station head there was the Dutch-born Count Frederick van den Heuvel, known as 'Fanny the fixer'.[35] A friend of Ian Fleming, the dandyish station head was described as 'the epitome of a diplomat with his imperial whiskers and black homburg'.[36] Van den Heuvel worked under the purview of Claude Dansey's Z Organisation, a clandestine network of British businessmen and journalists established during the 1930s to gather intelligence parallel to MI6, should the secret service ever find itself compromised.

Rather fittingly, Claude Dansey remains an elusive character in British intelligence history. He began his clandestine career during the Boer War, taking part in the relief of Mafeking. Hard to pin down by historians, Dansey had been with MI6 since 1917, having served with MI5 before that.[37] He was a professional and pragmatic spymaster who purposefully shied away from being photographed, even on his wedding day. However, like all intelligence officers, he could not escape having his passport photograph taken, which finally came to light in 1982.[38] The middle-aged, bespectacled spymaster with a penetrating stare was the ultimate puppeteer, pulling multiple strings at any time. When it came to women, 'Uncle Claude' never baulked at the idea of sending female agents behind enemy lines nor appointing them as officers, as would be the case with Rita Winsor. What he did take issue with were blown agents who requested a return to occupied Europe knowing full well that their lives were in danger.[39]

Dansey exercised a duty of care towards those who worked for him. He recruited individuals with the right qualities for specific roles. During the Second World War, one of his best agents was the 31-year-old, mother-of-two Marie-Madeleine Fourcade, who ran a major MI6 network in France that supplied vital intelligence on German submarine activity and weapons development.[40] The versatile spymaster wore many masks, leaving some with a bad impression of his character and behaviour. To the French Resistance heroine, he could not have been more caring and commendatory of her achievements. Dansey told Fourcade, 'You're the only network covering the whole of France. You work regularly and systematically and have a remarkable *esprit de corps*.[41] He genuinely admired women with such formidable executive capacity, a quality both Rita and Ena demonstrated throughout their MI6 careers.

Following the outbreak of war, Dansey moved his Z Organisation headquarters from Bush House in London, to neutral Switzerland.[42] Better placed there to penetrate Germany, 'Colonel Z' initially worked under consular cover in German-speaking Zurich before the new head of MI6, Stewart Menzies, recalled his assistant chief to London in November 1939.[43] Van den Heuvel later took charge of Swiss operations and located the main office in Geneva's French-speaking canton. Based at 41 Quai Wilson, Ena and the rest of the station staff enjoyed a beautiful view of Lake Geneva with its serene turquoise waters. But, beneath its peaceful and picturesque exterior, Switzerland was a hotbed of friendly and hostile foreign intelligence services using the neutral island at the heart of Western Europe as an operating base for running spy rings and escape networks.[44] Dansey's people hid among the flood of diplomats and refugees who arrived in Switzerland after September 1939. However, the Swiss valued their neutrality and did not look kindly on the cloak-and-dagger antics of other countries' secret services that risked jeopardising relations between Switzerland and Germany. Swiss authorities did all they could to monitor foreign missions through informants and by restricting the transmission of enciphered messages, which had to be sent via the Swiss post office.[45]

In May 1940, the German invasion of Western Europe called into question MI6 operations in the sanctuary that was Switzerland. There was a great sense of confusion and panic as Hitler's expansionist ambitions appeared to have no limits, leading London headquarters to entertain the possibility that Hitler might invade yet another neutral country, in addition to Denmark and Norway which had been occupied one month earlier. MI6 could not afford for its staff to be captured and interned, so Dansey sent word to the Swiss stations to prepare to leave.[46] In March 1987, Ena compiled a detailed account of what happened next. Her memoir 'A Journey to Bordeaux' is a rare document that names several other MI6 women working at the

Geneva MI6 station.[47] Having lost Rita unexpectedly to a heart attack in October 1986, Ena revealed to a close friend that she was 'shaken to the foundations'.[48] The two women had spent most of their lives together, and Ena suddenly found that she was alone. With only her memories to console her, the grieving MI6 veteran ensured that the story of how she became firm friends with Rita would survive long after her own death in May 1990.

Nearly forty-six years after the event, Ena described their ten-day journey across France with astonishing detail, recalling each stage of the adventure as if it had happened yesterday. The MI6 stations at Geneva and Zurich watched apprehensively as the battle for France unfolded. German troops marched into Paris on 14 June 1940, and the French government fled south to Bordeaux. Fighting continued as Hitler's panzers raced across northern France. They would soon reach the French–Swiss border. On 16 June, van den Heuvel urgently rang Ena at 7.30 a.m. and informed her that Rita Winsor was on her way to rendezvous with the evacuating staff based in Geneva. Having undertaken two evacuations in Berlin, Ena was well versed in speedy exit procedures. Within the next hour, she had received three further telephone calls from her boss. At the same time, she rallied her three colleagues: 'Momett' Whitcombe, Christine Robinson and Ann Mulholland (known affectionately as 'Nit Wit').

Having drunk an entire bottle of champagne, which a never wasteful Ena could not leave behind, she threw a rucksack over her shoulders, grabbed a shopping basket full of fresh oranges, and exited the office with her suitcases. The party made their way to the railway station, where Rita was waiting for them. Tall and elegant, the energetic Zurich station 'secretary' was admired wherever she went. Rita had always been a woman of action from a very young age. She had left school in 1926 when only sixteen and had worked as a typist at the Regent telephone exchange.[49] That same year, during the General Strike, Rita joined thousands of volunteers who acted as porters and train drivers on the London underground. The recent school-leaver helped keep the Bakerloo line running for nine days during the nationwide strike.[50] Rita's movements over the next ten years remain unknown. She may have worked for Dansey's Z Organisation before the war, but how she came to his attention remains a mystery. By September 1939, she was in Zurich working alongside the *Lederhosen*-wearing Edgeworth Leslie, who had previously worked for the 'prestigious firm of solicitors Slaughter and May, which supplied numerous recruits to the intelligence services'.[51]

As they arrived at the railway station, Rita introduced herself to the anxious MI6 'secretaries'. The party boarded the afternoon train across the French frontier to Lyon, where they arrived without incident. Unfortunately, however, they were too late to catch their Bordeaux connection. With thunderstorms breaking out periodically, they dashed across the road to the Hotel Terminus, which would soon become the Lyon Gestapo headquarters, but which was currently bursting with refugees. Posters plastered on the walls urged people to remain calm and stay in the city. Rita and Ena left Momett, Christine and Nit Wit at the hotel while they visited the British Consulate at the other end of the city. Ena recalled how 'the Consul turned out to be a gentleman with an ear trumpet who had to be communicated with through a third party, who was the clerk whose voice he was used to'.[52] After a prolonged conversation, the consul informed the two women that the Germans had crossed the River Loire and were only 50km away from Lyon. He advised them to leave on the evening train bound for Bordeaux, as it would be the last one run for refugees.

Rita and Ena rushed back to the hotel, where they ate a hurried lunch before struggling to the station with their fifteen suitcases swaying precariously on rickety luggage trolleys. The party of five fought their way through the chaotic crowd to the platform. The train pulled into the station three hours ahead of departure. Crammed into a carriage with eighteen French airmen and soldiers, the women held their nerve for several hours until the engine suddenly came alive, and the train lunged forward. After a lengthy stop at a wayside station, the exhausted party reached Saint-Germain-des-Fossés at noon on Tuesday, 18 June. With only military personnel permitted to continue on the train to Bordeaux, civilian passengers had no choice but to disembark and find alternative modes of transport.

The women abandoned their fifteen suitcases, leaving them with a 'woman with a kind heart' who promised to store them indefinitely.[53] She was true to her word, and Rita collected the bags at the end of the war.[54] With no option but to walk to Vichy, Rita, Ena and Momett set off in the blazing hot sun. As they left the town behind, the three women realised that Christine and Nit Wit were not with them. Thinking they would quickly catch up, the trio continued walking. After an hour, the women hitched a short ride, hanging onto a small lorry by their fingernails as they stood on the running board. They arrived in the French spa resort windswept and covered in road dust. There, they passed nervous residents discussing the military situation, wondering how long it would be before the Germans arrived in the city. In need of a room for the night, the women tried their luck at the iconic Astoria Palace Hotel. The three exhausted travellers bathed and dined before they turned in for the night, ready for an early visit to the police station to enquire as to the whereabouts of their lost companions.

The following morning, Ena was soaking in the free-standing bath when Rita called her to the window. As she looked out on the street below, panic-stricken people were running madly, vanishing and re-appearing. A distraught French chambermaid burst into the room and declared that the Germans had arrived in Vichy. The three women threw their belongings into rucksacks, paid the hotel bill, and sat down to devise a plan of action. Ena was 'rather green and shaky' at the prospect of being caught as a British spy. Their only option was to leave. The French military commandant advised them of the best route out of Vichy and supplied them with a map. He promised to replicate the map for Christine and Nit Wit, should he come across them. The resourceful and determined MI6 'secretaries' avoided the Germans and left the city, where a lorry picked them up on the outskirts before hurtling into the hills.

The lorry stopped in dense woodland just before the town of Randan. The driver could take them no further, as German forces had blocked the roads. After some mediation, Rita, Ena and Momett walked the short distance to the town, where they found no evidence of any military personnel. With their iron rations depleted, Rita purchased bread. The women eyed a restaurant in the town square. While waiting for the food, they conversed with a Belgian judge at the next table, who informed them that officials from the Geneva office of the International Labour Organisation (ILO) had also arrived in the town. By sheer chance, Rita came across one of the ILO men, who suggested the women would travel better on bicycles. Using a little sex appeal to drive down the price, Rita procured three bicycles – one silver, one pale blue and one iridescent green. Rita had only ridden once in her life before and required some help to get going.

The cyclists then crossed the Massif Central, stopping in Riom and Volvic. The challenging terrain of extinct volcanoes and rugged expanses, combined with the high altitude, pushed the women to their physical limits. After an eight-hour climb between Pontgibaud and Pontaumur, the party of three reached the little village of Combrailles on Thursday, 20 June 1940. As the women dismounted and got used to walking on two legs again, Rita took the lead and initiated a conversation with a local woman outside the grocery shop. She somehow managed to elicit an invitation from the woman and her husband to stay overnight in their home. With their bikes safely stored in the barn, Rita, Ena and Momett enjoyed a comfy bed for the night. However, when they rose at dawn the following day, Momett discovered that two of their bikes were missing. The Frenchwoman and her husband were so distressed by the news that they pushed the women into a car with three French soldiers. The men had all been in England after Dunkirk. The driver, a former chauffeur, delivered a smooth drive, and one of the other two soldiers, a music-hall singer, entertained the women with his fine singing voice. As the party drove down the road, they could not believe their eyes when they came across two French soldiers riding their missing bicycles. With their companions' assistance, the MI6 women jumped out of the car and retrieved the stolen goods. With three cycles now strapped to the back of the vehicle, the party continued their journey through Bourg-Lastic and Ussel.

When they reached Tulle, the women parted ways with the French soldiers and remounted their bicycles. Still unsteady on two wheels and not helped by the torrential rain, Rita suffered several mishaps. The unstable cyclist collided with a parked car and nearly ran over a French officer before plummeting onto the grass verge. Black and blue from her falls, Rita bravely carried on to Brive. Her spirits soared when they spotted that the station was full of trains. Unfortunately, however, they were for military use only. The women learnt that they would require permits to pass through road control points if they wished to continue their journey. Faced with further heavy rain showers, the exasperated cyclists stormed an unshaven and irritable French officer, who eventually took their passports, leaving Rita, Ena and Momett sitting uncomfortably in the rain, 'facing an unconcealed and well patronised public convenience'.[55] After half an hour, the officer returned with three permits.

On Saturday, 22 June 1940, the women reached Perigueux, where a French colonel secured the group of British secretaries a ride with a lorry bound for Bordeaux. The driver managed to pass through two military control points before stopping at Libourne. Blackout restrictions meant that it was impossible to travel any further. They continued their journey at dawn the next day, reaching their destination at 6.30 a.m., where they split up briefly to gather information. Ena despaired when she discovered that the British Embassy had already been evacuated. Undeterred, she enjoyed croissants and coffee while waiting for the American Consulate to open at 9 a.m. As the doors opened, Ena pushed through with another British woman, who was carrying a meowing cat in a basket on her back. Unfortunately, the Americans could do nothing for them. In the meantime, Rita had discovered that the British Embassy was not entirely deserted and might be able to help the women. Ena was left to mind the bicycles, while Rita and Momett sped off. A young officer soon dashed past Ena, shouting in a cracked voice that the French had signed an armistice with Germany. Ena recalled that it was 'heart-rending' to hear that France had given up.[56]

Within twenty minutes, Momett and Rita returned and declared to Ena, 'Saved again – there's an Admiral who may do something.'[57] A Royal Navy officer drove the three dishevelled women to the quay, where the captain of a destroyer greeted them on the gangplank with his telescope under his arm. While the women slept in the captain's cabin, the warship steamed at half speed, zig-zagging its way to Plymouth, arriving two days later on Tuesday, 25 June 1940. Ena noted that 'had it not been for Rita's persistence, we should have been considerably longer en route and have missed the destroyer'.[58] Rita, Ena and Momett never forgot the kindness of the French people who opened their homes to them. The MI6 women had nerves of steel and stalwart hearts, and one has to hope that their two colleagues, Christine and Nit Wit, also made it back to England. Throughout the hazardous journey, Rita and Ena developed a lasting friendship. The two brave young women, now inseparable, spent the rest of the war in Lisbon, the espionage capital of Europe.

Portugal's capital city was just the tonic that the two experienced MI6 women needed after their French ordeal. As German bombers dropped their loads on London, and the British faced blackouts and food shortages, Portugal was the land of light, a heavenly vision of sprawling shops, restaurants and cafés offering diners fresh fish and fruit. Governed by António de Oliveira Salazar, the country's quiet autocrat adopted a strategy of flexible neutrality that favoured the Allies while maintaining cordial relations with Hitler.[59] Salazar faced many challenges to keep Portugal independent, which was often more complicated than choosing sides. Fearful that Germany or Spain might invade, or that their oldest ally, Britain, might attempt to take over the strategically located Azores, the Portuguese also had to contend with a growing refugee problem. Tens of thousands arrived in Lisbon hoping to get through the American or British visa offices' doors and secure passage aboard one of the ocean liners bound for the Americas.

Several wealthy exiles made the vibrant city their home, alongside those less fortunate. Prior to the former monarch's taking up his appointment as governor of the Bahamas, the Duke and Duchess of Windsor entertained their cosmopolitan friends in Lisbon before boarding the American liner *Excalibur,* bound for Bermuda. The Duke appears to have been unaware of a failed German plot to kidnap him in the Portuguese capital.[60] But behind the city's glamour and glitterati lurked perilous intrigues. Lisbon's sun-baked streets were teeming with Axis and Allied spies who appeared to be nothing more than business people. During the day, intelligence officers met secretly with their agents and assets in luxurious hotel lobbies. As soon as the sun set, spies rushed to the extravagant Estoril Casino on the Atlantic coast, a short distance from the city. Women dripping in jewellery hung on the arms of those who apparently had nothing better to do than play cards on the Portuguese Riviera. Intelligence officers drank with diplomats and socialites while they spied on their adversaries, periodically throwing their chips on the table and scanning the room for mysterious or unfriendly activity.

MI6 staff such as Rita and Ena hid in plain sight, adopting the cover of embassy secretaries. While very little is known about Ena's activities in Lisbon, enough broken shards of the looking glass survive to build a picture of Rita's operational movements and achievements. Both women were based at the Porto Covo Palace, located at 35–39 Rua de São Domingos. The stunning late-eighteenth-century palace was a 'forbidding-looking stone building jutting out almost to the edge of the pavement of this narrow street in the old quarter of the city'.[61] The large number of small embassy rooms which spread over several floors offered plenty of office space. MI6 was assigned rooms on the second floor of the embassy building, along with private access for its staff and privileged visitors. An MI6 wireless radio station occupied the room on the floor directly above.[62] Surprisingly, staff working in the overlooked office could be 'seen from the other side of the street photographing letters and every sort of thing'.[63] Perhaps the blatant disregard for secrecy was intentional, given that intelligence services on both sides operated freely and openly in Portugal. As they left the embassy, MI6 staff faced the challenge of shaking off Gestapo agents and the dreaded Portuguese secret police (Polícia Internacional e de Defesa do Estado [PIDE]), who had been trained and indoctrinated by the Nazis. One of the MI6 station heads, Philip Johns, recalled how, time and time again, the PIDE 'was a thorn in our side in the development of covert intelligence activities'.[64] Eyes were everywhere, with every fifth man or woman secretly watching and waiting.

Good tradecraft was therefore essential for everyday living in Lisbon. Dansey carefully selected seasoned professionals like Rita and Ena because of their training and extensive experience. When the two women arrived in the autumn of 1940, the MI6 station was one of four remaining operational posts in Europe, alongside Madrid, Stockholm and Berne. The station was under the command of an experienced former MI5 officer, Richman Stopford, a wealthy bachelor who had worked as a banker in London before the war. He operated under the cover of financial attaché at the embassy, aided by his secretary, Mary Grepe, who had accompanied him from MI5 to Lisbon in June 1940.[65] By 1941, the station had grown to include Bobby Johnstone, Mike Andrew, Trevor Glanville, Michael Andrews and Graham Maingot, Dansey's chief Z agent in pre-war Rome. Ralph Jarvis, another banker, joined in March 1941. The assistant financial attaché proved his worth in counterintelligence, as he succeeded in identifying and turning nearly every German Abwehr spy in Lisbon.[66] By the end of the war, Jarvis's extensive registry 'contained files on 1,900 confirmed enemy agents, 350 suspected enemy agents and 200 Germans with known intelligence connections'.[67]

Rita and Ena experienced a quick turnover of station chiefs. In the spring of 1941, a naval officer who had served at the MI6 station in Brussels replaced Richman Stopford.[68] Philip Johns, who brought his wife with him, as was permitted in neutral countries, demonstrated how much better he was than his predecessor at engaging with the ambassador, Ronald Campbell, and his prickly diplomats. Surprisingly perhaps, Johns lasted only a year. Considered by Dansey to be too closely involved with anti-Salazar groups, Johns left for Buenos Aires at the end of 1942.[69] The penultimate wartime station chief, Cecil Gledhill, was one of Dansey's recruits and the only male officer fluent in Portuguese.[70] According to Kim Philby, who oversaw the Iberian subsection in MI6, Gledhill charged 'around like a bull in a china shop, opening up vast vistas of the obvious'.[71] He remained in post until the end of 1943, when an officer from the Madrid station, 'Togo' McLaurin, took over.[72] When he reported for duty in Lisbon, Klop Ustinov, father of the actor Peter Ustinov, was not particularly impressed by Gledhill. Ustinov, who served both as an MI5 and an MI6 officer, and who was himself rather good at turning German agents, reported to Guy Liddell on his return to London in July 1944 that he was 'horrified by the way both Gledhill and [counterintelligence officer] Charles de Salis go about their business'.[73] Ustinov described both men as 'amateurs and pretty indiscreet ones at that'.[74] In his view, by 'far and away the best element in the office are the women'.[75]

One woman stood out above all others. Described as 'the most important member' of Philip Johns's team, Rita was an unorthodox quartermaster who worked behind the scenes to get things done.[76] Female MI6 officers were few and far between during the war, and none achieved station-head status.[77] Apart from Margaret 'Teddy' Dunlop, MI6's counterintelligence officer in Tangier,[78] Rita was the only other known female officer in the wartime service. Described by the Lisbon station chief Johns, Rita was tall and dark with an 'attractive personality'. She had 'an exceedingly genuine sense of the ridiculous', and 'was particularly suited for the job, very quick thinking and with just that devious approach to problems so important in our operations'.[79] Fluent in Portuguese, Johns's number two 'managed to propel the relevant Portuguese official into action' whenever required.[80]

Rita was a fixer who dealt with everything from running agents to overseeing the exfiltration of defectors, as well as providing quick solutions to pressing problems. In 1941, she vouched for the journalist Elizabeth Wiskemann, who found her identity questioned while she waited in Lisbon for several weeks.[81] Like many during the war, Elizabeth was waiting for transport to become available, which could take days or even weeks. Undercover as an assistant press attaché, Elizabeth had been working at the Berne embassy, where she covertly gathered information on Germany, such as public opinion and the deportation of Jews.[82] Meanwhile Rita, located at the gateway to global travel, was in charge of arrangements for intelligence personnel undertaking particular assignments that required passage between Lisbon, England and America.

Seats on Pan Am's four-engine Boeing 'clippers' were in high demand. Despite their enormous size and crew of ten, these luxury flying boats could carry only forty passengers in overnight sleeper configuration. In such competitive conditions, Rita had to exert her considerable influence in securing bookings for British intelligence officers, who sometimes adopted pseudonyms when they travelled, as German spies closely watched arriving and departing passengers making the weekly transatlantic crossings. With Lisbon–New York flights lasting as long as twenty-six hours, the giant flying hotels offered passengers every comfort, including a fourteen-seat dining room and a private 'honeymoon suite' at the tail end of each aircraft.[83] Before flying to New York in 1941, the Director of Naval Intelligence, John Godfrey, and his assistant Ian Fleming stayed at the Palacio Hotel in Estoril, Lisbon. The two men played the tables at the casino, and Fleming later took inspiration from the occasion when writing his debut book, *Casino Royale* (1953). However, unlike James Bond's high-stakes gamble against Le Chiffre, Fleming bet modest amounts only to be thoroughly cleaned out by the end of the night, leaving his boss, Godfrey, suitably unimpressed.[84]

During the Second World War, civilian airliners operated at their own risk, and those who travelled on them understood the danger. It would have not surprised some when, on 1 June 1943, BOAC's Flight 777A took off from Lisbon but never reached its destination, a small airfield at Whitchurch, near Bristol. The DC-3 aircraft, owned and operated by Royal Dutch Airlines (KLM), was carrying the renowned British film actor Leslie Howard. The fifty-year-old star of films such as the epic *Gone with the Wind* (1939) had been on a lecture tour in Spain and Portugal promoting British films. Several actors and directors had links with British intelligence, and Howard was rumoured to be working as a British spy.[85] Years later, Rita and Ena recalled Howard's Lisbon visit. Rita had organised the Hollywood star's return journey to England. The day before Howard boarded the ill-fated flight, the slim, fair-haired actor enjoyed a picnic on the beach at Praia das Maçãs, reportedly organised by the air attaché Jack Schreiber, but in reality arranged by Rita and Ena. When the two women said farewell to Howard on the beach, they never dreamt that it would be the last time they saw him.[86] The following day, his plane was shot down over the Bay of Biscay by a flight of eight Luftwaffe Junkers bombers. There were no survivors. Great mystery surrounds the incident as to whether it was accidental or murder. Perhaps the plane was mistaken for being a military transport, as a common military version of the same aircraft type did exist. Yet this was not an isolated incident; the Luftwaffe seem to have been well aware of the regular BOAC/KLM Lisbon–UK route and attacked it repeatedly. Or perhaps the Germans intentionally targeted one of the passengers, such as Leslie Howard, or his bald cigar-smoking friend and theatrical agent, Alfred Chenhalls, who bore a close resemblance to Winston Churchill.[87]

Whatever the truth, the death of Howard and all those travelling with him served as a grim reminder of the perils of flying in a combat zone. While the actor's links with British intelligence remain obscure, Rita continued facilitating the movements of intelligence officers such as Richard Gambier-Parry, Frank Foley and Malcolm Muggeridge. Rita lunched with the men at the English Club, 'a piece of land forever England' with 'leather chairs, subdued light' and 'florid men reading newspapers'.[88] They discussed the war, inching their chairs together while speaking in hushed voices. As the solitary female MI6 officer in Lisbon, Rita filled a position usually held by a man. She put aside their egos and worked closely with her male colleagues on complex operations. In many ways, being a woman had advantages when running male agents, who initially assumed Rita was a secretary.

In the two years leading up to the failed plot to assassinate Hitler in July 1944, Rita and her colleague Graham Maingot ran an important German agent codenamed WHISKY.[89] Otto John was a young lawyer who worked for the German airline Lufthansa. The ardent anti-Nazi had long been involved with the German opposition and was a close associate of Claus von Stauffenberg, the leading conspirator who hoped to kill Hitler and liberate Nazi Germany. In 1942, John visited Madrid for work purposes. He seized the opportunity to fly to Lisbon and meet with Rita and Maingot at the British Embassy. He must have found the two intelligence officers a formidable pair. Maingot, known affectionately as 'G.M.', was 'short and rather stubby in stature, with prematurely white hair, and could certainly have played a part as a romantic film star'.[90] Rita towered over her partner and matched his covert talents for running agents.

Between 1942 and 1944, John met his British handlers a dozen times. Though he supplied Rita and Maingot with detailed reports, London headquarters were apprehensive about entertaining contact with anyone purporting to be an envoy of the German opposition. The

Venlo disaster of November 1939 loomed large in the minds of MI6 senior personnel, who refused to be fooled a second time. One evening in January 1944, John met with Rita in Lisbon.[91] Following a careful plan, John made his way to a dimly lit side street and found Rita waiting for him in a parked car. The MI6 officer drove through the city listening to John's urgent request for British support of Stauffenberg's plot. She had to inform him that 'strict instructions had been received from London forbidding any further contact with emissaries of the German opposition'. Rita drew the meeting to a close by relaying a message from MI6 headquarters that 'the war would now be decided by force of arms'.[92]

John returned to Berlin that month and reported on his meeting with Rita to the German conspirators, who rallied and took action in March 1944, but were prevented from shooting Hitler dead at the Berghof, when SS guards acting on orders refused to let aides into the meeting. Undeterred, the conspirators made a second attempt on 20 July 1944, when the 37-year-old Stauffenberg entered the conference room at the 'Wolf's Lair' in Rastenburg, East Prussia, and placed a slab of explosive concealed in his briefcase under Hitler's huge map table. However, after Stauffenberg left the room to make a telephone call, an officer unknowingly moved the briefcase to the far side of the vertical table-support, further away from the Führer. Thus, when the bomb was detonated by time fuse a minute or two later, Hitler escaped most of the blast. Following the failed coup, John flew to Madrid on 24 July.[93] After three weeks, he was smuggled out of the city, avoiding German Abwehr officers who were hot on his heels.[94] For the next three months, John travelled through Spain, hiding in a succession of flats across the country, before he made it to Lisbon, where he finally took refuge in an MI9 safe house, adopting the cover identity of an RAF pilot.[95] While MI6 figured out what to do with their agent turned defector, the Portuguese secret police raided the safe house and arrested John on 23 October 1944.[96] News of the German defector's arrest quickly reached the German Embassy, who demanded that the Portuguese release the 'traitor' to them immediately. Rita acted quickly and informed the Salazar government that they would be held to account should anything happen to John while he was in their custody.[97]

Rita was puzzled by the speed with which the Portuguese secret police had moved against her agent. Otto John himself suspected that someone had been working against him from the start. At the time, Graham Greene was in charge of the Portuguese desk at MI6 in London, and his boss was the Soviet penetration agent Kim Philby, who did his best to keep John away from London. Philby's Soviet masters planned to install a puppet communist government in Germany after the war, and any separate British peace with Germany could scuttle Soviet plans, which, in part, did eventually come about.[98] Thanks to the strong note of protest she lodged with the Portuguese, John was released into Rita's custody on 3 November 1944.[99] The following day, John boarded a flight to Gibraltar, escorted by the plain-spoken wife of the former British ambassador, Alice Hopkinson. Alice was to vouch for John if they had any problems when they landed at the RAF airfield on the Rock. However, bad weather saw the plane return to Lisbon. The following night, Rita escorted her agent to the flying-boat station at Tejo and waved him off.[100] John later recalled that Rita confided to him 'that up to the very last moment someone in London had been resisting [his] entry into England – it was Philby'.[101]

John escaped with his life. Had he been caught by his fellow countrymen, he would have faced execution. Conscious of Rita's role in his exfiltration, John wrote in his post-war memoir, 'I owed my life to Miss Rita Winsor.'[102] After hearing of her death at the end of 1986, John travelled from Austria to England. The 78-year-old had spent the previous few decades trying to clear his name. As the first head of West Germany's intelligence service, John had been convicted of treason and sentenced in 1956 to four years in prison. In his defence, John had claimed that he had been drugged and abducted to East Berlin in 1954, whereas the German court had ruled that the wartime German resister movement member had voluntarily defected to the German Democratic Republic, from which he had subsequently returned.[103] Rita's former agent, who had arguably been at the centre of one of the greatest conspiracies of the war, found himself labelled a traitor not once but twice.

John had not seen Rita since his departure from Lisbon to England in 1944, but he knew that Ena was still alive. In 1987, John strolled up the path of Green Cottage in the quintessential English village of Old Newton, near Stowmarket, and knocked on the front door. While the full details of the subsequent conversation remain unknown, Ena did share several points with her neighbour, who asked the MI6 veteran over a late afternoon coffee how her day had gone. 'Most interesting,'

Ena replied.[104] She then described how Otto John had unexpectedly turned up at the cottage to say a very belated 'thank you'.

Rita Winsor and Ena Molesworth's clandestine endeavours did not end in 1945. After an eventful Second World War spent mostly overseas, these two highly capable MI6 women established and managed a successful high-end travel business with a long list of clients visiting out-of-the-way places. After all, who would suspect two middle-aged spinsters touring Russia, China and South America with small parties of wealthy tourists under the cover of 'International Services'?

13

The Inner Circle

The sound of clinking teacups and a young woman's laughter echoed down the underground corridor. Joan Bright was in raptures as her latest visitor recounted an amusing story. Admiral James Somerville, Commander-in-Chief Eastern Fleet, had just finished reviewing top-secret files in the Special Information Centre (SIC).[1] Only hours before she had prepared the room and laid out the files, the 32-year-old secretary had managed to squeeze in a visit to the hair salon. Immaculately presented, the slim brunette sported a stylish bob, swept back with carefully set waves that emphasised her strong cheekbones and mischievous look. Joan was just one of several hundred men and women who worked around the clock in the Cabinet War Rooms in the heart of Westminster. Winston Churchill referred to the bomb-proof command bunker as 'This Secret Place', but it was affectionately known as 'The Hole' by the military officers, staffers and secretaries who roamed the underground maze of tunnels. The War Rooms were located ten feet below ground in the basement of what is now the Treasury building, a short block from Number 10 Downing Street. Shielded by a thick reinforced concrete slab, the warren of offices and meeting rooms played home to the inner circle of British government. From here, the prime minister directed military operations and made decisions that changed the course of the war.

A telephone rang loud and clear in Joan's office, interrupting the visitor's storytelling. She lifted the receiver, taking note of the warning message displayed around the rotary dial that the line was not secure. The caller was a familiar and welcoming voice. Speaking with a faint lisp, the assistant to the Director of Naval Intelligence, Ian Fleming, enquired whether Joan could help find a position for a mutual friend, Mary Grepe. The MI6 secretary had returned from her posting in Lisbon in June 1942 and was in need of work. Mary had called upon Fleming at the Admiralty, and he promised to help. The handsome naval officer immediately rang Joan, who secured Mary an interview for a personal assistant post.[2] Joan was great friends with Fleming's older brother Peter, who had introduced her to the family.[3] Ian and Joan briefly dated during the war, and while she remained very fond of the Bond creator, she later revealed how 'he was a ruthless man – he would drop somebody if he didn't want them any more'.[4] She remained tight-lipped about the relationship, stating a few years before she died in 2008 that it was 'no torrid love affair. I've got nothing to tell you on that side.'[5]

Described as 'the organising genius of the War Cabinet Secretariat',[6] Joan arrived at the underground stronghold in December 1940.[7] Well-versed in secret matters, she had previously worked for Military Intelligence Research, a section of the War Office that had been established along similar lines to MI6 Section D, to sabotage and subvert the enemy. Joan belonged to a group of women who navigated the secret world of British intelligence, moving from one organisation to another as and when the need arose or circumstances dictated. Women were, and still are, an essential part of the secret fabric of covert and irregular warfare. The transfer of expertise and specialist knowledge facilitated a constant churn of innovation and enterprising administrative endeavours. Joan found that as the war progressed, stuffy old brigadiers with a penchant for strict adherence to military rules and procedures that excluded anyone not in uniform began to soften their attitude. The civilian women made themselves indispensable and became accepted couriers of red-lettered 'Top Secret' files intended for officers' eyes only. Joan recollected in her vivid wartime memoir, *The Inner Circle*, how 'there was scarcely a senior officer without his female "Personal Assistant" – a "Temporary Civil Servant" for the duration – her high heels beating an efficient and provocative tattoo up and down the murky corridors, in and out of the shabby rooms'.[8]

The addition of women significantly changed the atmosphere for the better in the War Cabinet offices.[9] Senior officers were proud of their attractive and intelligent female civilian staff, a feature 'that distinguished Britain's command centre from other allied powers'.[10] Joan was a great supporter of women and worked hard to establish the position of female staff in the War Cabinet secretariat. Having a thoughtful and independent mind, she remained a quiet feminist for the rest of her days.[11] From a young age, Joan was driven and determined to do something interesting with her life. Trevor and Mary

Bright served as excellent role models to their five daughters. The aspiring English squire and the 'sturdy Lowland Scot' gave Joan the freedom to pursue a path of her own choosing.[12] Joan's father was an accountant with Antony Gibbs & Sons, the well-known banking and shipping firm. His work took him and his family to Argentina, where Joan was born on 27 September 1910. She adored her father, who in Joan's eyes represented the very best of how a man should be. Kind, sensitive, modest and reserved, Trevor enjoyed the finer things in life but did not earn the money needed to live the lavish lifestyle he dreamt of. Mary, ever the realist, carefully monitored family spending.

Trevor took various jobs worldwide while Mary and the girls settled in England, first in Derbyshire, then Bath and finally Bristol. Unlike her sisters, who attended boarding school during their teenage years, Joan was considered nervous and difficult to manage. Days before her twelfth birthday, Joan went to live with friends of her father. She spent the next four years with the Birch family and their daughter Ruby, benefiting from 'strong clean air, the regular routine of early nights and generous meals' which built up for her 'a foundation of good health'.[13] After Joan returned home, she spent a year at Clifton High School. Her future was shaped by her next action when she stepped through the doors of Mrs Hoster's Secretarial Training College in Cromwell Road. The highly reputed establishment for well-educated girls had been emancipating women since 1887. The founder, Constance Hoster, was an ardent advocate of training educated women for secretarial work and securing permanent employment for 'her girls'.[14] The bold pioneer lived by the mantra that 'good work can always command good wages'.[15] With her knowledge of the social and business world, Constance trained women in typewriting and shorthand.[16] By the time of her death in 1939, the institution had graduated thirty thousand women over a fifty-year period.[17]

Famous for 'turning out gels for the establishment', the secretarial school was a prime recruitment ground for the Foreign Office.[18] With her feet set on the ladder of good fortune, Joan applied for a job replacing her soon-to-be-married sister at the British Legation in Mexico City. After five years working as a cipher clerk and falling 'unsuitably in love', Joan left Mexico and its cheerful marimba bands and made the long journey back to England in 1936.[19] She struggled initially to find work that satisfied her sense of value, turning down an English teaching position with Rudolf Hess and his family in Nazi Germany.

Joan flitted from one temporary post to another, working at the Royal Institute of International Affairs at Chatham House and briefly for the international revolutionary socialist Fenner Brockway. She lasted only three weeks in the offices of the disaffiliated Independent Labour Party as she could not stand being called 'comrade'.[20] In September 1938, the conservative secretary then began typing in the office of an anti-aircraft battery in Acton. By the time 1939 arrived, she found herself out of work, but it would not be for long. As Joan recollected years later, 'with a shorthand pad and a typewriter I could be a valuable and mobile interpreter of others' thoughts, a human machine with the power to give and receive confidence. Without them I could not have done any of the jobs I had had, and I certainly would not have had "such a marvellous war".'[21]

Joan's baptism into the world of secret intelligence came about by sheer chance. In April 1939, she had bumped into an old childhood friend at a cocktail party. After she had explained her jobless predicament, John Walter reassured Joan that he would help find her something suitable. The following day, she received a telephone call instructing her to wear a pink carnation and to arrive at St James's Park underground station at 11 a.m., where a lady would approach her. Intrigued by the cloak-and-dagger nature of the request, Joan duly made her way to the tube station, where she met a short and dark-haired woman by the name of Greta Lempriere.[22] A seasoned intriguer, the 38-year-old professionally trained opera singer later spent the war in Tehran, and from there, was posted to Algiers for the remainder of the war.[23] Greta's career in the Foreign Office eventually spanned thirty years, of which some were spent working for MI6.[24] As she led Joan from the tube station to the intended destination, Greta frequently changed direction, sometimes doubling back, to shake off possible unwanted tails.[25]

As the two women came full circle, they rounded the corner back at the tube station, where Greta directed Joan into the chambers next door to St Ermin's Hotel. Joan sat patiently as a short, dapper, red-haired colonel introduced himself. Montague Chidson of MI6's Section D had a precise way of speaking. He warned Joan of the dreadful things that would happen to her if the Germans caught her. The Gestapo were masters of interrogation and torture who inflicted unimaginable pain using cruel methods such as the insertion of needles beneath toenails.[26] Unperturbed by what she described as 'good clean fun', Joan signed the Official Secrets Act.[27] From April 1938, MI6 seconded its newest secretary to D/MI(R), the military intelligence research unit of the War Office that for a time fell under the remit of Section D.[28] MI(R), as it was later restyled, was responsible for researching, planning and executing guerrilla operations behind enemy lines. However, its men were uniformed and subject to the standard conventions of war.[29] Joan was undoubtedly more comfortable with a military approach to thwarting the enemy than with irregular methods and remained baffled by Section D's antics. She found the head, Laurence Grand, 'a bit mad' as he devised the most extraordinary agent-led sabotage operations that 'one couldn't really go entirely along with'.[30]

Joan slowly adjusted to the new kind of work, which was completely different from anything she had done. Her MI(R) bosses were the chain-smoking Joe Holland and his three staff officers: the quiet-spoken Colin Gubbins; Millis Jefferis, a red-faced genius inventor; and Dymock Watson, a blue-eyed naval man with an iron determination to destroy chosen targets. In the run-up to war, Joan was joined in the office by Isabel 'Lesley' Wauchope, whom she described as having 'the face of an untroubled Madonna'.[31] The women laughed their way through hectic months of typing at the MI(R) offices within the Section D headquarters in St Ermin's Hotel.[32] The hotel was conveniently tucked away down one of Westminster's quiet backstreets, a short walk from MI6 headquarters on Broadway, and its Caxton Bar became a popular meeting place for intelligence officers wishing to avoid prying eyes. Kim Philby was interviewed twice at the hotel, just days apart, for a position in MI6. During the summer of 1940, the Soviet penetration agent was put through his paces by Marjorie Maxse, an elderly MI6 recruiter, who had invited Philby on the recommendation of her colleague, Guy Burgess. Unbeknown to Marjorie, Burgess was also working for the Soviets.[33] At the second interview, Burgess joined Marjorie and Philby as they met in the resplendent hotel lobby, which had white Victorian plasterwork that gave the impression of being inside a giant wedding cake. The intricate rococo sculpting served as a suitable distraction from the secret tunnel rumoured to run from beneath the grand central staircase to the Palace of Westminster.

Joe Holland had no intention of conforming to the secret habits of his Section D associates. The MI(R) head loathed the clandestine practices performed by MI6 officers, who never left the hotel offices during daylight for fear of being discovered by the German agents thought to be lurking around every street corner. Years later, an elderly Joan sat in the Special Forces Club behind Harrods in Knightsbridge and recalled how Holland had been 'a man of remarkable drive'.[34] Speaking with a lovely soft dulcet tone, Joan described the bow-legged Holland as a tough man who was challenging to work with. She had occasionally opened his office door and instantly had to duck, as the unconventional army officer, an avid reader, was prone to throwing books at his staff. Holland's volatile streak contrasted greatly with that of his most devoted staff officer, the placid Colin Gubbins. Yet the two men got on exceptionally well. Joan admired Gubbins's 'gifts of leadership, courage and integrity'.[35] Such qualities would make him a daring and visionary head of the Special Operations Executive (SOE). Years after the war, Joan co-authored his biography with another MI(R) alumnus and SOE veteran, Peter Wilkinson.[36]

Vivacious and committed, Joan enjoyed the thrill of the work. She assisted Gubbins in compiling three illustrated pamphlets instructing Allied agents on sabotage in the event of a German invasion. From detailed drawings, future saboteurs learnt how to attach a stick of gelignite under a railway sleeper. Guidance in various languages informed readers how to bring down a bridge with a carefully placed brown-paper parcel packed with explosives, and, should agents need to dispose of the incriminating pocket-sized guides, the paper was edible.[37] Other duties saw Joan tasked with sorting through a list of men and identifying who was most qualified to join MI(R). She then sat in on the interviews and made notes. Those selected included Peter Fleming, Peter Wilkinson, who was a talented linguist, Douglas Dodds-Parker, formerly of the colonial Sudan Political Service, and Tommy Davies, a director of Courtaulds, all of whom had eventful wartime careers with the Special Operations Executive. Joan and Lesley Wauchope made all the arrangements for the men's training at Caxton Hall, a building that had previously served as a base for suffragettes who held meetings in its hall before marching to Parliament. In 1938, the public hall was used for weddings and meetings, providing the perfect cover for small groups of men attending secret lectures on guerrilla tactics and clandestine wireless communication.[38]

After Hitler invaded Poland, and France and Britain declared war on Germany, Joe Holland lost no time in unshackling MI(R) from Section D, and returning his staff to the War Office. Joan and Lesley staggered up Whitehall carrying mountains of files and heavy typewriters; their unburdened male colleagues followed at a discreet distance behind. As Joan reflected, 'we were not to know that we were the vanguard of a revolution'.[39] Based on the third floor in Rooms 364 and 365, Joan and Lesley grew accustomed to the War Office with its unwashed walls and smell of stale cigarette smoke. With funding for the research section still coming from MI6, the women purchased two Royal typewriters, much to the envy of the other War Office typists who struggled with government-issued Imperials, which required a heavy stabbing action to press each key.[40] Joan loved to type, and she was incredibly good at it. As a young girl, she dreamt of being a concert pianist, likening typing to playing the piano. Never swayed by brand, the typewriter connoisseur chose her machines based on their look and efficiency.[41]

As MI(R) numbers increased, Holland despatched various unsuccessful missions to Europe. Meanwhile, Joan had a 'riotous time' with recruits, such as the actor David Niven.[42] As the war progressed, the atmosphere changed. During the Dunkirk evacuation at the end of May 1940, Joan reflected on how she could not have been closer to the centre of the conflict than working in the War Office. Joan would ask how many men had made it off the beaches each day. The 'secretary' asserted, 'we were fighting for our lives, we needed these men'.[43] That summer, Churchill and his ministers authorised the establishment of a new dirty tricks department to co-ordinate and direct subversion and sabotage behind enemy lines. MI(R) staff dispersed as the SOE emerged. Joan said a sad farewell to Gubbins, Wilkinson and her typing partner Lesley, who all joined SOE's ranks.[44]

On Holland's advice and armed with a letter of introduction, Joan attempted to secure a post working for General Hastings 'Pug' Ismay at the Office of the War Cabinet and Minister of Defence. She left unsuccessful but not deterred. As the hopeful secretary returned to the War Office, Joan removed her blue corduroy hat to enjoy the October sunshine.[45] For the next two months, she worked in MO9, a new War Office department that would later become the Commandos. Her new boss, Dudley Clarke, was a master of military deception and a far more amiable character than the terrifying, book-throwing Joe Holland.[46] Reunited with David Niven, Joan was entertained by his quick wit and endless supply of funny stories, which made the hours pass while she worked on chronicling MI(R)'s actions over the course of its short eighteen-month existence.[47]

Joan returned to her top-floor flat on Curzon Street at the end of each working day. During the Blitz, she spent many nights sleeping on the staircase or in the basement, listening to the news with the caretaker, Hulford, and his ancient cat, which always seemed to know when there would be a bombing raid. Disaster struck one evening in November when Joan had nipped to Berkeley Square to have drinks with friends. The group had heard the bombs drop, and Joan rushed back to find the house no longer standing. The bomb had fallen at an angle, directly hitting the basement where she used to sit. The caretaker had survived and was recovering in hospital, but his elderly cat had not been so lucky.[48] Joan picked her way through the rubble towards St Ermin's Hotel, where she spent the night.[49] The next day, she attended an interview for a position in the secretariat of the Joint Planning Committee, a subcommittee of the Chiefs of Staff Committee based in the Cabinet War Rooms. Colonel Cornwall-Jones broke ranks when he offered Joan a job, as he faced significant resistance to employing a civilian woman.

On 21 December 1940, Joan moved with her trusted Royal type-writer to the underground bunker, which she approached along a corridor from Great George Street.[50] Concealed within her bag, Joan brought a good supply of hard-to-come-by sanitary towels.[51] Factories that used to manufacture women's hygiene products had turned to churning out items for the war effort. The shortage of essential sanitary towels grew so great that, by 1942, the government had no option but to purchase 8.5 million abroad.[52] Britain's servicewomen drew upon a stockpile generously donated by the car manufacturer Lord Nuffield. However, civilian women like Joan had to source their own or resort to time-old methods of dealing with their monthly periods.[53] No evidence survives on how the secret service responded to the potential challenge of female personnel ringing in sick due to the lack of available sanitary products, or how such constraints affected a woman's self-esteem in the office. Women like Joan adapted and adjusted, bearing the responsibility of wartime expectations without complaint.[54]

Joan's new office was a square box of a room with cream-painted walls. She navigated the low ceilings and quickly shook off any claus-trophobic feelings. The first-rate secretary was now working at the heart of Britain's war machine, where Churchill presided over more than one hundred meetings of his War Cabinet. Typists remembered the prime minister as a 'shortish, fatish, tubby man bouncing around in a siren suit'.[55] He rarely slept in his bedroom office, but the prime minister did deliver four stirring wartime addresses before a microphone standing on the desk. The nerve centre of operations was the central map room, where women plotted the progress of naval convoy routes and troop movements with push pins and coloured string. A bank of coloured telephones linked the underground complex with strategic command centres all over the world. Churchill made transatlantic calls to President Franklin Roosevelt on the world's first confidential hotline to be located in a former broom cupboard amusingly disguised with a recycled toilet lock on the door indicating 'vacant' or 'engaged'. A special cable ran from the soundproof cubicle to an enormous speech encryption device installed in the basement of Selfridges department store, some distance away on Oxford Street. An enthusiastic 22-year-old Ruth Ive monitored the VIP calls, listening in, ready to disconnect the line should Churchill share information that might compromise national security.[56]

Joan took time to get used to the strange subterranean way of life with its 'quiet dungeon galleries, where the only mechanical sounds were the tap of typewriters and the hum of air-conditioning fans'.[57] A weatherboard was the sole link to life above ground. A standing joke among staff was that, if it indicated it was windy, it meant that there was an air raid in progress. Joan preferred to rely on the red and green lights that indicated whether it was safe to leave the bunker or not.[58] She was one of the many sworn to secrecy who worked long hours underground. To keep healthy in the absence of exposure to daylight, some staff used ultraviolet lamp treatments to boost vitamin D production.[59] The work was relentless. Joan's new boss, Arthur Cornwall-Jones, gave her the impossible task of creating a card index system that recorded every meeting and decision taken using cards coloured for different parts of the world. As good an organiser as she was, Joan explained to Cornwall-Jones that his ambitious idea was unworkable. She then spent the rest of her time engaged in secretarial work and soon came to miss the excitement of MI(R) work. She felt that she was 'neither fish nor fry; I was nothing really'.[60]

A chance to escape her miserable existence in the Joint Planning Committee arrived in May 1941 when Joan received a lunch invitation from Churchill's closest military adviser, General 'Pug' Ismay. Known as 'Pug' on account of his heavy bulldog jaw, the six-foot-tall chief staff officer was an efficient career soldier who disliked nonsense and unnecessary paperwork. He informed Joan that Churchill wished to establish an information centre for commanders-in-chief to consult secret papers.[61] The prime minister no longer had the time to meet on a regular basis with his commanders. Over a chilled bottle of Chablis, Ismay offered Joan the chance to run the centre. However, there would be no pay rise and no chance of being paid overtime. Joan felt 'a sort of non-acquiescent reaction against General Ismay's charm and his assumption that [she] would jump at the chance of going up to the higher regions of war-planning'.[62]

Loyal to Cornwall-Jones and convinced that top military brass could get any information they wanted at any time and any place, Joan declined Ismay's work offer. However, she eventually reconsidered the invitation and joined Ismay in June 1941.[63] After just one month in post, Joan received some difficult news. Her father had complained of not feeling well and had collapsed. He was diagnosed with throat cancer and given a year to live, but Joan received the sad news of his death only a month later, on 3 July. She recorded in her memoir how, while at work, 'it was the open black telephone – not the top-secret red nor the security-equipped green – which brought my mother's voice with its sad news to my ear'.[64]

That same day, Joan welcomed the first visitor to the Special Information Centre, Sir Alexander Hardinge, private secretary to the King.[65] The new information centre had the appearance of a sitting room, with its long polished table, a comfortable armchair, and a well-placed blue vase of fresh flowers to brighten the surroundings.[66] Under controlled conditions, senior officers visited and consulted secret papers from various military and intelligence bodies. However, Joan had a difficult start. The young gatekeeper faced initial hostility from other subterranean staff, who questioned why she was selected to sit in such a lovely carpeted room when they worked in such austere offices. Proud of his latest innovation, Churchill urged his chiefs of staff, 'You must go along to my new information room. You'll find out everything you like up there.'[67] Joan waited for further visitors, but the SIC remained empty for several weeks. Ismay reassured her more would come, and they did.

On 22 July 1941, Joan finally greeted the long-awaited second visitor, Admiral Percy Noble, the handsome Commander-in-Chief of the Western Approaches.[68] He signed the visitors' book before going through the intelligence reports and war summaries laid out by Joan on the table. As Noble left, he remarked, 'A nice set-up, but not quite what I expected.'[69] The feeling was mutual. After a flurry of high-ranking curious callers, two months came and went before she received further visitors in November.[70] Joan realised that the SIC needed to offer more than just informative papers. The air marshals, generals and admirals wanted to review the rare files that detailed precisely how decisions were reached in every aspect of the war. Joan had one problem: those files were constantly in use. Ever resourceful, she begged, borrowed and stole to get what she needed. Joan even memorised specific files she planned to obtain copies of. She patiently waited until the war's end to get her hands on one particular green minute that discussed Stewart Menzies's job in 1940, as she knew it would be useful in the future.[71]

The solution to her dilemma lay in the simple but daunting task of creating her own files. The brilliant back-office organiser achieved this by overhauling the central filing system of the secretariat, which she eventually took over. In Joan's professional opinion, the system was not fit for purpose, as many files carried too many duplicates, and the numbering was inadequate for cross-referencing purposes.[72] With a staff of three conscientious women – Joan Umney-Gray, Laura Cooper and Winnie Spearing – Joan began to work through the two hundred files piled high in laundry baskets. Deliberately placed next door to the SIC, the women created complete sets of new files that covered all subjects brought before the daily meetings of the Chiefs of Staff Committee.[73] A total of nearly eight hundred files were created before the end of the war.[74] For Joan, each dossier needed to tell the whole story: 'When you open a file, it's got to speak to you as to what's in it, and there must be nothing left out.'[75] Once the women had hole-punched and tagged various colour-coded papers and ordered them, it became easy to feed in new files sent their way. Now deemed an integral part of the War Cabinet Rooms, Joan's information enterprise found its way onto the 'circulation list of minutes, memoranda, telegrams, reports, letters and comments'.[76]

The redoubtable secretary managed both the SIC and the filing section at the same time. If need be, Joan could always dash from the SIC to the adjacent office and grab a file from one of the filing cabinets. After they had visited the SIC several times, Joan got to know many high-ranking callers well. Overseas commanders made particularly good use of the SIC, and they enjoyed the lack of formality, wish-ing 'Joany' a good morning when they arrived rather than having to engage in the business of saluting.[77] General Wavell, Commander-in-Chief, India, preferred to sit in silence as Joan fed him various situation reports. In a dry and grating voice, Wavell had complained during one visit that the information telegrams that Joan and Ismay supplied commanders with were dull. As Joan and her boss prided themselves on maintaining exceptionally high standards, they agreed to implement a two-tier system of telegrams to keep commanders better informed. The SICHTEL took the form of a situation report reviewing the bigger strategic picture of the war; the CHIEFTEL con-veyed top-secret material about future operations and plans for their eyes only. The latter greatly pleased Wavell.[78] As Joan collected the information and prepared the telegrams for Ismay, she recorded in her memoir how it represented her first 'step into the inner circle of the War Cabinet Offices'.[79]

Brilliant administrators such as Joan were in high demand. In April 1942, Wavell wrote to Ismay enquiring whether Joan could go to India to help set up a secretariat on the War Cabinet Offices model. According to Ismay, Joan was keen to accept Wavell's offer and the substantial pay increase. However, reluctant to part with Joan, Ismay said no.[80] Instead, he offered his assistant a pay rise of £500 a year and the chance to serve as an administrative officer for the British delegation at the Quebec conference in August 1943, one of six Allied conferences attended by Joan before the end of the war.[81] Ismay looked upon his young secretary as a fourth daughter, and Joan had a strong relationship with her boss. She sometimes stayed with the Ismay family at Wormington Grange, and she actually lived with them for a time during the war.[82] She described Ismay as a 'marvellous man' who was fair and businesslike with a 'strong sense of humour'.[83]

Joan Bright exhibited many of the valuable attributes and talents assigned by Ian Fleming to the character 'Miss Moneypenny', such as trust, loyalty and good judgement. Ismay recognised her skill and ability in a personal note inscribed within a copy of his memoir gifted to Joan. He wrote: 'For Joan who was loved by admirals and liftmen alike, and who fought like a tigress for the comfort of the underdog at the conferences . . . and who made a far bigger contribution to the successful working of the defence machinery than has ever been rec-ognised.'[84] Modest to the core, Joan attributed her wartime success to good secretarial training.[85] As Ismay's personal assistant, she was arguably the closest woman to Churchill's inner circle of commanders-in-chief. Ismay placed his trust in Joan when he assigned to her the responsibility for handling all administrative arrangements for the British delegation at the 'Big Three' summits, where Churchill, Joseph Stalin and Franklin Roosevelt (later replaced by Harry Truman) decided the fate of the post-war world.

As Ismay's 'file-keeper', 'conference housekeeper' and private secretary, Joan spent the second half of the war travelling to Washington, Moscow, Tehran, Yalta and Potsdam.[86] Not fazed by anything, a confident Joan adopted dark tailored clothing for her big professional moments overseas. She helped organise the organisers and took charge of allocating bedroom and office accommodation for British VIPs and their large retinues of staff. The tactful 'housekeeper' proved so capable that she received a constant supply of bouquets from American delegates hoping to secure better rooms for their people.[87] With great skill, Joan deftly switched to secretarial mode in an instant when required for note-taking in meetings discussing D-Day and Operation OVERLORD, the planned invasion of Europe.

Joan dealt with the administrative nightmare of the final wartime conference at Yalta on the Black Sea in February 1945. Many of the problems involved Churchill. Regardless of where the prime minister was during the war, he slept in a double bed. A big bed provided plenty of space for papers, books and newspapers, and his mind worked well and quickly with his feet up under the covers. The Russians were unaware of the prime minister's sleeping needs. Joan navigated several logistical challenges to fly a suitable bed from Moscow to Yalta.[88] When Churchill was defeated by Russian plumbing as he struggled with a cold bath due to a malfunctioning tap, Joan was on hand to assist.[89] Evenings were more relaxing, as the glamorous secretary attended parties where she was introduced to Mrs Roosevelt and took in a performance of Tchaikovsky's *Swan Lake* at the famous Bolshoi Theatre in Moscow.[90] Less glamorous entertainment, but no less fun, included a game of bridge in Ismay's cabin with Ian Fleming and stenographer Jean Crawford, who entertained everyone with Shirley Temple impersonations.[91]

While away from London, Churchill ensured that he was kept up to date with ULTRA intelligence reports from Bletchley Park. With security paramount, the prime minister was always trying to find out who was 'in the know' when it came to keeping the greatest secret of all. On the voyage to America in May 1943, Joan had been chatting in the bar aboard the *Queen Mary* when Churchill came in. She tried to back away discreetly, but the head of the Royal Air Force, Peter Portal, interrupted the prime minister as he passed by and asked him, 'May I introduce Joan Bright?' Joan shook Churchill's hand, and he looked her straight in the eyes and demanded, 'Do you know about BONIFACE?' Joan recollected that she had no idea who the mysterious BONIFACE was at the time.[92] The codename was a cover for intelligence drawn from enemy intelligence decrypts. Churchill liked to test people to see who knew, and who didn't. Joan passed the test. Not privy to ULTRA material, Joan was nevertheless aware of the weekly, sometimes daily, delivery of highly secret papers in a locked box. Ismay would read the material in his office while Joan gossiped with the despatch rider, Mrs Dunne, who returned the papers to Bletchley.[93] However, Joan was herself considered trustworthy enough to carry top-secret documents on journeys to the summits. When boarding a plane, she would hand the official papers in sealed containers to the pilot for safe custody.[94]

The burden of knowing secrets weighed heavily on Joan's conscience. She found herself in difficult circumstances throughout the war but demonstrated remarkable tact and resolve. On one occasion in May 1941, she had been running down the corridor from her underground office when she bumped into a grave-looking Ismay. He informed Joan: 'We have just had some ghastly news; the battleship *Hood* has been sunk, we think with few survivors.'[95] Running late for an appointment at an Elizabeth Arden beauty salon, she carried on her way. When Joan jumped into the chair and sat back, ready for her face massage, she asked the masseuse, who happened to be an old friend, how her brother was doing in the Royal Navy. She replied, 'Oh, so far as I know, he's all right; he's still on the *Hood*, you know.' After suppressing the secret for decades, Joan revealed in her memoir the emotional toll of harbouring undisclosed information from those she knew. She described her reaction to the conversation as if it were yesterday: 'I sank back unable to speak, all pleasure gone. I could not tell her what I knew, but I knew at that moment that her brother was dead.'[96]

Joan was a repository of secret knowledge. With an ordered mind and a love of keeping records, she stored everything away in her memory. Just as she maintained a highly confidential service in the SIC, Joan was a confidante at the major conferences. She befriended ambassadors, high-ranking military personnel and translators, keeping her eyes and ears open. The Russians had been generous and suspicious in turn at Moscow and Yalta, but the atmosphere was markedly different at the final conference in Potsdam in July 1945. Beyond the victory parades, cracks were beginning to appear in the facade of postwar peace.

The war in Europe was over, and the Allies were concerned with the reconstruction of the European continent. Germany was divided into occupied zones, with the Allied Control Commission co-ordinating overall policy. Tensions were rising, as is evident in the detailed instructions compiled by Joan which informed London that the chiefs of staff were not to fly-fish or go boating while in the Berlin area. They would be liable to be shot by the Russians on the other side of the lake in Babelsberg, an undamaged suburb southeast of Potsdam where the delegates were housed.[97]

Joan was particularly shocked by the state of Berlin when she accompanied the chiefs on a tour of the capital. Free to roam around Hitler's Chancellery in the Russian Zone, Joan and Mary Grepe, the former MI6 Lisbon secretary whom Joan had helped secure a position in the Air Ministry, climbed through the knee-high rubble and dust. In search of souvenirs, the tourists hammered away at Hitler's desk, and Mary managed to pillage a tile from the dead Führer's bathroom.[98] Joan described the visit to Hitler's headquarters in her memoir: 'There were hundreds of new Iron Cross medals strewn across the floor, their shining metallic faces a travesty ... It was a horrible and macabre place, its evil spirit hanging over the grim city it had destroyed. The smell of Berlin, as of the military suburb of Potsdam, was quite definitely the smell of decayed death.'[99]

When Joan returned to London at the beginning of August 1945, she was as exhausted as the rest of the nation. Britain had survived but was substantially broken and poor. Austerity and rationing continued for some time, and Churchill, whose towering presence had been at the centre of all things during the war, was replaced by Clement Attlee at the end of July. Joan continued working in the SIC, checking no longer needed files before archiving them. Files on Germany and the Far East Section remained open, and the thin folder marked 'A Certain High Explosive', which had sat in the filing cabinet since 1942, suddenly came into use in August 1945 when America dropped the two atomic bombs on Japan.[100]

The super-secretary admitted in her memoir that of all the jobs she did, the SIC files were nearest to her heart. Joan explained: 'I cared for them because I felt convinced they could contribute to the future histories.'[101] Through pure secretarial skill and talent, Joan had produced 'the history of the Second World War as it was fought and won on paper'.[102] Historians described the value of the SIC files as 'inestimable'.[103] Joan Bright remained a secret gatekeeper to all that went on in the Cabinet War Rooms for the rest of her life and took great pride when she attended the official opening of the Churchill Suite in the underground museum in 2003.[104] Fantastically sociable, she entertained a long list of fellow intelligence veterans, journalists and historians in her small London flat packed with books. Widely read, Joan maintained a keen interest in foreign affairs and knew only too well how nothing was as it appeared.[105]

The SIC closed its doors after receiving its final visitor on 30 November 1945.[106] But while one era ended, another began. As the shadowy war between the West and the Soviet Union resumed, a cold chill set in for those who continued their work in secret matters.

14

Tinker, Tailor, Spy, Secretary

As Kathleen Pettigrew came in from the cold, her desk lamp flickered, casting an intermittent shadow on her typewriter. After wisely deciding not to remove her coat, the MI6 secretary turned to acknowledge her office companion. Kathleen's pet parakeet greeted her with a piercing screech as the bird hopped to and fro on its perch. Visitors to the MI6 headquarters at 54 Broadway could not quite believe that C allowed his senior secretary to keep the talkative bird in the adjoining office.[1] The occupants of the unattractive nine-storey Broadway building shivered in their sweaters and scarves as they went about their secret work. Temperatures had plummeted as Londoners welcomed 1946. War-weary but hopeful for better times, they were unprepared for the big freeze that would follow at the end of the year. The city's gas supply had failed, and troops were called into the capital to help restore fuel lines. The British public were not permitted to know that Kathleen and her colleagues existed. MI6 was, and still is, the most secret intelligence organisation in the world. The men and women of Britain's espionage arm practised deception for King and country. Officers, agents, assets and secretaries operated on both sides of the covert battlefield between the West and Soviet Russia. Yet several rotten apples threatened to corrupt the class-bound spy establishment of MI6.

In January 1946, Kathleen was awarded the MBE for her secret wartime contribution.[2] The list of New Year's Honours was so long that the *London Gazette* ran to 165 pages: the longest in living memory, recognising military and civil war services in Britain, the European and Atlantic theatres, and the colonies. Cited simply as being 'Employed in a department of the Foreign Office', Kathleen attended the investiture at Buckingham Palace. As she waited to receive her medal, the 47-year-old servant of the secret state was joined in line by Jane Archer, MI5's first female officer, who, after being sacked from the Security Service, had joined MI6 in 1940. Jane received the OBE for her wartime exploits.[3] MI6 officer Kim Philby was also present and appointed OBE.[4] Not surprisingly, the MI6 chief, Stewart Menzies, had seen fit to put forward the names of several deserving men and women at the end of the war. However, little did he know that the MI6 rising star was leading a double life as a Soviet agent. Philby believed resolutely in the communist cause and served only one master.

After decades of deception, Philby's treachery was starting to unfold. As he left Buckingham Palace in the company of his good friend, James Jesus Angleton, one of the founding officers of the US Central Intelligence Agency (CIA), the newly decorated MI6 officer declared: 'What this country needs is a good stiff dose of socialism.'[5] The surprise and out-of-character statement left Angleton questioning Philby's true allegiance for the first time. MI6 also began to think something was amiss when Philby finally disclosed to his boss, Valentine Vivian, that he and Aileen Furse were not married. Philby revealed that his actual wife was the Austrian communist Litzi Friedmann, whom he had wed in the early 1930s. Granted leave in 1946 to apply for a divorce, by drawing attention to Litzi, Philby had made a grave error of judgement. Intrigued by Philby's revelation, Vivian looked into the matter and discovered with the aid of MI5 that Litzi was a suspected Soviet agent. Vivian shared his findings with Menzies. The exact way in which the MI6 chief reacted remains unknown. However, Menzies now shared the same belief held by the very first head of service, Mansfield Cumming, that Russia was the only enemy.

Like many in MI6, Kathleen had quietly observed Philby's career from a mid-level spy to being considered a possible future head of MI6. However, unlike the Soviet penetration agent, she had remained a faithful servant, having sworn allegiance to King and country. Through exemplary dedication to duty, Kathleen's personal and professional life became one, as a condition of the secrecy she lived with every day. But such devotion came with a heavy price. The majority of MI6's female staff could only have a career in the service if they remained unmarried. Officially, MI6 women worked for the Foreign Office and were therefore subject to the marriage ban, an arcane rule that remained in place until 1972.[6] Over the years, Kathleen had grown accustomed to being guarded in her relationships and in her choice of those in whom she placed her trust. She may have remained a spinster, but she did not live the life of a solitary, single woman.

In a rare letter to her cousin written in 1964, Kathleen described how, at the war's end, her long-term partner, a man whom she named 'Kit', was engaged on a lecture tour in America.[7] Nothing more is known about the mysterious man, who likely also worked for MI6 or the Foreign Office. Still, such a relationship suggests Kathleen was a woman who chose not to be constrained by the proper and expected ways of doing things. Confident in her identity, the ambitious secretary was a self-made woman who had risen from humble beginnings to serve in the upper echelons of Britain's foreign intelligence service. She did not need a ring on her finger to achieve ultimate success.

The war had created many opportunities for women who worked in the secret services. Some like Kathleen had taken on executive roles, while others were deployed overseas behind enemy lines. Yet, after 1945, British intelligence remained very much a man's world. Doors that had been open to women were now closed. New female recruits were told 'women are happier in subordinate positions'.[8] Dick White, appointed MI6 chief in 1956, claimed, 'Our secretaries need only two things: good legs and a good upbringing.'[9] Every day at lunchtime, a row of chauffeur-driven limousines appeared outside Broadway, ready to whisk their debutante owners to lunch at expensive restaurants.[10] Women remained stuck in low-paid clerical positions with little hope of career advancement. Kathleen witnessed a quick turnaround of female secretarial staff who joined hoping to find a husband, or who at least entertained work until they had secured a suitable match elsewhere.

Even before the war had ended, MI6 admitted it had been 'backward in employing women'.[11] In May 1946, regional controllers considered whether they should employ women as officers at home and overseas. Spurred into action by the report, MI6 identified several female officers for postings abroad. However, they refused to make it the rule, leaving most diplomatic and consular posts still held by men. In April 1949, MI6 proposed sending a woman to work in Tel Aviv, but the Foreign Office refused. And, when the secret service suggested sending a female secretary to Amman, the capital of Jordan, in August 1949, the ambassador stipulated that it had to be a woman who 'should be a person of a certain age and if possible of forbidding appearance, well able to take care of herself'.[12]

The situation in MI5 was no different. Women had made great strides by 1945, with fifty-nine serving in officer positions, but they did so without formal rank or pay.[13] By June 1950, only five women held positions of officer level or higher, compared to eighty-seven men who held the rank of director through to junior officer.[14] With female staff outnumbering men two to one in 1950, most of MI5's female work-force powered the Registry, the Security Service's principal weapon against internal and external enemies. Recruited from either the aris-tocracy or the families of MI5 officers, the 'Registry Queens' managed a vast emporium of information that poured into MI5 from a range of different sources.[15] These glamorous women with perfectly polished nails sorted, checked and filed all incoming material. MI5 records were 'to the Service what ammunition is to a combatant force'.[16] By 1951, the Registry held 700,000 index cards on suspect persons, firms, organisations and publications. Diligent women added new names to the index at a rate of two thousand a week. A total of 498,000 files were continually expanded and refreshed, with around 350 new files created each week. Whenever staff were available for the task, records were weeded and destroyed. From 1941 to 1951, the Registry Queens disposed of some 838,000 index cards and 180,000 files.[17]

By 1951, MI5 had compiled around 4,500 personal files on Soviet citizens arriving in Britain. From the end of the war to the early 1950s, MI5 had identified and 'immunised' seven Russian spies, while a further two were tried and convicted. The Security Service had procured one Russian defector, whom they successfully exploited for intelligence.[18] Yet Britain's secret services had long remained blissfully unaware of the traitors within their ranks, men who had sunk to the depths of duplicity for over a decade. Jane Archer had long suspected that a Soviet agent had penetrated an important government office, confirmed by the Soviet intelligence officer Walter Krivitsky, who defected to the West before the outbreak of war. Jane had identified several suspects in MI6, one of whom worked for Philby.[19] However, before she had the chance to interview those remaining on her list, MI5's best communist spy-catcher was sacked for insubordination in 1940.

Much to Philby's horror, Jane was taken on by MI6 for the rest of the war. In 1944, she moved to the new Soviet Section headed by Philby. Recognising Jane as 'the ablest professional intelligence officer ever employed by MI5',[20] Philby strategically moved his nemesis to the Eastern Europe desk, where she worked on intercepted radio traf-fic concerning communist activity. Ever the English gentleman, the discreet and charming Philby had skilfully neutralised a significant threat to his true identity being revealed. Then, during the late 1940s, colleagues consulted Philby on whether Jane Archer or Roger Hollis should interrogate a Russian agent detained in Canada named Igor Gouzenko. Knowing that Jane was by far the better interrogator, Philby ensured that Hollis was the first choice. According to her step-daughter, Jean Collard, Jane had 'expressed suspicions about Philby before she was eased out of the intelligence services'.[21] Jane eventually returned to MI5 before she retired in 1958, so that she could recuperate her long years of pensionable service.[22]

In the post-war world, Kathleen and Jane belonged to the old guard. A new generation of career-minded women stepped forward, ready to smash the glass ceiling and forge their place in MI6 history. The Oxford graduate and SOE veteran Daphne Park joined the service in 1948. After several years in London and learning Russian at Cambridge, she was posted to Paris for two years before her appointment at the Moscow embassy in 1954. Daphne was a formidable 'Miss Marple' type of character, a forthright woman who spoke her mind. A razor-sharp intellect and wit saw this future Baroness Park of Monmouth appointed Controller Western Hemisphere in 1975, the highest post ever occupied by a woman in MI6. The trailblazer celebrated her promotion with her favourite tipple, Earl Grey tea, 'stirred, not shaken' as she often joked.[23] Daphne may have formally been one of the first women to fulfil an operational MI6 role, but pioneers such as Rita Winsor and Teddy Dunlop paved the way during the war. After 1945, both women continued in their covert work but did so using very different cover identities.

A revealing internal document drafted towards the end of the war considered the future organisation of MI6 and the role of women working overseas. The use of Passport Control Offices was deemed too 'flimsy' a cover for overseas MI6 stations. The paper suggested MI6 representatives 'should be completely outside the orbit of the diplomatic mission' and that the best cover would be 'legitimate business interests'. The Travel and Industrial Association, founded during the 1930s, was provided as an example of a suitable organisation. Its offices were located in key European capitals and provided 'advertising and propaganda of British and Empire scenery, historical associations, and industrial facilities'. The government supported the association, which received the backing of 'all the main railways, shipping companies, and certain industrial and press interests'. After 1945, MI6 planned to post officers with 'experience of travel, shipping, journalistic and kindred professions' to work in one of the offices. The cover was perfect as 'persons of all nationalities would naturally visit such offices at all times and seasons'. The paper acknowledged that 'women may be suitable for key positions in MI6 work abroad, and where a woman is suitable, she will have remarkable cover by reason of her sex'.[24]

Rita Winsor was an ideal candidate. As an MI6 officer, she had proven that she could turn her hand to anything in wartime Lisbon, her speciality being the exfiltration of agents and defectors. The clandestine quartermaster had an impressive résumé that included everything from planning complex travel routes to carrying out reconnaissance missions and overseeing networks of safe houses used by both agents and officers. Fluent in French, German, Italian, Spanish and Portuguese, Rita possessed the necessary linguistic skills to work in international travel markets. She looked much like any other well-groomed English businesswoman and wore the latest fashions and unique jewellery, and she had all the right contacts with air travel and shipping companies, and with railway authorities. She was everything that MI6 was looking for – the perfect travel-agent spy.

Hiding in plain sight, Rita announced that she had left the Foreign Office, as she was supposedly tired of overseas postings.[25] She built a company that squashed suspicion and convinced others of her new post-war venture. Her high-end travel agency specialised in taking people who were 'somebody' to places no one else was going. Early customers included the film director Alexander Korda, the Scottish novelist A.J. Cronin, whose books outsold those of Agatha Christie at one point, and the film actress Diana Wynyard. The ex-British civil servant provided a unique personal service by supplying letters of introduction to clients from carefully sourced members of the Foreign Office.[26] With her inside knowledge of how to build covert identities, Rita followed a careful plan, creating a legend that would hide any clandestine work conducted for MI6, whether it be for scouting purposes, assisting in agent exfiltrations, acting as a courier, or meeting with representatives of friendly intelligence agencies. Over many years, Rita established her reputation in the field of travel, ensuring tours were reported in the press, creating a visible record should anyone wish to check or question her authenticity or that of the travel agency.[27]

International Services came into existence in December 1945.[28] With a suitably bland name for cover purposes, the travel agency was initially based at 60 Haymarket before it expanded from just one room to a suite of offices at 31 to 32 Haymarket in 1948. Rita eventually moved her business and twenty-five staff to 7 Haymarket in 1955. Located next door to the Theatre Royal Haymarket, the agency experienced a constant footfall of foreign tourists and cultured Londoners passing by on their way to attend a host of exciting new West End shows. Just a brisk walk across St James's Park from the MI6 headquarters on 54 Broadway, International Services was close enough to welcome intelligence officers needing specialist travel advice or to assist those with former intelligence links. Customers included the English anthropologist Geoffrey Gorer, who worked in psychological warfare during the Second World War, helping American and British intelligence services.[29]

From the company's inception, Rita served on the board of directors. For the travel business to appear legitimate, there was a regular turnover of other directors during the first few years of operation. Sir Oliver Welby and his wife, Barbara, served as founding directors for the first year. Residents of the sleepy rural Lincolnshire village of Sleaford, the Welbys had no tangible connections to the secret world of British intelligence. However, as part of the 'county set', they were acquainted with Ralph Jarvis, who conveniently lived twenty miles away in Doddington Hall, a grand Elizabethan mansion that stood at the centre of a tiny hamlet outside the city of Lincoln.[30] Jarvis had worked with Rita in Lisbon and most likely served as the point of contact with Sir Oliver Welby, a businessman in the brewery trade.

After a year, the Welbys resigned. Several months later, Rita's brother, Dennys Winsor, was appointed for one year before he resigned as a director on 16 September 1947. At this point, Ena Molesworth left MI6 and joined International Services. The two inseparable friends worked together until 1970, when they retired and sold the business to Bakar Travel, a Middle Eastern travel company that ran all money transactions through the British Bank of the Middle East. The two new owners, based in Beirut, supplied only PO Box addresses, suggesting a desire to avoid unwanted solicitations. Just as Rita had listed her occupation as 'none' on the company register in 1945, Bakar Travel built several layers of security around its business in the 1970s.

Unsurprisingly, International Services followed a similar schedule to other travel operators. A typical year for Rita included 'a trip to Canada in the spring, to Greece in midsummer, and a nine-week round-the-world tour in the autumn'.[31] Rita and Ena led guided tours in Afghanistan, Africa, America, Brazil and Japan.[32] Rita would often visit countries in advance to ensure that hotels were up to standard, to survey sites of interest, and to hold meetings with British Embassy officials. Communist countries such as Russia and China remained challenging to visit, as they viewed foreigners with extreme suspicion. After Stalin's death in 1953, the new Soviet premier, Nikita Khrushchev, began opening up international tourism. Rita recalled how she conducted a preliminary visit to Moscow at the end of the 1950s and discovered that one particular Russian hotel did not meet the high standards expected by her clients. The hotel and its bare floorboards were promptly struck from the itinerary.[33] Later, Rita led a small party to Moscow, Leningrad, Tashkent, Samarkand and Bokhara to study Russian art and architecture.[34]

Travel restrictions to the People's Republic of China began to loosen slightly in the 1960s. The previous decade saw the China International Travel Service set up by the Chinese government to shepherd select groups of foreigners from friendly countries. International Services was one of the first commercial travel companies permitted into China in 1963 and then again in 1965.[35] Chinese guides escorted travellers everywhere they went and were accompanied by a translator. Such an opportunity offered MI6 unique access to a country that feared outsiders and foreign interference. Set against the backdrop of the Vietnam War, Rita and Ena operated as clandestine observers, conducting intelligence without espionage, aware of the dangers if caught. Britain's foreign intelligence service had effectively weaponised tourism.

MI6 was not the only intelligence organisation that used travel businesses as covert cover for operatives. At the end of October 1966, a Czech-born American travel agent, Vladimir Kazan-Komarek, was arrested in Prague after his Aeroflot flight from Moscow to Paris made an unscheduled stop in the Czech capital. The 42-year-old American spy had attended a travel agents' conference sponsored by Intourist, the Soviet Travel Association. He confessed to being a spy and organising subversive activities in communist Czechoslovakia. Kazan spent three months in a Czech prison before he was released and able to return home to the United States.[36] But the naturalised American agent paid a heavy price for his patriotism. In 1972, Spanish police found his body in a hillside gully outside the coastal town of Estepona.[37]

A single man travelling alone to Russia was bound to catch the attention of Soviet intelligence. Yet two British businesswomen herding small groups of well-to-do men and women across Moscow and other red destinations failed to arouse suspicion. As the balance of power shifted during the Cold War, the two women travelled the world, advertising their tours in *The Times* newspaper and *Geographical* magazine. With professional accreditation awarded by the Association of British Travel, Rita and Ena were credible travel operators who proved good at their job.[38] As head of her own agency, Rita became the only woman to sit with thirty-one men on the International Federation of Travel Agencies council.[39] The press reported Rita's achievements, and she increased her visibility further by writing to the editor of *The Times* newspaper. Her letter concerning a lack of British typewriters appeared in print in January 1950.[40] She even found time to run as a prospective Liberal candidate in Somerset, which gave further credibility to her cover.[41]

The following year, Rita appeared on the popular BBC radio programme *In Town Tonight*, which invited celebrities and people of note and was broadcast on a Saturday evening. On it, Rita appeared as the eighth guest of the night, joining the renowned English stage actress Sybil Thorndike and the famous American actor and songwriter Hoagy Carmichael. As listeners tuned in at 7.15 p.m. on 24 March 1951, they were treated to some interesting vignettes about running a travel agency delivered by a woman at the top of her game. Rita recalled how one of her 'earliest customers was a man from Eastern Europe who said he was afraid the American customs would part him from his friend, and they had never been separated'. When asked by the interviewer, John Ellison, whether the man meant the immigration authorities, Rita replied, 'Well, I thought that, but he said "No, look",' and he pulled out from a hat box a large green snake.[42]

Rita revealed that she was not terrified by the incident, but that she had been scared out of her wits on a different occasion. She explained how 'One afternoon a woman came in wearing a black satin evening dress and carpet slippers and carrying an old-fashioned Gladstone bag. That in itself was sufficiently startling. But then she insisted that I got her a passage to South Africa in the *Vanguard*, the battleship which was taking the King and Queen there.' Executing infallible judgement and a certain coolness under pressure, Rita said, 'I couldn't do it, so she opened the bag and whipped out a revolver. I was petrified, but my secretary nipped out and dialled 999. The woman must have heard the phone, for she tore out the door like greased lightning and was never seen again.' The interview ended with Ellison remarking, 'It's a good thing all your customers don't try that sort of thing, Miss Winsor', to which Rita responded, 'Yes, isn't it. Otherwise I'd never stand the strain.'[43]

Publicity surrounding the travel agency continued. The launch of the Soviet Sputnik satellite in 1957 heralded the arrival of the Space Age. People from all countries went wild at the future prospect of travelling to different planets. At the same time, world leaders worried about national security threats. Several newspapers ran a quirky, funny story about International Services taking bookings for travel to the moon in 2040 and Mars in 2060. Schoolchildren worldwide wrote to Rita about booking a place, and clear-thinking, responsible businessmen enquired whether their children could perhaps inherit their spaceship seats. Rita duly kept a list of names for the day when space travel would become a real possibility.[44] As curious customers hung around the waiting room of 7 Haymarket, they admired a stunning mural commissioned from the artist Nadia Benois, mother of the actor Peter Ustinov, which depicted a party of travellers setting off for space.[45] Had Rita and Ena lived long enough to witness space travel, Rita would have been the first to secure her seat, while Ena would have preferred to keep her feet firmly on the ground.

Together, Rita and Ena made a formidable team. They navigated the immediate post-war years when travellers required endless pieces of paper before they could leave the country, and, somehow, they managed to handle 2,500 passport applications in their first year of working together.[46] These enterprising women gained an enviable reputation with consulates, leaving many believing that 'if Rita Winsor has made the arrangements, then everything is in order'.[47] Rita helped many notables of the day, such as the Countess of Eldon, a good friend of the young Princess Elizabeth, before she became Queen in 1952.[48] Others such as Somerset Maugham, the spy writer and secret agent, turned to Rita for help when needing travel assistance. After the war, Maugham's secretary was unable to get him to America to present a manuscript to his publisher. She asked Rita for help, and just like Mary Poppins, the extraordinary travel specialist set things right, and the eccentric novelist and dramatist made it across the Atlantic.[49] It wasn't the first time that Rita had helped him. As one of Rita's very first customers, Maugham had once sent her an urgent letter explaining how his niece wished to return to Turin but could not secure accommodation. Could Rita help?[50]

The answer was yes. It was always yes. Rita had a sparkling optimism and a unique way of approaching problems. By the late 1950s, her hard work in building the company had paid off. International Services was a bona fide travel agency with a store of helpful marketing materials and publicity records that were readily available and easily found. However, by the late 1950s, Rita and Ena sought an injection of youth into the company. Rather than recruit someone with previous experience in travel work, the two MI6 veterans recruited a 37-year-old naval man to work as general manager in 1958.[51] Ronald Ward was tall, dark and handsome. The former submariner possessed a confident manner marked by an element of coolness. Before joining the travel company, Ward had been seconded to the Naval Intelligence Division (NID) and attached to the Foreign Office from August 1955 to September 1956. The Director of NID, Rear Admiral John Inglis, described Ward's liaison work as 'a difficult job, requiring an unusual amount of tact, firmness and knowledge'.[52] It was then that Ward found himself caught up in one of the first great post-war spy scandals.

In April 1956, the warship *Ordzhonikidze* arrived in Britain on a goodwill visit carrying the Soviet leaders Nikita Khrushchev and Nikolai Bulganin. Once the Russian cruiser had dropped anchor, a decorated Royal Navy frogman by the name of Lionel 'Buster' Crabb slipped into the cold, murky waters of Portsmouth Harbour. The chain-smoking, heavy-drinking veteran diver was never seen again, although his headless corpse was washed up the following year. A bungled MI6 operation had deployed Crabb to investigate the ship's hull and propeller. The Director of Naval Intelligence, John Inglis, had requested intelligence on the propeller design to understand better how the cruiser could reach such fast speeds. Crabb's disappearance caused a major diplomatic row with the Soviet Union, humiliating Prime Minister Anthony Eden, who suspended British intelligence-gathering operations. As the NID liaison man with MI6, Ronald Ward dealt with the extreme fallout. He had placated, cajoled, avoided and delayed in any way he could to conceal the truth about MI5 and MI6. The relentless press, the Soviets and the public remained unconvinced by the official response that Crabb had merely been diving to test new equipment. While many persuasive explanations have since been offered, the disappearance of Buster Crabb remains unsolved.

By March 1958, Ward had experienced enough of the perils of having a desk job and requested retirement from the navy, even though Inglis considered him to be 'commander material'.[53] With his clandestine experience and strong character, Ward made an excellent addition to International Services. He was made a director in 1963 and led tours to Russia, China, Turkey and Iran. If Rita and Ena ever found themselves in a tight spot abroad, Ward was the man to help defuse or resolve any problems. Before his death, the intrepid tour guide spent considerable time disposing of private papers. When asked by his granddaughter what it all was, Ward responded that it was just rubbish, and that he was saving her a job when he died.[54] However, a letter written from Tehran in 1969 escaped the cull. In it Ward wrote to his wife, 'Have written pen portraits after one week together in a letter to Ena.'[55] This tantalisingly enigmatic statement implies that the travel agency was gathering information on its clients, whoever they were. Unsurprisingly, in later years, Rita and Ena purged any documents relating to International Services. Not one personal photograph or business record beyond those filed with Companies House has survived, suggesting that International Services was perhaps something more than just a travel agency.

While Rita and Ena toured remote and unfriendly countries carrying out undisclosed clandestine work, another lone female MI6 officer remained hard at work in Morocco. Teddy Dunlop was MI6's 'lady in Tangiers'.[56] Working under the cover of British vice-consul and Passport Control Officer, Margaret Isobel Dunlop had blazed a trail for women in Britain's foreign secret service during the war. Until now, she has remained elusive to historians, with very little known about her. While most women faced the stark choice between the secret service and a husband, Teddy found the normally impossible middle way. After a year of marriage to Dr Alexander Prentice, this headstrong diplomat had fallen desperately in love with a ship's doctor while travelling home to Scotland during the early 1930s.[57] The gentle and unobtrusive Dr Henry 'Harry' Dunlop had spent six years working on the British India line when he met Teddy. Resolved in her decision, Teddy divorced one Scottish doctor and married another. After 1935, Teddy and her new husband settled in Tangier, where the MI6 officer served as vice-consul, and Harry set up a general practice, devoting all of his spare time for the next twenty-two years to treating the poorer sections of the local population with no thought of payment.[58]

The couple took regular holidays at Teddy's family home on a remote Orkney island. Despite living overseas, Teddy and Harry retained a deep love of Scotland.[59] Teddy's father, Professor Ernest Shearer, was born into a humble farming family in Stromness. Academically bright, he attended Edinburgh University and graduated with a degree in Agriculture, which opened doors for him. With Orcadians renowned for their love of travel, Ernest Shearer set off for Bengal with his wife to take up his first academic appointment at Pusa Imperial College.[60] Teddy soon made her entrance in the world on 2 October 1906. Five years later, Ernest moved his family to Cairo, where he served as a technical adviser to the Egyptian Ministry of Agriculture, before returning to academia at the University of Edinburgh. Promoted to Professor of Agriculture in 1926, Ernest retired after eighteen years of service in 1944.[61] Just as his moustache had grown more prominent over the years, so had his bank account. The bold Scot had earned enough to purchase a grand house in Eskbank, south of Edinburgh, that he christened 'Zamalek' after the district in Cairo where he had lived. Complete with a tennis court and an extensive garden, the house accommodated the large family and their pet dogs. There was even money to purchase a Daimler car named Big Bertha. As the eldest of six children, Teddy took on a matriarchal role, policing the fun of her younger siblings. Fair-haired with piercing blue eyes, she was, both as a child and an adult, a seemingly serious character.[62]

However, there was also a caring side to the MI6 officer. Teddy found a way to bend the rules so that she could marry and entertain the prospect of having children. In May 1939, she and Harry welcomed their only child, a healthy girl. In a remarkable testament to modern motherhood, the MI6 officer fulfilled her vice-consular role and juggled motherhood with her clandestine responsibilities during the Second World War. In a lifestyle that would not suit everyone, Teddy attended lavish embassy parties at night and, during the day, she ran agent networks with a toddler kicking at her heels.

As the gateway between Europe and Africa, Tangier was considered a dangerous corner of the world. The port town stood on a hillside overlooking the Strait of Gibraltar. Agents from both sides wandered the narrow, winding alleys of the Casbah, with some taking rooms in the venerable El Minzah Hotel. In 1941, Ian Fleming took a short trip to Tangier to review naval intelligence in North Africa. However, he was far from discreet when he painted an enormous V sign on the airport runway, which caused a small diplomatic incident in Spanish-occupied Tangier.[63] Barbara Salt, who later became the first woman to receive a British ambassadorial appointment in 1962, was far more prudent when running SOE black propaganda campaigns in Tangier.[64] She recruited British nationals to help disseminate false rumours (known in the secret world as 'sibs'), hoping that they made it to German and Italian ears. In their roles, Margaret and Harry ensured that the 'news' travelled fast in the international community.[65]

After the war, Teddy continued to monitor the minor skirmishes occurring among North African Arabs.[66] In 1949, she met with the MI6 head of the Iberian Peninsula, Desmond Bristow, and agreed with his decision to reduce her network of agents.[67] Very little of note had happened since the war ended, and the Soviets had little influence in nearby Spain. As she set about identifying agents to lay off in January 1950, she found herself faced with a 'Guy Burgess problem'. The Soviet agent had taken a holiday from the Foreign Office and had effectively drunk his way through France and Spain. The pressures of leading a double life were taking their toll on him and the champion alcoholic caused major disruptions wherever he went. After stirring up trouble in Gibraltar, Burgess headed to Tangier for some North African sunshine.

Disturbed by Burgess's horrendous display of drunkenness, Teddy telephoned her boss, Desmond Bristow. He recalled the conversation in his memoir. An irritated Teddy informed him that Burgess was 'behaving in an appalling fashion' and pestering her for money.[68] She also struggled to keep him out of the office, as he knew everyone in the consulate. Teddy was truly horrified when Burgess blabbed secret information during one of his drunken escapades. She informed Bristow that Burgess had 'gone around broadcasting the name of the Swiss diplomat who allowed the British to use the Swiss diplomatic bag to bring rare pieces of equipment and information out of Switzerland'.[69] She then revealed to Bristow how Burgess had acted indiscreetly, setting 'the gays of Tangier alight'.[70] Teddy was left to deal with the destruction left in his wake. She submitted an official report to Bristow detailing Burgess's transgressions, and he duly sent it on to the Foreign Office, believing they would deal with their out-of-control employee. Surprisingly, Burgess received a mere rap on the knuckles and, as punishment, was packed off to Washington DC, where his bad behaviour continued.[71]

A baffled Teddy could not understand why Burgess had not been sacked. She met with Bristow and the other Iberian station heads in March 1950. Unaware that Burgess was actually a dangerous Soviet spy, the MI6 officers debated the situation and agreed that, should an employee of His Majesty's Government behave in their countries in such a monstrous way again, they would directly file a report with C himself.[72] Meanwhile, Burgess, still an obnoxious drunk, lived with Philby and his family in the American capital. By April 1951, Philby was growing uneasy at the speed with which American codebreakers were decrypting secret Soviet signals that identified a fellow Cambridge spy, Donald Maclean, as working for the Soviets. The senior British diplomat had attended Cambridge University in the 1930s with Burgess and Philby. Maclean's treachery peaked from 1947 to 1948, when he passed atomic secrets on to Moscow while serving in Washington.

Aware that British intelligence was closing in, Philby warned Maclean and Burgess. The two Foreign Office men slipped away to Russia before being unmasked as Soviet spies. Their defections sent shock waves across the intelligence services and the British government. The finger of suspicion now pointed at Philby, tainted by his association with Burgess. Philby returned from America to London to face the music, and, after a series of meetings at the end of 1951, the MI6 chief, Stewart Menzies, asked Philby for his resignation. With over four decades of service, Menzies was himself ready for retirement. The thought of managing further fallout from Burgess and Maclean's defection and the growing suspicion surrounding Philby most likely led Menzies to take retirement in 1952. Nevertheless, scandal followed the retiring C, casting doubt on his character.

On 30 June 1952, the 62-year-old chief announced his retirement in a signal to all MI6 stations. However, just before he left the Secret Intelligence Service, his secretary of many years, Muriel Jones, had attempted to take her life by overdosing on a controlled substance. Luckily, she was found unconscious at her Wandsworth flat and was revived in the nick of time, perhaps by her mother, with whom she lived, or by Kathleen Pettigrew, who must have known about the affair. Distraught at the thought of losing Menzies, the 49-year-old Muriel chose death in preference to life without him. Apart from Kathleen, nobody had any inkling that the two had been conducting an affair since the start of the war. Muriel's suicide attempt caused great alarm at headquarters. She spent considerable time in hospital before being discharged. MI6 moved the convalescing secretary and her mother to a flat on the corner of Ebury Street in Belgravia, not far from 54 Broadway. Paranoid MI6 staff wondered how Menzies and Muriel had conducted their affair undetected, questioning what other secrets the MI6 chief had taken with him into retirement.[73]

Desmond Bristow described how 'the climate in the Service was getting worse, not better. Everybody was suspicious of everybody else.'[74] For this reason, Teddy Dunlop resigned after her boss left in 1954.[75] At London headquarters, Kathleen was just as concerned as the rest of her colleagues, but work continued. It simply had to. On 1 October 1954, the senior 'secretary' returned an important paper to Jock Colville, private secretary to Winston Churchill, who had regained power in 1951. The paper concerned the neo-Nazi Werner Naumann, who was unsuccessfully trying to establish a Fourth Reich in Germany. Kathleen informed Colville that a complete report would arrive later that day. She then took a black ballpoint pen – not the green fountain pen famously favoured by her late boss – and signed her name, no longer having to wait for the ink to dry.[76] Kathleen now served under her fourth C, Major General John Sinclair, a soft-spoken 'tall, lean Scot with the angular, austere features of a Presbyterian minister'.[77] As she neared retirement, Kathleen maintained the same high standards that she had executed throughout her long career. One wonders whether she harboured suspicions about Philby, who had passed through her office numerous times to see Stewart Menzies. 'With sharp, intelligent eyes behind a pair of rimless spectacles', Kathleen saw everything.[78]

As the Philby saga continued, the vetting of recruits took on greater importance. Kathleen continued in her role of appointing suitable secretarial staff. On 8 December 1955, the now grey-haired senior executive officer sat at her trusted typewriter and compiled a standard reference request for a Miss Doreen Aizlewood. Kathleen had grown accustomed to the revolving door of young women who came and went after a few years of service. Kathleen required the recipient of the letter, former intelligence officer Peter Fleming, to comment on whether he considered Doreen to be reliable, discreet, of a suitable character and upbringing, and whether she was fit for 'employment in a Department where the work is of a confidential nature'.[79]

The striking young woman with dark curly hair and a twinkle in her eye had worked with Fleming from 1952 to 1953. Doreen came from a distinguished military family. Her great-uncle was General Meade Dennis, Montgomery's chief gunner in Normandy.[80] Doreen met with Kathleen's approval and joined MI6 on 23 January 1956. However, after only four years, she left the service, but not because of marriage. Unlike the debutantes she worked alongside, Doreen had no independent financial means to fall back on. Living and working in London simply proved too expensive for the secretary, who typically sought positions with accommodation included. Armed with a letter of recommendation from MI6, who considered Doreen to 'be a loyal and good secretary, very conscientious, methodical and intelligent', she soon secured another secretarial position outside the capital and outside the secret world.[81]

With Doreen's appointment in 1956, Kathleen welcomed Dick White as her fifth and final C. 'Immensely competent, she had acquired vast experience in the many years she had held her lonely post, raised high above the other women in the Service, and was looked upon by high and low with a respect not far removed from fear.'[82] Kathleen had borne witness to the emerging 'secret state', enjoying the good times and weathering the failures. In 1958, the sixty-year-old was finally ready to enjoy her retirement. But she was filled with a foreboding sense of doom. The 'third man' in the Cambridge spy ring was on the brink of being unmasked, and other Soviet moles were yet to be discovered.

With storm clouds brewing over MI6, Kathleen closed the office door at 54 Broadway for the final time, but the loyal 'secretary' would never truly leave the service. She had lived behind the looking glass for far too long. Privy to decades of secrets, Kathleen would carry them all to her grave.

EPILOGUE

A small group of mourners stood in silence at the cemetery. They dutifully listened to the clergyman as he spoke about the woman to whom they were paying their respects, but they had only known Kathleen Pettigrew as an elderly woman. They had no idea as to who she really was, and all that she had achieved in her life behind closed doors. The handful of staff from the Glenside Nursing Home had known Kathleen as 'Churchill's secretary'.[1] They were oblivious to the true facts of Kathleen's life, and that she had actually commenced her lifelong commitment to secret service during the First World War. At ninety-two years of age, Kathleen had long outlived those with whom she had worked closely in MI6. Her death marked the end of an era. The organisation she worked for and helped shape no longer existed. Britain's foreign intelligence service had been transformed into a professional and modern intelligence agency. Just as the typewriter had been replaced with the computer, the old guard had been consigned to the pages of the service history book.

While no MI6 representative was in attendance at Kathleen's funeral, there was only one family member present, for the rest of the Pettigrew family were long deceased.[2] Tim Warner lived nearby and had visited his distant cousin several times before her death. Along with his brother Richard, who lived in Ireland, the two were aware that Kathleen had worked for the Foreign Office in a secret capacity, but remained in the dark as to the exact nature of her work. Like so many who spent their careers in Britain's secret services, Kathleen had sworn an oath of secrecy; over the years, it had become the mask she wore. As a senior executive officer, she had retired to Sidmouth in 1958, and was awarded the OBE in recognition of her service.[3] She briefly returned to London in November of that year, when she wrote,

'I had, like the cat, to see the Queen, who gave me my last decoration.' Kathleen had intended to stay a couple of weeks, but she made her excuses instead. She revealed, 'I rushed back here after two days. I found I just couldn't take London any more.'[4]

Kathleen enjoyed the company of her older sister, Ellen, who also resided in Sidmouth. The Devonshire coastal town was a popular destination for secret service retirees wishing to escape London. After her sister's death in 1977, Kathleen lived a relatively solitary existence, until she moved into the nursing home. After her death, Tim Warner enquired with Kathleen's solicitor as to the whereabouts of family photographs and her OBE, which had disappeared from her flat and remain missing to this day.[5] Nearly all vestiges of Kathleen's work have vanished, and only her fading name inscribed on her sister's impressive granite headstone, now sunken into the ground on one side, bears witness to a life once lived. Kathleen had worked in complete secrecy, navigating a rigorous security system that was in many ways 'for her eyes only'. Privy to all the secrets, her career spanned the first half of the twentieth century and ended as clouds formed over the epicentre of deceit and disloyalty brought about by the Cambridge spies.

By the 1950s, women's careers in intelligence remained firmly rooted in paperwork. Progress was in many ways glacial. From 1909 to 1945, the women of Britain's intelligence services had proven themselves more than capable of holding a range of different roles and senior positions, but the opportunities offered them, with or without rank, were largely confined to the duration of each world war. At the end of both wars, the services contracted in size and experienced a talent drain, as many women left to resume their lives, with some returning to pre-war jobs and others choosing to wed and start a family. Women's careers in intelligence remained very much subordinate to men's. They only received opportunities if they were bestowed upon them by their male bosses. Those such as Winnie Spink, Jane Archer, Olga Gray, Mary Sherer, Rita Winsor and Teddy Dunlop broke barriers. They tested what could be achieved and determined what remained out of reach for women. Several paid the ultimate price for their career-ending achievements, ambitions and modern outlook, but as they tapped the glass ceiling, they ensured it would finally break for those who followed in their footsteps.

It was not until the end of the Cold War that women were finally ordained at the altar of power. Stella Rimington followed a slow path to leadership, but she eventually reached the pinnacle in 1992 when she became the first female Director General of MI5 – a marker we have seen in GCHQ, but have yet to witness in MI6. Stella joined MI5 in 1969, when she 'fell into intelligence by chance'.[6] She had worked as an archivist before she married, at which time she transformed herself into a diplomat's wife. It was then that she got the infamous tap on the shoulder and was offered a typing job in the service, a role that remained the entry point for all women. She could barely wait to escape the boredom of hosting coffee mornings, so she readily accepted. But her work in MI5 took her away from her small children, leaving her feeling detached from family life.

Stella wrote very candidly about her MI5 career in her memoir *Open Secret*, published in 2001. Her refreshing honesty provides an important window into the promotion path of MI5's first female head. In 1983, Stella was promoted, but she noted senior personnel were cautious and strategically chose to appoint her to a non-risk position that she considered a 'bit of a backwater'. She disclosed in her memoir:

> When I was summoned by Cecil to be told formally of my move, I tried to look both surprised and enthusiastic. I was indeed delighted to be promoted to Assistant Director, the first significant management level in the Service, which only one other woman had reached. But I was disappointed that it was not a more exciting job, and yet again I had a sense that they were being extremely cautious and that I was being tested in a way a man would not have been.[7]

She described how further promotions did not go down well with male colleagues who regarded her elevation as 'a step too far'.[8]

In 1986, Stella was promoted to Director of Counterespionage, a position that carried the title of 'K'. She reflected how, eighty years on, she had 'become the modern manifestation of Brigadier Vernon Kell, the founder of MI5'.[9] However, Stella's rise to power was ultimately decided by men who adopted a cautious path, choosing who to promote and when. She concluded: 'Had I allowed myself to brood on these things, I would have felt that I had been asked to prove myself for longer and more thoroughly than any man, but I didn't. I just felt pleased and satisfied to have made it.'[10] Today, with fewer than a third of senior posts currently occupied by women in both MI5 and MI6, there is still work to be done. The glass ceiling may have been broken, but it has yet to be smashed to pieces.

Kathleen Pettigrew inspired a powerful fantasy in the character of Miss Moneypenny. The Bond secretary truly represents the many extraordinary women who worked in British intelligence from its inception in 1909. Rescued from obscurity, these previously silenced voices provide a lasting legacy of women's contributions to the history of the intelligence services.

Women were, and still are, the true custodians of the secret world.

ENDNOTES

Prologue

1   Kathleen Pettigrew to Onslow Warner, 15 Jan. 1964, Tim Warner Private Collection (TW), p.1.
2   Ibid.
3   Dr Richard Warner, correspondence with author, 14 Feb. 2022.
4   'The Friends' is a euphemism used by Whitehall when referring to MI6.
5   The name 'Miss Pettavel' can also be found in Peter Fleming's unpublished manuscript *The Sett* written *c*.1946, MS 1390 B/6, University of Reading Special Collections. The novel deals with an imaginary invasion of the British Isles by German troops. Unlike his famous brother, Ian, Peter had actually seen action during the Second World War. As an intelligence officer, Peter had been engaged in secret commando operations, and was responsible for putting plans together for a 'stay behind' guerrilla army should Britain have been invaded. A good account of his wartime work can be found in Alan Ogden's biography *Master of Deception: The Wartime Adventures of Peter Fleming* (London: Bloomsbury Academic, 2019); First draft of Ian Fleming's *Casino Royale*.
6   Dr Richard Warner, correspondence with author, 4 Feb. 2022.
7   See note 1.
8   Ken Warner's full name was Onslow Boyden Waldo Warner (1902–1988).
9   Dr Richard Warner, correspondence with author, 14 Feb. 2022.
10 Ibid., 28 March 2022.
11 Ibid., 14 Feb. 2022.
12 Ibid., 1 July 2022.

1. The Real Miss Moneypenny

1   Malcolm Muggeridge, *The Infernal Grove: Chronicles of Wasted Time, vol. 2* (London: Collins, 1975), p.144.
2   Anthony Cave Brown, *'C': The Secret Life of Sir Stewart Menzies, Spymaster to Winston Churchill* (New York: Macmillan, 1987), p.228.
3   Ian Fleming, *Casino Royale* (London: Ian Fleming Publications, 2023), p.22.
4   A 'Most Secret' note addressed to Miss Pettigrew, 5 Oct. 1943, HW 1/1311, The National Archives (TNA).
5   Ibid.; A 'Most Secret' note addressed to Mr F. Brown from Kathleen Pettigrew, 5 Oct. 1943.
6   See Nadine Akkerman, *Invisible Agents: Women and Espionage in Seventeenth-Century Britain* (Oxford: Oxford University Press, 2018).

7   For an excellent overview of the Mata Hari story, see Julie Wheelwright, *The Fatal Lover: Mata Hari and the Myth of Women in Espionage* (London: Collins and Brown Limited, 1992).

8   Major Thomas Coulson's dubious biography *Mata Hari: Courtesan and Spy* (London: Hutchinson, 1930) served as a template for future books on Mata Hari, thus fuelling the femme fatale legacy.

9   Lisa Funnell, ed., *For His Eyes Only: The Women of James Bond* (New York: Columbia University Press, 2015). This anthology offers a detailed examination of the role and representation of women in the Bond franchise.

10   Fleming, *Casino Royale*, p.34.

11   Tammy Proctor's book *Female Intelligence: Women and Espionage in the First World War* (New York: New York University Press, 2003) paved the way for future scholarship on women in intelligence.

12   Christopher Andrew, *The Defence of the Realm: The Authorised History of MI5* (London: Allen Lane, 2009); Keith Jeffery, *MI6: The History of the Secret Intelligence Service 1909–1949* (London: Bloomsbury, 2010); John Ferris, *Behind the Enigma: The Authorised History of GCHQ, Britain's Secret Cyber-Intelligence Agency* (London: Bloomsbury, 2020).

13   Kate Vigurs, *Mission France: The True History of the Women of SOE* (New Haven, CT: Yale University Press, 2021). This book is the first collective biography of all the female agents of SOE's F Section.

14   H.L. Adam, 'Behind the Scenes in Scotland Yard', *Britannia* (19 Oct. 1928), p.130.

15   Roland Wild, *King's Counsel: The Life of Sir Henry Curtis-Bennett* (New York: J.J. Little and Ives, 1938), p.61.

16   Harold Brust, *In Plain Clothes: Further Memoirs of a Political Police Officer* (London: Stanley Paul, 1937), p.69.

17   Basil Thomson, *My Experiences at Scotland Yard* (New York: Doubleday, Page & Co, 1923), p.203.

18   Basil Thomson, *The Scene Changes* (New York: Doubleday, Doran & Co, 1937), p.300. Basil Thomson notes that a shorthand writer was hidden behind a screen while he questioned Sir Roger Casement on 24 April 1916.

19   Kathleen Pettigrew's work as a stenographer for Basil Thomson during the First World War is recorded by several newspapers. Examples include: 'Officer's Challenge to Duel', *Evening Standard*, 20 Aug. 1917; 'Mutilated Documents', *Manchester Evening News*, 17 Jan. 1918; 'An Altered Passport', *Nottingham Daily Express*, 18 Jan. 1918.

20   A typed copy of a confidential letter from Basil Thomson to His Excellency the Minister for the Netherlands, 16 Nov. 1916, MEPO 3/2444, TNA.

21   Cave Brown, *'C'*, p.227.

22   Helen Warrell, 'The Secret Lives of MI6's Top Female Spies', *Financial Times Weekend Magazine*, 10/11 Dec. 2022.

23   See Charles Dickens, *Oliver Twist* (London: Penguin, 1994).

24   60 Bolina Road no longer stands. The house was bombed during the Second World War and later cleared.

25 George H. Duckworth Notebook entry, 15 July 1899, Inquiry into the Life and Labour of the People in London, BOOTH/B/365, Collection UK-LSE-DL1CB01, Charles Booth Archive, LSE Digital Library.

26 For a good overview, see Peter Atkins, 'The Urban Blood and Guts Economy' in Peter Atkins, ed., *Animal Cities: Beastly Urban Histories* (London: Routledge, 2016), pp.77–106.

27 John Mackman was convicted for larceny and sentenced to six months' imprisonment and whipping. His trial was held on 26 May 1845, Surrey, HO 27/77, TNA.

28 'York Place and George Court', in *Survey of London, vol. 18, St Martin-in-the-Fields II: The Strand*, ed. G.H. Gater and E.P. Wheeler (London: London County Council, 1937), p.80; *British History Online,* http://www.british-history.ac.uk/survey-london/vol18/pt2/p80.

29 *The Speckled Band*, a theatrical adaptation written and produced by Sir Arthur Conan Doyle, was performed at the Adelphi Theatre in June 1910. See Janice M. Allan and Christopher Pittard, eds., *The Cambridge Companion to Sherlock Holmes* (Cambridge: Cambridge University Press, 2019), p.xvii.

30 *George Court, Looking towards The Strand, 1924* (Picture No 12917264), showing The George pub with aviary, *Illustrated London News,* Mary Evans Picture Library, available at: www.maryevans.com.

31 Kathleen left part of her estate to the Royal Society for the Protection of Birds.

32 *The Post Office London Directory* (London: Kelly's Directories Limited, 1905), p.1510.

33 The 1911 Census for the Pettigrew family resident at 1 George Court, Strand, London. RG 14/1188, TNA.

34 Kathleen Pettigrew to Ken Warner, 15 Jan. 1964, Tim Warner Private Collection (TW), p.2.

35 Ibid.

36 Ibid.

37 Ibid., p.1.

38 Ibid., p.4.

39 Ibid.

40 Mrs H. Waldo Warner [Rose Pettigrew], 'Memories of Philip Wilson Steer', Oct. 1947, GB 247 MS MacColl P64, University of Glasgow Archives and Special Collections (UGASC). Bruce Langton discovered the memoir and reproduced it in his book *Philip Wilson Steer, 1860–1942* (Oxford: Clarendon Press, 1971).

41 Langton, *Steer*, p.2.

42 Ibid., p.3.

43 Ibid., p.6.

44 The painting may be viewed at the Tate Gallery in London.

45 Dora H. Thomas, *A Short History of St. Martin-in-the-Fields High School for Girls* (London: John Murray, 1929), p.16. The school moved to Tulse Hill in 1928 where it remains today.

46 Ibid., p.101.

47   Thomas, *Short History*, p.64.
48   'The Pitman School Southampton Row', *Westminster Gazette*, 14 Aug. 1907, p.10.
49   'Pitman's Schools' (advertisement), *The Times*, 1 Jan. 1914.
50   The Pitman Collection is held by the University of Bath.
51   Cited in Michael Heller, *London Clerical Workers, 1880–1914: Development of the Labour Market* (London: Routledge, 2015), p.170.

2. Licence to Type

1   Andrew Lycett, *Ian Fleming* (London: Phoenix, 1996), p.216.
2   Michael H. Adler, *The Writing Machine* (London: Allen & Unwin, 1973), pp.32–3.
3   Cited in Jon Agar, *The Government Machine: A Revolutionary History of the Computer* (London: MIT Press, 2003), p.61.
4   See Gregory Anderson, ed., *The White-blouse Revolution: Female Office Workers since 1870* (Manchester: Manchester University Press, 1988).
5   The ability to analyse big data such as the 1901, 1911 and 1921 censuses by means of sophisticated search engines is a remarkable achievement, allowing historians to ask big questions and get answers within a matter of seconds.
6   See Suffragette Disturbances, 1910, HO 144/1107/200655, TNA.
7   See E. Phillips Oppenheim, *The Great Secret* (Boston: Little, Brown & Company, 1907).
8   William Le Queux, *The Invasion of 1910, With a Full Account of the Siege of London* (London: Eveleigh Nash, 1906).
9   William Le Queux, *Spies of the Kaiser: Plotting the Downfall of England* (London: Frank Cass, 1996), p.viii.
10   Ibid., p.xxxiv.
11   Cited in Thomas Boghardt, *Spies of the Kaiser: German Covert Operations in Great Britain during the First World War Era* (Basingstoke: Palgrave Macmillan, 2004), p.31.
12   See Nicholas Hiley, 'The Failure of British Counter-Espionage against Germany, 1907–1914', *The Historical Journal* 28, no. 4 (Dec. 1985), pp.835–62.
13   Physical descriptions of Mansfield Cumming can be found in the following works: Henry Landau, *All's Fair: The Story of the British Secret Service behind the German Lines* (New York: G.P. Putnam's Sons, 1934), pp.42–3; Compton Mackenzie, *Greek Memories* (London: Cassell, 1932), p.394.
14   Naval record of Mansfield Smith-Cumming, ADM 196/20/123, TNA.
15   Alan Judd, *The Quest for C: Sir Mansfield Cumming and the Founding of the British Secret Service* (London: HarperCollins, 1999), pp.20–21.
16   When Mansfield Smith married for the second time, he took his wife's surname by choice and became 'Smith-Cumming'.
17   Ian Fleming changed this designation to 'M' for the fictitious head of MI6 in his Bond novels.
18   Christopher Andrew, *Secret Service: The Making of the British Intelligence Community* (London: Heinemann, 1985), p.74.

19 Mansfield Cumming Royal Aero Club index card, 1913, *Great Britain, Royal Aero Club Aviators' Certificates, 1910–1950*, Royal Air Force Museum.

20 Vernon Kell accepted the post and a salary of £500 per annum on 19 September 1909. See Copy of Kell's Letter of Acceptance dated 19 Sept. 1909, KV 1/5, TNA.

21 Constance Kell, *A Secret Well Kept: The Untold Story of Sir Vernon Kell, Founder of MI5* (London: Conway, 2017), p.110.

22 Judd, *The Quest for C*, p.87.

23 The Formation of the Secret Service Bureau, KV 1/3, TNA.

24 MI5 World War I Branch Reports: H Branch Organisation and Administration 1915–1919, KV 1/53, TNA.

25 Judd, *Quest*, p.122.

26 Keith Jeffery, *MI6: The History of the Secret Intelligence Service, 1909–1949* (London: Bloomsbury, 2010), p.17.

27 The cost of a Caligraph typewriter in 1910 was £18 18s (= 18 guineas) as noted in: 'For Sale: Miscellaneous', *Hull Daily Mail*, 3 Nov. 1910, p.2.

28 Secret Service Bureau: Accounts 1909–12, FO 1093/109, TNA. Secret Service Accounts for December 1909 list the purchase of a typewriter for Mansfield Cumming on 31 December 1909 at the cost of £18 8s.

29 Pay List of Foreign Service from 1 April 1910 to 31 March 1911, ibid. From 1 July 1910, Miss Barnwell was paid an annual allowance of £10, paid in two instalments.

30 1911 Census entry for Miss Josephine Barnwell, RG 14/02388/0119, TNA.

31 Kate Crowe and Keith Hamilton, *History Note No. 6: Women and the Foreign Office* (Foreign and Commonwealth Office, 2018), p.9.

32 Ibid.

33 Stephen Limburn, interview with author, July 2021.

34 1901 Census entry for a Fanny L Limburne, RG 13/1053, TNA.

35 Jeffery, *MI6*, p.30.

36 Judd, *Quest*, p.135. It is the accepted convention within the world of secret intelligence that operational codenames are presented in upper case.

37 Keith Jeffery notes that Cumming and Kell were issued with basic advice on tradecraft such as the adoption of other names, not meeting agents for the first time at the office, and refraining from the use of paper with watermarks. See Jeffery, *MI6*, p.12.

38 For an excellent discussion concerning agent cover through the example of Freya Stark, see 'Prologue: Of Spies, Scouts, and Cover' in Adrian O'Sullivan, *The Baghdad Set: Iraq through the Eyes of British Intelligence, 1941–45* (London: Palgrave Macmillan, 2019), pp.1–29.

39 1911 Census entry for Agnes Joyce Blake, RG 15/ 00398, TNA.

40 1861 Census for the Garraway family resident at 94 Inverness Terrace, Paddington, RG 9/12, TNA. The Garraway household consisted of a governess, nurse, needlewoman, and several domestic servants.

41 Former British Colonial Dependencies, Slave Register, Dominica, 1823, T 71/358, TNA.

42   'Prince of Wales's Theatre', *Evening News,* 10 Feb. 1882. The article reports that a new comedietta had been presented at the theatre. The short play was adapted by Miss Agnes Garraway and Mr W.E. Rose from a German play by Moser. Examples of her translations include: Karl Rosner, *The King (Kaiser Wilhelm II)*, with an introduction by Viscount Haldane, trans. Agnes Blake (London: Methuen, 1922); Henry Kindermann, *Lola or The Thought and Speech of Animals*, trans. Agnes Blake (London: Methuen, 1922); Otto Ernst, ed., *Franz Joseph as Revealed by His Letters*, trans. Agnes Blake (London: Methuen, 1927); Wilhelm Hausenstein, *Fra Angelico*, trans. Agnes Blake (New York: Dutton, 1929).

43   'Women's Patents', *The Queen,* 25 Nov. 1893, p.37.

44   1911 Census entry for Agnes Joyce Blake, RG 14/394, TNA.

45   Secret Service Bureau: Accounts 1909–12, FO 1093/109, TNA. Accounts for December 1909 record Agent 'A' received £68 for the period 17 December 1909 to 17 March 1910.

46   Foreign Office: Staffing Matters. Handwritten letter from G.M.M. Macdonogh to Lord Errington, 4 July 1910, FO 1093/124, TNA. Lord Errington was the personal secretary of Sir Arthur Nicolson who succeeded Charles Hardinge as Foreign Office Permanent Under-Secretary in November 1910.

47   Judd, *Quest,* p.157.

48   Ibid., p.149.

49   Ibid.

50   Ibid., p.175.

51   Handwritten letter from G.M.M. Macdonogh to Lord Errington, 4 July 1910, FO 1093/124, TNA.

52   Letter from Mrs Agnes Blake to Mr Graves, 9 Nov. 1910, FO 1093/124, TNA.

53   Ibid.

54   Ibid.

55   Ibid.

56   Ibid.

57   Private letter from Charles L. Graves to Sir Edward Grey, 10 Nov. 1910, FO 1093/124, TNA.

58   Foreign Office Minute concerning Mrs Blake [S.S. Agent 'A'], 16 Nov. 1910, FO 1093/124, TNA; Secret Service Bureau: Pay List of Foreign Service from 1 October to 31 December 1910, FO 1093/109, TNA. On 16 November 'Agent A' was paid the balance of a year's salary, £58 10s.

59   Private letter from Charles L. Graves to Sir Edward Grey, 19 Nov. 1910, FO 1093/124, TNA.

60   Letter from Mrs Agnes Blake to Mr Graves, 9 Nov. 1910, FO 1093/124, TNA.

61   Handwritten letter from G.M.M. Macdonogh to Lord Errington, 4 July 1910, FO 1093/124, TNA.

62   See Rosamund Thomas, *Espionage and Secrecy: The Official Secrets Acts 1911–1989 of the United Kingdom* (London: Routledge, 1991).

63   Kell's 6-Month Reports, Nov. 1911, KV 1/9, TNA.

64   See Richard J. Aldrich and Rory Cormac, *The Black Door: Spies, Secret*

Intelligence and British Prime Ministers (London: William Collins, 2016). Chapter 1 covers the premiership of Herbert Asquith and the Secret Service Bureau, pp.21–43.

65 Security Intelligence Service, Seniority List and Register of Past and Present Members, December 1919, KV 4/127, TNA.

66 Formation of the Secret Service Bureau. The report records that there was a bell in the clerk's office, KV 1/3, TNA.

67 Security Intelligence Service, Seniority List and Register of Past and Present Members, December 1919, KV 4/127, TNA.

68 War Office Long Service and Good Conduct Awards, Register: James Westmacott, WO 102/17, TNA.

69 Obituary of James Richard Westmacott, *Norwood News,* 27 May 1938.

70 Security Intelligence Service, Seniority List and Register of Past and Present Members, December 1919, KV 4/127, TNA.

71 Christopher Andrew, *The Defence of the Realm. The Authorised History of MI5* (London: Penguin, 2010), p.35.

72 1911 Census entry for Frank Seymour Strong, RG 14/6597, TNA.

73 Medal card for Frank Seymour Strong, WO 372/19, TNA; Philip Strong, correspondence with author, 7 Sept. 2021.

74 Philip Strong, interview with author, 7 Oct. 2021.

75 'H' Branch Report, Organisation and Administration, Report on Women's Work in M.I.5, April 1920, KV 1/50, TNA.

76 Andrew, *Defence of the Realm*, p.48.

77 Cited in Andrew, *Defence of the Realm,* p.49.

78 Security Intelligence Service, Seniority List and Register of Past and Present Members, December 1919, KV 4/127, TNA.

79 Philip Strong, interview with author, 7 Oct. 2021.

80 Kell's 6-Month Reports, Apr. 1914, KV 1/9, TNA.

81 'The German Spy's Life Story', *The People*, 5 April 1914.

82 Boghardt, *Spies*, p.68.

83 'CID Meeting: Kell's presentation of the work and records of the Bureau', 3 March 1914, KV 1/6, TNA.

3. The Nameless

1 William Joseph Pettigrew, death certificate, 10 May 1915, General Register Office, copy in possession of author.

2 Of the 290,000 people buried in Nunhead Cemetery, only 44,000 have monuments. Garry Wiles, correspondence with author, 3 June 2023.

3 According to the 1921 Census records, Ellen Pettigrew was working as a Registry Clerk at Scotland Yard, RG 15/527, The National Archives (TNA).

4 The earliest evidence of Kathleen working for Thomson can be found on a typed copy of a confidential letter from Basil Thomson to His Excellency the Minister for the Netherlands, 16 Nov. 1916, MEPO 3/2444, TNA.

5 See Panikos Panayi, *Enemy in our Midst: Germans in Britain during the First World War* (New York: Berg, 1991).

6   Brust, *In Plain Clothes*, p.86.

7   Walter H. Thompson, *Guard from the Yard* (London: Jarrolds, 1938), p.46.

8   Kell, *A Secret Well Kept*, p.122.

9   *Scene at Buckingham Palace on the outbreak of war* (1914), picture ref. Q 65496, Photograph Archive Collection, Imperial War Museum (IWM).

10   For a forensic takedown of MI5's 'foundation myth' that Vernon Kell crushed the German espionage network on the first day of war with the arrest of twenty-one agents, see Nicholas Hiley, 'Entering the Lists: MI5's Great Spy Round-up of August 1914', *Intelligence and National Security* 21, no. 1 (Feb. 2006), pp.46–76; Nicholas Hiley, 'Re-entering the Lists: MI5's Authorized History and the August 1914 Arrests', *Intelligence and National Security* 25, no. 4 (Aug. 2010), pp.415–52.

11   'German Espionage during the War', *The Times*, 18 March 1920.

12   A number of post-war reports recorded the wartime work of MI5 branches and noted the contribution made by women. Several were written by women who were trained historians and writers. Mabel Esther Maynard authored the history of port controls and Lucy Eleanor Farrer was responsible for the 'G' Branch report. Mary Helen Shaw authored reports on 'A' and 'H' Branches. See 'H' Branch Report – Organisation and Administration, Annexure 22, Records of Service and Work, KV 1/53, TNA.

13   See Report on Cable Censorship during 1914–1919, DEFE 1/402, TNA; Report on Postal Censorship during the Great War (1914–1919), WO 33/3310, TNA.

14   Freya Stark, *Traveller's Prelude: An Autobiography* (London: John Murray, 1950), p.170.

15   'Recollections of Miss Mary Jenkins on Admiralty Intelligence cypher work', LIDDLE/WW1/DF/GA/CLE/2, The Liddle Collection, Brotherton Library, University of Leeds (BLUL).

16   For more details on Papen, see H.W. Blood, *Franz von Papen: His Life and Times* (London: Rich & Cowan, Ltd, 1939).

17   Report on Woman's Work, KV 1/50, TNA.

18   Ibid.

19   See Penny Summerfield, 'Women and the War in the Twentieth Century' in *Women's History: Britain, 1850–1945: An Introduction,* ed. June Purvis (London: UCL Press, 1995), pp.307–32.

20   'H' Branch Report – Organisation and Administration, Duties of H Branch, KV 1/54, TNA.

21   Report on Woman's Work, KV 1/50, TNA.

22   1921 Census entry for Miss Agnes Wilhelmina Masterton, RG 15/2151, TNA.

23   'H' Branch Report – Organisation and Administration, Report on Woman's Work, KV 1/50, TNA.

24   Tammy Proctor, *Female Intelligence: Women and Espionage in the First World War* (New York: New York University Press, 2003), p.55.

25   M.I.5. Chronological List of Staff taken to 31 December 1919, KV 4/127, TNA.

26 Donald Clarke, *A Daisy in the Broom: The Story of a School, 1820–1958* (London: Tweeddale, 1991), pp.280–82.

27 Ibid., p.206.

28 *Army Medical Department Report for the Year 1898 with Appendix: Volume XL* (London: Harrison, 1900), p.211.

29 1911 Census return for the Sissmore family, RG 14/6869, TNA.

30 Andrew, *Defence of the Realm*, p.122.

31 Report on Woman's Work, KV 1/50, TNA.

32 'H' Branch Report – Organisation and Administration, KV 1/49, TNA.

33 Report on Woman's Work, KV 1/50, TNA.

34 Lecture by Lieutenant Colonel Claude Dansey, 4 May 1917, Records of the War Department General and Special Staffs, RG 165, 9944-A-4/5, National Archives and Records Administration (NARA).

35 Report on Woman's Work, KV 1/50, TNA.

36 In 1916, Kell's organisation changed its name from MO5g to MI5.

37 Newport to Kell, 22 Sept. 1919, typed letter and handwritten note, KV 4/129, TNA.

38 'H' Branch Report – Organisation and Administration, Office Instructions, KV 1/56, TNA.

39 Ibid.

40 'H' Branch Report – Organisation and Administration, KV 1/49, TNA.

41 'Reminiscences of World War I', Private Papers of Mrs D.B.G. Line née Dimmock, Documents.1858, IWM.

42 Interview transcript of Lady Champion by Mr Liddle, Oct. 1976, LIDDLE/WW1/DF/148/1/24, TLC.

43 'H' Branch Report – Organisation and Administration, Annexure 9, Notes on the Registry, KV 1/53, TNA.

44 Ibid.

45 A list of alien passengers arriving in New York on 3 June 1934 describes Edith Lomax as being 5 feet 4 inches tall and having green eyes and grey hair. *Passenger and Crew Lists of Vessels Arriving at New York, New York, 1897–1957,* Microfilm Publication T715, 8892 rolls, NAID 300346, Records of the Immigration and Naturalization Service, RG 85, NARA.

46 The 1911 Census return for Edith Lomax, RG 14/3405, TNA.

47 The 1911 Census return for the Harrison family, RG 14/7242, TNA.

48 'H' Branch Report – Organisation and Administration, Annexure 9, Notes on the Registry, KV 1/53, TNA.

49 Ibid.

50 'H' Branch Report – Organisation and Administration, Annexure 6, 'Duties of H.7.', KV 1/53, TNA.

51 See the advert for 'Hartmann's Towelettes', *Hampstead News*, 5 April 1894.

52 'Now Science Solves Woman's Oldest Problem', *Daily Mirror*, 1 Oct. 1927.

53 Interview transcript of Lady Champion, Oct. 1976, LIDDLE/WW1/DF/148/1/24, TLC.

54 'H' Branch Report – Organisation and Administration, Annexure 9, Notes on the Registry, KV 1/53, TNA.

55 'H' Branch Report – Organisation and Administration, Annexure 4, 'Duties of H. And system of filing', KV 1/53, TNA.

56 Report on Woman's Work, KV 1/50, TNA.

57 Caswell, Florence May (oral history), 21 Oct. 1974, 513, IWM.

58 'H' Branch Report – Organisation and Administration, Office Instructions, KV 1/56, TNA.

59 Note to Miss Cribb, 24 Sept. 1918, KV 3/2, TNA.

60 Report on Woman's Work, KV 1/50, TNA.

61 'H' Branch Report – Organisation and Administration, Annexure 8, Notes on Records, Methods of Filing, Indexing and Registration, KV 1/53, TNA.

62 Report on Woman's Work, KV 1/50, TNA.

63 Ibid.

64 Ibid.

65 Kim Philby, *My Silent War: The Autobiography of a Spy* (London: Arrow, 2002), p.105.

66 Private Papers of Mrs D.B.G. Line née Dimmock, Documents.1858, IWM.

67 Dorothy Dimmock worked for MI5 from 14 August 1916 to 10 September 1917. M.I.5. Chronological List of Staff taken to 31 December, 1919, KV 4/127, TNA.

68 'Front Line Films', *Evening Mail*, 9 Aug. 1916.

69 Felicia Line, interview with author, 8 June 2023.

70 Peter Hopkirk, *On Secret Service East of Constantinople: The Plot to Bring Down the British Empire* (London: John Murray, 1994), pp.330–51.

71 'The Scene at Potters Bar', *Evening Mail*, 4 Oct. 1916.

72 'Reminiscences of World War I', Private Papers of Mrs D.B.G. Line née Dimmock, Documents.1858, IWM.

73 Ibid.

74 Ibid.

75 'H' Branch Report – Organisation and Administration, KV 1/49, TNA.

76 Andrew, *Defence of the Realm*, p.59.

77 Interview transcript of Lady Champion by Mr Liddle, Oct. 1976, LIDDLE/WW1/DF/148/1/24, TLC.

78 Mackenzie, *Greek Memories*, p.377; 'An Essay on the Girl Guide', *The Nameless Magazine*, March 1920, LBY E.J. 2710, IWM.

79 Report on Woman's Work, KV 1/50, TNA.

80 'H' Branch Report – Organisation and Administration, Annexure 6, 'Duties of H.7.', KV 1/53, TNA.

81 'H' Branch Report – Organisation and Administration, Annexure 9, Notes on the Registry, KV 1/53, TNA.

82 Report on Woman's Work, KV 1/50, TNA.

83 'H' Branch Report – Organisation and Administration, Annexure 9, Notes on the Registry, KV 1/53, TNA.

84 'Reminiscences of World War I', Private Papers of Mrs D.B.G. Line née

Dimmock, Documents.1858, IWM.

85 Ibid.

86 'H' Branch Report – Organisation and Administration, Annexure 9, Notes on the Registry, KV 1/53, TNA.

87 'H' Branch Report – Organisation and Administration, Annexure 21, 'War Museum', KV 1/53, TNA.

88 'Reminiscences of World War I', Private Papers of Mrs D.B.G. Line née Dimmock, Documents.1858, IWM.

89 'Spies in Scotland', *Aberdeen Daily Journal*, 7 Feb. 1920.

90 Ibid.

91 'The Kaiser-Moustache Spy', *The People*, 23 March 1924.

92 There is no official history of Special Branch, but the following two books offer an overview: Rupert Allason, *The Branch: A History of the Metropolitan Police Special Branch 1883–1983* (London: Secker & Warburg, 1983); Ray Wilson and Ian Adams, *Special Branch: A History 1883–2006* (London: Biteback, 2015).

93 Brust, *In Plain Clothes*, p.69.

94 Ibid., p.88.

95 Depiction of female stenographer, 'Fritz on the Rack', 1917 New Year Card, Museum of Military Intelligence (MMI).

96 Thompson, *Guard*, p.57.

97 Brust, *In Plain Clothes*, p.70.

98 Thomson, *My Experiences*, pp.220–21.

99 Ibid., p.221.

100 'Prodigy-ous', *The Clarion*, 1 May 1903.

101 'Blue Man's Colour Explained', *Witness (Belfast)*, 31 Aug. 1923.

102 Thomson, *My Experiences*, pp.220–21.

103 See Paul Lashmar, *Spies, Spin and the Fourth Estate: British Intelligence and the Media* (Edinburgh: Edinburgh University Press, 2020).

104 During the war, Basil Thomson wrote several topical articles such as 'Dartmoor – Stories of the Famous Prison', *Pall Mall Gazette*, 21 Feb. 1917.

105 Brust, *In Plain Clothes*, p.69.

106 Richard Deacon, *The Greatest Treason: The Bizarre Story of Hollis, Liddell and Mountbatten* (London: Century Hutchinson, 1989), p.69.

107 Basil Thomson, *Richardson Scores Again* (London: Eldon Press, 1934). Author's copy.

108 'Britain's Fourth Arm', *Sunday Dispatch*, 6 Feb. 1938.

109 Ibid.

110 'Mutilated Documents', *Manchester Evening News*, 17 Jan. 1918.

111 'Officer's Wife and "Count" – Lady's Confessions at Inquest', *Evening Standard*, 20 Aug. 1917.

112 Ibid.

113 An example of reporting that did not name Kathleen Pettigrew as the Special Branch shorthand writer can be found in 'Russian "Count" Shooting Case – Jury's Verdict at the Inquest', *The Times*, 21 Aug. 1917.

114 'Officer's Wife and "Count" – Lady's Confessions at Inquest', *Evening Standard*, 20 Aug. 1917.

115 Thomson, *My Experiences*, p.275.

116 Ibid.

117 'Lieut. Malcolm's Trial', *The Times*, 11 Sept. 1917.

118 'Lieut. Malcolm Acquitted – A popular verdict', *The Times*, 12 Sept. 1917.

119 'Lieut. Malcolm Acquitted', *Daily Mirror*, 12 Sept. 1917.

120 For a personal insight into the murder case see Derek Malcolm's *Family Secrets: The Scandalous History of an Extraordinary Family* (London: Hutchinson, 2003).

121 'Russian Pole's Death', *The Times*, 15 Aug. 1917.

122 'Russian "Count" Shooting Case', *The Times*, 21 Aug. 1917.

123 Alan Judd notes that Cumming recorded frequent meetings with Basil Thomson in his diary, *The Quest for C: Sir Mansfield Cumming and the Founding of the British Secret Service* (London: HarperCollins, 1999), p.310.

124 Ibid., p.290.

125 The late Keith Jeffery left a trail of breadcrumbs for future historians. One of which was the solitary mention of Miss W.V. Spink being a lone female in the First World War Russian Mission. See Keith Jeffery, *MI6: The History of the Secret Intelligence Service, 1909–1949* (London: Bloomsbury, 2010), pp.104, 807.

4. From Petrograd with Love

1 Descriptions of Mansfield Cumming's office and the MI6 headquarters located at 2 Whitehall Court can be found in Paul Dukes, *Red Dusk and the Morrow: Adventures and Investigations in Soviet Russia* (Garden City, NY: Doubleday, Page & Company, 1922), pp.5–11; Mackenzie, *Greek Memories*, pp.393–6; Valentine Williams, *The World of Action: The Autobiography of Valentine Williams* (London: Hamish Hamilton, 1938), pp.334–5.

2 In 1916, MI6, known as the Foreign Section of the Secret Service Bureau, adopted the cover of MI1(c) as part of the War Office.

3 Dukes, *Red Dusk*, pp.5–11; Mackenzie, *Greek Memories*, pp.393–6; Williams, *The World of Action*, pp.334–5.

4 Ibid.

5 Diary of Winifred Ramplee-Smith née Spink, 16 June 1916, David King Private Collection (DK).

6 Winifred Spink was awarded the British Service Medal (BSM) for intelligence duties in Petrograd and Rome during the First World War, but her employment was wrongly attributed to MI5, instead of MI6. Medal card of Winifred Verena Spink, WO 372/23/39050, The National Archives (TNA).

7 See Lloyd Eric Reeve, *Gift of the Grape* (San Francisco: Filmer, 1959); creative writing notebook belonging to Winifred Ramplee-Smith, DK.

8 Winifred Ramplee-Smith, 'Russian Reminiscence', 1961, DK.

9 David King, correspondence with author, 25 May 2022.

10 Ibid., 22 Feb. 2022.

11   Jane Gant, interview with author, 18 Feb. 2022.

12   Author correspondence with David King, 22 Feb. 2022.

13   Hilary Mantel, *Giving Up the Ghost: A Memoir* (London: Harper Perennial, 2004), p.151.

14   See Michael Smith, *Six: A History of Britain's Secret Intelligence Service. Part 1: Murder and Mayhem, 1909–1939* (London: Dialogue, 2010), pp.198–202.

15   Ramplee-Smith, 'Russian Reminiscence'.

16   Jane Gant, interview with author, 18 Feb. 2022.

17   1901 Census entry for Winifred Spink, RG 13/683, TNA.

18   Jane Gant, interview with author, 18 Feb. 2022.

19   See June Purvis, *Emmeline Pankhurst: A Biography* (London: Routledge, 2002).

20   The character of Mrs Banks, played by Glynis Johns, encouraged women to 'cast off the shackles of yesterday' when she sang the song 'Sister Suffragette' in Walt Disney's *Mary Poppins*, directed by Robert Stevenson, USA, 1964.

21   Diary of Winifred Ramplee-Smith, 2 Jan. 1913.

22   June Purvis, *Christabel Pankhurst: A Biography* (London: Routledge, 2018), p.315.

23   Diary of Winifred Ramplee-Smith, 27 Jan. 1913.

24   Ibid., 18 March 1913.

25   Curriculum Vitae of Winifred Ramplee-Smith, 1940, DK.

26   Walter Bersey, Membership list of the Automobile Club of Great Britain, 30 Oct. 1899, Royal Automobile Club Archive (RACA); Mansfield Cumming, Membership list of the Automobile Club of Great Britain, 30 Oct. 1902, RACA.

27   See Walter C. Bersey, *Electrically-propelled Carriages* (London: Morgan, Thompson and Jamieson, 1898).

28   Frederick Heelis (Principal of Pitman's School on Southampton Row) to Winifred Spink, 25 June 1913, DK.

29   Curriculum Vitae of Winifred Ramplee-Smith, 1945, DK.

30   Maurice Bailey, interview with author, 1 April 2022.

31   Keith Jeffery, *MI6: The History of the Secret Intelligence Service 1909-1949* (London: Bloomsbury, 2010), p.57.

32   Diary of Winifred Ramplee-Smith, 20 November 1916. Winnie recorded that she was paid £360 a year, the same as her male colleagues.

33   Ibid., 8 July 1916.

34   For more on Samuel Hoare see John A. Cross, *Samuel Hoare: A Political Biography* (London: Jonathan Cape, 1977).

35   During the Second World War, Cudburt Thornhill worked closely with Freya Stark in Cairo against the Italians.

36   Samuel Hoare, *The Fourth Seal: The End of a Russian Chapter* (London: William Heinemann, 1930), p.53.

37   Mansfield Cumming to Samuel Hoare, 11 May 1916, Templewood Papers, Part II File 38, UCL.

38   Diary of Winifred Ramplee-Smith, 12 to 15 July 1916.

39   Ramplee-Smith, 'Russian Reminiscence'.

40   Diary of Winifred Ramplee-Smith, 17 July 1916.

41   Ibid.

42   Hoare, *Fourth Seal*, p.48.

43   Smith, *Six*, pp.187–8.

44   Report on the British Intelligence Mission by Samuel Hoare, 29 Jan. 1917, Templewood Papers, Part II File 52, UCL.

45   Diary of Winifred Ramplee-Smith, 29 July 1916.

46   Curriculum Vitae of Winifred Ramplee-Smith, 1940, DK.

47   Samuel Hoare to Freddie Browning, 3 Aug. 1916, Templewood Papers, Part II File 42, UCL.

48   Ibid.

49   Hoare, *Fourth Seal*, p.49.

50   Ibid.

51   Diary of Winifred Ramplee-Smith, 25 Dec. 1916.

52   Ibid., 6 Aug. 1916.

53   Ibid., 14 Sept. 1916.

54   Ibid., 17 Sept. 1916.

55   Ibid., 11 Nov. 1915.

56   Ibid., 11 Jan. 1911; Georges Pancol, *Journal intime, lettres à la fiancée, poèmes* (Bordeaux: Opales, 1996), p.81.

57   David King, interview with author, 1 March 2022.

58   Diary of Winifred Ramplee-Smith, 7 Oct. 1916.

59   Georges Pancol, *Virginy: Tombe 556* (Paris: R. Chiberre, 1923).

60   Diary of Winifred Ramplee-Smith, 12 Dec. 1916. Winnie recorded in her diary that she had taken a walk along the Neva with a gentleman whose initials were 'F.M.P.' and against the entry she wrote 'Another scalp'.

61   David Hopper, interview with author, 1 Feb. 2022.

62   Anglo-Maikop Group Collection, 1910–1949, ClC/B/009, London Metropolitan Archives (LMA).

63   Report on the British Intelligence Mission by Samuel Hoare, 29 Jan. 1917, Templewood Papers, Part II File 52, UCL.

64   Ibid.

65   Diary of Winifred Ramplee-Smith, 30 Nov. 1916. The office moved from 58 Moika to 13 Moika.

66   Winifred Ramplee-Smith, small handwritten note, undated, DK.

67   Report on the British Intelligence Mission by Samuel Hoare, 29 Jan. 1917, Templewood Papers, Part II File 52, UCL; Diary of Winifred Ramplee-Smith, 18 Dec. 1916. Winnie moved to the Mission flat on this date.

68   Ibid., 16 Nov. and 4 Dec. 1916.

69   Ramplee-Smith, 'Russian Reminiscence'.

70   Hoare, *Fourth Seal*, p.160.

71   Ibid., p.68.

72   Smith, *Six*, p.199.

73   Oswald Rayner to Mrs Thomas Stanford, 14 Dec. 1916, P23/1/C/3, Oxfordshire

History Centre (OHC); Felix Yusupov to Oswald Rayner, postcard of L'Arc de Triomphe in Paris, 30 Jan. 1959, P23/1/C/9, OHC; Felix Yusupov to Oswald Rayner, postcard, 23 Feb. 1960, P23/1/C/10, OHC.

74 Felix Yusupov wrote several accounts of Rasputin's murder. See Felix Yusupov, *Rasputin: His Malignant Influence and His Assassination*, trans. Oswald Rayner (London: Jonathan Cape, 1927); *Lost Splendour* (London: Jonathan Cape, 1954).

75 See Andrew Cook, *To Kill Rasputin: The Life and Death of Grigori Rasputin* (Stroud: Tempus, 2005); Richard Cullen, *Rasputin: The Role of Britain's Secret Service in His Torture and Murder* (London: Dialogue, 2010).

76 'Croppy' (Colonel Henry Vere Benet) to Mrs Squire, 14 Feb. 1917 [Russian calendar], P23/1/C/3, OHC. Benet, a friend of Rayner's, was a military attaché in Petrograd during the war.

77 Diary of Winifred Ramplee-Smith, 30 Dec. 1916.

78 Ramplee-Smith, 'Russian Reminiscence'.

79 Hoare, *Fourth Seal*, p.156.

80 Ibid., p.157.

81 Ibid., p.160.

82 Samuel Hoare to Freddie Browning, 2 Jan. 1917, Templewood Papers, Part II File 49, UCL.

83 Diary of Winifred Ramplee-Smith, 2 Jan. 1917.

84 Samuel Hoare to Freddie Browning, 2 Jan. 1917, Templewood Papers, Part II File 49, UCL.

85 Diary of Winifred Ramplee-Smith, 21 Feb. 1917; Hoare, *Fourth Seal*, 207.

86 Diary of Winifred Ramplee-Smith, 3 March 1917. Winnie left Petrograd for Moscow on the 8 p.m. train. She also noted that Hoare had arrived safely in London that day.

87 Ibid., 21 Jan. 1917. Winnie recorded that she was in bed with yet another bad cold.

88 Ramplee-Smith, 'Russian Reminiscence'.

89 Ibid.

90 Ibid.

91 Ibid.

92 Ibid.; Diary of Winifred Ramplee-Smith, 13–15 March 1917.

93 Diary of Winifred Ramplee-Smith, 15 March 1917 (= 2 March [Russian Gregorian calendar]).

94 Ibid.

95 Winifred Spink to Samuel Hoare, 15 June 1917, Templewood Papers, Part II File 2, UCL. In 1963, Winnie donated a number of revolutionary newspapers and postcards to the Hoover Institution Library and Archive. Witold S. Sworakowski (Assistant Director) to Winifred Ramplee-Smith, 13 Dec. 1963, DK.

96 Ramplee-Smith, 'Russian Reminiscence'.

97 Ibid.

98 Ibid.; Diary of Winifred Ramplee-Smith, 2 April 1917. Winnie recorded that she went to the cinema with Reid to see films about the revolution.

99   Ramplee-Smith, 'Russian Reminiscence'.

100 Ibid.

101 Ibid.

102 Ibid.

103 Ibid.

104 Diary of Winifred Ramplee-Smith, 2 June 1917.

105 Ibid., 5 June 1917.

106 See Maria Bochkareva and Isaac Don Levine, *Yashka: My Life as a Peasant, Exile and Soldier* (New York: Frederick A. Stokes, 1919).

107 Ramplee-Smith, 'Russian Reminiscence'.

108 Diary of Winifred Ramplee-Smith, 7 July 1917.

109 Ramplee-Smith, 'Russian Reminiscence'.

110 Diary of Winifred Ramplee-Smith, 30 June 1917.

111 Diary of Winifred Ramplee-Smith, 12 July 1917.

112 See Smith, *Six*, p.208.

113 Diary of Winifred Ramplee-Smith, 19 March 1917.

114 Ibid., 16 July 1917; Ramplee-Smith, 'Russian Reminiscence'.

115 Ramplee-Smith, 'Russian Reminiscence'.

116 Ibid.

117 Diary of Winifred Ramplee-Smith, 1, 10, and 12 Aug. 1917.

118 Ibid., 13 Aug. 1917.

119 Frank Stagg to Samuel Hoare, 11 May 1916, Templewood Papers, Part II File 39, UCL.

120 Telegram to Mr Wardrop (Moscow), 9 April 1918, FO 371/3326, TNA.

121 Ramplee-Smith, 'Russian Reminiscence'.

122 Diary of Winifred Ramplee-Smith, 31 Aug. 1917.

123 Ibid., 20 Oct. 1917; Jeffery, *MI6*, pp.123–4.

124 '"Whitehall-Marked" – Winnie of the War Office', *The Tatler*, 9 Oct. 1918.

125 See Jessica Pallingston, *Lipstick: A Celebration of the World's Favourite Cosmetic* (New York: Saint Martin's Press, 1999).

126 Winifred Spink to Under Secretary of State (Foreign Office), 3 June 1918, FO 372/1139, TNA.

127 Diary of Winifred Ramplee-Smith, 8 June 1918.

128 Ibid., 8 Aug. 1918.

129 W. Langley (Foreign Office) to Winifred Spink, 13 June 1918, FO 372/1139, TNA.

130 Diary of Winifred Ramplee-Smith, 6 and 8 Aug. 1918.

131 Ibid., 29 April 1919; British Consul (Vladivostok) Marriage Register for Lionel Reid and Maria Evna Valli Klok, 28 Feb. 1919, FO 510/4, TNA.

132 Sarah Clark, correspondence with author, 25 Feb. 2022.

133 Lady Maud Hoare, Letter of Recommendation for Winifred Ramplee-Smith, 10 Nov. 1939, DK.

134 Samuel Hoare to Winifred Spink, 3 Jan. 1919, DK.

135 Winifred Ramplee-Smith to Lord Templewood (Samuel Hoare), 25 Nov. 1948, Templewood Papers, Part XVII File 4, UCL.

5. The Lunn Sisters

1   George A. Hill, *Go Spy the Land: Being the Adventures of I.K.8 of the British Secret Service* (London: Cassell, 1932), p.198.

2   Ibid., p.217; Captain G. A. Hill, 'Report on Work Done in Russia to End of 1917 [should read 1918]', 26 Nov. 1918, FO 371/3350, TNA.

3   Captain George A. Hill, 'Report on Work Done in Russia to End of 1917 [should read 1918]', 27 Nov. 1918, Major General Sir Frederick C. Poole Collection, Liddell Hart Centre for Military Archives (LHC).

4   Hill, *Go Spy the Land*, p.241.

5   Natalie Rothstein, 'The Lunn Family or Clogs to Clogs in Three Generations', Feb. 2001, Henry Rothstein Private Collection (HR).

6   Ibid.

7   List of British Subjects in Moscow District, August 1918, FO 369/1017, TNA. Pencil annotations to the typed list reveal that John Septimus Lunn, Lucy Winifred Lunn and Marjorie Nona Lunn had left and arrived in England. A second pencil annotation records 'a Mrs Lunn has left'.

8   Ibid.

9   Typed letter from Oliver Wardrop to the Foreign Office, 11 Sept. 1918, FO 369/1017, TNA.

10   James W. Ford-Smith, handwritten note entitled 'Escape from Russia', undated, MS. 1256/744, Leeds Russian Archive (LRA).

11   James W. Ford-Smith, handwritten note entitled 'Edwin Lunn', undated, MS. 1256/766, LRA.

12   MI5 Personal File (Communists and Suspected Communists) Edith Lunn, KV 2/2317 and KV 2/2318, TNA.

13   Major Ball (MI5), Typed Register Note, 5 Aug. 1925, KV 2/2317, TNA.

14   See Gill Bennett, *Churchill's Man of Mystery: Desmond Morton and the World of Intelligence* (London: Routledge, 2009).

15   Victor Madeira, *Britannia and the Bear: The Anglo-Russian Intelligence Wars 1917–1929* (Woodbridge: Boydell Press, 2014), pp.141–4; David Burke, *Russia and the British Left: From the 1848 Revolutions to the General Strike* (London: Bloomsbury Academic, 2020), p.197.

16   Jeffery, *MI6*, pp.231–2; Ferris, *Behind the Enigma*, p.89.

17   The MI5 Personal File on Edith Lunn wrongly describes her sister Marjorie (named Margaret in the file) as working for MI6 in Helsingfors (Helsinki) for one month before being dismissed for turning 'red', KV 2/2317, TNA. Natalie Rothstein records that her mother Edith was working briefly for MI6 in Helsinki. See Natalie Rothstein, 'The Lunn Family', HR.

18   List of Code and Cypher School Salaried Staff, undated, FO 1093/104, TNA. Marjorie Nona Lunn was employed as a GC&CS Lady Translator on 1 July 1921.

19   Rothstein, 'The Lunn Family', HR.

20   James W. Ford-Smith, Lunn family history, undated, MS. 1256/752, LRA.

21   Ibid.

22 Rothstein, 'The Lunn Family', HR. Owens College, which became Victoria University of Manchester in 1904, merged with the University of Manchester Institute of Science and Technology (UMIST) 100 years later to become the University of Manchester.

23 As an Anglican, Michael Lunn was buried just outside the orthodox cemetery of the Church of Nikolsky Trubetsky in Balashikha. He has a street named after him in the city, and indeed, locals have long referred to Balashikha as Michaylovka in his memory. The factory remained in continuous use, save for two months when Hitler was at the gates of Moscow, until well after the turn of the millennium.

24 Rothstein, 'The Lunn Family', HR.

25 Ibid.

26 Ibid.

27 Ibid. For more on Arthur Ransome see Roland Chambers, *The Last Englishman: The Double Life of Arthur Ransome* (London: Faber & Faber, 2009).

28 Rothstein, 'The Lunn Family', HR; James W. Ford-Smith, handwritten note entitled 'Catherine Louisa Lunn', undated, MS. 1256/761, LRA. Catherine had three sons and after the death of her husband became a magistrate. She died from lung cancer on 2 October 1956.

29 Rothstein, 'The Lunn Family', HR.

30 Ibid.; James W. Ford-Smith, handwritten note entitled 'Richard Arthur Lunn', undated, MS. 1256/790, LRA. Richard married Norah Peggy Smith, whom he met at his sister Catherine's wedding. They had no children.

31 Lunn and Smith Families Collection, 1870s–1995, MS. 1256, LRA.

32 Rothstein, 'The Lunn Family', HR; James W. Ford-Smith, handwritten note entitled 'Walter Stanley Lunn', undated, MS. 1256/794, LRA. Walter married and had two sons.

33 Rothstein, 'The Lunn Family', HR; James W. Ford-Smith, handwritten note entitled 'John Septimus Lunn', undated, MS. 1256/775, LRA. John lived with a woman until his forties when he married someone else. He had no children.

34 MI5 to Vivian, 19 Aug. 1940, KV 2/2318, TNA; Bletchley Park Roll of Honour entry for Flight Officer J. S. Lunn, who worked in Hut 3 and Block A (room 119) 1942–44.

35 Rothstein, 'The Lunn Family', HR; James W. Ford-Smith, handwritten note entitled 'Helen Clara Lunn', undated, MS. 1256/773, LRA.

36 Graduate Index Card for Helen Clara Lunn, 7 July 1919, University of Liverpool Library (ULL).

37 Passport Office papers forwarded by Mr Bloore, 3 Sept. 1925, KV 2/2317, TNA.

38 General Medical Council, *Medical and Dental Students' Register: Lists of Medical and Dental Students Registered during the Year 1926* (London: Constable, 1926), p.41.

39 Rothstein, 'The Lunn Family', HR; James W. Ford-Smith, handwritten note entitled 'Marjorie Nona Lunn', undated, MS. 1256/782, LRA.

40 MI5 to Morton (MI6), 13 Aug. 1925, KV 2/2317, TNA.

41 Rothstein, 'The Lunn Family', HR.

42 Arbuthnot (M.I.6.c) to M.I.5., 3 Dec. 1917, KV 2/2317, TNA.

43 Edith Lunn to Roberts, 15 Nov. 1917, KV 2/2317, TNA.

44 Rothstein, 'The Lunn Family', HR.

45 Arbuthnot (M.I.6.c) to M.I.5., 3 Dec. 1917, KV 2/2317, TNA.

46 Chief Constable of Cheshire to Kell, 19 Dec. 1917, KV 2/2317, TNA; Rothstein, 'The Lunn Family', HR.

47 Natasha Gelfand to Andrew Rothstein, 13 March 1970, HR.

48 Rothstein, 'The Lunn Family', HR.

49 Ibid.

50 Ibid.

51 See Dan Healey, *Homosexual Desire in Revolutionary Russia: The Regulation of Sexual and Gender Dissent* (Chicago: University of Chicago Press, 2001).

52 Rothstein, 'The Lunn Family', HR.

53 A.M. Liubarskaya to Andrew Rothstein, undated, HR.

54 Ibid.

55 Morton (MI6) to Philips (MI5), 6 Aug. 1925, KV 2/2317, TNA.

56 A.E. Hopper (British Consulate, Helsinki) to A. Allen Hopper, 29 May 1919, KV 2/506, TNA; Tania Rose and John Saville, 'Harold Grenfell', in Joyce Bellamy and John Saville, eds., *The Dictionary of Labour Biography*, vol. 9 (Basingstoke: Macmillan, 1993), pp.102–6.

57 Cross-reference from Scotland House concerning Salme Pekkala, 26 Nov. 1924, KV 2/513, TNA.

58 Admiralty Officer Service Record for Captain Harold Granville Grenfell, ADM 196/43/72, TNA.

59 See Personal File (Communists and Suspected Communists) Harold Grenfell, KV 2/506 and KV 2/507, TNA.

60 Home Office Circular against Salme Pekkala, 15 July 1921, KV 2/513, TNA. Notes that she arrived in England in February 1920.

61 Liddell (MI5) to Vivian (MI6), 4 April 1934, KV 2/513, TNA.

62 William Murphy, 'Lydia Stahl: A Secret Life, 1885–?', *Journal of Intelligence History* 18, no. 1 (Jan. 2019), pp.38–62; papers on Lydia Stahl can be found within the Personal File (Communists and Suspected Communists) Robert Switz, KV 2/1586–1590, TNA.

63 Admiralty Officer Service Record for Captain Harold Granville Grenfell, ADM 196/43/72, TNA.

64 Lansbury (*Daily Herald*) to Klishko (Secretary to the Russian Trade Delegation), 25 Nov. 1920, KV 2/2317, TNA; Ball (MI5) to Morton (MI6), 13 Aug. 1925, KV 2/2317, TNA.

65 Home Office Warrant imposed by Scotland House on Miss Edith Lunn, 25 March 1921, KV 2/2317, TNA.

66 Note from Colonel Carter, 31 May 1921, KV 2/2317, TNA.

67 Ibid.

68 Surveillance report on 100 Parliament Hill Mansions, 1 Sept. 1925, KV 2/2317, TNA.

69 Devon Constabulary to Kell, 31 Aug. 1925, KV 2/2317, TNA.

70 Mitroff to Rothstein ('Andriousha'), 17 Aug. 1925, KV 2/2317, TNA.

71 For the best overview to date that has come closest to the truth, see Gill Bennett, *The Zinoviev Letter: The Conspiracy that Never Dies* (Oxford: Oxford University Press, 2018).

72 Jeffery, *MI6*, p.218.

73 Clara Lunn to Edith Lunn, 13 Nov. 1925, KV 2/2317, TNA.

74 Salary list of GC&CS, 10 Jan. 1920, FO 1093/104, TNA.

75 Ferris, *Behind the Enigma*, p.78. John Ferris states that, when GC&CS began in 1919, there were 28 clerical staff, 2 cryptologic staff, 18 junior assistants, and 6 senior assistants.

76 Jackie Uí Chionna, *Queen of Codes: The Secret Life of Emily Anderson, Britain's Greatest Female Codebreaker* (London: Headline, 2023), p.79.

77 'History of Naval Section, 1919–1941' by W.F. Clarke, undated, HW 3/16, TNA.

78 Ferris, *Behind the Enigma*, p.78.

79 *London Gazette*, 7 Aug. 1925.

80 Ferris, *Behind the Enigma*, p.79.

81 GC&CS Billeting List, 12 July 1939, HW 3/1, TNA.

82 H.C. Lunn entry on the Bletchley Park Roll of Honour, Bletchley Park.

83 Rothstein, 'The Lunn Family', HR.

84 GC&CS Staff & Seniority Lists, Sept. 1939, HW 14/1, TNA.

85 Rothstein, 'The Lunn Family', HR.

86 MBE Award to Lucy Winifred Lunn, 14 June 1969, HR; 'John' to Lucy Lunn, 16 June 1969, HR.

87 Several private handwritten notes to Lucy Lunn, June 1969, HR.

88 Desmond Morton to Lucy Lunn, undated, HR.

89 Morton (MI6) to Philips (MI5), 6 Aug. 1925, KV 2/2317, TNA.

90 Christopher Andrew, *Secret Service: The Making of the British Intelligence Community* (London: Heinemann, 1985), p.284.

91 Judd, *The Quest for C*, p.203.

92 Ibid.

93 Jean Findlay, *Chasing Time: The Life of C.K. Scott Moncrieff: Soldier, Spy and Translator* (London: Vintage, 2015), p.260.

94 SOE Personnel File of Phyllis Mackenzie, HS 9/965/3, TNA.

95 Moncrieff to his mother, 29 Oct. 1928, cited in Findlay, *Chasing Time*, p.275.

96 Lucy Lunn to Helen Lunn, 2 Dec. 1925, KV 2/2317, TNA.

97 Moncrieff to Holland, Aug. 1929, MS-3760, Harry Ransom Center, University of Texas (HRC).

98 Rothstein, 'The Lunn Family', HR.

99 Ibid.

100 Ibid.

101 MI5 assessment on Edith, Helen, Lucy and 'Margaret' Lunn, 4 Feb. 1926, KV 2/2317, TNA.

102 Ibid.

103 MI5 note on the Lunn Case, 19 March 1926, KV 2/2317, TNA.

104 Christopher Andrew and Vasili Mitrokhin, *The Mitrokhin Archive: The KGB in Europe and the West* (London: Penguin, 2018), p.153. This book was originally published by Allen Lane in 1999 and caused a sensation, as it revealed, for the first time, the names of a number of British citizens who had worked as Russian spies, including Melita Norwood.

105 For more information on Melita Norwood see David Burke, *The Spy Who Came In from the Co-op: Melita Norwood and the Ending of Cold War Espionage* (Woodbridge: Boydell Press, 2008).

106 'The Spy Who Came In from the Co-op', *The Times*, 11 Sept. 1999.

107 For a grand narrative on the hundred-year intelligence war between Russia and the West see Calder Walton, *Spies: The Epic Intelligence War between East and West* (London: Abacus, 2023).

108 James W. Ford-Smith, Lunn family history, undated, MS. 1256/752, LRA.

109 Natasha Gelfand to Andrew Rothstein, 13 March 1970, HR.

6. Through the Looking Glass

1 Adrian O'Sullivan, *The Baghdad Set: Iraq through the Eyes of British Intelligence, 1941–45* (London/Cham: Palgrave Macmillan, 2019), p.13.

2 1921 Census entry for Mary Bidwell, RG 15/01261, The National Archives (TNA); pay estimate for Staff of the Secret Service Section of Special Branch, 1929, MEPO 2/9844, Metropolitan Police Service, FOIA, 01.FOI.21.022379. Miss Bidwell began work as a departmental secretary in the Directorate of Intelligence on 29 May 1920.

3 Diary of Major John Fillis Carre Carter, 1917, NAM 2004-06-94-1, National Army Museum (NAM); secret file marked 'Agent Dropping', 1918, NAM 2004-06-94-5, NAM.

4 For an example see Directorate of Intelligence. Supplementary Weekly Report, 15 Oct. 1920, CAB 24/112/72, TNA.

5 Cited in Richard C. Thurlow, *The Secret State: British Internal Security in the Twentieth Century* (Oxford: Blackwell, 1994), p.50.

6 Richard J. Aldrich and Rory Cormac, *The Secret Royals: Spying and the Crown, from Victoria to Diana* (London: Atlantic, 2021), p.196.

7 Confidential letter from Basil Thomson (Director Intelligence) to the Keeper of the Records (Public Record Office), 3 July 1920, EXT 11/18, TNA.

8 Three other women worked for Basil Thomson in the Directorate of Intelligence: Anna Kingham, Mary Bidwell and Maud Symons.

9 Confidential letter to Sir John Anderson, 1 Aug. 1928, MEPO 2/9844, Metropolitan Police Service, FOIA, 01.FOI.21.022379.

10 Secret Registry Schedule of Staff, undated, MEPO 2/9844, Metropolitan Police Service, FOIA, 01.FOI.21.022379; Hope Symons resigned from the SS Registry on 24 August 1928, MEPO 2/9844, FOIA.

11 Lilian Wyles was the daughter of Julia Grylls Symons (1852–1907), who was the niece of Frederick Symons (1833–1891), father to Maud and Eva 'Hope' Symons. Lilian Wyles wrote her memoir, *A Woman at Scotland Yard:*

Reflections on the Struggles and Achievements of Thirty Years in the Metropolitan Police (London: Faber & Faber, 1952).

12   Obituary of Frederick Gordon Symons, *Manchester Courier*, 14 Nov. 1891.

13   Thomson, *The Scene Changes*, pp.430–31.

14   Ibid.

15   Ibid., p.431; Andrew, *Secret Service*, p.283.

16   On 23 December 1919, Mansfield Cumming moved the MI6 headquarters from 2 Whitehall Court to 1 Melbury Road in Holland Park. See Keith Jeffery, *MI6: The History of the Secret Intelligence Service 1909–1949* (London: Bloomsbury, 2010), p.156.

17   In 1935, 1 Melbury Road was divided in two, and it became known as East and West House, 9–11 Melbury Road.

18   'Appointment of Standing for London Hackney Carriage within the Metropolitan Police District', *London Gazette*, 26 May 1922.

19   Jeffery, *MI6*, p.136.

20   Judd, *The Quest for C*, p.462.

21   Ibid.

22   Judd, *The Quest for C*, p.469.

23   1921 Census entry for Miss Beatrice Victoria Mortimer, RG 15/02902, TNA.

24   Arthur Lakey (alias ALLEN) statement to Mr Harker, 24 July 1928, KV 2/989, TNA.

25   Trial of Alfred John Mortimer, 9 Sept. 1920, CRIM 9/66, TNA.

26   Beatrice Victoria Mortimer, marriage certificate, 24 Oct. 1925, General Register Office, copy in possession of author.

27   1921 Census entry for Miss Gladys Lincoln, RG 15/00318, TNA.

28   These women have been identified on the 1921 Census as having worked for 'Captain Spencer' (an alias used by Mansfield Cumming) at 1 Adam Street, Adelphi, London. The final three women/secretaries named were left £100 after Cumming's death in 1923. Will of Mansfield George Smith Cumming, 10 Jan. 1923, General Register Office, copy in possession of author.

29   Georgina Knight, interview with author, 6 Aug. 2021.

30   Fort Sandeman, now known as Zhob, is a large castellated stronghold on the Afghanistan–Pakistan border.

31   Jeremy Baines, interview with author, 19 July 2021.

32   Emma Alexander, interview with author, 14 July 2022.

33   Williams, *The World of Action*, pp.337–8; Mackenzie, *Greek Memories*, p.395.

34   Emma Alexander, interview with author, 13 Aug. 2022.

35   Williams, *World of Action*, p.339.

36   Henslowe to Murray, 29 Aug. 1923, Henslowe Family Private Collection (HENS).

37   Admiral Sir Hugh 'Quex' Sinclair ran MI6 for sixteen years until his death in 1939 while still serving.

38   Typed letter of recommendation for Dorothy Henslowe supplied by Hugh Sinclair (signed in green ink), 10 July 1926 (HENS).

39 Jeffery, *MI6*, pp.222–5.

40 'Obituary of Admiral Sir Hugh Sinclair', *The Times*, 6 Nov. 1939.

41 Ibid.

42 Ibid.

43 Richard Deacon, *The British Connection: Russia's Manipulation of British Individuals and Institutions* (London: Hamish Hamilton, 1979), p.36.

44 Will of Evelyn Beatrice Sinclair, 10 July 1970, General Register Office, copy in possession of author.

45 Rupert Cooper, correspondence with author, 24 July 2022.

46 Scrapbook of Hugh Sinclair, 1914–1937, SCL/103/1, National Maritime Museum Caird Library and Archive, London (NMM).

47 List of Secretariat Staff with handwritten note concerning the appointment of three Special Temporary Clerks, 1935, FO 366/958, TNA.

48 Lakey statement to Harker, 20 Aug. 1928, KV 2/989, TNA.

49 A note by Harker, 1 Aug. 1928, KV 2/989, TNA.

50 Ibid.

51 Examples include Paul Dukes, *Red Dusk and the Morrow: Adventures and Investigations in Soviet Russia* (Garden City, NY: Doubleday, Page & Company, 1922); Basil Thomson, *My Experiences at Scotland Yard* (Doubleday, Page & Co, 1923); Samuel Hoare, *The Fourth Seal: The End of a Russian Chapter* (London: William Heinemann, 1930); George Hill, *Go Spy the Land* (London: Cassell, 1932); R.H. Bruce Lockhart, *Memoirs of a British Agent* (London: Putnam, 1932); Compton Mackenzie, *Greek Memories* (London: Cassell, 1932); and Henry Landau, *All Is Fair: The Story of the British Secret Service Behind the German Lines* (New York: G.P. Putnam's Sons, 1934).

52 'Official Secrets Charge Sensations', *Evening Despatch*, 3 Feb. 1938.

7. The Secretary Spy

1   'Official Secrets Charge Sensations – Story of Girl Who Foiled Plans', *Evening Despatch*, 3 Feb. 1938.

2   'Blonde Spy in Flat', *Daily Herald*, 4 Feb. 1938.

3   Ibid.; 'Girl at War Office Secret Agent', *News Chronicle*, 4 Feb. 1938.

4   Anthony Masters, *The Man Who Was M: The Life of Maxwell Knight* (Oxford: Blackwell, 1984), p.32.

5   Ibid., p.30.

6   Valarie Lippay, correspondence with author, 14 Jan. 2024.

7   The school has since been absorbed by Plymouth College.

8   Henry Hemming, *M: Maxwell Knight, MI5's Greatest Spymaster* (London: Penguin, 2017); Masters, *The Man Who Was M*.

9   Masters, *The Man Who Was M*, p.31.

10 Henry Hemming, 'The Peroxide Blonde Who Was Britain's Bravest Spy: How Olga Gray Risked Her Life to Stop the Soviets Stealing Our War Secrets Despite Being Crippled by Insecurity', *Daily Mail*, 1 Sept. 2017.

11 Francis Beckett, *Stalin's British Victims* (Abingdon: Routledge, 2016), p.97.

12 Vernon Kell lecture notes on 'Security Intelligence in War', 1934, PP/

MCR/120, SVK/2, Reel 1, Imperial War Museum (IWM).

13   Maxwell Knight, 'Report on the Work of M.S. (Agents) during the War, 1939–45', 4 April 1945, KV 4/227, TNA.

14   Ibid.

15   'The Woolwich Arsenal Case', 13 Feb. 1950, KV 2/1023, TNA.

16   Knight, 'Report on the Work of M.S.', KV 4/227, TNA.

17   Ibid.

18   Ibid.

19   Ibid.

20   Henry Hemming uncovered the names and activity of agents Mona Maund and Kathleen Tesch in his biography *M: Maxwell Knight*.

21   Knight, 'Report on the Work of M.S.', KV 4/227, TNA.

22   Masters, *The Man Who Was M*, p.32.

23   Joan Miller, *One Girl's War: Personal Exploits in MI5's Most Secret Station* (Dingle: Brandon, 1986), p.66.

24   'Statement of "X" the Informant in this case', 25 Jan. 1938, KV 2/1022, TNA.

25   'Communist in the Arsenal', *Morning Post*, 29 Nov. 1928.

26   'The Woolwich Arsenal Case', 13 Feb. 1950, KV 2/1023, TNA.

27   'Security Service Distribution of Duties', Oct. 1931, KV 4/127, TNA; Sheila Halliwell, correspondence with author, 2 Feb. 2023; Marcus Halliwell, interview with author, 25 Feb. 2023.

28   Vernon Kell, Recommendation for Kathleen Sissmore, 18 Aug. 1921, ADM/9/1921, The Honourable Society of Gray's Inn (HSGI).

29   'Women's Bar Successes', *Vote*, 7 Nov. 1924.

30   'Security Service Distribution of Duties', Oct. 1931, KV 4/127, TNA.

31   Kathleen Sissmore, 'B.3. note', 15 June 1931, KV 2/1020, TNA.

32   Knight, 'Report on the Work of M.S.', KV 4/227, TNA.

33   Masters, *The Man Who Was M*, p.33.

34   Ibid.

35   Knight, 'Report on the Work of M.S.', KV 4/227, TNA.

36   Masters, *The Man Who Was M*, p.34.

37   'Miss "X"', KV 2/1023, TNA.

38   Knight, 'Report on the Work of M.S.', KV 4/227, TNA.

39   Masters, *The Man Who Was M*, p.34.

40   Ibid.

41   'Statement of "X"', KV 2/1022, TNA.

42   Angus Macpherson, 'Olga the Beautiful Spy', *Mail on Sunday*, 29 July 1984.

43   Masters, *The Man Who Was M*, p.35.

44   Ibid.

45   Ibid., p.34.

46   Nigel West, *MASK: MI5's Penetration of the Communist Party of Great Britain* (Abingdon: Routledge, 2005), p.1.

47   'Statement of "X" the Informant in this case', 25 Jan.1938, KV 2/1022, TNA; Masters, *The Man Who Was M*, p.43.

48   'Statement of "X" the Informant in this case', 25 Jan. 1938, KV 2/1022, TNA.

49   'Poison Death Riddle of Author's Wife', *Evening Standard*, 17 Dec. 1936.
50   Tom Bower, *The Perfect English Spy: Sir Dick White and the Secret War 1935–90* (London: Heinemann, 1995), p.26.
51   'Miss X' testimony, 3, 7 and 11 Feb. 1938, CRIM 1/1003, TNA.
52   'The Woolwich Arsenal Case', 13 Feb. 1950, KV 2/1023, TNA.
53   Ibid.
54   Ibid.
55   Bryony Tillett, correspondence with author, 2 Jan. 2024.
56   Masters, *The Man Who Was M*, p.53.
57   'Official Secrets Act', *The Times*, 15 March 1938.
58   Miller, *One Girl's War*, p.18.
59   Masters, *The Man Who Was M*, p.54.
60   Letter to Miss Sissmore from SIS (MI6), 28 March 1938, KV 2/1022, TNA.
61   MI5 case file on the Soviet Intelligence agent Theodore Maly, KV 2/1009, TNA.
62   Theodore Maly was later found to have been executed on 20 September 1938, though evidence exists to suggest he may not have perished on this date.
63   'The Woolwich Arsenal Case', 18 Nov. 1950, KV 2/1023, TNA.
64   Vanessa Morrison, correspondence with author, 2 Jan. 2024.
65   Ibid.
66   Masters, *The Man Who Was M*, p.30.
67   Andrew, *The Defence of the Realm*, p.179.

8. Station X

1   'Government Buy Park', *Bletchley District Gazette*, 28 May 1938.
2   Ibid.
3   Michael Smith, *Station X: The Codebreakers of Bletchley Park* (London: Pan, 2004), p.1.
4   W.F. Clarke, 'B.P. Reminiscences', undated, HW 3/16, The National Archives (TNA).
5   The story was picked up by the *Bucks Examiner, Bucks Herald*, and the *Buckingham Advertiser and North Bucks Free Press,* all of which ran their stories at the beginning of June 1938.
6   The last story to appear in print before issue of the D-notice was 'Bletchley Park's Future', *Buckingham Advertiser and North Bucks Free Press*, 4 June 1938.
7   Jeffery, *MI6*, p.319.
8   See Frederick Winterbotham, *The Ultra Secret: The Inside Story of Operation Ultra, Bletchley Park and Enigma* (London: Weidenfeld & Nicolson, 1974). Winterbotham's book was the first to reveal the role and contribution of Bletchley Park and the Enigma machine.
9   See David Kenyon, *Bletchley Park and D-Day: The Untold Story of How the Battle for Normandy Was Won* (London: Yale University Press, 2019), pp.11–42.
10   Kerry Johnson and John Gallehawk, *Figuring It Out at Bletchley Park*

1939–1945 (Milton Keynes: BookTower, 2007), p.9.

11 W.H.W. Ridley to The Treasury Valuer, 16 April 1940, HW 64/42, TNA. Captain Ridley notes the occupation dates of the first eight huts at Bletchley Park.

12 See Patricia and Jean Owtram, *Codebreaking Sisters: Our Secret War* (London: Mirror, 2020); Mair and Gethin Russell-Jones, *My Secret Life in Hut Six: One Woman's Experiences at Bletchley Park* (Oxford: Lion, 2014); Tessa Dunlop, *The Bletchley Girls: War, Secrecy, Love and Loss: The Women of Bletchley Park Tell Their Story* (London: Hodder & Stoughton, 2015); and Michael Smith, *The Debs of Bletchley Park and Other Stories* (London: Aurum Press, 2015).

13 W.F. Clarke, 'B.P. Reminiscences', undated, HW 3/16, TNA.

14 'Notes of a Meeting held 23 December, 1941', HW 64/5, TNA; 'Administration of War Station', 14 Feb. 1942, HW 14/157, TNA.

15 There is no evidence to suggest that MI6 used the cover story of Captain Ridley's 'shooting party' in 1938.

16 W.F. Clarke, 'B.P. Reminiscences', undated, HW 3/16, TNA.

17 Ibid.

18 Ibid.

19 Evelyn Sinclair to Captain William Ridley, Christmas card, Dec. 1938, Peter Ridley Private Collection (PR).

20 In August 1939, the rose garden was removed to make way for Hut 4. Dorothy Hervieux (née McCarthy), interview, March 2017, Bletchley Park Trust Archive (BPTA); Eileen Moore (née McCarthy), conversation with David White, sound recording, 9 Dec. 2001, BPTA.

21 Jean Tingle, correspondence with author, 25 Feb. 2023; Anne Hubbard, correspondence with author, 6 March 2023.

22 Jean Tingle, interview with author, 18 Feb. 2023.

23 Julie Salmon, correspondence with author, 21 Jan. 2024.

24 Julie Salmon, interview with author, 19 Feb. 2023.

25 Dorothy Hervieux (née McCarthy), interview, March 2017, BPTA.

26 Ibid.

27 Geoffrey Pidgeon, 'Biography of Brigadier Sir Richard Gambier-Parry KCMG', D455, BPTA.

28 Richard Gambier-Parry in the grounds of Bletchley Park, 1939, photograph, P204, BPTA.

29 Eileen Moore (née McCarthy), conversation with David White, sound recording, 9 Dec. 2001, BPTA.

30 Ibid.

31 Dorothy Hervieux (née McCarthy), interview, March 2017, BPTA.

32 Pidgeon, 'Biography', D455, BPTA; Eileen Moore (née McCarthy), conversation with David White, sound recording, 9 Dec. 2001, BPTA.

33 Eileen Moore's visit to Bletchley Park, photographs, 9 Dec. 2001, Julie Salmon Private Collection (JS).

34 Eileen Moore (née McCarthy), conversation with David White, sound recording, 9 Dec. 2001, BPTA.

35 Joan Dunn (née King-Harman), Bletchley Park Oral History Interview 20181219, 20 July 2017, BPTA.

36 Dorothy Hervieux (née McCarthy), interview, March 2017, BPTA.

37 Jean Tingle, correspondence with author, 14 Feb. 2023.

38 1939 Register.

39 Ibid.

40 Private papers of Miss L Hamilton, Documents 16300, Imperial War Museum (IWM).

41 SOE Personnel File for Jessie Lois Hamilton, HS 9/650/5, TNA.

42 Private papers of Miss L Hamilton, Documents 16300, IWM.

43 Ibid.

44 Ibid.

45 *Report of an inquiry into the accident at Bletchley on the London Midland & Scottish Railway which took place on Friday 13th October 1939* (London: HMSO, 1939).

46 Eileen Moore (née McCarthy), conversation with David White, sound recording, 9 Dec. 2001, BPTA.

47 'Admiral Sir Hugh Sinclair', *The Times*, 8 Nov. 1939.

48 Sinclair to Cadogan, 3 Nov. 1939, FO 1096/127, TNA.

49 Cave Brown, *'C'*, p.14.

50 Robert Rhodes James, ed., *Memoirs of a Conservative: J.C.C. Davidson's Memoirs and Papers, 1910–37* (London: Weidenfeld & Nicolson, 1969), pp.381–2.

51 See S. Payne Best, *The Venlo Incident: A True Story of Double-Dealing, Captivity, and a Murderous Nazi Plot* (London: Hutchinson, 1950).

52 'Memorial Service – Admiral Sir Hugh Sinclair', *The Times,* 9 Nov. 1939.

53 Charles John Wharton Darwin, 'Formation of MI6 Communications – Section 8', undated, T2523, BPTA.

54 'Administration of Government Communications Headquarters', 8 Oct. 1940, HW 3/24, TNA.

55 Peter Ridley, interview with author, 17 Jan. 2023.

56 *London Gazette*, 31 Dec. 1948, p.14.

57 Service record for William Henry Wake Ridley, ADM 196/127/74, TNA.

58 Ibid.

59 Peter Ridley, correspondence with author, 8 Dec. 2022.

60 1939 Register.

61 Dorothy Hervieux (née McCarthy), interview, March 2017, BPTA.

62 Eileen Moore (née McCarthy), conversation with David White, sound recording, 9 Dec. 2001, BPTA.

63 In September 1939, Denniston first expressed his concerns that there was not enough space at Bletchley for both MI6 and GC&CS. See Denniston to Menzies, 12 Sept. 1939, HW 14/1, TNA.

64 Ferris, *Behind the Enigma*, p.192.

65 'Ruth Sebag-Montefiore', *The Times*, 18 July 2015.

66 Ruth Sebag-Montefiore, *Family Patchwork: Five Generations of an*

Anglo-Jewish Family (London: Weidenfeld & Nicolson, 1987), p.111.

67   Ibid.

68   Ibid.

69   Ibid., p.112.

70   Charmain Gladstone (née Prendergast), interview, Aug. 2015, BPTA.

71   Ibid.

72   Private Papers of Major General Leslie Rowley Hill, Documents.7354, IWM.

73   Joan Cash-Read (née Orchard), interview, 10 May 2014, BPTA.

74   Charmain Gladstone (née Prendergast), interview, Aug. 2015, BPTA.

75   Annette Salvesen, *Sworn to Secrecy: World War II Memoirs* (Palm Springs: Nelson Publishing Solutions, 2012), p.38.

76   Angela Pelly (née Gandell), interview, 4 July 2019, BPTA.

77   Sebag-Montefiore, *Family Patchwork*, p.112.

78   'Pond's Non-Detectable Face Powder', advertisement, *Daily Mirror*, 26 Nov. 1940.

79   'Women's Committee', March 1942, HW 64/75, TNA.

80   Lady Cynthia Tothill left Bletchley in June 1943 on health grounds. She suggested that Olive Montgomery should take her place on the Women's Committee representing Hut 10. 'Women's Committee', 5 June 1943, HW 64/75, TNA.

81   Sebag-Montefiore, *Family Patchwork*, p.112.

82   Ibid.

83   Pidgeon, 'Biography', D455, BPTA.

84   Ian Montgomery, interview with author, 24 Jan. 2023; *London Gazette*, 9 Jan. 1946, 300.

85   Linda Hughes, correspondence with author, 25 Jan. 2023.

86   Olive Winter Montgomery is remembered on her mother's headstone in St Margaret's Churchyard, Tylers Green, Buckinghamshire.

87   'Baronet's Death – Suffragette Incidence Recalled', *Evening Chronicle*, 24 July 1926.

88   Menzies to Brittain, 31 Jan. 1945, CAB 301/47, TNA.

89   Jeffery, *MI6*, p.626.

90   Cave Brown, *'C'*, pp.303–4.

91   For further information see David Kenyon, *Arctic Convoys: Bletchley Park and the War for the Seas* (London: Yale University Press, 2023).

92   Eileen Moore visit to Bletchley Park, written summary, 2001, T2817, BPTA.

93   1939 Register; First World War Medal Card for A.G.F. Ackary, WO 372/23/46749, TNA.

94   1939 Register.

95   Ibid.

96   Cave Brown, *'C'*, p.228.

97   Malcolm Muggeridge, *The Infernal Grove*, p.144.

98   The memorandum is missing from the original file, HW 1/1692, TNA. However, a transcribed summary of it may be found within the digital collection *Secret Files from World War to Cold War: British Government and Secret*

Intelligence and Foreign Policy Files (London: Routledge, 2016).

99   [Illegible signature] to Miss Pettigrew, 29 Dec. 1943, HW 1/2309, TNA.

100 See War Cabinet Memo to Miss Pettigrew, 24 May 1945, HW 1/3777, TNA.

101 BONIFACE précis from Miss Pettigrew to Captain Jones (Hut 3, Bletchley Park), 12 Sept. 1944, HW 1/3215, TNA.

102 Muriel Jones also assisted in this work. See HW 1/3792, TNA.

103 Nigel West, *MI6: British Intelligence Service Operations 1909–45* (London: Weidenfeld & Nicolson, 1983), p.108.

104 Cave Brown, *'C'*, p.228.

105 Ibid., p.414.

106 Ibid., pp.414–15.

107 Jeffery, *MI6*, p.478.

108 Liddell Diaries, Volume 7, 11 Dec. 1942, KV 4/191, TNA.

109 Cave Brown, *'C'*, p.716.

9. The Ministry of Unwomanly Warfare

1   Hugh Dalton, *The Fateful Years* (London: Frederick Muller, 1957), p.366.

2   See William Mackenzie, *The Secret History of SOE: The Special Operations Executive 1940–1945* (London: St Ermin's Press, 2000); Richard Duckett, *The Special Operations Executive in Burma: Jungle Warfare and Intelligence Gathering in World War II* (London: I.B. Tauris, 2017).

3   History of First Aid Nursing Yeomanry (FANY) Corps 1907–1947, HS 7/7, The National Archives (TNA).

4   Vigurs, *Mission France*, p.9.

5   Juliette Pattinson, *Behind Enemy Lines: Gender, Passing and the Special Operations Executive in the Second World War* (Manchester: Manchester University Press, 2007), p.26.

6   Martin Gilbert, *Winston S. Churchill, Volume 6 Finest Hour, 1939–41* (Boston: Houghton Mifflin, 1983), p.667.

7   Dorothy Furse Curriculum Vitae, undated, Private Collection of Nicholas Furse (NF).

8   KGB officer Yuri Modin wrongly describes Aileen Furse as working at MI5, when in fact it was her cousin Dorothy. Yuri Modin, *My Five Cambridge Friends: Burgess, Maclean, Philby, Blunt, and Caincross by Their KGB Controller* (London: Headline, 1994), p.61.

9   Ibid.

10 An SOE personnel file for Dorothy Furse could not be found in the National Archives. The file may have been destroyed in the fire that broke out at SOE headquarters shortly after the war. It may have been destroyed by MI6 who served as post-war custodians of the SOE archive.

11 Carlton to Furse, 1 May 1942, HS 9/605/5, TNA.

12 Dorothy Furse Curriculum Vitae, undated, NF.

13 Nicholas Furse, interview with author, 9 Sept. 2022; Noreen Riols, *The Secret Ministry of Ag. & Fish: My Life in Churchill's School for Spies* (London: Macmillan, 2013), p.137.

14 Confidential Letter of Recommendation from John Venner, Director of Finance and Administration, 18 March 1946, NF.

15 Nicholas Furse, interview with author, 9 Sept. 2022.

16 Ibid.

17 Flora Solomon and Barnet Litvinoff, *Baku to Baker Street: The Memoirs of Flora Solomon* (London: HarperCollins, 1984), p.172; M.R.D. Foot, *SOE: The Special Operations Executive 1940–46* (London: BBC, 1984), p.23.

18 Solomon, *Baku to Baker Street*, p.172.

19 Anthony Cave Brown, *Treason in the Blood: H. St. John Philby, Kim Philby, and the Spy Case of the Century* (New York: Houghton Mifflin, 1994), p.209.

20 Solomon, *Baku to Baker Street*, p.172.

21 Ibid.

22 Brown, *Treason in the Blood*, p.206.

23 Ibid.

24 Ibid., p.208.

25 Ibid.

26 Nicholas Elliott, *Never Judge a Man by His Umbrella* (Salisbury: Michael Russell, 1991), p.186.

27 Ben Macintyre, *A Spy Among Friends: Kim Philby and the Great Betrayal* (London: Bloomsbury, 2014), p.171.

28 Nicholas Furse, interview with author, 9 Sept. 2022.

29 Andrew Lownie, *Stalin's Englishman: Guy Burgess, the Cold War, and the Cambridge Spy Ring* (New York: St Martin's Press, 2016), p.107.

30 Kim Philby, *My Silent War: The Autobiography of a Spy* (London: Arrow, 2002), pp.9, 16.

31 Ibid., p.16.

32 For an excellent overview see Derwin Gregory, *The Global Infrastructure of the Special Operations Executive* (Abingdon: Routledge, 2022).

33 Private Papers of Miss L Hamilton, Oct. 1989, Documents.16300, Imperial War Museum (IWM).

34 Ibid.

35 Ibid.

36 Ibid.

37 Ibid.

38 Ibid.

39 SOE Personnel File for Barbara Keeley, HS 9/824/7, TNA. Barbara's pay rise was somewhere between £330 and £400 per annum.

40 Joyce Couper interview, 8 June 1995, 15482, IWM.

41 SOE Personnel File for Phyllis Mackenzie, HS 9/965/3, TNA. Phyl joined SOE on 8 November 1943; Organisational chart for SOE France (Appendix No. 10), HS 8/969, TNA.

42 See West, *MI6*, p.36.

43 Michael and Jill Mackenzie, interview with author, 9 Dec. 2021.

44 Gigliola Gori, *Italian Fascism and the Female Body: Sport, Submissive*

Women and Strong Mothers (London: Routledge, 2004), p.159.

45 Photographs of Phyl Mackenzie posing in various fencing positions, 1931, Mackenzie Family Private Collection (MF).

46 Diary of Winifred Ramplee-Smith née Spink, 10–12 June 1940, David King Private Collection (DK).

47 SOE Personnel File for Phyllis Mackenzie, HS 9/965/3, TNA.

48 Mills to Liddell, 3 March 1943, KV 4/206, TNA.

49 Catherine Jowett, interview with author, 9 Dec. 2021; Rufus Evill, interview with author, 13 Dec. 2021.

50 William Mackenzie, correspondence with author, 7 Dec. 2021.

51 Marcus Mussa, interview with author, 15 Nov. 2021; Michael and Jill Mackenzie, interview with author, 9 Dec. 2021; Rufus Evill, interview with author, 13 Dec. 2021.

52 Incoming Passenger List for SS *Esperance Bay*, 8 June 1943, Ancestry database on-line.

53 SOE Personnel File for Claire Woolf, HS 9/1620/5, TNA; Private Papers of Mrs C Wrench, undated, Documents.4898, IWM.

54 Maurice Buckmaster, *They Fought Alone: The True Story of SOE's Agents in Wartime France* (London: Biteback, 2014), p.68.

55 SOE Personnel File for Hugh Fraser, HS 9/540/4, TNA; Organisational chart for SOE France (Appendix No. 10), HS 8/969, TNA.

56 Private Papers of Mrs C Wrench, undated, Documents.4898, IWM.

57 Ibid.

58 Private Papers of Mrs C Wrench, undated, Documents.4898, IWM.

59 Careless Talk Costs Lives poster, INF 13/217, TNA.

60 D/CE.2 to D/CE.SS.1, 2 June 1943, HS 9/307/3, TNA.

61 Notes on Marie Christine Chilver, 28 Jan. 1942, HS 9/307/3, TNA.

62 'Christine Chilver', 16 Sept. 1942, HS 9/307/3, TNA.

63 Personal history of Christine Collard, undated, HS 9/307/3, TNA.

64 Memo regarding Christine Chilver, undated, HS 9/307/3, TNA.

65 Senter to Hinchley-Cooke, 13 Nov. 1941, HS 9/307/3, TNA.

66 Roche to Venner, 11 Sept. 1942, HS 9/307/3, TNA.

67 Christine Collard, Official Secrets Act Declaration, 31 Jan. 1943, HS 9/307/3, TNA.

68 Report on 96 Hour Exercise Manchester and Liverpool 25–29 October 1942, HS 9/307/3, TNA.

69 'FIFI', 2 July 1943, HS 9/307/3, TNA.

70 'Drill for Operating FIFI', 2 Jan. 1943, HS 9/307/3, TNA; SOE Personnel File for Prudence Willoughby, HS 9/1601/4, TNA.

71 Pattinson, *Behind Enemy Lines*, pp.71–2.

72 SOE Personnel File for Jose Tinchant, HS 9/1470/7, TNA.

73 'Report on Tas', 9 Dec. 1942, HS 9/307/3, TNA.

74 Ibid.

75 Ibid.

76 SOE Personnel File for Jose Tinchant, HS 9/1470/7, TNA.

77 [Illegible name] to Miss Collard (Christine Chilver), 17 April 1943, HS 9/307/3, TNA. Cecile Lefort is referred to as Mrs Cicely Humble. Humble was her mother's maiden name.

78 SOE Personnel File for Cecily Lefort, HS 9/908/1, TNA.

79 Ray Jenkins, *A Pacifist at War* (London: Hutchinson, 2009), pp.94–5.

80 Memo regarding pay increase for agent FIFI, undated, HS 9/307/3, TNA.

81 See SOE Personnel File for Joan Skinner, HS 9/1370/6; SOE Personnel File for Winifred Davidson, HS 9/398/6, TNA; Riols, *Secret Ministry.*

82 Report on 96 Hour Exercise at Birmingham 27 June to 2 July 1943, HS 9/307/3, TNA.

83 'Face of Fifi, Beauty Who Tested Our Spies' Resolve', *Sunday Telegraph*, 21 Sept. 2014.

84 AD/P to A/CD, 4 Nov. 1944, HS 9/307/3, TNA; Knight to Senter, 26 Feb. 1945, HS 9/307/3, TNA.

85 Solvita Viba, correspondence with author, 12 Feb. 2023.

86 Private Papers of Mrs C Wrench, undated, Documents.4898, IWM.

87 Ibid.

88 Ibid.

89 SOE Personnel File for Violette Szabo, HS 9/1435, TNA.

90 See Tania Szabó, *Violette: The Missions of SOE Agent Violette Szabó* GC (Stroud: History Press, 2018).

91 Selwyn Jepson interview, 3 July 1986, 9331, IWM.

92 SOE Personnel File for Vera Atkins, HS 9/59/2, TNA.

93 Vera Atkins Application for Naturalisation, HO 405/45567, TNA.

94 Liza Mundy, *The Sisterhood: The Secret History of Women at the CIA* (Cheltenham: History Press, 2023), p.13.

95 Clare Mulley, *The Spy Who Loved: The Secrets and Lives of Christine Granville* (New York: St Martin's Press, 2013), p.342.

96 Vera Atkins interview, 6 Jan. 1987, 9551, IWM.

97 See Sarah Helm, *A Life in Secrets: The Story of Vera Atkins and the Lost Agents of SOE* (London: Little, Brown, 2005).

98 SOE Personnel File for Noor Inayat Khan, HS 9/836/5, TNA.

99 Shrabani Basu, *Spy Princess: The Life of Noor Inayat Khan* (Stroud: Sutton, 2006), p.221.

10. Old Admiralty and the Citadel

1 The Admiralty complex consists of five historic Whitehall buildings: 1) the Admiralty Building (also known as the Ripley Building, built 1726); 2) Admiralty House (built 1788); 3) the Old Admiralty Building (also known as the Admiralty Extension, built 1904); 4) Admiralty Arch on Trafalgar Square (built 1910); and 5) the Citadel (built 1940–41).

2 Obituary of Lady Colefax, *The Times*, 26 Sept. 1950.

3 Maud Russell, *A Constant Heart: The War Diaries of Maud Russell, 1938–1945* (Wimborne Minster: The Dovecote Press, 2017), p.208.

4 Maud Russell began working (unpaid) in subsection 17 Z on 6 May 1943.

See Naval Intelligence Division Directory, Nov. 1942, ADM 223/257, The National Archives (TNA).

5   Godfrey Papers, Memoirs, vol. 5, Part I, GOD/171, National Maritime Museum, Greenwich, London (NMM).

6   See Peter Hore, *Bletchley Park's Secret Source: Churchill's Wrens and the Y Service in World War II* (Barnsley: Greenhill, 2021); Hannah Roberts, *The WRNS in Wartime: The Women's Royal Naval Service 1917–1945* (London: I.B. Tauris, 2017), published during the centenary of the WRNS.

7   In his book, Donald McLachlan likened the men and women of the Naval Intelligence Division to a Lowry canvas. Donald McLachlan, *Room 39: Naval Intelligence in Action 1939–45* (London: Weidenfeld & Nicolson, 1968), p.12.

8   'The Admiralty at War' by Pam Cuthbert, 15 Sept. 2005, A2329634, BBC WW2 People's War Archive (BBC).

9   McLachlan, *Room 39*, p.1.

10   Ibid., p.10.

11   GOD/171, NMM.

12   McLachlan, *Room 39*, p.2.

13   GOD/171, NMM.

14   McLachlan, *Room 39*, p.3.

15   Patrick Beesly, *Very Special Admiral: The Life of Admiral J.H. Godfrey, C.B.* (London: Hamish Hamilton, 1980), p.321.

16   Ibid., p.217.

17   Civil Service Record of Joyce Cameron, Charles Gardner Private Collection (CG).

18   Charles Gardner, interview with author, 1 Feb. 2022.

19   Report on the 'Conduct of Vassall's P.V. Enquiry; and his employment in N.I.D. on return from Moscow', undated, CAB 301/266, TNA.

20   For more on John Vassall see his autobiography: *Vassall: The Autobiography of a Spy* (London: Sidgwick & Jackson, 1975); Alex Grant, *Sex, Spies and Scandal: The John Vassall Affair* (London: Biteback, 2024).

21   Charles Gardner, interview with author, 1 Feb. 2022.

22   Handwritten note from John Godfrey to Joyce Cameron regarding the reunion of the Naval Intelligence Division, 3 Aug.1948, CG; Typed list of attendees for the 1949 naval intelligence reunion, 1949, CG.

23   Charles Gardner, interview with author, 1 Feb. 2022.

24   Memorandum of Joyce Cameron's service from 7 February 1939 to 27 November 1942 under Vice Admiral John Godfrey, 23 Feb. 1943, CG.

25   Beesly, *Very Special Admiral*, p.216.

26   Handwritten correspondence from John Godfrey to Joyce Cameron, 25 Nov. 1950, CG.

27   GOD/171, NMM.

28   Beesly, *Very Special Admiral*, p.213.

29   McLachlan, *Room 39*, p.388. Godfrey encouraged his officers to dictate instead of drafting by hand.

30   Charles Gardner, correspondence with author, 5 April 2022.

31　McLachlan, *Room 39*, pp.8–9.

32　Ibid., p.126.

33　GOD/171, NMM.

34　Beesly, *Very Special Admiral*, p.217.

35　'War Work: MI6 Naval Intelligence Department' by Joyce Williams, 23 Feb. 2004, A2335349, BBC.

36　Charles Gardner, correspondence with author, 16 Feb. 2022.

37　See Donald P. Steury, 'Naval Intelligence, the Atlantic Campaign and the Sinking of the *Bismarck*: A Study in the Integration of Intelligence into the Conduct of Naval Warfare', *Journal of Contemporary History* 22, no. 2 (April 1987), pp.209–33.

38　DNI Memo, NID Monograph: NID 9(I), ADM 223/467, TNA.

39　Beesly, *Very Special Admiral*, p.62.

40　Ibid., p.208.

41　See S.J.W. Bassett, *Royal Marine: The Autobiography of Colonel Sam Bassett, CBE, RM* (London: Frontis, 1962).

42　Beesly, *Very Special Admiral*, p.210.

43　McLachlan, *Room 39*, p.312.

44　For more about ISTD and the career of Sam Bassett, see Bassett, *Royal Marine,* passim.

45　McLachlan, *Room 39*, p.417.

46　Ben Macintyre, *Operation Mincemeat: The True Spy Story That Changed the Course of World War II* (London: Bloomsbury, 2016), p.27.

47　Ewen Montagu, *Beyond Top Secret Ultra* (New York: Coward, McCann & Geoghegan, 1978), p.49.

48　'N.I.D. Section 12 – organisation and duties', Naval Intelligence Department: selections from history including Enigma and Ultra, ADM 223/298, TNA

49　Andrew Boyd, *British Naval Intelligence through the Twentieth Century* (Barnsley: Seaforth, 2020), p.395.

50　Ibid., p.394.

51　Pauline Trumpler married Lieutenant Fenley on 28 February 1942. Lt Fenley worked as Ned Denning's assistant in the OIC.

52　Interestingly, Ben Macintyre has Juliet Ponsonby working as a secretary in subsection 17 M in May 1943 (Macintyre, *Operation Mincemeat*, p.243), yet the records reveal she was employed much later, on 27 March 1944. See ADM 223/298, TNA.

53　Montagu, *Beyond Top Secret Ultra*, p.99.

54　ADM 223/298, TNA.

55　'The Admiralty at War' by Beryl Embert, 15 Sept. 2005, A5760029, BBC.

56　'N.I.D. Section 12 – Health of the Section', Naval Intelligence Department: selections from history including Enigma and Ultra, ADM 223/298, TNA.

57　Montagu, *Beyond Top Secret* Ultra, p.99.

58　McLachlan, *Room 39*, p.61.

59　'Working for the Admiralty' by Gladys Mooge, 12 June 2004, A2769113, BBC.

60   McLachlan, *Room 39*, p.59.

61   Ibid., p.61.

62   'The Admiralty at War' by Beryl Embert, BBC.

63   The 'Secret Ladies' were: 'Bob' Benton, Eileen Nimms, Sheila Yoemans, Ann Cheshire, Sybil Hay and Pauline Trumpler. See correspondence with Gwen Clarke, MLBE 2/22, Churchill Archive Centre, Cambridge (CAC).

64   McLachlan, *Room 39*, p.120.

65   Operational Intelligence Centres: formation and history, ADM 223/286, TNA.

66   ADM 223/286, TNA.

67   Letter to Patrick Beesly from Doris Salmon, 6 Jan. 1976, MLBE 2/22, CAC.

68   Letter to Patrick Beesly from Margaret Stewart, *c*.1975, MLBE 2/13, CAC.

69   D.B. Taylor, 'Obituary – Margaret E. C. Stewart', *Proceedings of the Society of Antiquaries Scotland* 118 (1988), p.1.

70   MLBE 2/13, CAC.

71   Ibid.

72   Ibid.

73   Ibid.

74   Henrietta McMicking, correspondence with author, 9 March 2021.

75   McLachlan, *Room 39*, p.115.

76   See Ed Offley, 'Moving to Contact' in *Turning the Tide: How a Small Band of Allied Sailors Defeated the U-boats and Won the Battle of the Atlantic* (New York: Basic, 2012).

77   Alan Mooge, correspondence with author, 29 March 2021.

78   MLBE 2/22, CAC.

79   ADM 223/286, TNA.

80   MLBE 2/13, CAC.

81   Official History of 30 AU, ADM 223/214, TNA.

82   'NID 30: A Personal Memoir', Private Papers of Margaret Priestley, 16907, Imperial War Museum, London (IWM).

83   Peter Singlehurst, *British Navy Lists, Volume II* (Feb. 1944) [database on-line], 1916.

84   Bletchley Park Roll of Honour; https://bletchleypark.org.uk/roll-of-honour/7431 (accessed 2 April 2021).

85   Nicholas Rankin mentions Margaret but once in his exhilarating history of 30 AU. Nicholas Rankin, *Ian Fleming's Commandos: The Story of 30 Assault Unit in WWII* (London: Faber & Faber, 2011), p.224. No biography of Ian Fleming to date makes any reference to Margaret Priestley.

86   The best example of this is the rare collection edited by David Nutting, *Attain by Surprise: Capturing Top Secret Intelligence in World War II* (Chichester: David Colver, 2003), which consists of recollections and papers pertaining to thirty-three commandos.

87   Marilyn Monkhouse, correspondence with author, 8 March 2021.

88   16907, IWM.

89   Margaret Priestley described encounters such as this in her personal memoir. The example of the marine Ron Guy's encounter with Margaret can be found

in Guy Allan Farrin, *Beau Bete: The True Story of a Royal Marine Sniper Assigned to Ian Fleming's WWII Intelligence Unit* (Amazon Digital Services, 2020), p.42.

90 Patrick Dalzel-Job, *Arctic Snow to Dust of Normandy: The Extraordinary Wartime Exploits of a Naval Special Agent* (Barnsley: Pen & Sword, 2013), p.115.

91 Private Papers of Margaret Priestley, 16907, IWM.

92 Dalzel-Job, *Arctic Snow*, p.116.

93 Russell, *A Constant Heart*, p.247.

94 Neil Bax, 'Margaret Allnutt Bax' (In Memoriam: Life Stories), *Newnham College Roll Letter* (2006), p.126.

95 Nutting, *Attain by Surprise*, p.222.

96 Private Papers of Margaret Priestley, 16907, IWM.

97 Boyd, *British Naval Intelligence*, p.536.

98 ADM 223/214, TNA.

99 Private Papers of Margaret Priestley, 16907, IWM.

100 Ibid.

101 Ibid.

102 Marilyn Monkhouse, correspondence with author, 8 March 2021.

103 Russell, *A Constant Heart*, p.291.

11. MI5 Trailblazers

1 Liz Denno, interview with author, 19 Jan. 2023.

2 'Mainly about women', *Middlesex County Times*, 26 Aug. 1939; 'Marriages', *The Times*, 5 Sept. 1939; 'Mainly about women', *Middlesex County Times*, 9 Sept. 1939.

3 1939 Register.

4 Andrew, *Defence of the Realm*, p.220.

5 Ibid., p.217.

6 Ibid.

7 Mary Beevor interview, 20 Jan. 1987, 9599, Imperial War Museum (IWM).

8 Andrew, *Defence of the Realm*, pp.217–18.

9 Ibid., p.218.

10 Barbara Price-Smith interview, 13 Aug. 2004, 27196, IWM.

11 Report on the Operation of the Registry during the War, 12 Dec. 1945, KV 4/21, The National Archives (TNA).

12 John Curry, *The Security Service 1908–1945: The Official History* (London: PRO, 1999), p.170.

13 Mary Tackley, interview with author, 1 Nov. 2022.

14 Alice Roach, interview with author, 28 Aug. 2022.

15 Mary Tackley, interview with author, 1 Nov. 2022.

16 John Collard, interview with author, 21 Aug. 2022.

17 Alice Roach, interview with author, 28 Aug. 2022.

18 Ibid.

19 Mary Tackley, interview with author, 1 Nov. 2022.

20   Basil Denno, *A Trail of Pistachio Nutshells: The Memoirs of Basil Denno* (CreateSpace, 2018), p.246; Liz Denno, interview with author, 19 Jan. 2023.

21   Archer to Vivian, 10 Nov. 1939, KV 2/802, TNA.

22   Vivian to Harker, 15 Jan. 1940, KV 2/802, TNA.

23   Archer to Harker, 8 Jan. 1940, KV 2/802, TNA.

24   Guy Liddell Diaries, 20 Jan. 1940, KV 4/185, TNA.

25   Archer to Harker, 8 Jan. 1940, KV 2/802, TNA.

26   Guy Liddell Diaries, 20 Jan. 1940, KV 4/185, TNA.

27   Report regarding the interview with Krivitsky, 23 Jan. 1940, KV 3/804, TNA.

28   Nigel West, ed., *The Guy Liddell Diaries. Vol. I: 1939–1942* (London: Routledge, 2005), p.62.

29   Kevin Quinlan, *The Secret War Between the Wars: MI5 in the 1920s and 1930s* (Woodbridge: Boydell Press, 2014), p.140.

30   'Information obtained from Krivitsky', KV 2/805, TNA.

31   Ibid.

32   Ibid.

33   Kim Philby, *My Silent War: The Autobiography of a Spy* (London: Arrow, 2002), p.105.

34   An example of a severe confrontation between Jack Curry of MI5 and Felix Cowgill of MI6 'that made even Jane Archer uneasy' can be found in Nigel West, ed., *The Guy Liddell Diaries. Vol. II: 1942–1945* (London: Routledge, 2005), p.110.

35   West, *Liddell Diaries, I*, p.112.

36   Ibid.

37   Guy Liddell Diaries, 6 Dec. 1940, KV 4/187, TNA.

38   Morton to Churchill, 27 Nov. 1940, PREM 7/6, TNA.

39   Andrew, *Defence of the Realm*, p.220.

40   Mary Sherer report on TREASURE, 24 Aug. 1943, KV 2/464, TNA.

41   See John Masterman, *The Double Cross System in the War of 1939–1945* (New Haven, CT: Yale University Press, 1972).

42   See Ben Macintyre, *Double Cross: The True Story of the D-Day Spies* (London: Bloomsbury, 2012).

43   Security Service Staff List, Sept. 1938, KV 4/127, TNA.

44   Rufus Evill, interview with author, 13 Dec. 2021.

45   Sue Carden, correspondence with author, 17 April 2023; for a history of the school written by two former pupils, see Honor Osborne and Peggy Manisty, *A History of the Royal School for Daughters of Officers of the Army, 1864–1965* (London: Hodder & Stoughton, 1966). Peggy Manisty was recruited by MI5 straight from school and served in Malta during the Second World War.

46   Royal Bath School Magazine, July 1933, The Royal School Bath Archive (RSBA).

47   Sherer to Manisty, 28 Feb. 1940, Henry Manisty Private Collection (HM).

48   Mills to Liddell, 3 March 1943, KV 4/206, TNA.

49   Mary Sherer, Summary of TREASURE Case, 4 July 1944, KV 2/466, TNA.

50   Mary Sherer report on TREASURE, 24 Aug. 1943, KV 2/464, TNA.

51 Mary Kathryn Barbier, ed., *I Worked Alone: Diary of a Double Agent in World War II Europe* (Jefferson, NC: McFarland, 2014), p.202. Lily's diary was originally published in French in 1966; an English translation was published in 1968. See Lily Sergueiew, *Secret Service Rendered: An Agent in the Espionage Duel Preceding the Invasion of France* (London: William Kimber, 1968).

52 Barbier, *I Worked Alone*, p.203.

53 Another female Double Cross agent was Elvira Chaudoir, the daughter of a Peruvian diplomat, codenamed BRONX. See KV 2/2098, TNA.

54 Curry, *Security Service*, p.225.

55 Marcus Mussa, interview with author, 15 Nov. 2021.

56 Ibid.

57 Sherer to Robertson, 17 Nov. 1943, KV 2/464, TNA.

58 Barbier, *I Worked Alone*, p.232.

59 Kate Jowett, interview with author, 9 Dec. 2021.

60 Barbier, *I Worked Alone*, p.284.

61 Ibid., p.232.

62 Rufus Evill, interview with author, 13 Dec. 2021.

63 Mary Sherer, Summary of TREASURE Case, 4 July 1944, KV 2/466, TNA.

64 Sherer to Robertson, 8 Dec. 1943, KV 2/465, TNA.

65 Mary Sherer, Summary of TREASURE Case, 4 July 1944, KV 2/466, TNA.

66 Sherer to Foley, 7 Jan. 1944, KV 2/465, TNA.

67 Twenty Committee, 17 Feb. 1944, KV 4/67, TNA.

68 Mary Sherer, Summary of TREASURE Case, 4 July 1944, KV 2/466, TNA.

69 Page to Masterman, 26 May 1944, KV 2/466, TNA.

70 Mary Sherer, Summary of TREASURE Case, 4 July 1944, KV 2/466, TNA.

71 Marriott to A.D.B, 19 May 1944, KV 2/466, TNA.

72 Twenty Committee, 15 June 1944, KV 4/68, TNA.

73 Robertson to A.D.B., 15 June 1944, KV 2/466, TNA.

74 Note on TREASURE, 17 June 1944, KV 2/466, TNA.

75 Photograph of Mary Sherer in NAAFI uniform, undated, HM; Henry Manisty, correspondence with author, 31 May 2023.

76 Rufus Evill, interview with author, 13 Dec. 2021.

77 Marcus Mussa, correspondence with author, 27 Feb. 2023; Marcus Mussa, interview with author, 15 Nov. 2021.

12. Rita and Ena

1 'Graham Greene Really Was Our Man in Havana', *Daily Telegraph*, 9 July 1994.

2 Barbara Bilston, interview with author, 16 Aug. 2022; Howard Bailes, correspondence with author, 10 Sept. 2022.

3 Philip Jeffries, interview with author, 10 Aug. 2022.

4 Daphne Spencer, interview with author, 10 Aug. 2022.

5 Philip Jeffries, interview with author, 10 Aug. 2022.

6 'Death of an O.C.', *Gloucestershire Echo*, 29 Aug. 1933.

7   Bridget Heyworth, interview with author, 15 Sept. 2022.

8   FO 850/37, The National Archives (TNA).

9   Secret Service Clerical List, undated, MEPO 2/9844, Metropolitan Police Service, FOIA, 01.FOI.21.022379.

10   Anderson to Horwood, 21 May 1928, MEPO 2/9844, FOIA.

11   Graham to Anderson, 30 March 1928, MEPO 2/9844, FOIA.

12   Secret Memo, 7 Feb. 1929, MEPO 2/9844, FOIA.

13   Jeffery, *MI6*, p.232.

14   Andrew, *Defence of the Realm*, p.330.

15   West, *MI6*, p.59; Philip Jeffries, interview with author, 10 Aug. 2022; Barbara Bilston, interview with author, 16 Aug. 2022; Bridget Heyworth, interview with author, 15 Sept. 2022.

16   Michael Smith, 'Foley – The Spy Who Saved 10,000 Jews', *Daily Telegraph*, 2 Jan. 1999.

17   West, *MI6*, p.59.

18   Helen Fry, *Spymaster: The Man Who Saved MI6* (London: Yale University Press, 2021), pp.121–2.

19   Thomas Harding, *The Maverick: George Weidenfeld and the Golden Age of Publishing* (London: Weidenfeld & Nicolson, 2023), p.24.

20   Fry, *Spymaster*, p.141.

21   Jeffes to Rance, 10 Oct. 1938, FO 366/1036, TNA.

22   West, *MI6*, p.59.

23   Michael Smith, *Foley: The Spy Who Saved 10,000 Jews* (London: Biteback, 2016), p.140.

24   Margaret Reid to her mother, 12 Dec. 1938, MS 708/9/2, Brotherton Library, University of Leeds (BLUL).

25   Ibid.

26   Margaret Reid to her mother, 1938, MS 708/9/3, BL.

27   Ibid.

28   Philip Jeffries, interview with author, 10 Aug. 2022.

29   Ibid.

30   Robert Hutchinson, *German Foreign Intelligence from Hitler's War to the Cold War: Flawed Assumptions and Faulty Analysis* (Lawrence, KS: University Press of Kansas, 2019), p.31.

31   Smith, *Foley*, pp.200–201.

32   William Shirer, *The Rise and Fall of the Third Reich: A History of Nazi Germany* (New York: Simon & Schuster, 1990), p.616.

33   Philip Jeffries, interview with author, 10 Aug. 2022.

34   Private papers of Miss L. Hamilton, Documents 16300, Imperial War Museum (IWM).

35   Tom Bower, *Maxwell: The Final Verdict* (London: HarperCollins, 1996), p.158.

36   Joe Haines, *Maxwell* (London: Macdonald, 1988), p.134.

37   Philip H.J. Davies, *MI6 and the Machinery of Spying* (Abingdon: Frank Cass, 2005), p.101.

38 Jack Fishman, *And the Walls Came Tumbling Down* (London: Souvenir Press, 1982), pp.30–33, photographic insert.

39 Antony Read and David Fisher, *Colonel Z: The Secret Life of a Master of Spies* (London: Hodder & Stoughton, 1984), pp.268–9. Dansey ordered that Mary Lindell should not be sent back to France as her cover was blown. Despite his best efforts to safeguard his agent, Mary demanded her return, which was eventually approved.

40 See Lynne Olson, *Madame Fourcade's Secret War: The Daring Young Woman Who Led France's Largest Spy Network Against Hitler* (New York: Random House, 2019).

41 Marie-Madeleine Fourcade, *Noah's Ark: A Memoir of Struggle and Resistance* (New York: E.P. Dutton, 1974), pp.259–60.

42 Davies, *MI6*, p.74.

43 Jeffery, *MI6*, p.378.

44 See Józef Garliński, *The Swiss Corridor: An Amazing Account of Spy-Rings in World War II* (London: Dent, 1981).

45 Jeffery, *MI6*, pp.378–9.

46 Read and Fisher, *Colonel Z*, p.238. While this book paints a fascinating picture of Claude Dansey, readers should be wary, as it contains a number of historical inaccuracies and should therefore be treated with caution.

47 Georgina Molesworth, 'A Journey to Bordeaux', March 1987, Barbara Bilston Private Collection (BB).

48 Derek Graham, interview with author, 8 Aug. 2022.

49 Postal Service Appointment Book, 23 Sept. 1926, POST 58, The Postal Museum (TPM).

50 Selbie to Winsor, 17 May 1926, Claire Hubbard-Hall Private Collection (CHH).

51 Stephen Dorril, *MI6: Inside the Covert World of Her Majesty's Secret Intelligence Service* (London: Simon & Schuster, 2000), p.124.

52 Georgina Molesworth, 'A Journey to Bordeaux', March 1987, BB.

53 Ibid.

54 'Passage to the Moon', *The Times*, 6 May 1957.

55 Georgina Molesworth, 'A Journey to Bordeaux', March 1987, BB.

56 Ibid.

57 Ibid.

58 Ibid.

59 See Neill Lochery, *Lisbon: War in the Shadows of the City of Light, 1939–1945* (New York: PublicAffairs, 2011).

60 See Andrew Lownie, *Traitor King: The Scandalous Exile of the Duke and Duchess of Windsor* (London: Blink, 2021).

61 Philip Johns, *Within Two Cloaks: Mission with SIS and SOE* (London: William Kimber, 1979), p.71.

62 Ibid., p.73.

63 Liddell Diaries, 14 July 1944, KV 4/194, TNA.

64 Johns, *Within Two Cloaks*, p.78.

65 Mary Beevor interview, 20 Jan. 1987, 9599, IWM.
66 West, *MI6*, p.136.
67 Ibid., p.186.
68 Juan Pujol García and Nigel West, *Operation Garbo: The Personal Story of the Most Successful Spy of World War II* (London: Biteback, 2011), p.63.
69 Jeffery, *MI6*, p.409.
70 West, *MI6*, p.83.
71 Cited in Norman Sherry, *The Life of Graham Greene, Volume Two: 1939–1955* (London: Jonathan Cape, 1994), p.168.
72 West, *MI6*, p.188.
73 Liddell Diaries, 14 July 1944, KV 4/194, TNA.
74 Ibid.
75 Ibid.
76 Johns, *Within Two Cloaks*, p.74.
77 Jeffery, *MI6*, p.245.
78 Desmond Bristow with Bill Bristow, *A Game of Moles: The Deceptions of an MI6 Officer* (London: Little, Brown, 1993), p.186.
79 Johns, *Within Two Cloaks*, p.74; Mary Beevor interview, 20 Jan. 1987, 9599, IWM.
80 Malcolm Muggeridge, *The Infernal Grove: Chronicles of Wasted Time, vol. 2* (London: Collins, 1975), p.155.
81 Wiskemann to Barman, 25 April 1941, FO 898/256, TNA.
82 See Geoffrey Field, *Elizabeth Wiskemann: Scholar, Journalist, Secret Agent* (Oxford: Oxford University Press, 2024); Elizabeth Wiskemann, *The Europe I Saw* (New York: St Martin's Press, 1968).
83 'Boeing B-314', *Pan Am Clipper Flying Boats*, www.clipperflyingboats.com/pan-am/boeing-b314.
84 John Pearson, *The Life of Ian Fleming: Creator of James Bond* (London: Jonathan Cape, 1966), pp.113–14.
85 See Wesley K. Wark, ed., *Spy Fiction, Spy Films and Real Intelligence* (Abingdon: Routledge, 1991); Christopher Andrew and Julius Green, *Stars & Spies: Intelligence Operations and the Entertainment Business* (London: Bodley Head, 2021).
86 Barbara Bilston, interview with author, 16 Aug. 2022.
87 See Ian Colvin, *Flight 777: The Mystery of Leslie Howard* (London: Evans, 1957); Ronald Howard, *In Search of My Father: A Portrait of Leslie Howard* (London: William Kimber, 1981).
88 Malcolm Muggeridge, *Like It Was: A Selection from the Diaries of Malcolm Muggeridge* (London: Collins, 1981), p.178.
89 Hart to Baxter, 4 Nov. 1944, KV 2/2465, TNA.
90 Johns, *Within Two Cloaks*, p.76.
91 Oratory School Notes, 8 Nov. 1944, KV 2/2465, TNA.
92 Otto John, *Zweimal kam ich heim: Vom Verschwörer zum Schützer der Verfassung* (Düsseldorf: Econ, 1969), pp.147–8.
93 Oratory School Notes, 8 Nov. 1944, KV 2/2465, TNA.

94   Ibid.
95   West, *MI6*, p.187.
96   Oratory School Notes, 8 Nov. 1944, KV 2/2465, TNA.
97   West, *MI6*, p.188.
98   Philip Knightley, *The Master Spy: The Story of Kim Philby* (New York: Knopf, 1988), p.109.
99   Oratory School Notes, 8 Nov. 1944, KV 2/2465, TNA.
100 Otto John, *Twice through the Lines: Autobiography of a Super-Spy* (Aylesbury: First Futura, 1974), p.141.
101 'How Greene Helped the Men Who Tried to Kill Hitler', *Sunday Telegraph*, 17 July 1994.
102 John, *Twice through the Lines*, p.140.
103 See Keith R. Allen, *Interrogation Nation: Refugees and Spies in Cold War Germany* (Lanham, MD: Rowman & Littlefield, 2017).
104 Barbara Bilston, interview with author, 16 Aug. 2022.

13. The Inner Circle

1   Joan Bright Astley, *The Inner Circle: A View of War at the Top* (London: Hutchinson, 1971), p.73.
2   Mary Beevor interview, 20 Jan. 1987, 9599, Imperial War Museum (IWM).
3   Richard Astley, interview with author, 16 Oct. 2023.
4   Joan Bright Astley Obituary, *Independent*, 28 Jan. 2009.
5   Ibid.
6   Harry Grattidge and Richard Collier, *Captain of the Queens: The Autobiography of Captain Harry Grattidge, Former Commodore of the Cunard Line* (New York: E.P. Dutton, 1956), p.180.
7   Bright Astley, *The Inner Circle*, p.56.
8   Ibid., p.41.
9   Joan Bright Astley interview, 25 March 1999, 19836, IWM.
10   Richard Holmes, *Churchill's Bunker: The Secret Headquarters at the Heart of Britain's Victory* (London: Profile, 2009), p.138.
11   Richard Astley, interview with author, 16 Oct. 2023.
12   Bright Astley, *The Inner Circle*, p.14.
13   Ibid., p.18.
14   'Woman's World and Its Ways', *Evening Standard*, 22 Feb. 1917.
15   'What Women Say and Do', *New York Tribune*, 10 Dec. 1899.
16   See Ellen Countess of Desart and Constance Hoster, *Style and Title: A Complete Guide to Social Forms of Address* (London: Christophers, 1925).
17   'Carried the Torch', *Brooklyn Daily Eagle*, 3 Sept. 1939.
18   '"Secretary" to Churchill's War Planning', *Financial Times*, 9 Jan. 2009; Joan Dunn (née King-Harman), Bletchley Park Oral History Interview 20181219, 20 July 2017, Bletchley Park Trust Archive (BPTA).
19   Bright Astley, *The Inner Circle*, pp.25, 28.
20   Joan Bright Astley interview, 25 March 1999, 19836, IWM.
21   Bright Astley, *The Inner Circle*, p.13.

22   Joan Bright Astley interview, 17 Jan. 2002, Documents.16248, IWM.

23   'A Belief in Making Way for the Young', *Saffron Walden Weekly News*, 21 May 1970; 'Ex-Councillor Dies at 83', *Saffron Walden Weekly News*, 1 March 1984.

24   Greta Lempriere was awarded the MBE when she retired from the Foreign Office in 1959. See *London Gazette*, 29 Dec. 1959, p.18

25   Bright Astley, *The Inner Circle*, p.31.

26   Joan Bright Astley interview, 17 Jan. 2002, Documents.16248, IWM.

27   Bright Astley, *The Inner Circle*, p.31.

28   Laurence Grand, Notes and Lessons, 1946, HS 7/5, The National Archives (TNA).

29   Bright Astley, *The Inner Circle*, p.33.

30   Joan Bright Astley interview, 17 Jan. 2002, Documents.16248, IWM.

31   Bright Astley, *The Inner Circle*, p.35.

32   Joan Bright Astley interview, 17 Jan. 2002, Documents.16248, IWM.

33   Kim Philby, *My Silent War*, pp.9–10.

34   Joan Bright Astley interview, 17 Jan. 2002, Documents.16248, IWM.

35   Bright Astley, *The Inner Circle*, p.34.

36   Peter Wilkinson and Joan Bright Astley, *Gubbins and SOE* (London: Leo Cooper, 1993).

37   Bright Astley, *The Inner Circle*, p.38.

38   Ibid., pp.36–7.

39   Ibid., p.40.

40   Ibid.

41   Richard Astley, interview with author, 16 Oct. 2023.

42   Joan Bright Astley interview, 17 Jan. 2002, Documents.16248, IWM.

43   Joan Bright Astley interview, 25 March 1999, 19836, IWM.

44   SOE Personnel File for Isabel Wauchope, HS 9/1565/2, TNA.

45   Bright Astley, *The Inner Circle*, p.53.

46   To learn more about Dudley Clarke's impressive wartime exploits, see Robert Hutton, *The Illusionist: The True Story of the Man Who Fooled Hitler* (London: Weidenfeld & Nicolson, 2024).

47   Bright Astley, *The Inner Circle*, p.54; MI(R) Functions and Organisation, HS 8/258, TNA; MI(R) Strategy, HS 8/259, TNA; MI(R) War Diary and Notes, HS 8/263, TNA.

48   Bright Astley, *The Inner Circle*, p.55; Joan Bright Astley interview, 25 March 2003, Documents.16248, IWM.

49   Bright Astley, *The Inner Circle*, p.62.

50   Longhurst to Cornwall-Jones, 29 Nov. 1940, Documents.20514, IWM.

51   Bright Astley, *The Inner Circle*, p.56; Joan Bright Astley interview, 25 March 1999, 19836, IWM.

52   'Shipping Official and Cargo Scandal', *Liverpool Echo*, 23 Sept. 1942; 'Cargo', *Daily Mirror*, 24 Sept. 1942.

53   Julie Summers, *Fashion on the Ration: Style in the Second World War* (London: Profile, 2015), pp.68–9.

54 See Penny Summerfield, *Reconstructing Women's Wartime Lives: Discourse and Subjectivity in Oral Histories of the Second World War* (Manchester: Manchester University Press, 1998).

55 Margaret Walker interview, 2012, 34169, IWM.

56 See Ruth Ive, *The Woman Who Censored Churchill* (Stroud: History Press, 2014).

57 Bright Astley, *The Inner Circle*, p.61.

58 Ibid., pp.61–2.

59 Joanna Moody, *From Churchill's War Rooms: Letters of a Secretary 1943–45* (Stroud, Tempus, 2007), pp.46–7.

60 Joan Bright Astley interview, 17 Jan. 2002, Documents.16248, IWM.

61 Defence Committee Meeting Note, 17 June 1941, Documents.20514, IWM.

62 Bright Astley, *The Inner Circle*, p.64.

63 Ismay to [unspecified], 15 July 1942, Documents.20514, IWM.

64 Bright Astley, *The Inner Circle*, p.65.

65 Visitors' Book, 3 July 1941, Documents.20514, IWM.

66 Bright Astley, *The Inner Circle*, pp.66, 74.

67 Joan Bright Astley interview, 17 Jan. 2002, Documents.16248, IWM.

68 Visitors' Book, 22 July 1941, Documents.20514, IWM.

69 Bright Astley, *The Inner Circle*, p.67.

70 Visitors' Book, 13 Nov. 1941, Documents.20514, IWM.

71 Joan Bright Astley interview, 17 Jan. 2002, Documents.16248, IWM.

72 Ibid.

73 Bright Astley, *The Inner Circle*, p.75.

74 The files of the Special Information Centre (CAB 121) are available to view at the National Archives.

75 Joan Bright Astley interview, 17 Jan. 2002, Documents.16248, IWM.

76 Bright Astley, *The Inner Circle*, p.76.

77 Joan Bright Astley interview, 17 Jan. 2002, Documents.16248, IWM.

78 Bright Astley, *The Inner Circle*, pp.88–9.

79 Ibid., p.69.

80 Ibid., p.83; Ismay to [unspecified], 15 July 1942, Documents.20514, IWM.

81 Bright Astley, *The Inner Circle*, p.86; Ismay to [unspecified], 15 July 1942, Documents.20514, IWM.

82 Richard Astley, interview with author, 16 Oct. 2023.

83 Joan Bright Astley interview, 25 March 1999, 19836, IWM.

84 Roderick Bailey, 'Obituary of Joan Bright Astley', *Guardian*, 11 March 2009.

85 Joan Bright Astley interview, 25 March 2003, Documents.16248, IWM.

86 Bright Astley, *The Inner Circle*, p.122.

87 Ibid., p.150.

88 Ibid., p.193.

89 Ibid., p.162.

90 Ibid., p.164.

91 Ibid., p.134.

92 Joan Bright Astley interview, 25 March 2003, Documents.16248, IWM.
93 Ibid.
94 Authority to carry 'Top Secret' and 'Secret' Documents Abroad, 4 Oct. 1944, Documents.20514, IWM.
95 Bright Astley, *The Inner Circle*, p.139.
96 Ibid., pp.139–40.
97 Ibid., p.215.
98 Mary Beevor interview, 20 Jan. 1987, 9599, IWM.
99 Bright Astley, *The Inner Circle*, p.219.
100 Ibid., p.206.
101 Ibid., p.204.
102 Ibid.
103 Howard to Astley, 4 Sept. 1978, Documents.20514, IWM.
104 'Cabinet War Rooms', *Daily Telegraph*, 11 April 2003.
105 Richard Astley, interview with author, 16 Oct. 2023.
106 Visitors' Book, 30 Nov. 1945, Documents.20514, IWM.

14. Tinker, Tailor, Spy, Secretary

1   Cave Brown, *'C'*, p.689.
2   *London Gazette*, 9 Jan. 1946, p.301.
3   Ibid., p.275.
4   Ibid., p.282.
5   Cave Brown, *'C'*, p.694.
6   See Helen McCarthy, *Women of the World: The Rise of the Female Diplomat* (London: Bloomsbury, 2014).
7   Pettigrew to Warner, 15 Jan. 1964, Tim Warner Private Collection (TW), p.4.
8   Andrew, *The Defence of the Realm*, p.339.
9   Paddy Hayes, *Queen of Spies: Daphne Park, Britain's Cold War Spy Master* (London: Duckworth Overlook, 2015), p.68.
10 Ibid.
11 Jeffery, *MI6*, p.598.
12 Ibid., p.696.
13 Andrew, *Defence of the Realm*, p.325.
14 Security Service Statistics on Male and Female Staff, 1 June 1950, CAB 301/20, The National Archives (TNA).
15 See Charlotte Bingham, *MI5 and Me: A Coronet among the Spooks* (London: Bloomsbury, 2018).
16 'Security Service Records', 5 April 1951, CAB 301/20, TNA.
17 Ibid.
18 Counter-Espionage Statistics, 5 April 1951, CAB 301/20, TNA.
19 Guy Liddell Diary, 5 Jan. 1945, KV 4/196, TNA.
20 Philby, *My Silent War*, p.105.
21 'Woman Who Suspected Philby Is Ignored', *Daily Telegraph*, 23 April 2003.
22 Guy Liddell Diary, 6 Sept. and 5 Nov. 1947, KV 4/469, TNA.
23 Baroness Park of Monmouth Obituary, *Daily Telegraph*, 26 March 2010.

24 Boyle to Loxley, 'Some Reflections on the Future Organisation of SIS', 22 March 1944, FO 1093/194, TNA.
25 'Successful Women in a Man's World', *Birmingham Post*, 8 Nov. 1962.
26 Roderick Cameron, *The Golden Haze: With Captain Cook in the South Pacific* (London: Weidenfeld & Nicolson, 1964), p.xv.
27 'Saleswoman', *Evening Standard*, 21 June 1948.
28 Registration certificate of International Services Limited, 13 Dec. 1945, Companies House, copy in possession of author.
29 Molesworth to Gorer, 1965, SxMs52/4/1/1/13/82, Special Collection at the University of Sussex Library (USL); Winsor to Gorer, 1966, SxMs52/4/1/22, USL.
30 Richard Welby, correspondence with author, 7 Sept. 2022.
31 'Specialist in Travel', *Observer*, 9 Aug. 1957.
32 Travel advert, *The Times*, 19 Aug. 1961; Travel advert, *Observer*, 28 June 1970; Sacheverell Sitwell, *Bridge of Brocade Sash: Travels and Observations in Japan* (London: Weidenfeld & Nicolson, 1959), p.13.
33 Philip Jeffries, interview with author, 10 Aug. 2022.
34 Magazine clipping, undated, Claire Hubbard-Hall Private Collection (CHH).
35 Travel advert, *Geographical*, May 1963; Hugh Trevor Roper and Richard Davenport-Hines, *The China Journals: Ideology and Intrigue in the 1960s* (London: Bloomsbury, 2022), p.73.
36 'Czechs Charge Yank's a Spy', *Daily News*, 18 Nov. 1966.
37 'Body Found in Spain Thought to Be American Once Jailed by Prague', *New York Times*, 12 Dec. 1972.
38 'Successful Women in a Man's World', *Birmingham Post*, 8 Nov. 1962.
39 Ibid.
40 'Typewriters for Export', *The Times*, 11 Jan. 1950.
41 'Special Visit – Miss Marguerite Lea Winsor', *The West Briton*, 24 Jan. 1952.
42 'In Town Tonight' Script, 24 March 1951, CHH.
43 Ibid.
44 'Specialist in Travel', *Observer*, 9 Aug. 1957.
45 'Passage to the Moon', *The Times*, 6 May 1957.
46 Magazine clipping, undated, CHH.
47 'Successful Women in a Man's World', *Birmingham Post*, 8 Nov. 1962.
48 Eldon to Winsor, late 1940s, CHH.
49 'Successful Women in a Man's World', *Birmingham Post*, 8 Nov. 1962.
50 Somerset Maugham to Winsor, *c*.1946, CHH.
51 Ronald Ward Curriculum Vitae, undated, Sophie Floate Private Collection (SF).
52 Ronald Ward Royal Navy Service Record, SF.
53 Ibid.
54 Sophie Floate, interview with author, 7 July 2022.
55 Ward to Ward, 1969, SF.
56 Bristow, *A Game of Moles*, p.186.
57 Judy Shephard, interview with author, 20 Feb. 2024.

58 Obituary of Henry H. Dunlop, *British Medical Journal*, 26 Dec. 1959, p.1490.

59 Ibid.

60 'Personal and Social', *Evening Standard*, 20 Sept. 1904.

61 'Agriculture at Edinburgh', *Nature*, 2 Sept. 1944.

62 Judy Shephard, interview with author, 20 Feb. 2024.

63 John Pearson, *The Life of Ian Fleming: Creator of James Bond* (London: Jonathan Cape, 1966), p.111.

64 Barbara Salt SOE Personnel File, HS 9/1301/6, TNA.

65 Richard Pennell, 'Propaganda and Its Target: The Venom Campaign in Tangier during World War II', in Driss Maghraoui, ed., *Revisiting the Colonial Past in Morocco* (Abingdon: Routledge, 2013), p.164.

66 Bristow, *Game of Moles*, p.206.

67 Ibid., p.207.

68 Ibid., p.212.

69 Ibid.

70 Ibid.

71 See Guy Burgess MI5 Personal File, KV 2/4101, TNA.

72 Bristow, *Game of Moles*, pp.217–18.

73 Cave Brown, *'C'*, pp.716–17.

74 Ibid., p.248.

75 Ibid., p.256.

76 Pettigrew to Colville, 1 Oct. 1954, PREM 11/762, TNA.

77 George Blake, *No Other Choice: An Autobiography* (London: Jonathan Cape, 1990), p.157.

78 Ibid.

79 Pettigrew to Fleming, 8 Dec. 1955, MS 1391 A/9/104, University of Reading Special Collections (URSC).

80 Robin Aizlewood and Sue Wingfield Digby, interview with author, 30 May 2022.

81 Establishment Officer to Rendel, 5 Oct. 1962, Robin Aizlewood Private Collection (RA).

82 Blake, *No Other Choice*, p.157.

Epilogue

1 John McCarthy, correspondence with author, 19 Nov. 2021.

2 Lorelei Warner, interview with author, 6 July 2022.

3 *London Gazette*, 12 June 1958, 3525.

4 Pettigrew to Warner, 15 Jan. 1964, Tim Warner Private Collection (TW), p.1.

5 Lorelei Warner, interview with author, 6 July 2022.

6 'Stella Rimington: I Fell into Intelligence by Chance', *Guardian*, 23 April 2022.

7 Stella Rimington, *Open Secret: The Autobiography of the Former Director-General of MI5* (London: Hutchinson, 2001), p.159.

8   Ibid., p.185.
9   Ibid.
10   Ibid.

SELECT BIBLIOGRAPHY

ARCHIVES

Bletchley Park Trust Archive (BPTA)
Brotherton Library, University of Leeds (BLUL)
Cambridge University Library (CUL)
Churchill Archive Centre, Cambridge (CAC)
Imperial War Museum (IWM)
Leeds Russian Archive (LRA)
Liddle Hart Centre for Military Archives (LHC)
London Metropolitan Archives (LMA)
Museum of Military Intelligence (MMI)
National Archives and Records Administration, College Park, MD
    (NARA)
National Army Museum (NAM)
National Maritime Museum Caird Library and Archive (NMM)
Oxfordshire History Centre (OHC)
Royal Automobile Club Archive (RACA)
The Honourable Society of Gray's Inn (HSGI)
The National Archives, Kew (TNA)
The Royal School Bath Archive (RSBA)
University of Glasgow Archives and Special Collections (UGASC)
University of Liverpool Library (ULL)
University of Reading Special Collections (URSC)

PRIVATE COLLECTIONS

Doreen Aizlewood Papers, Robin Aizlewood Collection (RA)
Joyce Cameron Papers, Charles Gardner Collection (CG)
Dorothy Furse Papers, Nicholas Furse Collection (NF)
Dorothy Henslowe Papers, Henslowe Family Collection (HENS)
Lunn Family Papers, Henry Rothstein Collection (HR)
Phyllis Mackenzie Papers, Mackenzie Family Collection (MF)
Peggy Manisty Papers, Henry Manisty Collection (HM)
Georgina Molesworth Papers, Barbara Bilston Collection (BB)
Kathleen Pettigrew Papers, Tim Warner Collection (TW)
William Ridley Papers, Peter Ridley Collection (PR)
Winifred Spink Papers, David King Collection (DK)
Ronald Ward Papers, Sophie Floate Collection (SF)
Rita Winsor Papers, Claire Hubbard-Hall Collection (CHH)

PUBLISHED WORKS

Adler, Michael H., *The Writing Machine* (London: Allen & Unwin, 1973).

Agar, Jon, *The Government Machine: A Revolutionary History of the Computer* (London: MIT Press, 2003).

Akkerman, Nadine, *Invisible Agents: Women and Espionage in Seventeenth-Century Britain* (Oxford: Oxford University Press, 2018).

Aldrich, Richard J. and Rory Cormac, *The Black Door: Spies, Secret Intelligence and British Prime Ministers* (London: William Collins, 2016).

———, *The Secret Royals: Spying and the Crown, from Victoria to Diana* (London: Atlantic, 2021).

Allason, Rupert, *The Branch: A History of the Metropolitan Police Special Branch 1883–1983* (London: Secker & Warburg, 1983).

Allen, Keith R., *Interrogation Nation: Refugees and Spies in Cold War Germany* (Lanham, MD: Rowman & Littlefield, 2017).

Anderson, Gregory, ed., *The White-blouse Revolution: Female Office Workers since 1870* (Manchester: Manchester University Press, 1988).

Andrew, Christopher, *Secret Service: The Making of the British Intelligence Community* (London: Heinemann, 1985).

——, *The Defence of the Realm: The Authorised History of MI5* (London: Allen Lane, 2009).

Andrew, Christopher and Julius Green, *Stars & Spies: Intelligence Operations and the Entertainment Business* (London: Bodley Head, 2021).

Andrew, Christopher and Vasili Mitrokhin. *The Mitrokhin Archive: The KGB in Europe and the West* (London: Penguin, 2018).

Barbier, Mary Kathryn, ed., *I Worked Alone: Diary of a Double Agent in World War II Europe* (Jefferson, NC: McFarland, 2014).

Basu, Shrabani, *Spy Princess: The Life of Noor Inayat Khan* (Stroud: Sutton, 2006).

Beckett, Francis, *Stalin's British Victims* (Abingdon: Routledge, 2016).

Beesly, Patrick, *Very Special Admiral: The Life of Admiral J.H. Godfrey, C.B.* (London: Hamish Hamilton, 1980).

Bennett, Gill, *Churchill's Man of Mystery: Desmond Morton and the World of Intelligence* (London: Routledge, 2009)

——, *The Zinoviev Letter: The Conspiracy that Never Dies* (Oxford: Oxford University Press, 2018).

Bersey, Walter, *Electrically-propelled Carriages* (London: Morgan, Thompson & Jamieson, 1898).

Bingham, Charlotte, *MI5 and Me: A Coronet among the Spooks* (London: Bloomsbury, 2018).

Blake, George, *No Other Choice: An Autobiography* (London: Jonathan Cape, 1990).

Blood, H.W., *Franz von Papen: His Life and Times* (London: Rich & Cowan, Ltd, 1939).

Bochkareva, Maria and Don Levine, *Yashka: My Life as a Peasant, Exile and Soldier* (New York: Frederick A. Stokes, 1919).

Boghardt, Thomas, *Spies of the Kaiser: German Covert Operations in Great Britain during the First World War Era* (Basingstoke: Palgrave Macmillan, 2004).

Bok, Sissela, *Secrets: On the Ethics of Concealment and Revelation* (Oxford: Oxford University Press, 1984).

Bower, Tom, *The Perfect English Spy: Sir Dick White and the Secret War 1935–90* (London: Heinemann, 1995).

——, *Maxwell: The Final Verdict* (London: HarperCollins, 1996).

Boyd, Andrew, *British Naval Intelligence through the Twentieth Century* (Barnsley: Seaforth, 2020).

Bright Astley, Joan, *The Inner Circle: A View of War at the Top* (London: Hutchinson, 1971).

Bristow, Desmond with Bill Bristow, *A Game of Moles: The Deceptions of an MI6 Officer* (London: Little, Brown, 1993).

Brust, Harold, *In Plain Clothes: Further Memoirs of a Political Police Officer* (London: Stanley Paul, 1937).

Buckmaster, Maurice, *They Fought Alone: The True Story of SOE's Agents in Wartime France* (London: Biteback, 2014).

Burke, David, *The Spy Who Came In from the Co-op: Melita Norwood and the Ending of Cold War Espionage* (Woodbridge: Boydell Press, 2008).

Burke, David, *Russia and the British Left: From the 1848 Revolutions to the General Strike* (London: Bloomsbury Academic, 2020).

Cave Brown, Anthony, *'C': The Secret Life of Sir Stewart Menzies, Spymaster to Winston Churchill* (New York: Macmillan, 1987).

——, *Treason in the Blood: H. St. John Philby, Kim Philby, and the Spy Case of the Century* (New York: Houghton Mifflin, 1994).

Chambers, Roland, *The Last Englishman: The Double Life of Arthur Ransome* (London: Faber & Faber, 2009).

Clarke, Donald, *A Daisy in the Broom: The Story of a School, 1820–1958* (London: Tweeddale, 1991).

Colvin, Ian, *Flight 777: The Mystery of Leslie Howard* (London: Evans, 1957).

Cook, Andrew, *To Kill Rasputin: The Life and Death of Grigori Rasputin* (Stroud: Tempus, 2005).

Coulson, Thomas, *Mata Hari: Courtesan and Spy* (London: Hutchinson, 1930).

Cross, John A., *Samuel Hoare: A Political Biography* (London: Jonathan Cape, 1977).

Cullen, Richard, *Rasputin: The Role of Britain's Secret Service in His Torture and Murder* (London: Dialogue, 2010).

Curry, John, *The Security Service 1908–1945: The Official History* (London: PRO, 1999).

Dalton, Hugh, *The Fateful Years* (London: Frederick Muller, 1957).

Dalzel-Job, Patrick, *Arctic Snow to Dust of Normandy: The Extraordinary Wartime Exploits of a Naval Special Agent* (Barnsley: Pen & Sword, 2013).

Davies, Philip H.J., *MI6 and the Machinery of Spying* (Abingdon: Frank Cass, 2005).

Deacon, Richard, *The British Connection: Russia's Manipulation of British Individuals and Institutions* (London: Hamish Hamilton, 1979).

——, *The Greatest Treason: The Bizarre Story of Hollis, Liddell and Mountbatten* (London: Century Hutchinson, 1989).

Desart, Ellen Countess of and Constance Hoster, *Style and Title: A Complete Guide to Social Forms of Address* (London: Christophers, 1925).

Dorril, Stephen, *MI6: Inside the Covert World of Her Majesty's Secret Intelligence Service* (London: Simon & Schuster, 2000).

Duckett, Richard, *The Special Operations Executive in Burma: Jungle Warfare and Intelligence Gathering in World War II* (London: I.B. Tauris, 2017).

Dukes, Paul, *Red Dusk and the Morrow: Adventures and Investigations in Soviet Russia* (Garden City, NY: Doubleday, Page & Company, 1922).

Dunlop, Tessa, *The Bletchley Girls: War, Secrecy, Love and Loss: The Women of Bletchley Park Tell Their Story* (London: Hodder & Stoughton, 2015).

Elliott, Nicholas, *Never Judge a Man by His Umbrella* (Salisbury: Michael Russell, 1991).

Farrin, Guy Allan, *Beau Bete: The True Story of a Royal Marine Sniper Assigned to Ian Fleming's WWII Intelligence Unit* (Amazon Digital Services, 2020).

Ferris, John, *Behind the Enigma: The Authorised History of GCHQ, Britain's Secret Cyber-Intelligence Agency* (London: Bloomsbury, 2020).

Field, Geoffrey, *Elizabeth Wiskemann: Scholar, Journalist, Secret Agent* (Oxford: Oxford University Press, 2024).

Findlay, Jean, *Chasing Time: The Life of C.K. Scott Moncrieff: Soldier, Spy and Translator* (London: Vintage, 2015).

Fishman, Jack, *And the Walls Came Tumbling Down* (London: Souvenir Press, 1982).

Fleming, Fergus, ed., *The Man with the Golden Typewriter: Ian Fleming's James Bond Letters* (London: Bloomsbury, 2015).

Fleming, Ian, *Casino Royale* (London: Ian Fleming Publications, 2023).

Foot, M.R.D., *SOE: The Special Operations Executive 1940–46* (London: BBC, 1984).

Fourcade, Marie-Madeleine, *Noah's Ark: A Memoir of Struggle and Resistance* (New York: E.P. Dutton, 1974).

Fry, Helen, *Spymaster: The Man Who Saved MI6* (London: Yale University Press, 2021).

Funnell, Lisa, ed., *For His Eyes Only: The Women of James Bond* (New York: Columbia University Press, 2015).

García, Juan Pujol and Nigel West, *Operation Garbo: The Personal Story of the Most Successful Spy of World War II* (London: Biteback, 2011).

Garliński, Józef, *The Swiss Corridor: An Amazing Account of Spy-Rings in World War II* (London: Dent, 1981).

Gilbert, Martin, *Winston S. Churchill, vol. 6, Finest Hour, 1939–41* (Boston: Houghton Mifflin, 1983).

Gori, Gigliola, *Italian Fascism and the Female Body: Sport, Submissive Women and Strong Mothers* (London: Routledge, 2004).

Grant, Alex, *Sex, Spies and Scandal: The John Vassall Affair* (London: Biteback, 2024).

Grattidge, Harry and Richard Collier, *Captain of the Queens: The Autobiography of Captain Harry Grattidge, Former Commodore of the Cunard Line* (New York: E.P. Dutton, 1956).

Gregory, Derwin, *The Global Infrastructure of the Special Operations Executive* (Abingdon: Routledge, 2022).

Haines, Joe, *Maxwell* (London: Macdonald, 1988).

Hanks, Tom, *Uncommon Type: Some Stories* (London: William Heinemann, 2018).

Harding, Thomas, *The Maverick: George Weidenfeld and the Golden Age of Publishing* (London: Weidenfeld & Nicolson, 2023).

Hayes, Paddy, *Queen of Spies: Daphne Park, Britain's Cold War Spy Master* (London: Duckworth Overlook, 2015).

Healy, Dan, *Homosexual Desire in Revolutionary Russia: The Regulation of Sexual and Gender Dissent* (Chicago: University of Chicago Press, 2001).

Heller, Michael, *London Clerical Workers, 1880–1914: Development of the Labour Market* (London: Routledge, 2015).

Helm, Sarah, *A Life in Secrets: The Story of Vera Atkins and the Lost Agents of SOE* (London: Little, Brown, 2005).

Hemming, Henry, *M: Maxwell Knight, MI5's Greatest Spymaster* (London: Penguin, 2017).

Hiley, Nicholas, 'The Failure of British Counter-Espionage against Germany, 1907–1914', *The Historical Journal* 28, no. 4 (Dec. 1985): 835–862.

———, 'Entering the Lists: MI5's Great Spy Round-up of August 1914', *Intelligence and National Security* 21, no. 1 (Feb. 2006): 46–76.

———, 'Re-entering the Lists: MI5's Authorized History and the August 1914 Arrests', *Intelligence and National Security* 25, no. 4 (Aug. 2010): 415–452.

Hill, George A., *Go Spy the Land: Being the Adventures of I.K.8 of the British Secret Service* (London: Cassell, 1932).

Hoare, Samuel, *The Fourth Seal: The End of a Russian Chapter* (London: William Heinemann, 1930).

Holmes, Richard, *Churchill's Bunker: The Secret Headquarters at the Heart of Britain's Victory* (London: Profile, 2009).

Hopkirk, Peter, *On Secret Service East of Constantinople: The Plot to Bring Down the British Empire* (London: John Murray, 1994).

Hore, Peter, *Bletchley Park's Secret Source: Churchill's Wrens and the Y Service in World War II* (Barnsley: Greenhill, 2021).

Howard, Ronald, *In Search of My Father: A Portrait of Leslie Howard* (London: William Kimber, 1981).

Hutchinson, Robert, *German Foreign Intelligence from Hitler's War to the Cold War: Flawed Assumptions and Faulty Analysis* (Lawrence, KS: University Press of Kansas, 2019).

Hutton, Robert, *The Illusionist: The True Story of the Man Who Fooled Hitler* (London: Weidenfeld & Nicolson, 2024).

Ive, Ruth, *The Woman Who Censored Churchill* (Stroud: History Press, 2014).

Jeffery, Keith, *MI6: The History of the Secret Intelligence Service 1909–1949* (London: Bloomsbury, 2010).

Jenkins, Ray, *A Pacifist at War* (London: Hutchinson, 2009).

John, Otto, *Zweimal kam ich heim: Vom Verschwörer zum Schützer der Verfassung* (Düsseldorf: Econ, 1969).

——, *Twice through the Lines: Autobiography of a Super-Spy* (Aylesbury: First Futura, 1974).

Johns, Philip, *Within Two Cloaks: Mission with SIS and SOE* (London: William Kimber, 1979).

Johnson, Kerry and John Gallehawk, *Figuring It Out at Bletchley Park 1939–1945* (Milton Keynes: BookTower, 2007).

Judd, Alan, *The Quest for C: Sir Mansfield Cumming and the Founding of the British Secret Service* (London: HarperCollins, 1999).

Kell, Constance, *A Secret Well Kept: The Untold Story of Sir Vernon Kell, Founder of MI5* (London: Conway, 2017).

Kenyon, David, *Bletchley Park and D-Day: The Untold Story of How the Battle for Normandy Was Won* (London: Yale University Press, 2019).

——, *Arctic Convoys: Bletchley Park and the War for the Seas* (London: Yale University Press, 2023).

Knightley, Philip, *The Master Spy: The Story of Kim Philby* (New York: Knopf, 1988).

Landau, Henry, *All's Fair: The Story of the British Secret Service behind the German Lines* (New York: G.P. Putnam's Sons, 1934).

Langton, Bruce, *Philip Wilson Steer 1860–1942* (Oxford: Clarendon Press, 1971).

Lashmar, Paul, *Spies, Spin and the Fourth Estate: British Intelligence and the Media* (Edinburgh: Edinburgh University Press, 2020).

Le Queux, William, *The Invasion of 1910, With a Full Account of the Siege of London* (London: Eveleigh Nash, 1906).

—— *Spies of the Kaiser: Plotting the Downfall of England* (London: Frank Cass, 1996).

Lochery, Neill, *Lisbon: War in the Shadows of the City of Light, 1939–1945* (New York: PublicAffairs, 2011).

Lockhart, R.H. Bruce, *Memoirs of a British Agent* (London: Putnam, 1932).

Lownie, Andrew, *Stalin's Englishman: Guy Burgess, the Cold War, and the Cambridge Spy Ring* (New York: St Martin's Press, 2016).

———, *Traitor King: The Scandalous Exile of the Duke and Duchess of Windsor* (London: Blink, 2021).

Lycett, Andrew, *Ian Fleming* (London: Phoenix, 1996).

Macintyre, Ben, *Double Cross: The True Story of the D-Day Spies* (London: Bloomsbury, 2012).

———, *A Spy among Friends: Kim Philby and the Great Betrayal* (London: Bloomsbury, 2014).

———, *Operation Mincemeat: The True Spy Story That Changed the Course of World War II* (London: Bloomsbury, 2016).

Mackenzie, Compton, *Greek Memories* (London: Cassell, 1932).

Mackenzie, William, *The Secret History of SOE: The Special Operations Executive 1940–1945* (London: St Ermin's Press, 2000).

Madeira, Victor, *Britannia and the Bear: The Anglo-Russian Intelligence Wars 1917–1929* (Woodbridge: Boydell Press, 2014).

Malcolm, Derek, *Family Secrets: The Scandalous History of an Extraordinary Family* (London: Hutchinson, 2003).

Mantel, Hilary, *Giving Up the Ghost: A Memoir* (London: Harper Perennial, 2004).

Masters, Anthony, *The Man Who Was M: The Life of Maxwell Knight* (Oxford: Blackwell, 1984).

McCarthy, Helen, *Women of the World: The Rise of the Female Diplomat* (London: Bloomsbury, 2014).

McLachlan, Donald, *Room 39: Naval Intelligence in Action 1939–45* (London: Weidenfeld & Nicolson, 1968).

Miller, Joan, *One Girl's War: Personal Exploits in MI5's Most Secret Station* (Dingle: Brandon, 1986).

Modin, Yuri, *My Five Cambridge Friends: Burgess, Maclean, Philby, Blunt, and Caincross by Their KGB Controller* (London: Headline, 1994).

Montagu, Ewen, *Beyond Top Secret Ultra* (New York: Coward, McCann & Geoghegan, 1978).

Moody, Joanna, *From Churchill's War Rooms: Letters of a Secretary 1943–45* (Stroud, Tempus, 2007).

Muggeridge, Malcolm, *The Infernal Grove: Chronicles of Wasted Time, vol. 2* (London: Collins, 1975).

Mulley, Clare, *The Spy Who Loved: The Secrets and Lives of Christine Granville* (New York: St Martin's Press, 2013).

Mundy, Liza, *The Sisterhood: The Secret History of Women at the*

CIA (Cheltenham: History Press, 2023).

Murphy, William, 'Lydia Stahl: A Secret Life, 1885–?', *Journal of Intelligence History*, 18, no. 1 (Jan. 2019): 38–62.

Nutting, David, ed., *Attain by Surprise: Capturing Top Secret Intelligence in World War II* (Chichester: David Colver, 2003).

Ogden, Alan, *Master of Deception: The Wartime Adventures of Peter Fleming* (London: Bloomsbury Academic, 2019).

Olson, Lynne, *Madame Fourcade's Secret War: The Daring Young Woman Who Led France's Largest Spy Network against Hitler* (New York: Random House, 2019).

Osborne, Honor and Peggy Manisty, *A History of the Royal School for Daughters of Officers of the Army, 1864–1965* (London: Hodder & Stoughton, 1966).

O'Sullivan, Adrian, *The Baghdad Set: Iraq through the Eyes of British Intelligence, 1941–45* (London: Palgrave Macmillan, 2019).

Owtram, Jean and Patricia Owtram, *Codebreaking Sisters: Our Secret War* (London: Mirror, 2020).

Pallingston, Jessica, *Lipstick: A Celebration of the World's Favourite Cosmetic* (New York: St Martin's Press, 1999).

Panayi, Panikos, *Enemy in Our Midst: Germans in Britain during the First World War* (New York: Berg, 1991).

Pattinson, Juliette, *Behind Enemy Lines: Gender, Passing and the Special Operations Executive in the Second World War* (Manchester: Manchester University Press, 2007).

Payne Best, S., *The Venlo Incident: A True Story of Double-Dealing, Captivity, and a Murderous Nazi Plot* (London: Hutchinson, 1950).

Pennell, Richard, 'Propaganda and Its Target: The Venom Campaign in Tangier during World War II' in *Revisiting the Colonial Past in Morocco*, ed. Driss Maghraoui (Abingdon: Routledge, 2013).

Philby, Kim. *My Silent War: The Autobiography of a Spy* (London: Arrow, 2002).

Phillips Oppenheim, E., *The Great Secret* (Boston: Little, Brown, 1907).

Proctor, Tammy, *Female Intelligence: Women and Espionage in the First World War* (New York: New York University Press, 2003).

Purvis, June, *Emmeline Pankhurst: A Biography* (London: Routledge, 2002).

————, *Christabel Pankhurst: A Biography* (London: Routledge, 2018).

Quinlan, Kevin, *The Secret War Between the Wars: MI5 in the 1920s and 1930s* (Woodbridge: Boydell Press, 2014).

Rankin, Nicholas, *Ian Fleming's Commandos: The Story of 30 Assault Unit in WWII* (London: Faber & Faber, 2011).

Read, Antony and David Fisher, *Colonel Z: The Secret Life of a Master of Spies* (London: Hodder & Stoughton, 1984).

Reeve, Lloyd Eric, *Gift of the Grape* (San Francisco: Filmer, 1959).

Rhodes James, Robert, ed., *Memoirs of a Conservative: J.C.C. Davidson's Memoirs and Papers, 1910–37* (London: Weidenfeld & Nicolson, 1969).

Rimington, Stella, *Open Secret: The Autobiography of the Former Director-General of MI5* (London: Hutchinson, 2001).

Riols, Noreen, *The Secret Ministry of Ag. & Fish: My Life in Churchill's School for Spies* (London: Macmillan, 2013).

Roberts, Hannah, *The WRNS in Wartime: The Women's Royal Naval Service 1917–1945* (London: I.B. Tauris, 2017).

Roper, Hugh Trevor and Richard Davenport-Hines, *The China Journals: Ideology and Intrigue in the 1960s* (London: Bloomsbury, 2022).

Russell, Maud, *A Constant Heart: The War Diaries of Maud Russell, 1938–1945* (Wimborne Minster: Dovecote Press, 2017).

Russell-Jones, Mair and Gethin Russell-Jones, *My Secret Life in Hut Six: One Woman's Experiences at Bletchley Park* (Oxford: Lion, 2014).

Salvesen, Annette, *Sworn to Secrecy: World War II Memoirs* (Palm Springs: Nelson Publishing Solutions, 2012).

Sebag-Montefiore, Ruth, *Family Patchwork: Five Generations of an Anglo-Jewish Family* (London: Weidenfeld & Nicolson, 1987).

Sergueiew, Lily, *Secret Service Rendered: An Agent in the Espionage Duel Preceding the Invasion of France* (London: William Kimber, 1968).

Sherry, Norman, *The Life of Graham Greene, Volume Two: 1939–1955* (London: Jonathan Cape, 1994).

Shirer, William, *The Rise and Fall of the Third Reich: A History of Nazi Germany* (New York: Simon & Schuster, 1990).

Sitwell, Sacheverell, *Bridge of Brocade Sash: Travels and Observations in Japan* (London: Weidenfeld & Nicolson, 1959).

Smith, Michael, *Station X: The Codebreakers of Bletchley Park* (London: Pan, 2004).

——, *Six: A History of Britain's Secret Intelligence Service. Part 1: Murder and Mayhem, 1909–1939* (London: Dialogue, 2010).

——, *The Debs of Bletchley Park and Other Stories* (London: Aurum Press, 2015).

——, *Foley: The Spy Who Saved 10,000 Jews* (London: Biteback, 2016).

Solomon, Flora and Barnet Litvinoff, *Baku to Baker Street: The Memoirs of Flora Solomon* (London: HarperCollins, 1984).

Stark, Freya, *Traveller's Prelude: An Autobiography* (London: John Murray, 1950).

Summerfield, Penny, *Reconstructing Women's Wartime Lives: Discourse and Subjectivity in Oral Histories of the Second World War* (Manchester: Manchester University Press, 1998).

Szabó, Tania, *Violette: The Missions of SOE Agent Violette Szabó GC* (Stroud: History Press, 2018).

Thomas, Dora H., *A Short History of St. Martin-in-the-Fields High School for Girls* (London: John Murray, 1929).

Thomas, Rosamund, *Espionage and Secrecy: The Official Secrets Acts 1911–1989 of the United Kingdom* (London: Routledge, 1991).

Thompson, Walter H., *Guard from the Yard* (London: Jarrolds, 1938).

Thomson, Basil, *My Experiences at Scotland Yard* (New York: Doubleday, Page & Co, 1923).

——, *Richardson Scores Again* (London: Eldon Press, 1934).

——, *The Scene Changes* (New York: Doubleday, Doran & Co, 1937).

Thurlow, Richard C., *The Secret State: British Internal Security in the Twentieth Century* (Oxford: Blackwell, 1994).

Uí Chionna, Jackie, *Queen of Codes: The Secret Life of Emily Anderson, Britain's Greatest Female Codebreaker* (London: Headline, 2023).

Vassall, John, *Vassall: The Autobiography of a Spy* (London: Sidgwick & Jackson, 1975).

Vigurs, Kate, *Mission France: The True History of the Women of SOE* (New Haven, CT: Yale University Press, 2021).

Walton, Calder, *Spies: The Epic Intelligence War between East and*

West (London: Abacus, 2023).

Wark, Wesley K., ed., *Spy Fiction, Spy Films and Real Intelligence* (Abingdon: Routledge, 1991).

West, Nigel, *MASK: MI5's Penetration of the Communist Party of Great Britain* (Abingdon: Routledge, 2005).

——, *MI6: British Intelligence Service Operations 1909–45* (London: Weidenfeld & Nicolson, 1983).

——, ed., *The Guy Liddell Diaries, vol. I: 1939–1942* (London: Routledge, 2005).

——, ed., *The Guy Liddell Diaries, vol. II: 1942–1945* (London: Routledge, 2005).

Wheelwright, Julie, *The Fatal Lover: Mata Hari and the Myth of Women in Espionage* (London: Collins & Brown, 1992).

Wild, Ronald, *King's Counsel: The Life of Sir Henry Curtis-Bennett* (New York: J.J. Little & Ives, 1938).

Wilkinson, Peter and Joan Bright Astley, *Gubbins and SOE* (London: Leo Cooper, 1993).

Williams, Valentine, *The World of Action: The Autobiography of Valentine Williams* (London: Hamish Hamilton, 1938).

Wilson, Ray and Ian Adams, *Special Branch: A History 1883–2006* (London: Biteback, 2015).

Winterbotham, Frederick, *The Ultra Secret: The Inside Story of Operation Ultra, Bletchley Park and Enigma* (London: Weidenfeld & Nicolson, 1974).

Wiskemann, Elizabeth, *The Europe I Saw* (New York: St Martin's Press, 1968).

Wyles, Lilian, *A Woman at Scotland Yard: Reflections on the Struggles and Achievements of Thirty Years in the Metropolitan Police* (London: Faber & Faber, 1952).

Yusupov, Felix, *Rasputin: His Malignant Influence and His Assassination*, tr. Oswald Rayner (London: Jonathan Cape, 1927).

——, *Lost Splendour* (London: Jonathan Cape, 1954).

ACKNOWLEDGEMENTS

The power of a good book should never be underestimated. In fact, it can be transformative for the reader. Several years before the Covid-19 pandemic, I found myself in such a position. I was handed a signed copy of Stella Rimington's memoir, *Open Secret*, by my then university chaplain, Rev Dr Peter Green. The book belonged to his late mother, and he generously gifted it to an aspiring historian interested in all things related to the secret world of British intelligence. I was incredibly touched, and it remains a prized possession within my personal library. It took just one day for me to devour the contents. I was captivated by what the first female head of MI5 had to say about her journey to the top of Britain's Security Service. I was also impressed by her honesty, yet I was left with more questions than answers concerning the history of women in intelligence. Where was *their* history?

Stella Rimington's memoir has sparked a lifelong interest in retrieving the voices of women who worked for Britain's secret services, and in women's history more generally. The idea for my debut book, *Her Secret Service*, was born during one of my many countryside walks with the magnanimous Maxwell, whose company is missed more than I can express. However, the book would not have been possible had it not been for the steadfast support of the families and friends of the women (and men) contained within these pages. I am indebted to them all. Their positive engagement and willingness to reminisce and share private papers and family records with a perhaps sometimes overenthusiastic historian allowed me to bring a group of remarkable women to life. It has been a great honour to tell their stories for the first time.

From inception to publication, writing this book has been an amazing journey. As Arnold Schwarzenegger rightly reminds us, the achievements of any one person ride on the many people who have helped along the way, and my contributions are no different. Special thanks go to my dear friend and mentor, Professor Adrian O'Sullivan, who has spent endless hours discussing aspects of the book with me and reading through draft material. From one intelligence historian to another, thank you. I am indebted to Professor Andrew Boyd, Nicholas Rankin and Michael Smith, who generously shared historical records with me at a time when archives were closed during the pandemic. I greatly appreciate the support of John McCarthy, who served as a superb 'head of Sidmouth Station'. Thanks also go to Dr David Abrutat, Dr Jim Beech, Gill Bennett, Dr Krysten Blackstone, Jock Bruce, Dr Thomas Cheetham, Dr Tony Comer, Professor Rory Cormac, Michael Curtis, Guy Farrin, Dr Nicholas Hiley, Alan Judd, Dr Hazel Kent, Dr David Kenyon, Dr Patrick Kiernan, Dr Dan Lomas, Andrew Lycett, the late Professor Kristie Mackrakis, Lee Richards, Georgina Robinson, Emily Russell, Margaret Thomson, Phil Tomaselli, Nigel West and Dr Julie Wheelwright.

I wish to thank the wonderful team at Northbank Talent Management, who represent me. I am particularly indebted to Diane Banks who 'found' me, and set me on my present course as a published author and full-time writer. Sincere thanks to my agents Martin Redfern, who began the process, and Matthew Cole, who saw the book to completion. At Weidenfeld & Nicolson I must express a huge note of thanks to my editor Maddy Price, whose patience and understanding served as a welcome source of support during unforeseen challenges. As a cheerleader for women's history, I was honoured to be taken on by Maddy, and benefited greatly from her careful stewardship and sage advice. Writing the book, I was struck by the number of works I drew upon that had been published by Weidenfeld & Nicolson. I could not have wished for a better home for my book.

An army of friendly and expert archivists and librarians have also helped, and I am indebted to them. My sincere thanks also go to Charles Sebag-Montefiore and Mary Davidson for their kind permission to quote from their late mother, Ruth Sebag-Montefiore's insightful memoir, *Family Patchwork: Five Generations of an Anglo-Jewish Family* (London: Weidenfeld & Nicolson, 1987). Richard Astley entertained many questions about his marvellous mother, Joan Bright Astley, and kindly gave his permission to quote from her memoir, *The Inner Circle: A View of War at the Top* (London: Hutchinson, 1971).

I count myself very lucky to have such a loving and supportive family. My parents, Simon and Caroline Hall, really are the best parents any child could hope for. From a young age, they instilled in me and my sister the belief that anything is possible if you put your mind to it and work hard. I have passed this motivational message on to my daughter, Holly, who remains a constant source of joy in my life. Over the years, she has come to know the women whose stories feature in this book, and, despite the vast generation gap, they have empowered and inspired a young lady with big dreams. Finally, I must express my love and gratitude to my husband, David, who has patiently waited for the book to be completed and never once complained when I disappeared into my study to write. With many more incredible stories waiting to be told, I am blessed to have him by my side.

INDEX